2021 YEARBOOK

OF THE GENERAL ASSEMBLY

CUMBERLAND PRESBYTERIAN CHURCH

Office of the General Assembly

Cumberland Presbyterian Church

May 2021

8207 Traditional Place

Cordova (Memphis), Tennessee 38016

For information address Office of the General Assembly, Cumberland Presbyterian Center, 8207 Traditional Place, Cordova (Memphis), Tennessee, 38016-7414.

Compiled and edited by Elizabeth A. Vaughn for the Office of the General Assembly of the Cumberland Presbyterian Church.

Published and distributed exclusively by The Communications and Discipleship Ministry Teams, CPC, Memphis, Tennessee, for the Office of the General Assembly. Additional copies may be acquired through Cumberland Presbyterian Resources.

The Discipleship Ministry Team of the Ministry Council of the Cumberland Presbyterian Church is the successor organization to the Board of Christian Education of the Cumberland Presbyterian Church.

Funded, in part, by your contributions to Our United Outreach.

First Edition 2021 (First Printing)

ISBN: 978-1-945929-32-8

OUR UNITED OUTREACH
Made Possible In Part By Your Tithe To Our United Outreach

2021 YEARBOOK

General Assembly
Cumberland Presbyterian Church

Vision of Ministry

Biblically-based and Christ-centered
   born out of a specific sense of mission,
   the Cumberland Presbyterian Church strives to be true to its heritage:
   to be open to God's reforming spirit,
   to work cooperatively with the larger Body of Christ,
   and to nurture the connectional bonds that make us one.
The Cumberland Presbyterian Church seeks—to be the hands and feet of Christ in witness and service to the world and, above all, the Cumberland Presbyterian Church lives out the love of God to the glory of Jesus Christ.

Containing Statistics for the Year 2020

(<u>Note</u>: Statistical information for the year 2020 was impacted by the global coronavirus 2019 pandemic)

Changes Made to Other Data Through Print Time
(The Yearbook is updated periodically on our website www.cumberland.org/gao)

Edited by Elizabeth Vaughn

TABLE OF CONTENTS

GENERAL ASSEMBLY OFFICERS

MODERATOR
THE REVEREND SHELIA O'MARA
PO Box 170
Gadsden, TN 38337
chaplainshelia@aol.com
(443)699-2321

VICE MODERATOR
THE REVEREND MICHAEL CLARK
2353 Blue Springs Road
Decherd, TN 37324
mclark37398@gmail.com
(931)967-2121

STATED CLERK AND TREASURER
THE REVEREND MICHAEL SHARPE
8207 Traditional Place
Cordova, TN 38016
(901)276-4572
FAX (901)272-3913
msharpe@cumberland.org

ENGROSSING CLERK
THE REVEREND VERNON SANSOM
7425 Northampton Boulevard
Knoxville, TN 37931
(865)556-4107
vernon@sansom.us

THE BOARD OF DIRECTORS OF THE
GENERAL ASSEMBLY CORPORATION

(Members whose terms expire in 2021)
(2)MS. CALOTTA EDSELL, PO Box 172103, Memphis, TN 38187
    cedsell@hotmail.com
(2)REV. NORLAN SCRUDDER, 1514 Irene Lane, Fort Gibson, OK 74434
    ndscrudder@gmail.com
(Members whose terms expire in 2022)
(3)REV. BOBBY COLEMAN, 107 E Henson, Springdale, AR 72764
    bobby.coleman@gmail.com
(1)REV. RICKEY PAGE, 1369 Black River Drive, Mt Pleasant, SC 29466
    rickey.page59@gmail.com
(Members whose terms expire in 2023)
(3)REV. JOHN BUTLER, 501 Cherokee Drive, Campbellsville, KY 42718
    rev.butlerj8134@gmail.com
(3)MS. BETTY JACOB, PO Box 158, Broken Bow, OK 74728
    chocpres@pine-net.com

*Ecumenical Partners
+Cumberland Presbyterians in America
Numbers in parenthesis denote number of terms.

MINISTRY COUNCIL

(Members whose terms expire in 2021)
(2)REV. KENNY BUTCHER, 403 Kalye Court, Mt Juliet, TN 37122
(1)MS. AMY CRESSWELL, 1822 Glen Oaks Lane, Dyersburg, TN 38024
(2)REV. PHILLIP LAYNE, 10699 Griffith Highway, Whitwell, TN 37397
(2)MS. VICTORY MOORE, 17388 Chandlerville Road, Virginia, IL 62691
(1)MS. MELINDA REAMS, 10 W Azalea Lane, Russellville, AR 72802
(Members whose terms expire in 2022)
(2)MS. CARLA BELLIS, 19264 Law 2170, Aurora, MO 65605
(1)MS. DEBBIE HAYES, 69 Cactus Drive, Benton, KY 42025
(1)MR. TED SHIRAI, 25 Minami Kibogaoka, Asahi-ku, Yokohama, Kanagawa, JAPAN
(1)REV. TIM SMITH, 214 Jeffery Drive, Fayetteville, TN 37334
(2)REV. MIKE WILKINSON, 1504 Clear Brook Drive, Knoxville, TN 37922
(Members whose terms expire in 2023)
(2)REV. DR. MICHAEL CLARK, 2353 Blue Springs Road, Dechard, TN 37324
(2)REV. JUAN DAVID CORREA, Calle 76 #87-14, Medellin, COLOMBIA, SOUTH AMERICA
(1)REV. DEREK JACKS, 341 Shadeswood Drive, Hoover, AL 35226
(1)MS. LORA ROGERS-KERNER, 156 State Route 348 W, Symsonia, KY 42082
(1)ANGELICA POVEDA, COLOMBIA, SOUTH AMERICA

YOUTH ADVISORY MEMBERS
(1)MR. LAKE PORTER 17 Lovers Lane, Fayetteville, TN 37334
(1)MS. RYLEE ROGERS, 314 Hampshire Drive, Clarksville, TN 37043
(2)MS. LACEY YOUNG, 1211 Michael Drive, Alabaster, AL 35007

ADVISORY MEMBERS
REV. SHELIA O'MARA, PO Box 170, Gadsden, TN 38337
REV. MICHAEL SHARPE, 8207 Traditional Place, Cordova, TN 38016

GENERAL ASSEMBLY BOARD OF:

I. TRUSTEES OF BETHEL UNIVERSITY

(Members whose terms expire in 2021)
(1)*MR. CLINTON FOX, 1850 South Boulevard, Houston, TX 77098
(3)+REV. ELTON C. HALL, SR., 305 Tiffton Circle, Hewitt, TX 76643
(1)MS. LINDA C. INGRAM, 203 Ballard Lane, Sparta, TN 38583
(3)MS. DEWANNA LATIMER, 193 Moses Drive, Jackson, TN 38305
(2)*DR. E. RAY MORRIS, PO Box 924628, Norcross, GA 30010
(2)MR. STEVE PERRYMAN, 535 Ranch Road, Rogersville, MO 65742
(1)REV. ROBERT TRUITT, 1238 Old Eastside Road, Burns, TN 37029
(Members whose terms expire in 2022)
(1)*MR. SCOTT ALLEN, 15 Pamela Lane, Crossville, TN 38558
(3)MR. JEFF AMREIN, 11711 Paramont Way, Prospect, KY 40059
(2)*MR. SCOTT CONGER, 143 Fawn Ridge Drive, Jackson, TN 38305
(3)MR. BILL DOBBINS 5716 Quest Ridge Road, Franklin, TN 37064
(1)MS. VICKI H. HOOVER, 200 N Poplar Street, Paris, TN 38242
(1)MR. WILLIAM TERRY HOWELL, 205 Como Street, McKenzie, TN 38201
(2)*DR. BROCK MARTIN, 419 Browning Avenue, Huntingdon, TN 38344
(1)MR. KEITH PRIESTLEY, 780 Old McKenzie Road, McKenzie, TN 38201
(1)+ELDER CRAIG A. WHITE, 240 Waters Edge Lane, Madison, AL 35758

*Ecumenical Partners
+Cumberland Presbyterians in America
Numbers in parenthesis denote number of terms.

(Members whose terms expire in 2023)
(2)DR. NANCY BEAN, PO Box 205, McKenzie, TN 38201
(1) *JUDGE BEN CANTRELL, 1485A Woodmont Boulevard, Nashville, TN 37215
(1)*MRS. PATRICIA KAHLDEN, PO Box 909, Caldwell, TX 77836
(3)MR. KENNETH (KEN) D. QUINTON, 2912 Waller Omer Road, Sturgis, KY 42459
(1)+DR. BERNICE C. RICHARDSON, 5902 Fortune Drive NE, Huntsville, AL 35811
(2)MR. TOMMY SURBER, 825 Hico Road, McKenzie, TN 38201
(3)REV. ROBERT (BOB) WATKINS, 5405 Kacena Avenue, Marion, IA 52302

II. TRUSTEES OF CUMBERLAND PRESBYTERIAN CHILDREN'S HOME

(Members whose terms expire in 2021)
(1)BRIAN MARTIN, 614 CR 4608, Troup, TX 75789
(1)MRS. GUIN TYUS, 903 W Hickory Boulevard, Madison, TN 37115
(Members whose terms expire in 2022)
(1)MS. MICHELE BLAND, 6837 Roberts Lane, Fort Worth, TX 76140
(1)*MR. BRIAN CARWRIGHT, 3218 Northwood Drive, Highland Village, TX 75077
(3)MR. RICHARD DEAN, 2140 Cove Circle North, Gadsden, AL 35903
(1)*MR. CAMERON MARONE, 6085 Water Street, Plano, TX 75024
(1)MS JACQUELINE SAN MIGUEL-LOZANO, 4005 Paradise Lane, Sanger, TX 76266
(1)MR. SAM SUDDARTH, 206 Ha Le Koa Court, Smyrna, TN 37167
(1)*MR. MATTHEW WHITTEN, 3909 Fawn Drive, Denton, TX 76208
(Members whose terms expire in 2023)
(2)MR. PETE CARTER, 306 Jackson Hills Drive, Maryville, TN 37804
(3)*MR. CHARLES W. HARRIS, 3293 Birch Avenue, Grapevine, TX 76051
(3)*MR. KNIGHT MILLER, 509 Brixham Park Drive, Franklin, TN 37069

III. TRUSTEES OF HISTORICAL FOUNDATION

(Members whose terms expire in 2021)
(2)REV. LISA OLIVER, 110 Allen Drive, Hendersonville, TN 37075
(1)MS. KELLY SHANTON, 3932 W Beaver Creek Drive, Powell, TN 37849
(Members whose terms expire in 2022)
(2)MS. ROBIN MCCASKEY HUGHES, 1205 Olde Bridge Road, Edmond, OK 73034
(2)MS. ASHLEY LINDSEY, 403 College Street, Smiths Grove, KY 42171
(1)MS. MARTHA JO MIMS, 3011 Wolfe Road, Columbus, MS 39705
(2)+WILLIE LYNK, 932 Valley Square Road, Morganfield, KY 42437
(Members whose terms expire in 2023)
(2)+REV. JOE HOWARD, III, 2903 Al Lipscomb Way, Dallas, TX 75215
(1)MS. CATHY LITTLEFIELD, PO Box 125, Booneville, AR 72927
(3)+MS. PAT WARD, 2620 Rabbit Lane, Madison, AL 35756

IV. TRUSTEES OF MEMPHIS THEOLOGICAL SEMINARY OF THE CUMBERLAND PRESBYTERIAN CHURCH

(Members whose terms expire in 2021)
(1)REV. DANIEL BARKLEY, 2732 Rexford Street, Hokes Bluff, AL 35903
(1)REV. GLORIA VILLA DIAZ, 2425 Holly Hall Street B42, Houston, TX 77054
(1)REV. YOONG KIM, 2770 Farmstead Way, Suwanee, GA 30024
(1)REV. RIAN PUCKETT, 55 Ham Street, Batesville, AR 72501
(3)MS. SONDRA RODDY, 628 Mannington Place, Lexington, KY 40503
(3)*REV. MELVIN CHARLES SMITH, 1263 Haynes Street, Memphis, TN 38114
(3)*MS. LATISHA TOWNS, Regional One-The Med, 877 Jefferson Avenue, Memphis, TN 38103

*Ecumenical Partners
+Cumberland Presbyterians in America
Numbers in parenthesis denote number of terms.

(Members whose terms expire in 2022)

(1)MR. GREG ALLEN, 1138 Balbade Drive, Nashville, TN 37215
(1)REV. JILL CARR, 1601 Arbour Drive, Lebanon, MO 65536
(2)*MS. JANE ASHLEY FOLK, 4123 Chanwil Place, Memphis, TN 38117
(2)*REV. LARRY HILLIARD, 102 Johnson Street, Waveland, MS 39576
(1)MS. CHERYL LESLIE, 3374 Walnut Grove Road, Memphis, TN 38111
(1)*MS. LISANNE MARSHALL, 325 Meadow Grove Lane, Memphis, TN 38120
(1)*REV. KEITH NORMAN, 2835 Broad Avenue, Memphis, TN 38112
(2)*REV. DEBORAH SMITH, 584 E McLemore Avenue, Memphis, TN 38106

(Members whose terms expire in 2023)

(3)REV. ANNE HAMES, 118 Paris Street, McKenzie, TN 38201
(2)REV. WES JOHNSON, 6222 Crestmoore Lane, Sachse, TX 75048
(2)+MS. VANESSA K. MIDGETT, 118 Thunderbird Drive, Huntsville, AL 35749
(2)REV. JASON MIKEL, 410 Ramblewood Lane, Nolensville, TN 37135
(2)*REV. JIMMY MOSBY, PO Box 45843, Little Rock, AR 72214
(2)REV. KIP RUSH, 516 Franklin Road, Brentwood, TN 37027

V. STEWARDSHIP, FOUNDATION AND BENEFITS

(Members whose terms expire in 2021)

(1)MS. DEBBIE SHANKS, 3997 N 100th Street, Casey, IL 62420
(2)MR. JAMES SHANNON, 2307 Littlemore Drive, Cordova, TN 38016
(3)MR. MICHAEL ST. JOHN, 324 Carriage Place, Lebanon, MO 65536

(Members whose terms expire in 2022)

(2)REV. KEN BYFORD, 23716 Highway 9 N, Piedmont, AL 36272
(1)MRS. MARY JO RAY, 16 Nottingham Lane, Columbus, MS 39705
(2)MS. ANDREA SMITH, 1715 Water Cure Road, Winchester, TN 37398 (resigned)
(1)MR. OWEN SMITH, 119 Pine Island Drive, Marshall, TX 75672

(Members whose terms expire in 2023)

(3)MR. RANDY DAVIDSON, PO Box 880, Ada, OK 74821
(1)MR. JOHN KOELZ, 4498 S Carothers, Franklin, TN 37064
(2)REV. GARY TUBB, 103 Forest Drive, Mountain Home, AR 72653
(2)REV. DWAYNE TYUS, 426 W Old Hickory Boulevard, Madison, TN 37115

GENERAL ASSEMBLY COMMISSIONS:

I. MILITARY CHAPLAINS AND PERSONNEL

(2) Term Expires in 2021–REV. TONY JANNER, 104 Northwood Drive, McKenzie (deceased) TN 38201
(1) Term Expires in 2022–REV. SHELIA O'MARA, PO Box 170, Gadsden, TN 38337
(1) Term Expires in 2023–MR. TOMMY CRAIG, 8958 Carriage Creek Road, Arlington, TN 38002

These three persons and the Stated Clerk represent the denomination as members of the Presbyterian Council for Chaplains and Military Personnel, 4125 Nebraska Avenue NW, Washington, DC 20016

---

*Ecumenical Partners
+Cumberland Presbyterians in America
Numbers in parenthesis denote number of terms.

GENERAL ASSEMBLY COMMITTEES

I. JUDICIARY

(Members whose terms expire in 2021)

(3)REV. ANNETTA CAMP, 2303 Mill Creek Road, Halls, TN 38040
anetta@cumberlandchurch.com

(1)REV. JIM RATLIFF, 13 Hernando Drive, Cherokee Village, AR 72529
kudzu8161@yahoo.com

(2)MR. BILL TALLY, 907 Tipperary Drive, Scottsboro, AL 35768
wtally@scottsboro.org

(Members whose terms expire in 2022)

(2)MS. RACHEL MOSES, 1138 Blaine Avenue, Cookeville, TN 38501
coachrach@aol.com

(2)REV. JAN OVERTON, 3320 Pipe Line Road, Birmingham, AL 35243
jan@crestlinechurch.org

(1)REV. ROGER REID, 637 Colburn Drive, Lewisburg, TN 37091
drrtr@yahoo.com

(Members whose terms expire in 2023)

(2)MS. PAMELA BROWN, 6400 North Grove Avenue, Warr Acres, OK 73012
pambrownlaw@cox.net

(3)REV. HARRY CHAPMAN, 4908 El Picador Court SE, Rio Rancho, NM 87124
wrightrev@gmail.com

(2)REV. GEOFFREY KNIGHT, 2119 Avalon Place, Houston, TX 77019
geoff@cphouston.org

II. JOINT COMMITTEE ON AMENDMENTS

The committee consists of five members of the Judiciary Committee of the Cumberland Presbyterian Church in America and the Cumberland Presbyterian Church.

III. NOMINATING

(Members whose terms expire in 2021)

(1)MR. ETHAN MORGAN, 119 Mountain Top Lane, Cookeville, TN 38506
remorgan8@gmail.com

(1)REV. RANDY SHANNON, 30282 Highway H, Marshall, MO 65340
pastor_randy_shannon@yahoo.com

(Members whose terms expire in 2022)

(1)MS. ALLISON CARR, PO Box 1547 Lebanon, MO 65536
owilsonhoo@gmail.com

(1)MS. DIANN PHELPS, 4743 Happy Hollow Road, Hawesville, KY 42348
diannphelps@att.net

(1)REV. MICAIAH TANCK, 3218 Scenic Drive, Scottsboro, AL 35769
micaiah.thomas@gmail.com

(1)REV. BRENT WILLS, 4607 E Richmond Shop, Lebanon, TN 37090
bwills9185@yahoo.com

(Members whose terms expire in 2023)

(1)MS. JENNIFER BYRD, 176 E Valley Road, Whitwell, TN 37397
jennkbyrd@gmail.com

(1)MR. VICTOR HASSELL, 510 N Main Street, Sturgis, ky 42459
hassellvictor@hotmail.com

(1)MR. KEN SMITH, 6197 34th Street, Lubbock, TX 79407
knsmith@earthlink.net

(1)REV. MARION SONTOWSKI, 17101 N Western Avenue, Edmond, OK 73012
sontowski_tn@yahoo.com

*Ecumenical Partners
+Cumberland Presbyterians in America
Numbers in parenthesis denote number of terms.

IV. OUR UNITED OUTREACH COMMITTEE

(Members whose terms expire in 2021)
(1)MS. GWEN RODDYE, 3728 Wittenham Drive, Knoxville, TN 37921
(3)MS. ROBIN WILLS, 4607 E Richmond Shop Road, Lebanon, TN 37090
(Members whose terms expire in 2022)
(2)REV. BRUCE HAMILTON, 203 W Fifth Street, Mountain View, MO 65548
(Members whose terms expire in 2023)
(2)MR. MIKEL DAVIS, 102 Willow Wood Lane, Ovilla, TX 75154
(1)REV. EDUARDO MONTOYA, 2436 Anna Way, Elgin, IL 60124

YOUTH ADVISORY MEMBERS:
(1)MS. SIERRA ALEXANDER, 1014 Wren Street, Dyersburg, TN 38024
(1)MS. KAILEY SUNDSTROM, 309 Bryson Lane, Clarksville, TN 37043
(1)MR. NATE WOOD, 17246 Highway K, Aurora, MO 65605

V. PLACE OF MEETING

THE STATED CLERK OF THE GENERAL ASSEMBLY
THE MODERATOR OF THE GENERAL ASSEMBLY
A REPRESENTATIVE OF WOMEN'S MINISTRIES OF THE MISSIONS MINISTRY TEAM

VI. UNIFIED COMMITTEE ON THEOLOGY AND SOCIAL CONCERNS

(Members whose terms expire in 2021)
(1)REV. MITCH BOULTON, 80 Topsy Lane, Savannah, TN 38372
        steelermitch@gmail.com
(1)+REV. BOBBY HAWKINS, 220 S. Foxwell Street, Providence, KY 42450
        hawk49@bellsouth.net
(1)REV. MICHAEL QUALLS, 5355 June Cove, Horn Lake, MS 38637
        mqualls1@yahoo.com
(1)+MR. JAMES REYNOLDS, 128 Heritage Lane, Madison, ALabama 35758
        jwreyns@aol.com
(1)MS. MELISSA WILSON, 107 Hillwood Drive, Dickson, TN 37055 **(resigned)**
        milzwilz@yahoo.com
(Members whose terms expire in 2022)
(3)+REV. JIMMIE DODD, 1798 Campbell Street, Jackson, TN 38301 **(resigned)**
        dodd125@gmail.com
(1)REV. VIRGINIA ESPINOZA, PO Box 132, Boswell, OK 74727
        vespinoza@choctawnation.com
(1)REV. TERRA SISCO, 811 W Cheyenne Street, Marlow, OK 73055
        terrasisco@hotmail.com
(3)+ELDER JOY WALLACE, 541 Glenn Arbor, Dallas, TX 75240
        jlwallace1951@gmail.com
(1)REV. JO WARREN, 811 Wall Street, Morrilton, AR 72110
        jmw364@yahoo.com

(Members whose terms expire in 2023)

(2)+REV. EDMUND COX, 249 Mimosa Circle, Maryville, TN 37801
  edmundcox765@gmail.com
(3)+REV. NANCY FUQUA, 1963 County Road 406, Towncreek, AL 35672
  fuq23@bellsouth.net
(2)REV. RICHARD MORGAN, 1468 Williams Cove Road, Winchester, TN 37398
  icthuse3@gmail.com
(2)REV. LISA SCOTT, (address on file in GA office)
  lascott1979@att.net
(2)+REV. RICK WHITE, 1544 Herring Avenue, Waco, TX 76708
  rickwaco3@aol.com

President of Memphis Theological Seminary - Ex-officio Member

OTHER DENOMINATIONAL PERSONNEL
REPRESENTATIVES TO:

Caribbean and North American Area Council, World Communion of Reformed Churches:
STATED CLERK MICHAEL SHARPE, 8207 Traditional Place, Cordova, TN 38016

(Member whose terms expire in 2023)

(2)MS. SHERRY POTEET, PO box 313, Gilmer, TX 75644
  spoteet1@aol.com

*Ecumenical Partners
+Cumberland Presbyterians in America
Numbers in parenthesis denote number of terms.

LIVING GENERAL ASSEMBLY MODERATORS

2020—REV. SHELIA O'MARA, PO Box 170, Gadsden, TN 38337

2019—REV. SHELIA O'MARA, PO Box 170, Gadsden, TN 38337

2018—REV. DANIEL J. EARHEART-BROWN, 475 N Highland Street Apt 9L, Memphis, TN 38122

2017—REV. DAVID LANCASTER, 426 Fuqua Road, Martin, TN 38237

2016—REV. DWAYNE TYUS, 426 Old Hickory Boulevard, Madison, TN 37115

2015—REV. MICHELE GENTRY, Urb San Jorge casa 28, Km 8 via a La Tebaida
    Armenia, Quindio, COLOMBIA, SA

2014—REV. LISA HALL ANDERSON, 1790 Faxon Avenue, Memphis, TN 38112

2013—REV. FOREST PROSSER, 1157 Mountain Creek Road, Chattanooga, TN 37405

2012—REV. ROBERT D. RUSH, 12935 Quail Park Drive, Cypress, TX 77429

2011—REV. DON M. TABOR, 9611 Mitchell Place, Brentwood, TN 37027

2009—ELDER SAM SUDDARTH, 206 Ha Le Koa Court, Smyrna, TN 37167

2007—REV. FRANK WARD, 46 Henderson Cove, Atoka, TN 38004

2006—REV. DONALD HUBBARD, 2128 Campbell Station Road, Knoxville, TN 37932

2005—REV. LINDA H. GLENN, 49 Mason Road, Threeway, TN 38343

2004—REV. EDWARD G. SIMS, 1176 Warfield Boulevard #410, Clarksville, TN 37043

2003—REV. CHARLES MCCASKEY, 679 Canter Lane, Cookeville, TN 38501

1999—ELDER GWENDOLYN G. RODDYE, 3728 Wittenham Drive, Knoxville, TN 37921

1998—REV. MASAHARU ASAYAMA, 3-15-9 Higashi, Kunitachi-shi, Tokyo, JAPAN

1996—REV. MERLYN A. ALEXANDER, 80 N. Hampton Lane, Jackson, TN 38305

1995—REV. CLINTON O. BUCK, 4912 Essexshire Avenue, Memphis, TN 38117

1990—REV. THOMAS D. CAMPBELL, 7437 Old Clinton Pike, Powell, TN 37849

IN MEMORY OF:

Moderator of the162nd General Assembly
REV. JOHN DAVID HALL
Died August 2, 2020

SYNOD AND PRESBYTERY CLERKS

SYNOD OF GREAT RIVERS
(GR)

The Reverend Andy McClung
919 Dickinson Street
Memphis, TN 38107
(901)606-6615
scubarev@att.net

Arkansas Presbytery (GRAR)

Janie Stamps
4008 Logan Lane
Fort Smith, AR 72903
(479)478-0161 (Home)
(479)883-5633 (Cell)
(479)782-0454 FAX
bjstamps@msn.com (Home)

Missouri Presbytery (GRMI)

The Reverend Michael Reno
52 Rolla Gardens
Rolla, MO 65401
(573)578-5321
pastormikecpc@gmail.com

West Tennessee Presbytery (GRWT)

The Reverend Andy McClung
919 Dickinson Street
Memphis, TN 38107
(901)606-6615
scubarev@att.net

SYNOD OF MIDWEST
(MI)

Debra Shanks
3997 N 100th Street
Casey, IL 62420
(217)932-2995
royndebbie@hotmail.com

Covenant Presbytery (MICO)

Reese Baker
1175 Rowland Cemetery Road
Fredonia, KY 42411
(270)625-0912
rbaker@kynet.biz

Cumberland Presbytery (MICU)

The Reverend Darrell Pickett
113 Woods Drive
Glasgow, KY 42141
(270)834-6102
dpickett@glasgow-ky.com

North Central Presbytery (MINC)

The Reverend J C McDuffee
1985 County Road 1325 N
Fairfield, IL 62837
(618)599-0652
statedclerk@ncpwebsite.com

SYNOD AND PRESBYTERY CLERKS

MISSION SYNOD
(MS)

The Reverend Randy Hardisty
4908 Redondo Street
N Richland Hills, TX 76180
(817)821-9665
trinitycpc@sbcglobal.net

Andes Presbytery (MSAN)

The Reverend Liliana Sarmiento
Calle 51 #15-32
Los Naranjos Dosquebradas
Colombia, South America
(57)321-622-2797
lilianasarmi23@gmail.com

Cauca Valley Presbytery (MSCA)

Jairo Lopez
Paraiso la Morada
5ta Etapa, Casa 36, Jamundi
Colombia, South America
011-5726-615410

Choctaw Presbytery (MSCH)

The Reverend Virginia Espinoza
PO Box 132
Boswell, OK 74727
(580)434-7971
vespinoza@choctawnation.com

Presbytery del Cristo (MSDC)

Karen Avery
9420 Layton Court NE
Albuquerque, NM 87111
(505)821-7668
kavery5@comcast.net

Emaus Presbytery (MSEM)

Cecilia Tarborda
Calle 20D #42C-56
Bello, Colombia
(57)300-783-5638
chilalu1147@hotmail.com

Hong Kong Presbytery (MSHK)

The Reverend So Li Wong
2/F Welland Plaza
188 Nam Cheong Street
Sam Shui Po, Kowloon
HONG KONG, CHINA
(011)852-3705-8390
soliwong@gmail.com

Japan Presbytery (MSJA)

The Reverend Takehiko Miyai
4-13-24 Higashihara Zama-shi
Kanagawa-ken
252-0004 JAPAN
(011)81-46-255-6441
tacke.m@gmail.com

Red River Presbytery (MSRR)

Barbara Isaacs
PO Box 1294
Ada, OK 74821
(580)320-3270
clerk@rrpcpc.org

SYNOD AND PRESBYTERY CLERKS

Trinity Presbytery (MSTR)

Paula Hayes
PO Box 5449
Longview, TX 75608
(903)759-1896 (Home)
(903)759-0092 (Work)
phayes7442@aol.com

**SYNOD OF SOUTHEAST
(SE)**

The Reverend Cliff Hudson
7407 Bonny Oaks Drive
Chattanooga, TN 37421
(423)892-8710
gchudson3@gmail.com

Cumberland East Coast Presbytery (SEEC)

The Reverend Seung N Kim
3714 190th Street Apt 133
Flushing, NY 11358
(646)479-2305
seungno@gmail.com

Presbytery of East Tennessee (SEET)

The Reverend Ronald L. Longmire
2041 Eckles Drive
Maryville, TN 37804
(865)984-1647
ronaldlongmire@charter.net

Grace Presbytery (SEGR)

Jessie Dunnaway
New Hope CP Church
5521 Double Oak Lane
Birmingham, AL 35242
(205)937-3684
jessie@newhopecpc.org

Hope Presbytery (SEHO)

Dianne Vandiver
4500 County Road 50
Lexington, AL 35648
(256)247-3827 (Home)
(256)222-8434 (Cell)
diannevandiver08@gmail.com

Korean Cumberland Presbytery of Southeast (SEKP)

The Reverend Enoch Yu
2012 Shenley Park Lane
Duluth, GA 30097
(678)600-2787
jaeyu117@yahoo.com

Robert Donnell Presbytery (SERD)

Frances Dawson
PO Box 904
Scottsboro, AL 35768
(256)244-0554 (Cell)
francescdawson@gmail.com

Tennessee-Georgia Presbytery (SETG)

The Reverend Kriss McGowan
885 Mount Calvary Road
Whitwell, TN 37397
(423)432-0037 (Cell)
(423)463-8609 (Home)
tngastatedclerk@gmail.com

SYNOD AND PRESBYTERY CLERKS

**TENNESSEE SYNOD
(TN)**

The Reverend Charles McCaskey
565 East Tenth Street
Cookeville, TN 38501
(931)526-6585 (Office)
(931)372-2620 FAX
charles@cookevillecpchurch.org

Columbia Presbytery (TNCO)

George Ladd
4521 Turkey Creek Road
Williamsport, TN 38487
(931)682-2263
george.caleb.ladd@gmail.com

Murfreesboro Presbytery (TNMU)

The Reverend Charles McCaskey
565 East Tenth Street
Cookeville, TN 38501
(931)526-6585 (Office)
(931)528-2273 FAX
charles@cookevillecpchurch.org

Nashville Presbytery (TNNA)

Keith Vanstone
3803 Plantation Drive
Hermitage, TN 37076
(615)454-1600
keithv@bellsouth.net

MINISTERS GAINED AND LOST IN 2020

MINISTERS RECEIVED BY ORDINATION

NAME	PRESBYTERY	DATE
Carwheel, Greg	Red River	11/15/20
Correa, Juan David	Emaus	12/12/20
Craddock, Barry	Cumberland	10/11/20
Lofton, Kathy	Red River	10/04/20
Luthy, Dusty	Covenant	01/11/20
Moore, Kimberly	Nashville	09/20/20
Spenkle, David	West Tennessee	10/16/20
Tucker, Dave	Red River	09/27/20
Velez, Gloria	Emaus	12/18/20
Westfall, Justin	Red River	10/04/20

MINISTERS WHO HAVE MOVED TO OTHER DENOMINATIONS

NAME	DENOMINATION	DATE
Thomas, Cassandra	PCUSA	10/07/2020

MINISTERS DROPPED FROM MINISTRY BY PRESBYTERY

NAME	PRESBYTERY	DATE
Doles, Steve	del Cristo	03/13/2020
Mitchum, Mark	Trinity	2020
Turner, Steve	Trinity	2020

MILITARY CHAPLAINS

Logan, Jason B   (M8)
  709 Cavalier Drive
  Clarksville, TN 37040
  jason.b.logan.mil@mail.mil
  (609)556-3128   TNMU#7200
Park, Jin Ho   (M8)
  4510 161st Street
  Flushing, NY 11358
  wlsgh527@yahoo.com
  (917)971-0293   SETG#2100
Phelps, John   (M8)
  361 Chaco Road
  jbphelps75@yahoo.com
  (671)689-6764
  Yona, GUAM 96915   MICU#3100
Santillano, Ray Paul   (M8)
  10515 Lupine Canyon
  Helotes, TX 78023
  ramon.santillano.mil@mail.mil
  (210)425-1789   MSTR#8100
Turner, Glyn   (M8)
  601 Wynfal Drive
  Holly Ridge, NC 28455
  (585)307-7715
  glynturner@hotmail.com

NON-MILITARY CHAPLAINS

Aden, Marty   (M9)
  202 Bennington Place
  Wilmington, NC 28412
  maden@ec.rr.com
  (910)274-8465   MSRR#8400
Brown, Mark   (M9)
  752 Hawthorne Street
  Memphis, TN 38107
  dmbrown@utmem.edu
  (901)274-1474   GRWT#9100
Burns, Garrett   (M9)
  387 Forest Avenue
  McKenzie, TN 38201
  burnsg@bethelu.edu
  (731)535-3126   GRWT#9100
Chall-Hutchinson, Deborah   (M9)
  190 Ussery Road
  Clarksville, TN 37043
  challhut@gmail.com
  (931)905-1671   TNNA#7300
Cook, Lisa   (M9)
  4101 Dalemere Court
  Nashville, TN 37207
  sacredsparksministry@gmail.com
  (615)868-4118   TNNA#7118
Gentry, Michele   (M9)
  Urb San Jorge casa 28
  Km 8 via a La Tebaida
  Armenia, Quindio, Colombia
  South America
  gentry.andes@yahoo.com
  (318)285-1161   MSAN#8900

Hames, Anne   (M9)
  118 Paris Street
  Mc Kenzie, TN 38201
  FAX: (731)352-4069
  hamesa@bethel-college.edu
  (731)352-4066   GRWT#9100
Hartung, J Thomas   (M9)
  2291 Americus Boulevard W Apt 1
  Clearwater, FL 33763
  revtom6@aol.com
  (727)797-2882   SEGR#0100
Hayes, Jennifer   (M9)
  7005 Woodmoor Road
  Fort Worth, TX 76133
  hayesj712@gmail.com
  (205)533-1018   TNMU#7200
Headrick, Anthony   (M9)
  625 Bakers Bridge Avenue
  Suite 105 PMB 197
  Franklin, TN 37067
  anthony.headrick@va.gov
  (208)972-7602............. SEGR#0100
Jackson, Terry   (M9)
  1461 Mt Pleasant Road
  Hernando, MS 38632
  tjackson48@comcast.net
  (662)429-9741   GRWT#9100
Kelly, Patrick L   (M9)
  1449 Rainbow Road
  Mountain City, TN 37683-2110
  (423)727-4067   SEET#2200
Kennemer, Darren   (M9)
  8828 Highway 119
  Alabaster, AL 35007
  (205)663-3152
  darren.kennemer@va.gov
                        SERD#0107
Knight, Melissa   (M9)
  3514 Westbrook Drive SE
  Smyrna, GA 30082
  (530)632-6472
  revlissa@gmail.com   MSDC#8700
Lefavor, David   (M9)
  414 S Monroe Siding Road
  Xenia, OH 45395
  david.lefavor@va.gov
  (937)262-3394   SEGR#0100
Lewis, Emily Fowler   (M9)
  5225 Maple Avenue Apt 5309
  Dallas, TX 75235
  emilykaye.fowler@gmail.com
  (817)983-3559   MSRR#8400
McCarty, John   (M9)
  305 W Martindale Drive
  Marshall, TX 75672
  mtsjohn@gmail.com
  (423)650-8788   SETG#2100
Messer, James C   (M9)
  3653 Old Madisonville Road
  Henderson, KY 42420
  jcmess@hotmail.com
  (270)827-0711   MINC#5304

Oliver, Lisa   (M9)
  110 Allen Drive
  Hendersonville, TN 37075
  (615)474-3954   TNMU#7230
Pickett, Patricia   (M9)
  1460 Cheatham Dam Road
  Ashland City, TN 37015
  tovahtoo@aol.com
  (615)792-4973   TNNA#7300
Richards, Carroll   (M9)
  210 Allison Drive
  Lincoln, IL 62656
  FAX: (217)732-7894
  dr_cr@comcast.net
  (217)732-7894   MINC#5200
Ruggia, Mario (Bud)   (M9)
  603 Rumsey Street
  Kiowa, KS 67070
  ruggia@aol.com
  (620)825-4076   MSRR#8400
Scott, Lisa   (M9)
  (address on file)
  lascott1979@att.net
  (816)332-0604   GRMI#4100
Smith, James A   (M9)
  309 Lutes Road
  Paducah, KY 42001
  james1493@att.net
  (901)574-2345   MICO#3400
Snelling, Linda   (M9)
  240 Dakota Drive
  Waxahachie, TX 75167
  lsnelling50@gmail.com
  (469)550-9074   MSRR#8400
Sumrall, Phil   (M9)
  107 Barnhardt Circle
  Fort Oglethorpe, GA 30742
  phil.sumrall@gmail.com
  (423)903-1938   SETG#2100
Travis, Kermit   (M9)
  3220 Sharon Highway
  Dresden, TN 38225
  (731)364-2315   GRWT#9415
Varner Villa, Susan   (M9)
  11299 Herschel Loop
  Daphne, AL 36526
  smvarner76@yahoo.com
  (804)304-4642   GRAR#1100
West, David   (M9)
  2027 Lucille Street
  Lebanon, TN 37087
  drdavidlwest@aol.com
  (217)732-7568   TNNA#5405
Wilson, Don   (M9)
  7300 Calle Montana NE
  Albuquerque, NM 87113
  don-wilson07@comcast.net
  (505)823-2594   MSDC#8700

IN MEMORY OF
MINISTERS LOST BY DEATH

NAME	PRESBYTERY	AGE	DATE
Acton, Wade	Grace	90	03/24/21
Alhart, Daryl	Murfreesboro	79	05/17/20
Barnett, David Rudolph	North Central	92	12/26/20
Barrett, Geoffry	Cumberland	77	05/24/20
Bayer, David	West Tennessee	73	04/09/20
Board, Newman Ray	Covenant	82	08/19/20
Bone, Howard Leslie	Missouri	81	05/10/21
Brown, Rex	East Tennessee	82	07/27/20
Campbell, Gordon	Missouri	92	04/01/21
Craig, Robert A.	North Central	86	10/24/20
Estes, Sam	del Cristo	101	02/09/21
Gary, Brian	Cumberland	76	02/27/21
Haire, Shelby O.	Cumberland	82	02/03/20
Hall, John David	Robert Donnell	88	08/02/20
Hancock, B J	Murfreesboro	86	01/20/21
Harris, Ernest	Trinity	97	09/24/20
Ivey, Billy F	East Tennessee	87	02/04/20
Janner, Tony	West Tennessee	75	11/05/20
Jaramillo, Luciano	Grace	86	02/01/21
Jett, Mace, Jr.	West Tennessee	89	03/25/20
Lovelace, John G	North Central	91	04/30/21
McCoy, Kenneth	West Tennessee	72	07/12/20
McSpadden, Nancy	Arkansas	67	05/12/20
Melson, Glenda	East Tennessee	79	02/14/20
Melton, Sam	Tennessee-Georgia	84	02/28/20
Meredith, Charles	Cumberland	79	06/22/20
Miller, James R	Columbia	82	01/16/20
Nunn, Don	Trinity	85	02/05/20
Pejendino, Fhanor	Cauca Valley	64	02/02/21
Pinnell, James (Jim)	West Tennessee	63	05/25/20
Ryan, James (Jack)	Arkansas	69	01/06/21
Shanley, Dwight	Arkansas	76	01/11/21
Shoulta, John	Covenant	72	04/04/20
Shugert, Rich	Red River	75	04/26/21
Vaught, Joseph (Joe)	Cumberland	73	04/01/21
Williams, Bobby D	West Tennessee	84	10/19/20
Woodliff, George	Arkansas	83	04/18/20

SURVIVING SPOUSES OF MINISTERS BY PRESBYTERY

(Deceased spouse in parenthesis.)

ANDES

Carmen S de Ortiz
(Arturo Ortiz)
127 Pennsylvania Avenue
Somerville, MA 02145
(617)718-9144

Myriam de Ortiz
(Jaime Ortiz)
Cra 50D #62-69 Barrio Prado Centro
Medellin, Antioquia
Colombia, South America
(574)551-6267

ARKANSAS

Batholomew, Maudline
(Harold Bartholomew)
13395 Highway 265
Prairie Grove, AR 72753
(479)846-2850

Blackburn, Nathalee
(Samuel Blakeburn)
6706 S 6th Street
Fort Smith, AR 72908
(479)649-9436

DuBose, Sandra
(Paul DuBose)
207 7th Street
Cotter, AR 72626
(870) 373-1021

Elkins, Patsy
(Robert Harold Elkins)
525 Elkins Road
Magazine, AR 72943
(479)637-3723
robtelkins@cej.net

Faith, Jeannine
(Charles Faith)
4710 Mount Olive Road
Melbourne, AR 72556
(870)368-4069

Fleming, Angela
(Patrick Fleming)
616 N Border Street
Benton, AR 72015
(501)994-4678
ptfleming@live.com

Hollenbeck, Linda
(Edward B. Hollenbeck)
409 Carson Drive
Benton, AR 72015
(501)315-9737

Kinslow, Jean
(Alfred Kinslow)
29209 Perdido Beach Blvd
Vista Bella #701
Orange Beach, AL 36561
(251)981-8385

Ryan, Barbara
(James Ryan)
8806 Kennesaw Mountain Drive
Mabelvale, AR 72103

Shanley, Martha
(Dwight Shanley)
16904 Old Mill Road
Little Rock, AR 72206

Wynne, Glenna
(W. J. Wynne)
1501 W Block
El Dorado, AR 71730
(870)863-9444

CAUCA VALLEY

Munoz, Aliria Correal de
(Gerardo Munoz)
5405 Robelene Drive
Metaire, LA 70003
gwilson54@cox.net

Pejendino, Socorro
(Fhanor Pejendino)
24 Avenida 0-97 Zona
7 Ciudad de GUATEMALA
(317)654-5750

Wallace, Beth
(Boyce Wallace)
Cra 101 No 15-93
Cali, COLOMBIA, SA
(352)339-1579
hbwcali@yahoo.com

Yepez, Mrs. (??)
(Juan Yepez)
Colombia, South America

CHOCTAW

Jacob, Betty
(Randy Jacob)
PO Box 158
Broken Bow, OK 74728
(580)584-2099
chocpres@pine-net.com

COLUMBIA

Barker, Mickey
(Jack Barker)
40 Watson Street
Savannah, TN 38372
(731)926-1577

Bates, Betty Ruth
(Harold Bates)
204 Apache Trail
Columbia, TN 38401
(931)381-6737

Burns, Angela C.
(Bobby G. Burns)
328 Dunnaway Road
Shelbyville, TN 37160
(931)294-5105

Denton, Virgie
(Clyde Denton)
2538 County Club Lane
Columbia, TN 38401
(931)388-7154

Green, Marie
(Odis Green)
18 Oakwood Street NW
Rome, GA 30165
(706)291-1738

Miller, Carolyn
(James R Miller)
1214 Whitney Drive
Columbia, TN 38401
(931)381-3367

Sain, Sally
(Edwin Sain)
27 Hilltop Road
Fayetteville, TN 37334
(931)433-8708
ssain@fpunet.com

Seaton, Whitney
(Charlie Seaton)
111 W Hardin Drive
Columbia, TN 38401
(931)388-0319

Wilkins, Dianne S
(Marvin Edward Wilkins)
209 Mackey Street
Rogersville, AL 35652
(256)247-5557
marvinwilkins@msn.com

COVENANT

Atchison, Cheryl
(Dean Atchison)
206 Marsha Drive
Ledbetter, KY 42058

Cannon, Joyce
(Chester Cannon)
1026 W Center Street
Madisonville, KY 42431

Clark, Eileen
(Morris Clark)
8720 State Route 132 W
Clay, KY 42404

Dixon, Sonja
(Robert Dixon)
8550 Lafayette Road
Hopkinsville, KY 42240
(270)886-7647
sonjadixon@earthlink.net

Gerard, Vanda
(Eugene "Stan" Gerard)
615 N 42nd Street
Paducah, KY 42001
(270)443-2889

Marsiglio, June
(Roger Marsiglio)
505 Logan
Providence, KY 42450)

Moss, Lou
(Larry Moss)
167 Bluegrass Drive
LaCenter, KY 42056
(270)292-2000

Owen, Pat
(Bert Owen)
7906 Manner Pointe Drive
Louisville, KY 40220
(502)749-1940
bertorpatowen@insightbb.com

Shirey, Althea (Suzie)
(John H. Shirey)
10181 State Route 56 W
Sturgis, KY 42459
(270)389-3562

Shoulta, Brenda
(John Shoulta)
11504 Mount Carmel Road
White Plains, KY 42464
(270)676-3563
bshoulta@bellsouth.net

Vasseur, Loretta
(Terry Vasseur)
121 Crossland Road
Murray, KY 42071
(270)876-8083

CULLMAN

Kimbrell, Glenda
(Bobby Kimbrell)
9479 Cumberland Oaks Drive
Pinson, AL 35126
(205)680-1743

SURVIVING SPOUSES OF MINISTERS BY PRESBYTERY CONTINUED
(Deceased spouse in parenthesis.)

Weathersby, Dorothy
(E.W. Weathersby)
1203 2nd Avenue NE
Cullman, AL 35055
(256)734-2886

CUMBERLAND

Bruington, Myrna
(Donald Bruington)
105 Bank Street Apt 3
Hardinsburg, KY 40143
(270)257-2228

Gary, Cathy
(Brian Gary)
105 Wilma Avenue
Radcliff, KY 40160

Graham, Mary
(Harold Graham)
103 Freeman Green Drive
Elizabethtown, KY 42701
(270)360-1191

Haire, Betty
(Shelby O Haire)
3179 Meeting Creek Road
Eastview, KY 42732
(270)862-3887

Hatcher, Cherry Lee
(Carlton Hatcher)
2111 Robin Road
Bowling Green, KY 42101
(270)842-8488

Johnson, Genevie
(Robert Johnson)
351 Bacon Court
Harrodsburg, KY 40330
(859)734-3789

Jones, Peggy
(Joseph Jones)
405 Lakeview Drive
Campbellsville, KY 42718

Milam, Dona
(Robert Milam)
9294 Owensboro Road
Falls of Rough, KY 40119
(270)879-8985

Mouser, Wynemia Despain
(Calvin Mouser)
16305 Highland Drive
McKenzie, TN 38201
(270)932-7377

Phelps, Diann
(John Phelps)
4743 Happy Hollow Road
Hawesville, KY 42348
(270)927-9835
haor@juno.com

Renner, Wallace
(Patricia Renner)
1648 Griffith Avenue
Owensboro, KY 42301
(270)685-4359
pwrenner@adelphia.com

Sprague, Rose
(George Sprague)
101 Clyde Morris Hall #242
Ormond Beach, FL 32174

Vaught, Amy
(Joseph Vaught)
208 Carters Creek Pike
Columbia, TN 38401

DEL CRISTO

Appleby, Judy
(Bob Appleby)
3265 16th Street
San Francisco, CA 94103
(415)703-6090
gfcc@gum.org

Chang, Grace
(John Chang)
1753 Castro Drive
San Jose, CA 95130
(408)370-0643

Ellis, Ernestine
(John Ellis)
1432 Cape Verde Place
Tucson, AZ 85748
(520)296-9027

Freeman, ??
(Jack Freeman)
3559 Cody Way
Sacramento, CA 95864
(916)489-2567

Hom, Christina
(Paul Hom)
722 24th Avenue
San Francisco., CA
(415751-9766

Kennedy, Louise
(John F Kennedy)
4916 44th Street
Lubbock, TX 79414
(806)796-0738

Matlock, Bettye
(Joe Matlock)
5905 Hickory Grove Lane
Bartlett, TN 38134
(901)937-8457

EAST TENNESSEE

Alexander, Carolyn Roberts
(Don Charles Alexander)
220 107 Cutoff
Greeneville, TN 37743
(423)638-8453
alexandercda@msn.com

Blakeburn, Wiletta
(Roy E Blakeburn)
111 Park Place
Greeneville, TN 37743
(423)787-9609
blakeburnr@aol.com

Brooks, Dianna
(Wayne Brooks)
215 Love Street
Greeneville, TN 37745
(423)329-5209

Broyles, Elizabeth
(Lon Broyles)
753 Snapp Bridge Road
Limestone, TN 37681
(865)483-8433

Broyles, Minnie
(Raymond Broyles)
4944 Kilaminajaro
Old Hickory, TN 37138-4102
(615)428-8640

Dobson, Valdean
(Howard Dobson)
150 Liberty Way
Greeneville, TN 37645
(423)798-8947

Ivey, Edna
(Billy F Ivey)
409 Rodeo Drive
Knoxville, TN 37934
(865)966-5946

Johnson, Mary Louise
(Beverly Johnson)
801 Riverhill Drive Apt 421
Athens, GA 30606
(865)977-0405
bevloujohnson@aol.com

Johnson, Rebecca
(Scott Johnson)
512 Rolling Creek Circle
Knoxville, TN 37922
(865)966-3699

Richardson, Regena
(W. Jean Richardson)
7533 Lancashire Boulevard
Powell, TN 37849
(865)947-3111
jeanandregena@frontier.com

Scott, Betty
(Lee Scott)
1580 Dover Road
Morristown, TN 37813
(731)415-2936

GRACE

Acton, Virginia
(Wade Acton)
1615 Estes Drive
Glencoe, AL 35905

Benson, Annette
(William Benson)
137 W Lowndes Drive
Columbus, MS 39701
(662)386-3433
willardb715@gmail.com

Brown, Marye
(Richard C Brown)
2100 NE 140th Street Apt 510E
Edmond, OK 73013
(205)663-5486

Buerhaus, Charity
(Chuck Buerhaus)
313 S Main Street
Piedmont, AL 36272
(256)447-6195

Johnson, Barbara
(Thomas "Tommy" Johnson)
PO Box 566
Helena, AL 35080
revtomjohnson@aol.com

Maynard, Jackie
(Terrell Maynard)
3 Nelson Cove
Milan, TN 38358
(731)437-0026

Athala Jaramillo
(Luciano Jaramillo)
6248 SW 14th Street
West Miami, FL 33144
lucatha@aol.com
(305)264-107410

Mims, Martha Jo
(Howell "Gay" Mims)
3011 Wolfe Road
Columbus, MS 39705
(662)328-3778
mjmims@muw.edu

SURVIVING SPOUSES OF MINISTERS BY PRESBYTERY CONTINUED
(Deceased spouse in parenthesis.)

Phillips, Edna
(Troy Phillips)
  2024 Hilltop Road
  Rock Hill, SC 29732
  (803)325-1416

Tant, Becky
(Robert H Tant)
  516 Davis Drive
  Glencoe, AL 35905
  (256)494-9450
  rtant82091@aol.com

HOPE

Copeland, Frances S.
(Bill Copeland)
  142 Thornton Terrace Drive
  Rogersville, AL 35652
  (256)247-1688

Hyden, Mae
(Lee Hyden)
  2195 Allsboro Road
  Cherokee, AL 35616
  (256)360-2896

MISSOURI

Bone, Beverly
(Leslie Bone)
  16504 George Franklyn Drive
  Independence, MO 64055

Cravens, Doris
(Marvin L Cravens)
  604 N Hovis Street
  Mountain Grove, MO 65711
  (417)926-5778

Cravens, Hallie
(Ellis Cravens)
  9566 Highway Z
  Hartville, MO 65667
  (417)668-5954

Dailey, Sarah
(Larry Dailey)
  11412 W 57th
  Shawnee, KS 66203
  (573)374-9537

Hensley, Jean Ann
(Howard Hensley)
  537 Piperpoint
  Rogersville, MO 65742
  (414)753-1108

McCloud, Johnnie
(Theron McCloud)
  419 Magnolia Court
  Lebanon, MO 65536
  (417)532-3388
  jmccloud@advertisenet.com

Scobey, Darlis
(James Scobey)
  105 Oak Hill Downs Street
  Farmington, MO 63640
  (573)756-1683

MURFREESBORO

Alhart, Reba Kay
(Daryl Alhart)
  215 Fairview Street
  Estill Springs, TN 37330
  (931)349-7104

Basham, Earline
(Willard Basham)
  335 Myers Road
  Winchester, TN 37398

Breeding, Karen
(Gordon Breeding)
  1907 Susan Drive
  Murfreesboro, TN 37129
  (615)867-3660
  zanylady1000@yahoo.com

Campbell, Grace
(Coyle Campbell)
  186 Old Limestone Road
  New Market, AL 35761
  (256)379-4932

Clark, Barbara
(Jonathan Clark)
  88 Woodcrest Drive
  Winchester, TN 37398
  (931)967-9613
  bjhclark@bellsouth.net

Dickerson, Helen
(Andrew Mizel Dickerson, Jr.)
  914 Dogwood Drive
  Murfreesboro, TN 37129

Hancock, Rose
(B J Hancock)
  103 Cowan Street W
  Cowan, TN 37318
  (931)967-8491

Martin, Peggy
(James W Martin)
  1922 Battleground Drive
  Murfreesboro, TN 37129
  (615)896-4442

Martindale, Dana
(J. Craig Martindale)
  2913 Pellas Place
  Murfreesboro, TN 37127
  (615)653-0858
  w5bu@hotmail.com

Salisbury, Rebecca
(Loyce Estes)
  1033 Twin Oaks Drive
  Murfreesboro, TN 37130
  (615)410-7801

Watson, Mary Leota
(David E Watson)
  804 W Main Street
  McMinnville, TN 37110
  (931)473-7561
  leotaw@blomand.net

Walkup, Joyce
(Lyon Walkup)
  225 Bertha Owen Road
  Morrison, TN 37357
  (931)607-3233
  dirtroad@blomand.net

NASHVILLE

Andrews, Jane
(Leonard Andrews)
  7390 Cabot Drive
  Nashville, TN 37209
  (615)352-0145

Burnett, Mary Lee
(Cecil Burnett)
  321 Raindrop Lane
  Hendersonville, TN 37075

Maxedon, Chris
(Julian Maxedon)
  2260 Highway 31
  White House, TN 37188

Parish, Rita
(Johnny Parish)
  114 Savo Bay
  Hendersonville, TN 37075
  (615)824-5842
  rfbparish@comcast.net

Schott, Mary Ann
(Fred Schott)
  606 Taylor Trail
  Springfield, TN 37172
  (615)384-8572

Smith, Dolores
(Billy T Smith)
  c/o Brookdale of Clarksville
  2183 Memorial Drive
  Clarksville, TN 37043
  (931)358-3765

Stiles, Peggy
(John Stiles)
  300 Bantam Court
  Clarksville, TN 37043

NORTH CENTRAL

Barnett, Jeanne
(Rudy Barnett)
  3014 Mockingbird Lane
  Evansville, IL 47710
  (618)643-3253

Gross, June
(Ronald Gross)
  2436 N 420th Street
  Oblong, IL 62449
  (217)932-2788

McCain, Violet
(Terence McCain)
  15804 Camden Avenue
  Eastpointe, MI 48021
  (586)774-4861

Smith, Evelyn June
(Albert J. Smith)
  15740 Millbank Street
  Huntersville, NC 28078
  (704)975-2990

Springer, Eileen
(Robert Springer)
  403 Prairie Ridge Court
  Eureka, IL 61530
  (309)467-5030

RED RIVER

Brown, Beth
(LaRoyce Brown)
  311 S 8th Street
  Marlow, OK 73055
  (580)658-3989

Dewhirst, Robin
(Tim Dewhirst)
  3609 Oakbriar Lane
  Colleyville, TX 76034
  (817)605-8147
  timdew@sbcglobal.net

Morgan, Sharon
(Jerome Morgan)
  8420 Baumgarten Drive
  Dallas, TX 75228

Shelton, Barbara Ann
(Robert E Shelton)
  10508 Royalwood Drive
  Dallas, TX 75238
  (214)349-7162
  bshelton67@yahoo.com

SURVIVING SPOUSES OF MINISTERS BY PRESBYTERY CONTINUED
(Deceased spouse in parenthesis.)

Fran Shelton
(Robert M Shelton)
7128 Lakehurst Avenue
Dallas, TX 75230
(214)348-2133
ftshelton@gmail.com

Hall, Carol
(John David Hall)
109 Oddo Lane SE
Huntsville, AL 35802
(256)447-8817

Shugert, JoAnn
(Rich Shugert)
5208 Bellis Drive
Fort Worth, TX 76244
(817)913-7243
jashugert@gmail.com

Turpen, Mary Lou
(Brent Turpen)
1722 E Elm Street
New Albany, IN 47150
(918)803-2281
mlturpen@hotmail.com

Ward, Suzie
(Kevin Ward)
216 E Caroline
Marshall, TX 75672

ROBERT DONNELL

Hunter, Jean
(James E. Hunter)
1905 Delynn
Hazel Green, AL 35750
(256)838-3902

TENNESSEE-GEORGIA

Galloway, Katherine
(Cliff Galloway)
7127 White Oak Valley Road
McDonald, TN 37353

Kapperman, Linda
(Glenn Kapperman)
2719 Rio Grande Road
Chattanooga, TN 37421
(423)894-7924

Marsh, Mary Elizabeth
(Allan Marsh)
1000 Media Road
Minneola, FL 34715

Melton, Wanda
(Samuel D Melton)
2249 Bucks Pocket Road SE
Old Fort, TN 37362
(423)472-8467

Naugher, Catherine
(Doyce Naugher)
985 Mt Pleasant Road
Rydal, GA 30171
(770)382-1982

TRINITY

Leslie, Jenann
(Marvin E. Leslie)
300 Henley Perry Drive
Marshall, TX 75670
(903)938-6642
jenann.leslie@gmail.com

Nunn, Helen
(Donald W. Nunn)
203 Bridgers Hill Road
Longview, TX 75604
(903)297-6074
nunnh@earthlink.net

Harris, Jeri
(Ernest Harris)
759 S State Street #133
Ukiah, CA 95482
(903)782-9712

Rustenhaven, Dolores
(William (Bill) Rustenhaven, Jr.)
703 W Burleson Street
Marshall, TX 75670
(903)935-7056
rustenhavendolores@yahoo.com

WEST TENNESSEE

Brown, Beverly
(Paul B. Brown)
406 N McNeil Street
Memphis, TN 38112
(901)278-6909

Brown, Phyllis
(David Brown)
1930 Mignon
Memphis, TN 38107
(901)274-1513

Butler, Shirley
(George A Butler)
306 Flora Circle
Newbern, TN 38059

Caperton, Julia
(Donald Caperton)
137 Park Street
Camden, TN 38320
(731)593-5096

Cook, Marcine
(Paul V. Cook)
144 Big John Drive
Martin, TN 38237
(731)587-0787
marcine175@aol.com

Davis, Willene
(Harold Davis)
333Thompson Street, Apt 327
Hendersonville, NC 28792
(901)757-1394

Drylie, Linda
(James Drylie)
512 JE Blaydes Parkway
Atoka, TN 38004
(901)837-1627

Forester, Willie Mae
(J. C. Forester)
833 Main Street
McKenzie, TN 38201
(731)352-3107

Hall, Patsy
(Charles R. Hall)
4341 Pebble Garden Court
Birmingham, AL 35235
(205)538-7993

Hicks, Ruby
(Willam D. Hicks)
3938 Cardinal Drive
Union City, TN 38261
(731)885-5887

Janner, Mary Ann
(Tony Janner)
294 Buxtons Way
Freeport, FL 32439
(731)352-9566

Jett, Shirley
(Mace Jett, Jr)
109 Park Street
Martin, TN 38237
(731)587-0805

Knight, Helen
(James Knight)
8081 Jills Creek Drive
Bartlett, TN 38133
(901)387-0675

Laurence, Brenda
(G. Larry Laurence)
2823 Nine Mile Road
Enville, TN 38332
(731)687-2022
southernmoma@hotmail.com

Leslie, Cheryl
(Randall Leslie)
3374 Walnut Grove Road
Memphis, TN 38111
(901)458-4413

Leslie, Marilyn
(Eugene Leslie)
13155 Center Hill Road
Olive Branch, MS 38654
(731)613-0425
eleslie1@bellsouth.net

McClanahan, JoAnn
(H Walter McClanahan)
215 White Brothers Road
Humboldt, TN 38343
(731)784-1176
joannmcclanahan@hughes.net

McMahen, Sandra
(Rowe Gene McMahen)
92 Stonewall Circle
McKenzie, TN 38201
(731)352-3067

Phelps, Doris
(Earl Phelps)
172 Michie-Pebble Hill Road
Stantonville, TN 38379
(731)632-5107

Pinnell, Carol
(James Pinnell)
1525 Parks Well Road
Gleason, TN 38229
(731)648-5078

Schwarz, Betty
(Karl Schwarz, Sr.)
83 W Curtis Street
Bells, TN 38006
(901)663-3987

Reid, Donna
(Richard Reid)
104 Gregg Street
Jackson, TN 38301
(731)453-5302

Smith, Genelle
(Jerry Smith)
502 Blackpatch Drive Apt A102
Springfield, TN 37172

Stott, Beverly
(Melvin Buddy Stott)
911 Low Gap Road
Princeton, WV 24740
(731)364-5863
bevstott@frontiernet.net

Williams, Beth
(Bobby D Williams)
844 W Highway 22
Union City, TN 38251
(731)885-1710

CUMBERLAND PRESBYTERIANS
SERVING OUTSIDE THE UNITED STATES

Please e-mail missionaries before mailing anything to them to determine the best way to send them letters or packages. If you want to communicate with missionaries in closed countries, first e-mail the Missions Ministry Team (Lthomas@cumberland.org) and we will forward your e-mail to the missionary.

Jose & Sara Guerrero—Brazil
e-mail: josueggutierez@yahoo.es

Beth Wallace (Missionary Emeritus)—Colombia
e-mail: hbwcali@yahoo.com
oovoo and facetime: Boyce Wallace

Patrick & Jessica Wilkerson—Colombia
e-mail: patrickwilkerson3@gmail.com

Socorro Pejendino—Guatemala
email: pastorasocorrod@hotmail.com

T T G—Kyrgyzstan
email: lynndont@gmail.com

D S L—Laos and Cambodia
email: lynndont@gmail.com

Daniel & Kay Jang—Philippines
Ilollo Cumberland Mission Church
email: goingup129@hanmail.net

Wilson & Diana Lopez—Spain
email: wilsonlg7@gmail.com

Kenneth & Delight Hopson—Uganda
Under the care of World Gospel Missions
e-mail: ken.hopson@wgm.org
skype: Delight Hopson
oovoo: Kenneth Hopson

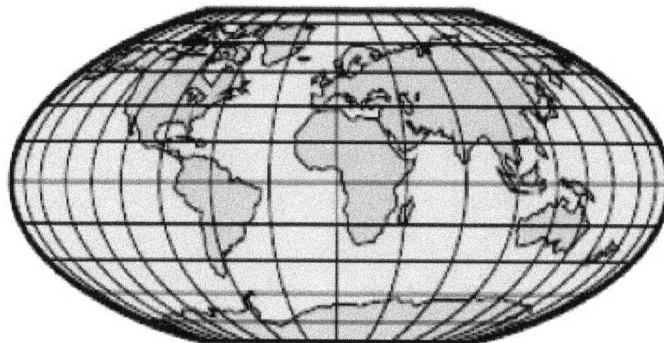

The Cumberland Presbyterian Church
has five families working in closed countries as
humanitarian workers.

NEW CHURCH DEVELOPMENTS & MISSION PROBES

ANDES

Aguadas
Cra 3 #7-14
Aguadas, Caldas
Colombia, SA
(576)851-4773
jeob40@hotmail.com
Pastor: Joaquin Orozco   (M1)
Began: 1996 (as re-development)

Chinchina
Mz 2 Casa 21, Urb. Milan
Dosquebradas, Ris
Colombia, SA
(476)322-2177
oikoninonia@gmail.com
Pastor: Rodrigo Martinez   (M1)

CAUCA VALLEY

Bugalagrande
Cra 8 No 7A-12
Bugalagrande, Colombia, SA

Carmelo
Veredo Carmelo
Limones, Cauca, Colombia, SA
Pastor: Juan Ventura   (M3)

Casa de Oracion

Dia de Salvacion
Pastor: Luis Cantor
(   )256-2835

Golondrinas
Corregimiento Golondrinas
Montebello, Colombia, SA
vallejo0903@hotmail.com
Pastor: Ariel Vallejo   (M3)
(312)853-3138

Guachucal
Centro
Guachucal, Colombia, SA
Iflesianuevavida15@gmail.com
Pastor: Martin Termal   (M3)
(317)458-3294

Ipiales
Cra 2A No 12-54
Ipiales, Colombia, SA
(316)705-5551
pastoscarealpe@hotmail.com
Pastor: Oscar Realpe   (M1)

Juanico
Vereda Juanico
Guapi, Colombia, SA
Pastor: Bernabe Angulo   (M3)
(310)364-9445

Limones
Corregimiento Limones
Guapi, Colombia, SA
Pastor: Henry Angulo   (M3)

Los Monos
Vereda Los Monos
Sapuyes, Colombia, SA
Pastor: Mario Paredes   (LS)

Manantial de Vida
Vereda de Brazo Seco
El Charco, Colombia, SA
Pastor: Sofinias Velazco   (M3)

Morales
Morales, Colombia, SA
johnydiana7@hotmail.com
Pastor: Jhon Agredo   (M3)
(310)436-0141
jhonydiana7@hotmail.com

Rios de Agua Viva
Trav 87 No 2-24
Buenatura, Colombia, SA
(314)752-2207
euripidesmoreno1@hotmail.com
Pastor: Euripides Moreno   (M1)

Sapuyes
Iglesia Presbiteriana C
Sapyues, Colombia, SA
walterviteri@gmail.com
Pastor: Oscar Rosero   (M3)

Villa Gorgona
Manzana C Casa 5 Santa Ana
Villa Gorgona, Colombia, SA
(311)627-4274
montesdesalvacion@gmail.com
Pastor: Daniel Blanco   (M3)

Villavicencio
Villavicencio, Colombia, SA
german_millanco1@yahoo.com.mx
Pastor: German Millan   (M3)
(311)510-5964

COLUMBIA

Williamson County
101 Valley Ridge Road
Franklin, TN 37064
(731)780-1004
ellen.hudson17@icloud.com
Pastor: Ellen Hudson

COVENANT

Cadiz
Cadiz, KY
Pastor: Danny York   (M1)
Began: 2000

DEL CRISTO

Agape (formerly Marantha East)
12008 Fred Carter
El Paso, TX 79936
(915)857-1343
yaanaivitaly@yahoo.com
Pastor: Alfredo Rincon   (M1)
Began: 2007

Bethesda Korean Fellowship
139 Silverado Drive
Santa Teresa, NM 88008
(915)329-3451
pyongsanyu@hotmail.com
Pastor: Pyong San Yu   (M1)
Began: 03/10

EMAUS

Amaga
Cra 49 #49-18
Amaga, Antioquia
Colombia, South America
(574)847-3250
rebcaldas@une.net.co
Pastor: Jhon Jairo Arias   (M1)
Began: 1997

Envigado
Calle 38 Sur #40-25
Envigado, Antioquia
Colombia, South America
Pastor: Juan Fernando Morales
(M3)
juanfer0116@gmail.com

Istmina
San Barrio San Francisco
Istmina, Choco
Colombia, South America
Pastor: Yeison David Lopez
(57)315-2901817
yeisondavidlopez@outlook.com

La America
Carrera 99 #41a-21
Medellin, Antioquia
Colombia, South America
adanvarilla@hotmail.com
Pastors: Lida Patricia Vargas(M3)
Adan Manuel Varilla   (M3)

GRACE

_____ (0312)
Comunidad Biblica of Miami
6375 W Flagler Street
Miami, FL 33144
(305)801-6424
tonymardo@comcast.net
Pastor: Mardoqueo Munoz
Began: 01/16

_____ (0309)
Naples Fellowship
842 Bent Creek Way
Naples, FL 34114
(931)273-0768
revga@hotmail.com
Pastor: Ramon Garcia   (M1

Jacksonville, FL NEI
401 Monument Road Apt 74
Jacksonville, FL 32225
Pastor: Janina Barrios   (M1)

Ministerio Hosanna Group
10922 SW 243 LN
Homestead, FL 33032
Pastor: Carlos Daza

Casa de Gracia CP Ministry
1680 West 56 Street Apt 105C
Hialeah, FL 33012
Pastor: Yoel rodriguez
yoelaymee@hotmail.com

Panamericana Ministry
412 SW 87 Place
Miami, FL 33174
Pastor: Aida Diego   (M1)
revaidamd@yahoo.com

NEW CHURCH DEVELOPMENTS & MISSION PROBES (continued)

Tiempos de Fe NEI
488 SW 126th Terrace
Davie, FL 33325
Pastor: Sandra Castellanos
sandramcastellanos@hotmail.com

RED RIVER

Church of St. Giles
3500 S Peoria Avenue
Tulsa, OK 74105
(918)760-6145
Pastor: William G. Webb, Jr. (M1)

El Lugar De Su Gracia
1415 W Wheatland Road
Duncanville, TX 75116
(972)748-4752
Pastor: Josue Rodriguez
josuehrodriguez@hotmail.com

_____ (8426)
Marantha
2801 Biway Street
Fort Worth, TX 76114
(817)210-5571
sledadmartinez164@gmail.com
Pastor: Soledad Martinez (M1)
Began: 2015

TENNESSEE-GEORGIA

GJHS Ministries
3327 Duluth Highway
Duluth, GA 30096
(770)940-2365
gjhministryatl@gmail.com
Pastor: Jung Hee Jung (M1)
Began: 10/08/16

WEST TENNESSEE

_____ (9437)
Comunidad Cristiana Amor Y Fe
3427 Appling Road
Bartlett, TN 38133
(830)872-6090
paul-tuba@hotmail.com
Pastor: Lugwin Paul Puloc Munoz
Began: 3/2016

_____ (9323)
Grace Fellowship
9160 Tchulahoma Road
Southaven, MS 38671
(662)393-2552
tthompson393@aol.com
Pastor: Tommy Thompson (M1)

Iona Community of Faith
1790 Faxon Avenue
Memphis, TN 38112
website: www.iona.gutensite.com
(901)283-8062
wa4mff@aol.com
Pastor: Barry Anderson (M1)

PROVISIONAL CHURCHES

"A provisional fellowship is a pre-existing non-English congregation that is being received into the Cumberland Presbyterian Church through an authorized assimilation process.

ARKANSAS

_____ (2135)
Arkansas Korean Loving Church
8201 Frenchmans Lane
Little Rock, AR 72209
(501)247-9527
Pastor: Jinook Jung

CUMBERLAND
EAST COAST

_____ (2445)
Immanuel Presbyterian Church
67-17 215th
Oakland Gardens, NY 11364
Pastor: Soo Yeol Park
(646)599-4941
shwbpark@naver.com

_____ (2138)
Our Good Presbyterian Church
32132 Huntly Circle
Salisbury, MD 21804
(443)783-3809 (cell)
Pastor: Hyoung Sik Choi   (M1)
Began: 2001

DEL CRISTO

_____
El Paso Hope Presbyterian
4600 La Luz Avenue
El Paso, TX 79903
(916)305-9119
Pastor: Myungsik Kang   (M2)

_____
Lord's Joyful Church
605-H S Palm
La Habra, CA 90631
(949)241-6167
Pastor: Kun Ho Cho   (M1)

EAST TENNESSEE

_____ (2332)
Pilgrim
300 Cabot Street
Beverly, MA 01915
(978)712-0877
Pastor: Valerie Crisman
pilgrimchurchbeverlyma@gmail.com
Began: April 2017

KOREAN OF SE

_____(2126)
Baek Seok Church
3075 Landington Way
Duluth, GA 30096
(404)398-8469
mnb0924@yahoo.co.kr
Pastor: Seung Chon Han   (M1)

_____
Ecclesia
105 Mandarin Drive
Oak Grove, KY 42262
(931)802-8485
Pastor: Choil Ma   (M1)
choilma@yahoo.com

_____ (2130)
Korean Livingstone Presbyterian Church
3340 Bentbill xing
Cumming, GA 30041
(770)912-8477
barkmoksa@hanmail.net
Pastor: Young Rae Park   (M1)

_____
Nahnum Mission
550 Pleasant Hill Road
Lilburn, GA 30047
(404)667-1800
Pastor: Seok Heon Lim   (M1)
slim3398@gmail.com

_____ (2160)
True Light Jesus
3972 Stillwater Drive
Duluth, GA 30096
(678)822-1508
Pastor: Paul Kim   (M1)

RED RIVER

_____
El Lugar De Su Gracia
1415 Wheatland Road
Duncancille, TX 75116
(972)748-4752
Pastor: Josue Rodriguez
josuehrodriguez@hotmail.com

WEST TENNESSEE

_____
Redeemer Evangelical Church
7011 Poplar Avenue
Germantown, TN 38138
(901)737-3370
jimmylatimer@redeemerevangelical.com
Pastor: James M. Latimer

MISSION CHURCHES AND PASTORS UNDER CARE OF MISSIONS MINISTRY TEAM
(General Assembly Ministry Council)

AUSTRALIA
"Australia CP Council of Churches"

Darwin Dasom Korean
(Provisional)
  44 Dripstone Road
  Causurina, NT 0820
  lee7315465@naver.com
  Pastor: Seok Yun Lee   (M1)

Joyful Message Church
(Disciple)
  237 Botany Road
  Waterloo
  oldrooney@hotmail.com
  Pastor Sung Yong Cho   (M1)

Jupum Mission Church
(Mission)
  Goulburn Christian Life Centre
  148 Sloan Street
  Goulbourn NSW
  morning0588@gmail.com
  Pastor: Young Chul Park   (M1)

Penrith Church (Citizen)
(Mission)
  15 Evan Street
  Penrith NSW 2750
  rsk2002@empal.com
  Pastor: Suk Kyu Ryu   (M1)

Sydney Hiel Church
  247 Old Northern Road
  Castle Hill
  lovepresage@naver.com
  Pastor Jiho Kim   (M1)

ORDAINED:

Cho, Sung Yong
  6/58-62 Carnarvon Street
  Silverwater, NSW
  oldrooney@hotmail.com
Hwang, Sun Hee
  1512 Lindsay Street
  Darwin, NT 0800
  hangsongwee2@gmail.com
Kim, Jiho
  31 Olga Street
  Chatswood NSW 2067
  lovepresage@naver.com
Lee, Joung Me (Sharon)
  2 Belmore Street
  Ryde NSW 2112
  jmlee153@naver.com
Lee, Seok Yun
  18 Queen Street
  NT0820
  lee7315465@naver.com
Park, Yong Chul (John)
  2 Belmore Street
  Ryde NSW 2112
  morning0588@gmail.com
Ryu, Suk Kyu
  9155 Manson Road
  Strathfield, NSW 2131
  rsk2002@empal.com

PROVISIONAL PASTORS:

Huh, Min
  2112 Eunka Street
  Chadstone, VIC 3148
  min0430446647@gmail.com
Kim, Young Kwang
  25 Clemsford Avenue
  Epping, NSW 2121
  basskk77@naver.com
Lim, Kiho
  kiholim72@gmail.com

LICENTIATES:

Jang, Suk Jin
  sjjang2@msn.com
Park, Myung Soon
  237 Botany Road
  Waterloo NSW
  chlpjs17@gmail.com

CANDIDATES:

Kim, In Jae
  david.injae@gmail.com
Kim, Jae Kyoung
  kjk6662@gmail.com
Lee, Donghyung
  7/1-3 Mary Street
  Lidcombe NWS 2141
  ldh8940@gmail.com
Nam, Mee Yae
  10 Blain Street
  Toongabbie NSW 2146
  ehddid2@daum.net

BRAZIL
Hosted by Missions Ministry Team

_____ (8313)
Mata De Sao Joao Church
  Nucleo Colonial JK Lote 56
  Mata De Sao Joao 48280-000
  Bahia, BRAZIL
  (5571)99699-5348
  Pastor: Carlos Santos da Silva (M1)
  (5571)99699-5348
  san_coc@hotmail.com

ORDAINED:

Santos da Silva, Carlos
  Nucleo Colonial JK Lote 56
  Mata De Sao Joao 48280-000
  Bahia, BRAZIL
  (5571)99699-5348
  san_coc@hotmail.com

CANDIDATES:

Silva, Priscilla Santos Cerqueira
  Nucleo Colonial JK Lote 56
  Mata de Sao Jao 48280-000
  Bahia, BRAZIL

MISSIONARIES:

Josue and Sarah Guerrero
  Salvador, BRAZIL
  josueggutierrez@yahoo.es

MISSION CHURCHES AND PASTORS UNDER CARE OF
MISSIONS MINISTRY TEAM (General Assembly Ministry Council)
(continued)

GUATEMALA
"Guatemala CP Council of Churches"
24 Avenida 0-97 Zona 7
Colonia Altamira II Ciudad De
Guaremala, Guatermala

Casa de Fe y Oracion
31 calle 9-75 Colonia Miralvally
Zona 6 de Mixco
Guatemala

Comunidad de Fe
13 Avenida 20-58
Colonia La Reformita Zona 12
Ciudad de Fuatemala
Guatemala

MISSIONS

La Vid
Guatemala City
Pastor: Oscar Ramirez   (M2)

Nueva Esperanza
17 Avenida 50-51 Zona 12
Colonia La Colina Cuidad de
Guatemala

MISSIONARIES:

Reverend Socorro Pejendino
pastorasocorrod@hotmail.com

LICENTIATES:

Ramirez, Oscar
35 Ave 28-09 zona 5 Colonia Santa Ana
Ciudad de Guatemala
Guatemala
oscar.ramirez@lavid.church

HAITI
"Haiti CP Council of Churches"
Hosted by Hope Presbytery

PROVISIONAL CHURCHES:

Eglise Evangelique de Dufour
Pastor: Jean Joab St Louis   (M1)

Eglise E U-Chunen Gris de Gris-Gris
Pastor: Kemson Lundy   (M1)

Eglise Evangelique de Lexi
Pastor: Fauvelt Smith   (M1)

Eglise Evangelique de Mache Kabrit
Pastor: Evetuel Theissaint   (M1)

Eglise Evangelique de Nan Akou
Pastor: Sheslaire Georges   (M1)

Eglise Evangelique de Saint-Jules
Pastor: Eddy Eddouard   (M1)

MEXICO
"Mexico CP Council of Churches"
Hosted by Red River Presbytery

Fuente de Vida - Ajusco
(Mission)
Calle Primera Cerrada de Hombres
Ilustres 2B Colonia Santa Ceilia
Tepetlapa Delebacion
Xochimilco CP
Ciudad Mexico

PROVISIONAL CHURCHES:

Casa del Alfarero
C Norte 12 A Esq OTE 53
Chalco Edo
Mexico
54-4-627-5570
alaprep28@hotmail.com
Pastor: Alejandro Alejo   (M1)

Iglesia Marantha
Arroyo de Miumbre #1749
Col Felipe Augeles
Ciudad Juarez
Mexico
54-53-67-9103
jessevega69@gmail.com
Pastor: Jedidiah Vega   (M1)

Restauration de Vida
Calle C Col San Marcos
Azcapotzalco C P 02020
Mexico
55-53-18-7622
castro_dan@hotmail.com
Pastor: Jose Dan Castro   (M1)

PASTORS

Castro, Jose Dan (Solis)
(see address Restauration de Vida)

PROVISIONAL PASTORS:

Alejo, Alejandro (Robledo)
Casa del Alfarero CP Church
C Norte 12 Esq Ote 53 Col Union
de GPE
Chalco Mexico
Phone: 46-27-5570
aleprep28@hotmail.com
Castro, Jose Dan (Solis)
Restauracion de Vida CP Church
Calle C Col San Marcos
Azcapotzalco C P 02020 Mexico
Phone: 55-53-18-7622
castro_dan@hotmail.com
Mata, Jorge Fernando
Marantha CP Church Towi 8127 Sta
Fe Cd C Jaurez
Chihuahua Mexico
Phone: 656-62-59-975
pastormata@hotmail.com

MISSION CHURCHES AND PASTORS UNDER CARE OF
MISSIONS MINISTRY TEAM (General Assembly Ministry Council)
(continued)

PHILIPPINES
"Philippine CP Council of Churches"

_____
Gracious Jesus Cumberland
Presbyterian
(Church)
  Cabang
  Oton, Iloilo
  Pastor: Alexander Duyac, Jr.   (M1)
_____(2321)
Iloilo Cumberland Presbyterian
(Church)
  Brgy Airport, Mandurriao
  Iloilo City 5000, Philippines
  Pastor: Daniel Wonjeon Jang   (M1)
      Harold Bonete   (M1)

_____
Mostro Cumberland Presbyterian
(Mission)
  Brgy Mostro Anilao
  Iloilo, Philippines

_____
Pavia Cumberland Presbyterian
(Mission)
  Brgy Anilao Pavio
  Iloilo, Philippines
  Pastor: Manual Job Baldevia   (M1)

_____
Sohoton Cumberland Presbyterian
(Mission)
  Brgy Sohoton Barotac Nuevo
  Iloilo, Philippines
  Pastor: Romeo Agana   (M2)

MISSIONARIES:

Mr Daniel Wonjeon (M1) and Kay Jang

PASTORS:

Baldevia, Manuel Job
  (no address on file)
Bonete, Harold Henry
  c/o Iloilo CP Church
Duyac, Alexander, Jr.
  Brgy, Cabang, Oton, Iloilo

LICENTIATES:

Agana, Romeo G, Jr.
  c/o Iloilo CP Church

CANDIDATES:

Clarice Anne C, Sapu-ay
  c/o Iliolo CP Church
Dyuac, Aldrandreb D
  c/o Gracious Jesus CP Church
Garnica, Darrel Von
  c/o Gracious Jesus CP Church
Yutig, Lucelle E
  c/o Gracious Jesus CP Church

SOUTH KOREA
"Korean CP Council of Churches"

_____(2221)
First Cumberland Presbyterian Church
of Korea
(Church)
  Hyundai I-park B-02
  Burim-dong 113
  Dongan-gu, Anyang-si
  Gyeonggi-do, Korea 431-787
  Phone: 82-70-8872-8033
  Pastor: Heungsoo Kang   (M1)
  Clerk: Yoon JinSub
  303-101 Raenian Ever heim Apt
  Naeson 2-dong, Uiwangsi
  Gyeonggi-do, Korea 437-761
  jinsyoon@gmail.com

_____
Glory Church
(Mission)
  302 Si-Bum Building
  1342 Seocho 2-dong, Seocho-gu
  Seoul, Korea 137-861
  Phone: 82-2-3474-8405
  Pastor: Geumtaek Lim   (M1)
_____(2323)
New Life Church
(Mission)
  325-1 Donghyeon-dong
  Jecheon-si
  Chungcheongbud-do, Korea 390-190
  Phone: 82-10-6655-9188
  Pastor: Woonyong Yu   (M1)

_____
Seum Church
(Mission)
  Seobu-ro 2105 beongil 26-6 101 ho
  Jang-gu, Suwan City, South Korea
_____(2324)
Ye-ll Church
(Mission)
  15 Seogyeong-ro, 28beong-gil
  Heungdeok-gu, Cheongiu-si
  Chungcheongbuk-do, Korea 361-803
  Phone: 82-42-232-6000
  Pastor: Dawie Ahn(M1)

PASTORS:

Ahn, Dawit (David)
  606-304 Gapyeong Jugong Apt
  Jungnim-dong, Heungdeck-gu
  Cheongju-si
  Chungcheongbuk-do
  Korea 361-850
  Phone: 82-10-2421-0219
  ankim91@hanmail.net
Kang, Huengsoo
  Hyundai I-park B-02, Burim-dong 113
  Dongan-gu, Anyang-si
  Gyeonggi-do, Korea 431-787
  Phone: 82-10-8428-0084
  halieus@hanmail.net
Kim, YoungHo (Steve)
  B02 Hyundai I-Space 1608-2
  Burim Dong, Dong An Gu
  AnYang City, Kyunggi Do S Korea
  Phone: 231-348-8033
  paidion4377@naver.com

Lee, Sangdo
  507-1501 Samik Green Apt
  Myeongil 1-dong, Gngdong-gu
  Seoul, Korea 134-782
  Phone: 82-10-3353-2907
  humanolsd@hanmail.net
Lee, Yongrae
  507 Je-ll Officetel, 99-20
  Yulgeon-dong, Jangan-gu
  Suwon-si, gyeonggi-do, Korea
  Phone: 82-10-9928-9012
  path0316@naver.com
Lim, Geumtaek
  302-si-Bum Building
  1342 Seocho 2dong, Seccho-gu
  Seoul, Korea 137-861
  Phone: 82-11-9044-5250
  limkt114@hanmail.net
Park, Bo-Seong
  304-28 Sinlim-Dong, Kwanak-Gu
  Seoul, Korea
  Phone: 002-884-3474
Yu, Woonyong
  325-1 Donghyeon-dong, Jecheon-si
  Chungcheongbuk-do, Korea 390-190
  Phone: 82-10-6655-9188
  lifeyu@hanmail.net

LICENTIATES:

Choi, Justin
  823-4 Naeson 1-dong, Uiwang-si
  Gyeonggi-do, Korea 437-838
  Phone: 82-10-2668-8795
  rev.choi@hotmail.com
Lee, Il-Do (Derek)
  151-2 Ongnyeon-dong
  Yeonsu-gu, Incheon, Korea
  Phone: 82-10-2627-2152
  monya215@naver.com

MISSION CHURCHES AND PASTORS UNDER CARE OF
MISSIONS MINISTRY TEAM (General Assembly Ministry Council)
(continued)

SPAIN/FRANCE

MISSION CHURCHES

Renacer Madrid
   Pastor: Adriana Amorocho Fernandez
                                 (M3)

Banyeres Spain
   Pastor: Adriana Galeano Cano   (M3)
          Edision Echeverry
          Hernandez   (M3)

Lyon France
   Magarita Mendez
   Jairo Mendez

CANDIDATES

Adriana Galeano Cano   (M3)
   (Banyeres, Spain)
Edison Echeverry Hernandez   (M3)
   (Banyeres, Spain)
Luiz Fernando Cespedes Nuñes   (M3)
   (Zaragoza, Spain)
   lf1120@Jotmail.com
Damaris Vasquez Blandino   (M3)
   (Zaragoza, Spain)
   Dama_vp@hotmail.com
Adriana Amrocho Fernandez   (M3)
   (Madrid, Spain)
   adrianamorochof@hotmail.es
Margarita Mendez   (M3)
   (Lyon, France)
   margaritaflorez47@hotmail.com
Jairo Mendez   (M3)
   (Lyon, France)
   jairomendezs@hotmail.com

MISSIONARIES

Diana Lopez   (M1)
   gutierrezdp21@hotmail.com
Wilson Lopez   (M1)
   wilsonlg7@gmail.com

CAMP GROUNDS

ARKANSAS PRESBYTERY

Camp Peniel
83 Camp Peniel Drive
Solgohachia, AR 72156
(501)354-5282
camp@camp-peniel.com
Camp Manager: Dustin Taylor
(479)285-2369

CHOCTAW PRESBYTERY

Camp Israel Folsom
Box 158
Broken Bow, OK 74728
(580)584-2099

COLUMBIA PRESBYTERY

Crystal Springs Camp, Inc.
21 Crystal Springs Camp Road
Kelso, TN 37348
(615)449-3258
bwills9185@yahoo.com
Camp Manager: Brent Wills

PRESBYTERY OF EAST TENNESSEE

Camp Chilhowee
c/o Bill & Traci Pressley
1920 Old Chilhowee Loop Road
Maryville, TN 37865
(865)983-7084

Camp John Speer
c/o Dennis Elwell
2154 Viking Mountain Road
Greeneville, TN 37743
(423)636-1366
dpelwell@gmail.com
www.campjohnspeer.com

GRACE PRESBYTERY

Camp Bailey
c/o Ryan Burkes
11590 Road 101
Union, MS 39365
(601)481-4693

MISSOURI PRESBYTERY

Camp Cumberland
16 Church Camp Road
South Greenfield, Missouri 65752
(417)682-3425
Barb Parrish, Business Manager
(417)718-0311
Rev. Jill Carr, Camp Chaplain

MURFREESBORO PRESBYTERY

Crystal Springs Camp, Inc.
21 Crystal Springs Camp Road
Kelso, TN 37348
(615)449-3258
bwills9185@yahoo.com
Camp Manager: Brent Wills

NASHVILLE PRESBYTERY

Crystal Springs Camp, Inc.
21 Crystal Springs Camp Road
Kelso, TN 37348
(615)449-3258
bwills9185@yahoo.com
Camp Manager: Brent Wills

TENNESSEE-GEORGIA PRESBYTERY

Camp Glancy
1370 Coppinger Cove Road
Sequatchie, TN 37374

WEST TENNESSEE PRESBYTERY

Camp Clark Williamson
390 Mason Road
Humboldt, TN 38343
(800)655-8204
(731)784-3221
Mike Hannaford, Administrator
www.campclarkwilliamson.com

Explanation of Symbols

MC=
    Abbreviation for name of
county or state if more
than one church in the
presbytery has the same
name.

4= The number of Sundays
    each month the church
    engages in worship
M= Manse
E= Every Home Plan for The
    Cumberland Presbyterian
W= Organized women's
    ministry

P = Provisional Church
C = Church
F = Fellowship
U = Union Church

Synod/Presbytery
Abbreviations

Church Name

Church Number

Telephone
Number

Little Brown Church (MC) (4MEWC) GRWT9450
2307 Country Lane
Pleasant Valley, TN 37001
(901)654-0058 <Kingdom>

County

PA: John Doe
          1 Church St.
          Pleasant Valley, TN 37001
          (901)654-3210

        <M1>

AP: Mary Smith
          20 Serenity Lane
          Pleasant Valley, TN 37001
          (901)654-0123

        <M1>

CL: Jane Doe
          30 Charity Rd.
          Pleasant Valley, TN 37001
          (901)654-2345

CL= Clerk of Session
CO= Chair of commission
      appointed to govern
      church

AP = Associate/AssistantPastor
IP = Interim Pastor
LS = Layperson serving church
OD= Member of another
      denomination
PA = Installed Pastor
SS = Stated Supply

DE = Denominational Employee
ED = Editor
FM = Former Moderator
IT = In Transit to another Presbytery
M1 = Ordained Minister
M2 = Licentiate
M3 = Candidate
M4 = Minister of another denomination
       enrolled as a member through
       reciprocal agreement
       (Constitution 5.3)
M5 = Member of another denomination
M6 = Layperson serving church
M7 = Associate or Assistant Pastor
M8 = Military Chaplain
M9 = Non-Military Chaplain
M0 = Mentored Minister
MY = Missionary
OM = Other approved ministry
OP = Member of another presbytery
PR = Professor, Teacher
RT = Retired **or HR (honorably retired)**
ST = Student
WC - **Without Charge**

SUMMARY OF STATISTICS OF PRESBYTERIES BY SYNODS

GENERAL		MEMBERSHIP			CHANGES				FINANCES				
(Number of Ministers)	1.Church Number	2.Active	3.Total	4.Church School	5.Prof. of Faith	6.Gains	7.Losses	8.Children Baptized	9. OUR UNITED OUT-REACH	10. Total Out-Reach Giving	11. All Other Expenses	12. Total Income Received	13. Value Church Prop. 1=1000
	1	2	3	4	5	6	7	8	9	10	11	12	13

GR: SYNOD OF GREAT RIVERS

	1	2	3	4	5	6	7	8	9	10	11	12	13
Arkansas (53)	54	1,706	2,574	819	27	43	108	8	91,197	434,207	1,871,422	2,230,880	20,588
Missouri (20)	21	571	946	300	0	9	22	2	49,010	148,113	415,561	565,364	8,039
West Tennessee (122)	93	5,191	8,008	2,636	63	73	614	16	280,248	670,099	4,320,928	5,303,994	62,813
SYNOD TOTALS (195)	168	7,468	11,528	3,755	90	125	744	26	420,455	1,252,419	6,607,911	8,100,238	91,440

MI:SYNOD OF THE MIDWEST

	1	2	3	4	5	6	7	8	9	10	11	12	13
Covenant (43)	44	2,317	4,935	1,367	9	32	57	1	132,242	336,897	1,437,001	1,895,328	30,281
Cumberland (54)	62	2,364	3,735	1,493	12	32	72	10	98,201	280,703	1,697,817	1,901,435	25,602
North Central (24)	30	911	1,695	731	1	26	69	0	71,119	243,780	959,999	1,118,388	11,888
SYNOD TOTALS (121)	136	5,592	10,365	3,591	22	90	198	11	301,562	861,380	4,094,817	4,915,151	67,771

MS:MISSION SYNOD

	1	2	3	4	5	6	7	8	9	10	11	12	13
Andes (16)	7	8,867	15,795	5,815	35	148	339	21	470,882	1,385,863	6,752,633	7,934,974	105,261
Cauca Valley (16)	21	2,987	3,642	2,309	0	462	73	0	2,750	6,940	19,763	412,167	23730
Choctaw (3)	7	63	109	48	0	7	2	0	0	2,701	15,637	23,234	641
del Cristo (51)	11	1,259	3,634	469	2	3	138	4	75,638	392,908	2,745,163	3,454,792	19,425
Emaus (7)	5	596	634	113	0	0	0	0	0	0	0	0	769
Hong Kong (2)	10	1376	2,489	384	62	41	21	12	12,193	325,565	2,939,371	3,400,609	4,657
Japan (18)	13	984	2,221	434	23	35	48	4	4,989	243,468	1,294,802	1,434,994	3,116
Red River (58)	22	2,663	4,254	1,286	41	118	55	7	121,255	612,025	5,771,387	6,471,032	36,026
Trinity (41)	21	1,085	1,722	531	15	34	56	5	99,004	292,114	1,873,007	1,944,947	25,972
SYNOD TOTALS (212)	117	19,880	34,500	11,389	178	848	732	53	786,711	3,261,584	21,411,763	25,076,749	219,597

SE:SYNOD OF THE SOUTHEAST

	1	2	3	4	5	6	7	8	9	10	11	12	13
Cum East Coast (1)	7	143		52	0	10	3	0	500	10,400	81,915	92,315	280
East Tennessee (63)	37	2,528	4,159	1,337	17	53	151	7	285,434	605,359	3,647,467	4,503,085	40,433
Grace (104)	33	2,161	3,192	1,045	9	35	140	16	141,008	330,957	2,128,593	2,682,899	29,013
Hope (10)	16	763	1,353	407	2	7	18	0	51,853	195,894	725,006	721,552	10,579
Korean of SE	2	150	169	19	0	23	21	0	0	12,900	155,600	172,000	2
Robert Donnell (27)	14	735	1,413	257	0	10	12	3	65,976	164,847	942,712	1,131,560	12,981
Tenn-Georgia (39)	22	1,225	2,211	550	10	241	52	10	32,085	150,733	1,670,462	1,828,521	18,754
SYNOD TOTALS (244)	131	7,705	12,671	3,667	38	379	397	36	576,856	1,471,090	9,351,755	11,131,932	112,042

TN:TENNESSEE SYNOD

	1	2	3	4	5	6	7	8	9	10	11	12	13
Columbia (30)	37	1,071	1,989	607	5	19	135	2	56,629	256,069	1,563,754	1,838,846	20,152
Murfreesboro (52)	44	2,730	3,992	1,674	11	70	136	9	276,446	547,960	2,774,527	3,499,118	35,970
Nashville (55)	36	2,408	3,477	1,443	29	48	402	7	179,107	456,425	3,736,067	4,519,609	51,127
SYNOD TOTALS (137)	117	6,209	9,458	3,724	45	137	673	18	512,182	1,260,454	8,074,348	9,857,573	107,249

	1	2	3	4	5	6	7	8	9	10	11	12	13
GRAND TOTALS (881)	669	46,854	78,522	26,126	373	1,579	2,744	144	2,597,766	8,106,927	49,540,594	59,081,643	598,099

Andes Presbytery
MISSION SYNOD

GENERAL		MEMBERSHIP			CHANGES				FINANCES			
1.Church Number	2.Active	3.Total	4.Church School	5.Prof. of Faith	6.Gains	7.Losses	8.Children Baptized	9. OUR UNITED OUT-REACH	10. Total Out-Reach Giving	11. All Other Expenses	12. Total Income Received	13. Value Church Prop. 1=1000
1	2	3	4	5	6	7	8	9	10	11	12	13
Armenia	8903	348	483	85	0	12	14	0	0	0	46,884	45,922	450
Cartago	8906	60	73	15	0	0	8	0	0	0	7,594	7,623	100
Dosquebradas	8907	152	164	25	0	4	17	0	0	0	14,811	14,417	112
La Virginia Mis	8913	15	21	15	0	NRR	0	0	0	0	0	0	21
Manizales	8914	73	73	51	0	0	4	0	0	0	18,343	19,511	13
Pereira	8916	220	230	30	0	0	25	0	0	0	104,663	105,008	500
Quimbaya	8920	59	59	18	0	0	0	0	0	0	3,593	4,230	0
Presbytery	8900												
TOTALS	**7**	**927**	**1,103**	**239**	**0**	**16**	**68**	**0**	**0**	**0**	**195,888**	**196,711**	**1,196**

*Math error corrected. **Purged roll.. NRR - No Report Received

---

CHURCHES, PASTORS, AND CLERKS:

Armenia   (4MWC)MSAN8903
Cra 15 #16-39
Armenia, Quindio
Colombia, South America
(574)745-4860   <S America>
FAX: (574)745-4895
ipc-armenia@hotmail.com
PA: John Jairo Correa   <M1>
Calle 2 Norte #16-39
Armenia, Quindio
Colombia, South America
(574)745-0496
jjcedp07@hotmail.com
AP: Esperanza Diaz   <M1>
Calle 2 Norte #16-19
Armenia, Quindio
Colombia, South America
(576)745-0496
CL: Jose Leobardo Castro
Calle 16 #14-43
Armenia, Quindio
Colombia, South America
57(310)-389-2361

Cartago   (4MW C)MSAN8906
Cra 12 #8-47
Cartago, Valle
Colombia, South America
(572)214-5060   <S America>
FAX: (572)214-5060
presbicartago@gmail.com
PA: Juan Alexander Castano   <M1>
Cra 9 norte #18-09 Barrio Villa Elena
Colombia, South America
(314)539-6086
juanalexandercastanovelez@yahoo.es
CL: Anciana Claudia Milena Munoz
Cra 4 #16-54
Colombia, South America
(311)753-5212
clamile74@hotmail.com

Dosquebradas   (4MWC)MSAN8907
Calle 51 #15-32 (mailing)
Cra 15 A #50-31 (physical)
barrio Los Naranjos
Dosquebradas, Risaralda
Colombia, South America
(574)322-2938   <S America>
PA: Juan Esteban Blandon   <M1>
Calle 51 #15-32
barrio Los Naranjos
Dosquebradas, Risaralda
Colombia, South America
(574)322-2938
juanestebanblandon@yahoo.com
CL: Anciana Diana Carolina Pineda
Cra 15 #56-33 Barrio Santa Teresita
Colombia, South America
(321)253-5887
dicapina18@gmail.com

La Virginia   (4WMF)MSAN8913
Cra 4 bis #10-35
La Virginia, Risalda
Colombia, South America
(576)368-3589   <S America>
CL: Nora Patricia Diaz
Cra 4 bis #10-35
LaVirginia, Risalda
Colombia, South America
(311)312-2349
noris_1985@hotmail.com

Manizales   (4WMC)MSAN8914
Calle 22 #25-33
Manizales, Caldas
Colombia, South America
(576)883-0383   <S America>
FAX: (576)833-0383
manizales50ipc@hotmail.com

PA: William Diaz   <M1>
Calle 42 #26B-68
Manizales, Caldas
Colombia, South America
(574)890-2972
manizales50ipc@hotmail.com
CL: Luz Dary Herrera
Calle 5 #22-56
Manizales, Caldas
Colombia, South America
(576)889-0994

Pereira   (4MWC)MSAN8916
Cra 12 bis #11-69
Pereira, Risaralda
Colombia, South America
(574)333-9295   <S America>
FAX: (574)324-4110
cumberlandpres@une.net.co
PA: David Montoya   <M1>
Cra 12 bis #11-69
Pereira, Risaralda
Colombia, South America
(574)324-4109
FAX: (574)324-4110
adamonva@gmail.com
AP: Luz Maria Heilbron   <M1>
Cra 12 bis #11-51
Pereira, Risaralda
Colombia, South America
(576)333-9295
pastorapresbi@hotmail.com
AP: Ricardo Castaneda
Urbanizacion Casas de Milan
Manzana 2 Casa 21
(305)337-5131
rijcha@gmail.com
AP: Diana Maria Valdez   <M1>
Urbanizacion Casas de Milan
Manzana 2 Casa 21
(305)240-3165
dianamariavaldezduque@gmail.com

ANDES PRESBYTERY CONTINUED

AP: Geovanny Lopez   <M2>
  Jardin Etapa 1 Manzana 11 Casa 9
  Colombia, South America
  (314)347-5132
  carlogyo@hotmail.com
CL: Shirley Murillo
  Cra 12 bis #11-69
  Pereira, Risaralda
  Colombia, South America

_____

Quimbaya   (C)MSAN89220
  Cra 6 #25-54
  Quimbaya, Quindio
  Colombia, SA
  (576)752-3570
SS: Jorge Enrique Jimenez   <M2>
  Urb Manantiales MzC Casa 6
  Armenia, Quindio
  Colombia, South America
  (321)643-0693
  joenjimu@yahoo.es
CL: Session Clerk
  Cra 6 #25-54
  Quimbaya, Quindio
  Colombia, SA

_____

OTHERS ON MINISTERIAL ROLL:

Arias, John Jairo   <M1 WC>
  Calle 144 sur #196-08 / Apto 202
  Caldas, Antioquia
  Colombia, South America
  (57)317-693-1162
  sajoarias@hotmail.com
Cardona, Nancy   <M1 WC>
  Calle 51 #15-32
  Dosquebradas, Risaralda
  Colombia, South America
  (576)322-2938
  nancycardona10@yahoo.com
Gentry, Michele   <M1 M9>
  Urb San Jorge casa 28
  Km 8 via a La Tebaida
  Armenia, Quindio
  Colombia, South America
  (318)285-1161
  gentry.andes@yahoo.com
Guerrero, Luz Dary   <M1 MY>
  Cra 26D #385-15 Apt 101
  Ed Itaparica
  Envigado-Antioquia
  Colombia, South America
  (315)412-1100
  guerrerol500@yahoo.com
Munoz, Gerardo   <M1 WC>
Orozco, Joaquin   <M1 OM>
  Cra 3 #7-14
  Aguadas, Caldas
  Colombia, South America
  (576)851-4773
  jeob40@hotmail.com
Rivera, Carlos A   <M1 WC>
  Calle Dr Jose Maria Vertiz 1410
  Departmento 202B, Colonia Portales
  Delegacion Benito
  Juarez, C.P. 03300 MEXICO
  (52)1-55-31058377
  caralrifra@une.net.co

Sarmiento Paez, Liliana   <M WC>
  Calle 51 #15-32
  Los Naranjos Dosquebradas
  Colombia, South America
  (321)622-2797
  lilianasarmi23@gmail.com
Valencia, Nulbel   <M1 RT>
  Diag 11D Casa 11 urbGemelas
  Dosquebradas, Risaralda
  Colombia, South America
  (576)330-7704
  nava1928@hotmail.com
Velez, Gabriel   <M1 RT>
  Calle 8A #16A-26, Villa Fanny
  Dosquebradas, Risaralda
  Colombia, South America
  (576)330-1168

_____

OTHER LICENTIATES ON ROLL:

Giraldo, Juan Pablo   <M2>
  Calle 51 #15-32
  barrio Los Naranjos
  Dosquebradas, Risaralda
  Colombia, South America
  (576)322-2938

_____

OTHER CANDIDATES ON ROLL:

Castaneda, Liliana   <M3>
  Cra 4 #21-39 Barrio La Paz Quimbaya
  Colombia, South America
  (317)290-0110
  licabo2008@hotmail.com
Giraldo, Marcela   <M3>
  Calle 68 D #40-15
  Manizales, Caldas
  Colombia, South America
  (576)878-5412
Llanos, Victor Hugo   <M3>
  Calle 22 #25-33 Manizales
  Colombia, South America
  (316)285-4359
  victorllanos40@hotmail.com
Lopez, Martin Emilio   <M3>
  Calle 15 #10-22
  La Virginia, Risaralda
  Colombia, South America
  (310)820-6216
  lopezrestrepomartinemilio@yahoo.es
Osorio, Jorge   <M3>
  Cra 16 #11-07
  Colombia, South America
  (320)757-1888
  jopingo@hotmail.es
Rodriquez, Luz Adriana   <M3>
  Calle 15 #10-22 La Virginia
  (314)612-9702
  annasantilo2@hotmail.com

Arkansas Presbytery
GREAT RIVERS SYNOD

GENERAL	1.Church Number	2.Active	3.Total	4.Church School	5.Prof. of Faith	6.Gains	7.Losses	8.Children Baptized	9. OUR UNITED OUT-REACH	10. Total Out-Reach Giving	11. All Other Expenses	12. Total Income Received	13. Value Church Prop. 1=1000
	1	2	3	4	5	6	7	8	9	10	11	12	13
Appleton	1202	12	12	12	0	0	0	0	250	2,519	11,608	14,127	40
Arkansas Loving	2135	23	23	12	0	0	0	0	2,000	9,611	152,734	175,364	549
Barren Fork	1501	111	124	50	5	6	3	0	8,940	16,297	85,667	78,620	400
Ben Lomond	1301	6	7	8	0	0	0	0	0	939	16,332	18,203	80
Bethesda	1302	54	54	30	0	0	2	0	0	21,720	83,015	94,872	957
Booneville	1401	34	42	5	0	0	3	0	5,041	10,074	51,689	50,404	317
Byron*	1508	13	13	10	2	0	0	0	0	460	3,171	8,457	247
Calico Rock*	1503	60	60	11	0	1	31	0	0	33,370	54,300	112,834	1,524
Camden	1303	35	48	27	1	1	5	0	486	6,524	59,981	61,603	400
Camp Ground	1101	35	83	15	0	NRR	0	0	5,294	0	0	0	500
Caulksville	1402	200	256	20	5	5	4	1	0	32,856	89,420	132,267	750
Crossroads	1102	34	34	20	0	0	0	0	1,654	4,216	54,019	36,680	0
Dilworth	1304	7	7	8	0	0	0	0	0	900	15,512	23,960	75
Dover	1203	25	25	12	0	0	1	0	3,051	7,777	39,477	61,028	175
E. T. Allen	1307	17	17	12	0	NRR	0	0	0	0	0	0	225
Faith-Hopewell	1502	103	117	42	0	1	1	0	12,779	27,443	91,480	127,703	400
Falls Chapel	1308	17	17	10	0	0	3	0	0	17,258	34,853	29,079	200
Fellowship (BC)	1505	81	184	22	0	2	6	2	0	25,843	108,078	135,545	1,465
Fellowship (OC)	1309	34	68	46	1	4	1	0	5,353	14,928	26,247	53,529	117
Fomby	1310	5	18	5	0	0	1	0	0	1,778	13,019	11,552	138
Fort Smith	1406	20	166	7	0	0	1	1	689	1,333	25,362	23,330	400
Grace	1405	30	31	16	0	0	3	0	5,196	23,146	54,102	75,488	500
Gum Springs	1205	6	7	9	0	0	1	0	0	1,281	9,081	9,322	n/a
Hector	1207	11	45	12	0	0	0	0	0	1,100	24,985	26,085	54
Lake Hamilton	1221	24	24	19	1	0	5	0	236	236	60,544	63,212	400
Lockesburg	1311	7	11	4	0	NRR	0	0	0	0	0	0	40
Marietta	1408	38	38	20	0	0	2	0	2,000	9,578	40,821	41,047	350
Mars Hill	1211	18	34	16	0	0	0	0	500	500	25,896	20,900	240
Mt. Carmel*	1212	31	31	15	0	0	6	0	5,420	1,298	58,670	63,386	349
Mt. Olive	1517	24	42	7	3	7	1	0	0	17,300	25,715	42,230	230
New Hope	1510	14	14	0	0	0	1	0	0	6,332	16,605	26,719	375
Old Union	1409	25	25	20	0	0	0	1	5,493	11,384	18,410	41,570	123
Oxford	1511	35	35	30	0	0	0	0	0	11,392	8,083	25,901	550
Palestine	1103	71	71	54	0	4	6	0	4,550	11,314	52,135	107,121	1,000
Pilot Prairie	1411	8	14	6	0	NRR	0	0	0	0	0	0	50
Pine Bluff, 1st	1104	14	14	6	0	NRR	0	0	0	0	0	0	750
Pine Ridge	1105	13	26	10	1	2	2	0	0	7,881	39,302	32,788	402
Pineville	1512	56	83	16	3	4	3	3	0	27,308	57,751	100,291	750
Pleasant Grove	1214	5	9	5	0	NRR	0	0	0	0	0	0	70
Provo	1314	11	38	25	0	NRR	0	0	0	0	0	0	125
Rodney	1513	16	16	14	0	0	1	0	0	550	19,159	22,569	65
Rose Hill	1106	57	57	23	0	0	6	0	5,134	10,484	82,787	51,339	1,000
Russellville	1216	67	196	28	5	5	6	0	12,000	20,129	141,222	106,895	1,015

Arkansas Presbytery (continued)
GREAT RIVERS SYNOD

GENERAL		MEMBERSHIP			CHANGES				FINANCES				
1.Church Number	2.Active	3.Total	4.Church School	5.Prof. of Faith	6.Gains	7.Losses	8.Children Baptized	9. OUR UNITED OUT-REACH	10. Total Out-Reach Giving	11. All Other Expenses	12. Total Income Received	13. Value Church Prop. 1=1000	
	1	2	3	4	5	6	7	8	9	10	11	12	13
Salem (FC)	1514	15	17	10	0	0	0	0	0	0	0	0	250
Searcy	1218	24	54	11	0	0	0	0	1,201	28,020	26,000	29,000	500
Shaver	1413	1	1	0	0	NRR	0	0	0	0	0	0	12
Shell Chapel	1108	6	28	0	0	0	0	0	682	1,505	4,895	8,869	500
Sherwood	1220	14	22	0	0	1	1	0	275	900	44,706	34,454	777
Sidney	1515	9	18	9	0	NRR	0	0	0	0	0	0	200
Sulphur Springs	1315	48	48	5	0	NRR	0	0	0	0	0	0	27
Trimble Camp G.	1504	36	36	33	0	NRR	0	0	0	0	0	0	365
Trinity	1219	26	40	0	0	0	0	0	0	500	19,535	18,192	200
Walkerville	1317	6	6	4	0	0	0	0	2,973	4,470	10,084	14,640	185
Walnut Grove	1414	14	68	8	0	0	2	0	0	1,753	14,970	19,705	175
TOTALS	**54**	**1,706**	**2,574**	**819**	**27**	**43**	**108**	**8**	**91,197**	**434,207**	**1,871,422**	**2,230,880**	**20,588**

*Math error corrected. **Purged roll. NRR - No Report Received

CHURCHES, PASTORS, AND CLERKS:

Appleton (W4C)GRAR1202
608 McGowan Road (mailing)
320 Tate Street (physical)
Atkins, AR 72823
( ) <Pope>
CL: Pam Simpson
3 Highway 124
Jerusalem, AR 72080
(501)669-2999

Arkansas Loving (C)GRAR2135
8201 Frenchmans Lane
Little Rock, AR 72209 <Pulaski>
PA: Jinook Jung <M1>
1603 Coolhurst Avenue
Sherwood, AR 72120
(501)247-5953
swcho100491@gmail.com
CL: Sun Cha Stamp
121 Gravel Lane
Sherwood, AR 72120

Barren Fork (4MWC)GRAR1501
782 Barren Fork Road
Mount Pleasant, AR 72561
(870)346-5121 <Izard>
PA: Alan Meinzer <M1>
780 Barren Fork Road
Mount Pleasant, AR 72561
(870)612-3936
brotheralan@centurylink.net
CL: Brandon Love
PO Box 262
Mount Pleasant, AR 72561
(870)291-0772

Ben Lomond (4C)GRAR1301
180 LR 39 (mailing)
Ogden, AR 71853
495 N Main Street (physical)
Ben Lomond, AR 71823
( ) <Sevier>
kmillz13@hotmail.com
OD: Herman R Welch <M5>
180 LR 39
Ogden, AR 71853
(903)748-2126
herawe@yahoo.com
CL: Kimberly Hatridge
PO Box 53
Ben Lomond, AR 71823
(870)287-4215

Bethesda (4MW C)GRAR1302
395 Ouachita 47
Camden, AR 71701
(870)231-4909 <Ouachita>
CL: Ben Fields
451 Ouachita 47
Camden, AR 71701
(870)231-5080
bfields2011@hotmail.com

Booneville (4MEW C)GRAR1401
PO Box 163 (mailing)
355 Sharp Street (physical)
Booneville, AR 72927
( ) <Logan>
cpcbooneville@gmail.com

PA: Henry Jenkins <M1>
PO Box 148 (mailing)
90 W Grove (physical)
Magazine, AR 72943
(479)969-8351
henryj@magtel.com
CL: Diane Buffington
7910 Jack Creek Road
Booneville, AR 72927
(479)675-1961
mdbuffington@gmail.com

Byron (4WC)GRAR1508
PO Box 524 (mailing)
Byron Road, Viola, AR (physical)
Calico Rock, AR 72519
(870)291-8542 <Fulton>
calicowild@hotmail.com
CL: Jeanne Perry
PO Box 524
Calico Rock, AR 72519
(870)291-8542
calicowild@hotmail.com

Calico Rock (4MEWC)GRAR1503
PO Box 315 (mailing)
692 AR 56 Highway E (physical)
Calico Rock, AR 72519
(870)297-3931 <Izard>
FAX: (870)297-3151
crcpc01@gmail.com
CL: Carolyn Jeffery
PO Box 183
Calico Rock, AR 72519
(870)297-8530
cjeffery6@gmail.com

ARKANSAS PRESBYTERY CONTINUED

Camden (4MEWC)GRAR1303
1545 California Avenue
Camden, AR 71701
(870)836-8712 <Ouachita>
PA: Nicholas Chambers <M1>
362 Ouachita 54
Camden, AR 71701
(870)807-0279
nachambrs@hotmail.com
CL: Jimmy Vaughan
1607 W 3rd Street
Fordyce, AR 71742
(870)818-1512
jvaughan103@hotmail.com

Camp Ground (4WMC)GRAR1101
1548 E AR 274 Highway
Hampton, AR 71744
(870)798-4302 <Calhoun>
PA: Garland Skidmore <M1>
2083 US Highway 278 E
Hampton, AR 71744
(870)798-4634
CL: Shirley Strickland
1783 E AR 274 Highway
Hampton, AR 71744
(870)918-2344
strick6@sat-co.net

Caulksville (4MWC)GRAR1402
PO Box 2 (mailing)
23 W Main, Caulksville, AR (physical)
Ratcliff, AR 72951
(479)635-4301 <Logan>
PA: Bill Van Meter <M1>
10626 Highway 41
Charleston, AR 72933
(479)965-2998
revbill46@gmail.com
CL: Cherre Nietert
10201 Nietert Lane
Branch, AR 72928
(479)438-0673

Crossroads (4C)GRAR1102
3600 Market Place Avenue
Bryant, AR 72022
(501)888-4190
CL: Betty Kettles
16904 Old Mill Road
Little Rock, AR 72206
(501)888-4190
r.kettles@yahoo.com

Dilworth (4C)GRAR1304
153 Wall Road (mailing)
2517 N Red Bridge Road (physical)
Horatio, AR 71842
(870)642-8051 <Sevier>
mtcarmel2@windstream.net
CL: Charla Conatser
153 Wall Road
Horatio, AR 71842

Dover (4MWC)GRAR1203
10022 State Route 27 (mailing)
Hector, AR 72843
96 Waters Street (physical)
Dover, AR 72837
(479)331-3130 <Pope>
markoe@centurytel.net

OD: Mike Galloway <M5>
2821 Linker Mount Road
Dover, AR 72837
(479)331-0254
markoe@centurytel.net
CL: Jana Bartlett
10022 State Route 27
Hector, AR 72843
jkb10022@gmail.com

E T Allen (4WC)GRAR1307
PO Box 822 (mailing)
153 Highway 71 N
Ashdown, AR 71822
( ) <Little Rive>
CL: Glen Ray Bowman
1050 Oak Place
Ashdown, AR 71822
(903)824-5000

Faith-Hopewell (4WC)GRAR1502
3895 Harrison Street
Batesville, AR 72501
(870)612-5949 <Independence>
PA: Rian Puckett <M1>
55 Ham Street
Batesville, AR 72501
(731)288-7742
bro.rianpuckett@gmail.com
CL: Sue Turner
155 Red Cut Road
Batesville, AR 72501
(870)307-1983
bsturner01@yahoo.com

Falls Chapel (4MC)GRAR1308
PO Box 93 (mailing)
127 LW Davis Road (physical)
Lockesburg, AR 71846
( ) <Sevier>
CL: Brenda Michaels
PO Box 93
Lockesburg, AR 71846
(870)289-5959

Fellowship (BC) (4EWC)GRAR1505
PO Box 866 (mailing)
1206 E 9th Street (physical)
Mountain Home, AR 72653
(870)425-5419 <Baxter>
info@fellowshipcumberland.org
PA: Gary Robert Tubb <M1>
103 Forest Drive
Mountain Home, AR 72653
grtubb@yahoo.com
(870)424-0603
CL: Andy Marts
393 County Road 1085
Mountain Home, AR 72653
(870)481-6092
amarts@centurytel.net

Fellowship (OC) (4WC)GRAR1309
397 Ouachita 54 (mailing)
2855 Ouachita 3 (physical)
Camden, AR 71701
( ) <Ouachita>

SS: Jimmy Vaughan <M2>
1607 W 3rd Street
Fordyce, AR 71742
(870)818-1512
jvaughan103@hotmail.com
CL: Martha Chambers
389 Ouachita 54
Camden, AR 71701

Fomby (4C)GRAR1310
704 Highway 317 (mailing)
1215 Highway 32 E (physical)
Ashdown, AR 71822
(870)898-2856 <Little Rive>
carole4485@att.net
CL: Carole C Booth
704 Highway 317
Ashdown, AR 71822
(870)898-2856
carole4485@att.net

Fort Smith (4MEWC)GRAR1406
605 N 47th Street
Fort Smith, AR 72903
(479)782-0454 <Sebastian>
FAX: (479)782-0454
ksstamps@msn.com
CL: Janie Stamps
4008 Logan Lane
Fort Smith, AR 72903
(479)478-0161
bjstamps@msn.com

Grace (4C)GRAR1405
2451 Wedington Drive
Fayetteville, AR 72701
(479)442-6772 <Washington>
PA: Tom Merchant <M1>
18784 Shoreline Way
Fayetteville, AR 72703
(231)557-5435
merchantt48@gmail.com
CL: Robin Thomas
1195 N White Rock Lane
Fayetteville, AR 72704
(479)521-0371
rthomas@mman.com

Gum Springs(WC) (4C)GRAR1205
27 Meadowview Drive (mailing)
Gum Springs Road (physical)
Searcy, AR 72143
(501)278-9750 <White>
SS: Jim Bradberry <M3>
120 Hummingbird Lane
Searcy, AR 72143
(501)278-9750
CL: Kimberly Holleman
27 Meadowview Drive
Searcy, AR 72143
(501)268-6920
kdholle1@cablelynx.com

Hector (4MWC)GRAR1207
PO Box 53 (mailing)
29 Maple (physical)
Hector, AR 72843
(479)747-7561 <Pope>

ARKANSAS PRESBYTERY CONTINUED

CL: Beth McAlister
PO Box 53
Hector, AR 72843
(479)747-7561
beth.ann56@hotmail.com

_____

Lake Hamilton   (4C)GRAR1221
2891 Airport Road
Hot Springs, AR 71913
(501)760-3800   <Garland>
lakehamiltoncpc@gmail.com
IP: Steve Mosley   <M1>
320 N Sherman Circle
Russellville, AR 72802
(479)880-9498
stevemosley@hotmail.com
CL: Tamara Stroope
2891 Airport Road
Hot Springs, AR 71913
info@lakehamiltonchurch.com

_____

Lockesburg   (1C)GRAR1311
128 Cherokee Trail (mailing)
114 W Walnut (physical)
Lockesburg, AR 71846
( )   <Sevier>
CL: Joe E Bush
128 Cherokee Trail
Lockesburg, AR 71846
(870)289-2433

_____

Marietta   (4C)GRAR1408
623 Church Street (mailing)
2604 West Main (physical)
Charleston, AR 72933
(479)965-0224   <Franklin>
CL: Tim Aldridge
623 Church Street
Charleston, AR 72933
(479)965-7639
dcotim58@live.com

_____

Mars Hill   (4WC)GRAR1211
172 Thompson Lane (mailing)
1224 State Route 363 (physical)
Pottsville, AR 72858
( )   <Pope>
PA: Jo Warren   <M1>
811 Wall Street
Morrilton, AR 72110
(501)354-4139
pastorjo47@ymail.com
CL: Gary Thompson
172 Thompson Lane
Pottsville, AR 72858
(479)970-4652
thompgary@gmail.com

_____

Mt Carmel   (4C)GRAR1212
1470 Mt Carmel Road W
London, AR 72847
(479)293-4447   <Pope>
mtcarmel@centurylink.net
CL: Jennifer Metz
276 Metz Lane
London, AR 72847
(479)293-4229
jmetz54@hotmail.com

_____

Mt Olive   (4EC)GRAR1517
214 Bear Trail Hollow (mailing)
5539 Mt Olive Road (physical)
Melbourne, AR 72556
(870)368-4923   <Izard>
bobeth@centurytel.net
PA: Christopher Anderson   <M1>
117 Big Pine Road
Batesville, AR 72501
(870)805-0886
pastorcsa@gmail.com
CL: Mary Beth Jeffery
214 Bear Trail Hollow
Melbourne, AR 72556
(870)368-4923
bobeth@centurytel.net

_____

New Hope   (2C)GRAR1510
25 Pine Hill Road (mailing)
3655 Bethesda Road (physical)
Batesville, AR 72501
( )   <Independence>
verenaaherrin@yahoo.com
PA: Rian Puckett   <M1>
55 Ham Street
Batesville, AR 72501
(731)288-7742
bro.rianpuckett@gmail.com
CL: Verena Herrin
25 Pine Hill Road
Batesville, AR 72501
(870)793-6145
verenaaherrin@yahoo.com

_____

Old Union   (4C)GRAR1409
3184 Cotton Road (mailing)
Old Union Road (physical)
Magazine, AR 72943
( )   <Logan>
PA: Henry Jenkins   <M1>
PO Box 148
Magazine, AR 72943
(479)969-8352
henryj@magtel.com
CL: Carla Sims
3184 Cotton Road
Magazine, AR 72943
(479)675-6590
carlasims@live.com

_____

Oxford   (4U)GRAR1511
PO Box 824 (mailing)
Melbourne, AR 72556
211 Main Street (physical)
Oxford, AR 72565
( )   <Izard>
SS: Bobby D Coleman   <M1>
107 E Henson
Springdale, AR 72764
(870)213-5410
bobby.coleman@gmail.com
CL: Lee Melton
PO Box 824
Melbourne, AR 72556
(870)373-0178
lmeltonrtr@yahoo.com

_____

Palestine   (4MEWC)GRAR1103
PO Box 98 (mailing)
223 South Main Street (physical)
Palestine, AR 72372
(870)581-2600   <St. Francis>
FAX: (870)581-2600
CL: Lisa Alldredge
PO Box 803
Palestine, AR 72372
(870)581-2913
lsatmall@yahoo.com

_____

Pilot Prairie   (4MC)GRAR1411
PO Box 1873
Waldron, AR 72958
(479)637-3938   <Scott>
CL: Lee Ann Forest
PO Box 1873
Waldron, AR 72958

_____

Pine Bluff 1st   (4W C)GRAR1104
2401 Camden Road
Pine Bluff, AR 71603
( )   <Jefferson>
CL: Catherine Currington
205 Moss Road
White Hall, AR 71602
(870)247-3839

_____

Pine Ridge   (4C)GRAR1105
4890 Grant 14
Grapevine, AR 72057
(870)942-1827   <Grant>
CL: Buren Walker
336 Grant 748
Sheridan, AR 72150
(870)942-4790

_____

Pineville   (4MWC)GRAR1512
PO Box 256 (mailing)
1229 AR 223 Highway (physical)
Pineville, AR 72566
(870)297-4104   <Izard>
CL: Janie Jenkins
PO Box 504
Calico Rock, AR 72519
(870)297-3991
djjenkins@centurytel.net

_____

Pleasant Grove   (2C)GRAR1214
1083 Highway 305 S
Searcy, AR 72143
(501)796-3466   <White>
CL: Robbie Stroud
1922 Highway 31 N
Beebe, AR 72012
(501)882-3262

_____

Provo   (4C)GRAR1314
131 LR 47 (mailing)
Ashdown, AR 71822
125 Dooley Road (physical)
Lockesburg, AR 71846
( )   <Sevier>

CL: Betty Crow Ward
180 B McHorse Road
Lockesburg, AR 71846

ARKANSAS PRESBYTERY CONTINUED

Rodney   (2EC)GRAR1513
  1364 Rodney Road (mailing)
  1333 Rodney Road (physical)
  Jordan, AR 72519
  ( )   <Baxter>
PA: Dave Williamson   <M1>
  PO Box 67
  Dolph, AR 72528
  (870)499-7448
CL: Carol Lee
  1364 Rodney Road
  Jordan, AR 72519
  (870)499-3238
  txgrany69@yahoo.com

Rose Hill   (4MWC)GRAR1106
  1031 Binns Drive (mailing)
  2133 Highway 83 N (physical)
  Monticello, AR 71655
  (870)367-5114   <Drew>
  gsaray@att.net
PA: Bruce Hamilton   <M1>
  203 W Fifth Street
  Mountain View, MO 65548
  (352)408-0873
  behamilton@gmail.com
CL: Jeff Loveless
  2821 Highway 278 East
  Monticello, AR 71655
  (870)460-5164
  jeff_loveless@yahoo.com

Russellville   (4WC)GRAR1216
  1200 N Arkansas Avenue
  Russellville, AR 72801
  (479)968-1061   <Pope>
  FAX: (479)880-0071
  fcpcrussellville@yahoo.com
PA: James R Fisk   <M1>
  9 Mills Drive
  Bella Vista, AR 72714
  jimfisk95@yahoo.com
  (479)886-1216
CL: Deanna Boston
  721 Kovel Court
  Russellville, AR 72801
  (479)890-3880
  fcpcrussellville@yahoo.com

Salem (FC)   (4MWC)GRAR1514
  1003 Flint Springs Road (mailing)
  Viola, AR 72583
  Highway 5 S, Salem, AR (physical)
  ( )   <Fulton>
  salemcumberlandchurch@gmail.com
SS: Bobby D Coleman   <M1>
  107 E Henson
  Springdale, AR 72764
  (870)269-6010
  bobby.coleman@gmail.com
CL: Bonnie Brown
  1003 Flint Springs Road
  Viola, AR 72583
  (870)458-2657
  bbrown325@centurytel.net

Searcy   (4MWC)GRAR1218
  100 E Race Street
  Searcy, AR 72143
  (501)268-8278   <White>

SS: Jim Bradberry   <M3>
  120 Hummingbird Lane
  Searcy, AR 72143
  (501)278-9750
CL:Howard Johnson
  2180 Holmes Road
  Searcy, AR 72143
  (501)268-3071
  howardwjohnson@gmail.com

Shaver   (1C)GRAR1413
(no longer has services 10/30/13)
  401 Shaver Road (mailing)
  1448 Shaver Road (physical)
  Paris, AR 72855
  ( )   <Logan>

Shell Chapel   (4WC)GRAR1108
  2143 Grider Field Road (mailing)
  3110 Highway 425 (physical)
  Pine Bluff, AR 71601
  (870)535-5408   <Jefferson>
CL: Joyce Shell
  2143 Grider Field Road
  Pine Bluff, AR 71601
  (870)535-5408
  mkshell@earthlink.net

Sherwood   (4WC)GRAR1220
  1402 E Kiehl Avenue
  Sherwood, AR 72120
  (501)835-8889   <Pulaski>
PA: William Guthrie   <M1>
  3217 Miracle Heights Cove
  Sherwood, AR 72120
  (501)584-0019
  billybarloe@yahoo.com
CL: Olive Snow
  5907 Woodview Drive S
  Sherwood, AR 72120
  (501)835-7819
  ladysnow64@yahoo.com

Sidney   (2U)GRAR1515
  Batesville, AR 72501
  ( )   <Sharp>
PA: Alan Meinzer   <M1>
  780 Barren Fork Road
  Mount Pleasant, AR 72561
  (870)612-3936
  brotheralan@centurylink.net
CL: Jodi Moody
  127 Arkansas Highway 58
  Sidney, AR 72577
  (870)283-6766

Sulphur Springs   (4C)GRAR1315
  3225 Ouachita 2 (mailing)
  3086 Ouachita 2 (physical)
  Louann, AR 71751
  (870)689-3598   <Ouachita>
  mdarden@oeccwildblue.com
CL:Peggy Muckelrath
  128 Ouachita 55
  Louann, AR 71752
  (870)689-3409
  pmukelrath@oecc.com

Trimble Camp G   (4WC)GRAR1504
  PO Box 150 (mailing)
  Trimble Camp Ground Road (physical)
  Dolph, AR 72528
  (870)297-8088   <Izard>
PA: Joel Snyder   <M1>
  224 Lord Lane
  Mountain View, AR 72560
  (870)269-9743
  synyder.joel@ymail.com
CL: Jana Cowgill   <M3>
  1037 Chriswood Drive
  Clarkridge, AR 72623
  (870)421-2106
  jana.cowgill@gmail.com

Trinity   (4MEWC)GRAR1219
  809 W Wall Street
  Morrilton, AR 72110
  (501)354-4139   <Conway>
PA: Gordon Warren   <M1>
  811 Wall Street
  Morrilton, AR 72110
  (501)208-1120
  jogordonwarren@suddenlink.net
CL: Jo Beth Hoyt
  187 Francis Street
  Morrilton, AR 72110
  (501)354-4139

Walkerville   (4MEWC)GRAR1317
  10160 Highway 19 S
  Magnolia, AR 71753
  ( )   <Columbia>
CL: Stella Ball
  10570 S Highway 19
  Emerson, AR 71740
  (870)696-3973
  jse10570@gmail.com

Walnut Grove   (4WC)GRAR1414
  4724 N State Highway 23 (mailing)
  1294 Six Mile Road (physical)
  Magazine, AR 72943
  ( )   <Logan>
  danekas@centurytel.net
CL: Debbie Danekas
  4724 N State Highway 23
  Booneville, AR 72927
  (479)675-5004
  danekas@centurytel.net

OTHERS ON MINISTERIAL ROLL:

Blanton, D B   <M1 RT>
  ADDRESS UNKNOWN
Bowling, Andrew   <M1 WC>
  20945 Highway 16 E
  Siloam Springs, AR 72761
  (479)524-6576
Bradshaw, James (Jim)   <M1 WC>
  415 S Red Street
  Sheridan, AR 72150
  (870)942-2525
Brewer, Barbara   <M1 WC>
  500 N Persimmon Circle Apt 501
  Rogers, AR 72756
  (870)325-6449

ARKANSAS PRESBYTERY CONTINUED

Brown, Amy   <M1 WC>
679 Freeze Bend Road
Newport, AR 72112

Cadenbach, Mark   <M1 OM>
91 Elzadah Lane
Salem, AR 72576
(890)955-9250
cadenbm@nctc.net

Chang, Leo   <M1 WC>
819 W Division SE
Springfield, MO 65803
(901)287-9901

Chambers, Jason   <M1 WC>
555 Blue Hole Road
Beebe, AR 72012
(870)807-1930
jmchambers@memphisseminary.edu

Davenport, Vondal   <M1 WC>
57 Main Street
Ratcliff, AR 7951
(479)965-2036

Davis, Robert (Toby)   <M1 WC>
PO Box 21
Archer City, TX 76351
(901)826-5755
pastortobydavis@gmail.com

Deere, Thomas (Tom)   <M1 WC>
460 Yukon Drive
Russellville, AR 72811
(479)498-0318
tdeere@suddenlinkmail.com

Hamelink, Ronald L   <M1 WC>
5045 Starlite Court
Las Cruces, NM 88012
(575)640-4341
hamronelink@yahoo.com

Holley, Ann   <M1 WC>
PO Box 345
Lockesburg, AR 71846
(870)289-3421
ladyrev1115@yahoo.com

Jeffrey, Sarah Ann   <M1 WC>
5271 Highway 202 E
Yellville, AR 72687
(870)453-7076

Johnson, Roberta Smith   <M1 WC>
397 Ouachita 54
Camden, AR 71701
(870)231-5827

Jones, Michael   <M1 WC>
120 Jennifer Lane
Branson, MO 65616
(417)334-2058

Jones, Victor   <M1 WC>
7017 Highway 177 S
Jordan, AR 72519
(870)499-5882
pam.jones@centurytel.net

Mars, Stan   <M1 WC>
PO Box 274
Mt Pleasant, AR 72561
(217)254-5120
smars2@liberty.edu

Niswonger, Richard   <M1 WC>
20941 Highway 16 E
Siloam Springs, AR 72761
(479)524-4081
rniswonger@cox.net

O'Neal Danhof, Clair   <M1 WC>
301 Whispering Hills Street
Hot Springs, AR 71901
acglenn@aol.com

Pedigo, Russell   <M1 WC>
289 Cemetary Street
Morgantown, KY 71730
(870)862-4689
russell_pedigo@hotmail.com

Suttle, Michael   <M1 WC>
159 Ouachita 593
Camden, AR 71701
(870)836-0008
m_s_suttle@msn.com

Sweigart, John M   <M1 WC>
PO Box 876
Dover, AL 72837
(479)229-4041

Terrell, Elizabeth   <M1 WC>
2073 Vinton Avenue
Memphis, TN 38104
(901)647-2788

Tompkins, Wayne   <M1 WC>
548 E Columbia Road 23
Emerson, AR 71740
(870)807-2874
wtministries1947@gmail.com

Treadaway, Kenneth A   <M1 WC>
172 Miller County 494
Texarkana, AR 71854
treadaways@ark.net
(870)574-1609

Varner Villa, Susan   <M1 M9>
11299 Herschel Loop
Daphne, AL 36526
(804)304-4642
smvarner76@yahoo.com

Washburn, Gloria   <M1 WC>
PO Box 1000
Mountain Home, AR 72654
(870)321-3539
grwashburn07@gmail.com

Wood, Wayne   <M1 WC>
HC 61 Box 600
Calico Rock, AR 72519
(870)297-2205
FAX: (870)297-3151
bexarwood@centurytel.net

OTHER LICENTIATES ON ROLL:

Harbour, Ethan   <M2>
77 Burton Road
Booneville, AR 72927
(479)849-6329
ethanharbour@gmail.com

OTHER CANDIDATES ON ROLL:

Cowgill, Jana   <M3>
1037 Chriswood Drive
Clarkridge, AR 72623
(870)421-2106
jana.cowgill@gmail.com

Dixon, Wendall Logan   <M3>
201 Pine Hill Road
Dover, AR 72837

Fisk, Matthew
Benton, AR

Shatley, Melissa   <M3>
339 Ouachita 54
Camden, AR 71701

Walsh, Devin   <M3>
801 East "M" Street
Russellville, AR 72801
(479)890-6716

Warren, Elizabeth
811 W Wall Street
Morrilton, AR 72110
(501)354-4139

Cauca Valley Presbytery
MISSION SYNOD

GENERAL		MEMBERSHIP			CHANGES					FINANCES			
1.Church Number	2.Active	3.Total	4.Church School	5.Prof. of Faith	6.Gains	7.Losses	8.Children Baptized	9. OUR UNITED OUT-REACH		10. Total Out-Reach Giving	11. All Other Expenses	12. Total Income Received	13. Value Church Prop. |1=1000
1	2	3	4	5	6	7	8	9		10	11	12	13
Betania Mission	8204	42	42	36	0	2	0	0	0	63	375	4,130	868
Bethel	8205	150	210	65	0	10	0	0	0	67	263	12,423	445
Caleb Mission	8223	65	65	15	0	0	0	0	0	312	1,384	12,296	556
Central	8208	100	106	40	0	0	6	0	0	1,027	3,006	39,624	3,641
Divino Redentor	8206	150	156	130	0	4	1	0	0	1,056	3,370	33,703	863
Emaus	8219	41	44	20	0	3	1	0	2,750	37	470	5,544	202
Filipos	8211	70	69	20	0	0	2	0	0	40	431	6,642	722
Getsemani	8210	55	67	83	0	12	0	0	0	25	19	4,904	881
Guabas	8229	59	57	34	0	3	0	0	0	100	73	7,293	47
Maranatha	8220	169	169	90	0	6	2	0	0	388	1,515	14,188	147
Nueva Esperanza	8221	49	90	12	0	2	0	0	0	481	1,844	15,905	5,934
Nueva Jerusalen	8222	75	80	50	0	0	5	0	0	22	472	8,167	807
Popayan	8227	900	1,136	800	0	346	6	0	0	0	0	97,492	514
Principe De Paz	8201	10	15	10	0	0	0	0	0	0	0	0	181
Renacer	8225	569	603	367	0	55	21	0	0	1,656	833	82,952	3,508
Rey de Reyes	8228	88	227	137	0	5	5	0	0	157	71	8,819	159
Samaria	8217	55	73	60	0	0	18	0	0	207	762	7,076	666
San Lucas	8215	52	78	75	0	2	2	0	0	364	802	13,544	918
San Marcos	8218	76	85	30	0	7	2	0	0	265	1,439	10,157	1,200
San Pablo	8212	150	180	150	0	5	2	0	0	290	1,320	16,915	1,012
Tulua Mission	8226	62	90	85	0	0	0	0	0	383	1,314	10,393	459
TOTALS	**21**	**2,987**	**3,642**	**2,309**	**0**	**462**	**73**	**0**	**2,750**	**6,940**	**19,763**	**412,167**	**23,730**

*Math error corrected. **Purged roll.

CHURCHES, PASTORS, AND CLERKS:

Betania   (4WF)MSCA8204
   Av 5 No 20-12
   Cali, Colombia, South America
   ( )391-3975   <S America>
   ipcbetania@gmail.com
PA: Mario Gaviria   <M1>
   Calle 2 A73-75
   Cali, Colombia, South America
   ( )484-6805
   mariogaviria50@hotmail.com
CL: Ana Bechara de Montoya
   Aereo 851
   Cali, Colombia, South America

Bethel   (4MWC)MSCA8205
   Calle 14 Oeste No 48-17
   Cali, Colombia, South America
   ( )554-7514   <S America>
   iglesiapcbethel20@hotmail.com
SS:Rodrigo Torres   <M2>
   Av 6 A Oeste No 15-87
   Cali, Colombia, South America
   (312)207-8319
   rojo_nana@hotmail.es

CL: Ana Leyda Meneses
   Aereo 10701
   Cali, Colombia, South America

Caleb   (4F)MSCA8223
   Av 47 Oeste No 9 A-24
   Montebello, Colombia, South America
   ( )323-8070   <S America>
   ipccentral@hotmail.com
PA: Gildardo Agudelo   <M1>
   Cra 74C No 1B-90
   Cali, Colombia, South America
   ( )323-8070
   pastorgildardoaguedelo@outlook.com.ar
CL: Carmen Rosa
   Ave 47 Oe 9-51
   Montebello, Colombia, South America

Cali Central   (4MWC)MSCA8208
   Av De Las Americas 19N-18
   Cali, Colombia, South America
   ( )668-7109   <S America>
   ipccentral@hotmail.com
PA: Sergio Betancur   <M1>
   Cra 96 No 48-53 Bloque 2 Apt 101
   Cali, Colombia, South America
   (313)629-6604
   sergiobetancurposada@hotmail.com

CL: Nancy Trejos
   Av De Las Americas 19N-18
   Cali, Colombia, South America
   nantre6@hotmail.com

Divino Redentor   (4MWC)MSCA8206
   Cra 3 No 36-29
   Juan XXIII
   Buenaventura, Colombia, South America
   (092)242-8399   <S America>
   ipc.divinoredentor@gmail.com
PA: Wilfrido Quinonez   <M1>
   Cra 36B No 4-18
   Juan XXIII
   Buenaventura, Colombia, South America
   (315)532-5070
   wilqui07@hotmail.com
CL: Marlen Palacios
   Cra 3 No 36-29
   Juan XXIII
   Buenaventura, Colombia, South America

Emaus   (4WC)MSCA8219
   Diag 1 sur Cra 49-1
   Buenaventura, Colombia, South America
   (092)244-2624   <S America>
   emauspres@hotmail.com

CAUCA VALLEY PRESBYTERY CONTINUED

SS: Manuel Medina   <M1>
   Diag 1 sur Cra 49-1
   Buenaventura, Colombia, South America
   (316)339-1735
   emauspres@hotmail.com
CL: Omairo Valasco Cosme
   Aereo 969
   Buenaventura, Colombia, South America

Filipos   (4WF)MSCA8211
   Calle 34 No 24A-36
   Cali, Colombia, South America
   ( )438-2563   <S America>
   i.p.c.filipos@hotmail.com
PA: Roberto Fonseca   <M1>
   Cra D1 No 46C-22
   Cali, Colombia, South America
   ( )446-7370
   robertoaltafuya@yahoo.com.ar
CL: Nancy Cortez
   Calle 34 No 24A-36
   Cali, Colombia, South America

Getsemani   (ARC)MSCA8210
   Cra 15 No 8-43
   El Cerrito, Colombia, South America
   (092)256-4261   <S America>
SS: Luis Cantor   <M3>
   Cra 15 No 8-43
   El Cerrito, Colombia, South America
   (315)775-8238
   pastoralberto7328@hotmail.com
CL: Amparo Renjifo
   Cra 15 No 8-43
   El Cerrito, Colombia, South America

Guabas   (4WF)MSCA8229
   Corregimiento Guabas
   Guacari, Colombia, South America

Maranatha   (4WF)MSCA8220
   Calle 12 No 4-69
   Guapi, Colombia, South America
   (092)840-0424   <S America>
   ipcmarantha@yahoo.com
CL: John Fredy Zamora
   Calle 12 No 4-69
   Guapi, Colombia, South America

Nueva Esperanza   (F)MSCA8221
   Cra 89 4C-35
   Cali, Colombia, South America
   (318)666-5314   <South America>
   ipcnuevaesperanzacali@gmail.com
PA: Jorge Valencia   <M1>
   Cra 17-1 29-36
   Cali, Colombia, South America
   ( )383-4124
   jorgevalencia65@hotmail.com
CL: Janeth Zuniga
   Cra 89 4C-35
   Cali, Colombia, South America
   tinta_y_papel@hotmail.com

Nueva Jerusalen   (4F)MSCA8222
   Cra 73 CN No 1A-54 (Lourdes)
   Cali, Colombia, South America
   ( )377-3837   <S America>
   cdi434herederosdevidaplena@hotmail.com
SS: Fabian Florez   <M3>
   Cll 2 80-27
   Cali, Colombia, South America
   (310)597-7268
   fabianflorezpastor@yahoo.es
CL: Adriana Montenegro
   Aereo 6365
   Cali, Colombia, South America

Popayan   (ARC)MSCA8227
   Cra 9 No 6N-87
   Popayan, Colombia, South America
   (092)823-8988   <S America>
   jesucristoeslasolucionipc@gmail.com
PA: Johnny Montano   <M1>
   Anticua 4 Casa 25
   Popayan, Colombia, South America
   (318)286-7264
   jmonsolis@gmail.com
CL: Diego Orlando Golu
   Cra 9 No 6 6N-87
   Popayan, Colombia, South America

Principe De Paz   (4WC)MSCA8201
   Cra 27 No 7-48
   Cali, Colombia, South America
   ( )484-9511   <S America>
CL: Mismery Garcia
   Cra 27 No 7-48
   Cali, Colombia, South America

Renacer   (4WF)MSCA8225
   Diag 26M Trv 73A-69
   Cali, Colombia, South America
   ( )422-3940   <S America>
   ipcrenacer@gmail.com
PA: Wilson Lopez   <M1>
   Cra 100 No 34-65
   Cali, Colombia, South America
   (317)516-3225
   wilsonlg7@gmail.com
CL: Sucelly Zamora
   Diag 26M Trv 73A-69
   Cali, Colombia, South America

Rey de Reyes   (4WC)MSCA8228
   Calle 6A No 17-03
   Tulua, Colombia, South America
   (311)615-5006
   presbireydereyes@hotmail.com
PA: Bertulio Toro   <M1>
   Calle 5A No 22-03
   Tulua, Colombia, South America
   (311)615-5006
   bertulioevangelista@hotmail.com
CL: Jeymi Jimenez
   Calle 6A No 17-03
   Tulua, Colombia, South America

Samaria   (4MWC)MSCA8217
   Trans 30 No 17F-122
   Cali, Colombia, South America
   ( )381-1515   <S America>
   ipcsamaria@hotmail.com
PA: Juan Bautista Reina   <M1>
   Dig 23 T 31-60
   Cali, Colombia, South America
   (316)404-1528
   juanbautistareina@hotmail.com
CL: Maria Josefa Martinez
   Aereo 4290
   Cali, Colombia, South America

San Lucas   (4WC)MSCA8215
   Calle 26 No 29-53
   Palmira, Colombia, South America
   ( )287-8038   <S America>
   ipc_sanpablo@yahoo.com
SS: Alexander Quintero   <M2>
   Calle 26 No 29-53
   Palmira, Colombia, South America
   (317)573-8198
   maalgo75@hotmail.com
CL: Leydi Marcela Quintero
   Calle 26 No 29-53
   Palmira, Colombia, South America

San Marcos   (4MWC)MSCA8218
   Calle 46 A No 4N-25
   Cali, Colombia, South America
   ( )446-3311   <S America>
   ipcsanmarcos@gmail.com
SS: Diego Palomino   <M3>
   Calle 55 Bis #9-14
   Cali, Colombia, South America
   (314)858-2006
   diegofdopalomino@gmail.com
CL: Luz Dazy Ceballos
   Calle 46 A No 4N-25
   Cali, Colombia, South America

San Pablo   (4MWC)MSCA8212
   Cra 8 No 5-27
   Guacari, Colombia, South America
   ( )253-8245   <S America>
   ipc_sanpablo@yahoo.com
PA: Aldrin Calero   <M1>
   Cra 6 No 4-26
   Guacari, Colombia, South America
   ( )253-1473
   aldrin_calero@hotmail.com
CL: Liliana Soto
   Cra 8 No 5-27
   Guacari, Colombia, South America

Tulua Central   (4WF)MSCA8226
   Calle 41A No 26-26
   Tulua, Colombia, South America
   ( )224-5004   <S America>
   iglesiacentraltulua@hotmail.com
SS: Orlando Mendez   <M3>
   Cra 20 39-17 Apar 104
   Tulua, Colombia, South America
   (310)891-5453
   orlandomendezf@hotmail.com
CL: Luz Miria Montoya
   Calle 41A No 26-26
   Tulua, Colombia, South America

OTHERS ON MINISTERIAL ROLL:

Aguirre, Luciria   <M1 WC>
   Calle 3B No 97-05
   Cali, Colombia, South America
   (301)775-9464
   pastorluciana50@yahoo.com.co
Ariza, Fabiola   <M1 WC>
   Calle 25 No 5A-54
   Cali, Colombia, South America
   fatvioleta@hotmail.com
   (316)419-8414
Caicedo, Efrain   <M1 WC>
   Calle 29 No 29A-03
   Cali, Colombia, South America
   ( )326-8794
Camacho, Blanca   <M9>
   Calle 4D 89-26 Apto 205
   Cali, Colombia, South America
   (301)401-2094
   blancanidiacamacho@yahoo.com
Cuartas, Joel   <M1 WC>
   Cll 14 Oeste 52-100
   Cali, Colombia, South America
   ( )513-7756
   pastorjoelcuartas@hotmail.com
Fonseca, Roberto   <M1 WC>
   CRA D2 46C-22
   Cali, Colombia, South America
   ( )446-5351
   robertoaltafuya@yahoo.com.ar
Gaviria, Mario   <M1 WC>
   Cll 2 A 73-75
   Cali, Colombia, South America
   ( )484-6805
   mariogaviria50@hotmail.com

CAUCA VALLEY PRESBYTERY CONTINUED

Giraldo, William <M1 WC>
 Trv 21 10 180
 Pereira, Colombia, South America
 (315)782-5045
 giraldo_william@yahoo.com
Gonzalez, Rito <M1 MY>
 Cra 25C No 123-27
 Cali, Colombia, South America
 (316)650-1370
Jimenez, Raul <M9>
 Calle 3B No 97A-05 Apto 102C
 Cali, Colombia, South America
Madrid, Alejandro <M1 WC>
 Calle 12 No 4-69
 Guapi, Colombia, South America
Pejendino, Socorro <M1 MY>
 24 Avenida 0-97 Zona
 7 Ciudad de GUATEMALA
 (317)654-5750
 pastorasocorrod@hotmail.com
Racines, Jairo <M1 WC>
 Calle 23 No 3-28
 Cali, Colombia, South America
 (314)632-2375
 senicartheos@live.com
Rodriguez, Jairo <M1 WC>
 Calle 39 No 13-40
 Cali, Colombia, South America
 (310)437-6316
 jairo.hrodriguez@hotmail.com
Sanchez, Sol Maria <M9>
 CRA 96 48 53, Bloque 2 Apt 101
 Cali, Colombia, South America
 (314)689-2322
 sol.marias@hotmail.com
Solis, Arcadio <M1 WC>
 Cra 42 D1 No 55-69
 Cali, Colombia, South America
 ( )328-9693
Torres, Mariano <M1 WC>
 Cra 34 No 4-34A 34
 Buenaventura, Colombia, South America
 (317)733-7335

OTHER LICENTIATES ON ROLL:

Gutierrez, Diana <M2>
 Cra 100 No 34-65
 Cali, Colombia, South America
 (318)772-8053
 gutierrezdp21@hotmail.com
Paredes, Flavio <M2>
 Cra 7 No 1-76
 Ipiales, Colombia, South America
 (301)501-7891
 fepa5308@hotmail.com

OTHER CANDIDATES ON ROLL:

Angulo, Henry <M3>
 Verdeda Limones
 (311)734-2253
Artega, Jose Felix <M3>
 Ipiales, Colombia, South America
Caicedo, Jose Urier <M3>
 Cra 4 sur 9C-15
 Jamundi, Colombia, South America
 (317)675-2580
 joseurier@hotmail.com
Garcia, Jesus Maria <M3>
 Mazma 38 Casa 34 Barrio Bosques de
 Maracibo
 (318)463-7302
 jesus.garciagil@hotmail.com
Garcia, Luz Stella <M3>
 Cll 33 No 34A-22
 Cali, Colombia, South America
 ( )232-5868

Gonzalez, Carlos Humberto <M3>
 Cra 7 E 2-15
 Cali, Colombia, South America
 (312)889-7919
 carloshg@hotmail.com
Gonzalez, Patricia <M3>
 Tulua, Colombia, South America
 adriapatriciag@gmail.com
Guasaquillo, Samuel <M3>
 Calle 8 no 3-10 Bugalagrande
 Cali, Colombia, South America
 (311)619-9012
 reysoberano777@gmail.com
Gutierrez, Consuelo <M3>
 Calle 18N No 4N-49
 Cali, Colombia, South America
 consuelogutierrezrico@hotmail.com
Gutierrez, Gloria <M3>
 Cll 18 N 4N 49 Apt 202
 Cali, Colombia, South America
 (315)546-8125
 gloritabondadosa@hotmail.com
Guyara, Elizabeth <M3>
 Ave 3 No 19-18
 Cali, Colombia, South America
 bethgu00@hotmail.com
Hoyos, Javier <M3>
 Calle 44 12-36
 Cali, Colombia, South America
 (316)740-4168
 danlauyanjav@hotmail.com
Lerma, Andres Felipe <M3>
 Calle 2 Sur Cra 74 17
 Cali, Colombia, South America
 (316)563-8825
 andestey@hotmail.com
Madrid, Alejandro <M3>
 Cra 11 18 19
 Popayan, Colombia South America
 (313)676-7328
 ale.madrid@yahool.com
Madrid, Jorge Alexis <M3>
 Cra 9 #6 N 87 Bello Horizonte
 Cali, Colombia South America
 (310)436-0141
 jorgedmadrid@gmail.com
Micolta, Ruby Mabely <M3>
 Anticua 4 Casa 25
 Popayan, Colombia, South America
 (318)286-7264
 rumami@gmail.com
Mosquera, Luis Alfonzo <M3>
 Calle 3 #36-29, B Juan 23
 Cali, Colombia, South America
 (321)662-7191
 creer7@hotmail.com
Munoz, Arlex <M3>
 Ave 3N No 19-18
 Cali, Colombia, South America
 armisport2@gmail.com
Ocoro, Richard <M3>
 Guapi
 Cali, Colombia, South America
 (315)200-4727
 vpoera@hotmail.com
Ordonez, Jeason <M3>
 Diag 26 O 96 31
 Cali, Colombia, South America
 (312)898-9304
 jeamauri@hotmail.com
Paz, Ivan <M3>
 Pasto, Colombia, South America
 ivanpaz1234@hotmail.com
Ponce, Dennis Adrian <M3>
 Buenaventura, Colombia, South America

Ponce, Jesus Adriam <M3>
 Carrera 38 #3-31 14 De Julio
 Cali, Colombia, South America
 (318)526-6265
 dapcristo@hotmail.com
Restrepo, Johanna <M3>
 Ave 4 A Oeste 20-11
 Cali, Colombia, South America
 (318)655-9955
 rojo_nana@hotmail.es
Rizo, Yensy <M3>
 Diag 26 H 2 83-35 Marroquin
 Cali, Colombia, South America
 ( )403-7709
Rodriguez, Sofonias Velasco <M3>
 Brazo Seco Guapi-Cauca
 (317)885-9033
Rosero, Oscar <M3>
 Sapuyes Marino Los Monos
 (318)415-7077
Ruiz, Daveiva <M3>
 Diagonal 26 F 77-80
 Cali, Colombia, South America
 (314)668-2610
 daveiva61@gmail.com
Valencia, Ana Dolly <M3>
 Cll 18 50 C-17
 Cali, Colombia, South America
 ( )513-7754
 anadollycuartas@hotmail.com
Vargas, Guido <M3>
 Calle 73N 7B-08
 Popayan, Colombia, South America
 (315)326-0308
 g_varg@yahoo.com
Ventura, Juan <M3>
 El Carmelo
 (321)623-7234
 i.p.c.divinoredentor@hotmail.es
Viafara, Jesus David <M3>
 Cra 26 J 98 13
 Cali, Colombia, South America
 (312)203-9074
 viafarajdv@gmail.com

Choctaw Presbytery
MISSION SYNOD

	GENERAL	MEMBERSHIP			CHANGES					FINANCES			
	1.Church Number	2.Active 3.Total	4.Church School	5.Prof. of Faith	6.Gains 7.Losses 8.Children Baptized			9. OUR UNITED OUT-REACH		10. Total Out-Reach Giving	11. All Other Expenses	12. Total Income Received	13. Value Church Prop. 1=1000
	1	2	3	4	5	6	7	8	9	10	11	12	13
Coal Creek	6102	4	24	6	0	0	0	0	0	926	855	1,183	11
Lone Star	6105	5	16	5	0	0	0	0	0	250	2,920	4,014	68
McGee Chapel*	6106	30	30	8	0	6	0	0	0	1,000	5,000	10,000	500
Panki Bok	6108	2	4	2	0	NRR	0	0	0	0	0	0	6
Pigeon Roost	6109	5	16	5	0	0	1	0	0	500	1,250	2,400	30
Rock Creek	6111	10	10	12	0	1	1	0	0	25	5,612	5,637	24
Round Lake	6112	7	9	10	0	NRR	0	0	0	0	0	0	2
TOTALS	**7**	**63**	**109**	**48**	**0**	**7**	**2**	**0**	**0**	**2,701**	**15,637**	**23,234**	**641**

*Math error corrected. **Purged roll. NRR - No Report Received

CHURCHES, PASTORS, AND CLERKS:

Coal Creek   (4WC)MSCH6102
   13893 County Road 3830 (mailing)
   Route 1 Box 1215 (physical)
   Coalgate, OK 74538
   ( )   \<Atoka\>
SS: Virginia Espinoza   \<M1\>
   PO Box 132
   Boswell, OK 74727
   (580)775-4138
   vespinoza@choctawnation.com
CL: Lola Mae John
   13893 County Road 3830
   Coalgate, OK 74538
   (580)258-8244

Lone Star   (2WC)MSCH6105
   PO Box 44 (mailing)
   206 S Newell Street (physical)
   Coalgate, OK 74538
   ( )   \<Atoka\>
SS: Hannah Bryan   \<M1\>
   3601 Dana Drive
   Durant, OK 74701
   (580)775-4955
   hbryan@choctawnation.com
CL: Evangeline Robinson
   PO Box 44
   Boswell, OK 74727
   (580)513-0170
   erobinson@choctawarchiving.com

McGee Chapel   (2EW C)MSCH6106
   PO Box 158 (mailing)
   99 Chapel Circle (physical)
   Broken Bow, OK 74728
   (580)584-2099   \<McCurtain\>
   FAX: (580)584-2099
   chocpres@pine-net.com

SS: Nathan Scott   \<M1\>
   9696 S Katy Road
   Atoka, OK 74525
   (580)364-6155
CL: Betty Jacob
   PO Box 158
   Broken Bow, OK 74728
   (580)584-2099
   FAX: (580)584-2099
   chocpres@pine-net.com

Panki Bok   (2C)MSCH6108
   PO Box 158 (mailing)
   Broken Bow, OK 74728
   Eagletown, OK 74734 (physical)
   ( )   \<McCurtain\>

Pigeon Roost   (2C)MSCH6109
   PO Bo 132 (mailing)
   910 North 4000 Road (physical)
   Boswell, OK 74727
   (580)775-4138   \<Choctaw\>
PA: Virginia Espinoza   \<M1\>
   PO Box 132
   Boswell, OK 74727
   (580)775-4138
   vespinoza@choctawnation.com
CL: Virginia Espinoza
   PO Box 132
   Atoka, OK 74525
   (580)889-2292

Rock Creek   (2WC)MSCH6111
   c/o Dena Vielma (mailing)
   305 East Memorial Street
   Broken Bow, OK 74728
   (580)306-2920   \<LeFlore\>
SS: Nathan Scott   \<M1\>
   9696 S Katy Road
   Atoka, OK 74525
   (580)364-6155

CL: Dena Vielma
   305 East Memorial Street
   Broken Bow, OK 74728
   (580)5306-2920

Round Lake   (1WC)MSCH6112
   Box 127
   Tupelo, OK 74572
   (580)317-7427   \<Coal\>
PA: Hannah Bryan   \<M1\>
   3601 Dana Drive
   Durant, OK 74701
   (580)775-4955
   hbryan@choctawnation.com
CL: Vickie McClure
   Box 127
   Tupelo, OK 74572
   (580)317-7427

OTHERS ON MINISTERIAL ROLL:

OTHER CANDIDATES ON ROLL:

Columbia Presbytery
TENNESSEE SYNOD

GENERAL	1. Church Number	MEMBERSHIP: 2. Active	3. Total	4. Church School	CHANGES: 5. Prof. of Faith	6. Gains	7. Losses	8. Children Baptized	FINANCES: 9. OUR UNITED OUTREACH	10. Total Out-Reach Giving	11. All Other Expenses	12. Total Income Received	13. Value Church Prop. 1=1000
	1	2	3	4	5	6	7	8	9	10	11	12	13
Ash Hill	7101	31	63	23	0	2	2	0	2,816	7,224	24,123	27,982	260
Belleview	7104	10	20	7	0	0	1	0	0	670	12,705	11,092	650
Boonshill	7106	23	25	23	0	0	1	0	800	3,378	25,752	18,265	350
Champ	7108	11	11	4	0	0	0	0	0	200	14,738	16,700	40
Chapel Hill	7109	28	28	13	0	0	0	0	250	2,740	37,000	51,000	410
Columbia	7110	34	44	15	0	2	2	0	1,300	8,240	66,449	84,661	1,500
Elora	7111	5	5	8	0	0	0	0	0	300	7,846	11,020	296
Faith Fellowship	7146	50	75	14	0	0	5	0	2,400	8,000	17,432	48,375	750
Fayetteville	7112	86	273	30	1	1	4	0	14,400	24,400	157,482	209,972	2,400
Fiducia	7113	9	9	6	0	NRR	0	0	0	0	0	0	80
Flintville	7115	7	7	12	0	0	0	0	0	1,330	6,617	6,617	25
Franklin	7116	23	23	3	0	1	2	0	0	2,798	32,393	29,454	926
Green Hill	7118	11	11	6	0	0	2	0	3,175	9,914	31,930	33,409	86
Harpeth Lick	7119	15	16	0	0	0	25	1	1,600	2,719	24,528	29,411	250
Hohenwald	7120	12	12	0	0	0	0	0	188	388	25,949	40,577	250
Howell	7121	51	125	60	0	2	0	0	3,000	29,230	58,432	100,032	750
Jenkins	7144	69	156	25	0	3	6	0	2,568	32,201	219,456	198,392	3,296
Kelso	7122	27	53	10	1	1	0	0	643	349	53,527	66,416	258
Kingdom	7123	10	10	8	0	0	1	0	440	1,120	11,261	14,334	325
Lawrenceburg	7124	20	16	12	0	NRR	0	0	112	0	0	0	110
Lewisburg, 1st	7125	45	168	55	1	1	3	0	0	4,500	115,140	100,414	500
McCains	7126	23	23	19	0	0	18	0	2,000	11,866	45,791	50,133	414
Mt. Carmel	7127	51	101	12	0	0	2	0	0	14,978	124,639	150,277	900
Mt. Joy	7129	45	69	15	0	1	30	0	1,164	2,364	52,382	64,876	850
Mt. Lebanon	7130	36	36	10	0	0	2	0	0	726	28,110	26,559	125
Mt. Moriah	7131	37	127	15	0	0	1	1	0	27,356	13,724	47,408	250
Mt. Nebo	7132	5	5	5	0	1	1	0	0	460	22,699	19,563	90
Mt. Pleasant	7133	38	89	11	0	0	0	0	5,096	9,354	30,288	36,370	1,000
New Bethel	7134	10	10	10	0	NRR	0	0	132	0	0	0	100
Petersburg	7135	41	46	40	1	0	12	0	4,875	15,687	41,674	57,361	243
Pleasant Mount	7136	30	77	20	1	1	2	0	2,200	2,500	59,991	57,413	500
Richland	7137	46	114	49	0	0	0	0	1,500	0	0	0	150
Santa Fe	7138	20	20	18	0	0	1	0	0	2,314	15,718	18,982	0
Swan	7140	9	13	3	0	0	2	0	50	100	26,248	30,433	300
Union Grove	7141	8	8	0	0	0	0	0	0	1,800	11,722	16,034	100
Waynesboro	7142	43	43	15	0	3	7	0	5,920	18,187	70,439	88,626	618
West Point	7143	52	58	31	0	0	3	0	0	8,676	77,569	76,688	1,000
TOTALS	**37**	**1,071**	**1,989**	**607**	**5**	**19**	**135**	**2**	**56,629**	**256,069**	**1,563,754**	**1,838,846**	**20,152**

*Math error corrected. **Purged roll. NRR - No Report Received

COLUMBIA PRESBYTERY CONTINUED

CHURCHES, PASTORS, AND CLERKS:

_____
Ash Hill   (4WC)TNCO7101
  c/o Roger Cathey (mailing)
  4921 Ash Hill Road
  4930 Ash Hill Road Ophysical)
  Spring Hill, TN 37174
  (931)381-3367   <Williamson>
CL: Helen Logue
  1603 Emerald Court
  Franklin, 37064
  (615)599-6764

_____
Belleview   (4WC)TNCO7104
  1752 Burke Hollow Road (mailing)
  Nolensville, TN 37135
  4724 Murfreesboro Road (physical)
  Franklin, TN 37064
  ( )   <Williamson>
PA: James R Miller   <M1>
  1214 Whitney Drive
  Columbia, TN 38401
  (931)381-3367
  rev.james.miller@charter.net
CL: John Koelz
  4498 South Caruthers Road
  Franklin, TN 37074
  (615)595-7394
  koel3358@bellsouth.net

_____
Boonshill   (4C)TNCO7106
  91 Red Oak Road (mailing)
  Petersburg, TN 37144
  Rt 2 (physical)
  Boonshill, TN
  ( )   <Lincoln>
OD: Thomas Smith   <M5>
  2314 Old Columbia Road
  Lewisburg, TN 37091
  (931)607-6008
  tomandbobbi6764@gmail.com
CL: Sammy Luna
  91 Red Oak Road
  Petersburg, TN 37144
  (931)703-0536
  srluna@ardmore.net

_____
Champ   (2C)TNCO7108
  2800 Hillsboro Road (mailing)
  Huntsville, AL 35805
  61 Tucker Creek Road (physical)
  Mulberry, TN
  ( )   <Lincoln>
PA: Kirk Smith   <M1 RT>
  813 1st Avenue
  Fayetteville, TN 37334
  (931)438-8649
  kirks37334@att.net
CL: Diann Adams
  2800 Hillsboro Road
  Huntsville, AL 35805
  (256)534-6076

_____
Chapel Hill   (4MWC)TNCO7109
  PO Box 72 (mailing)
  302 N Horton Parkway (physical)
  Chapel Hill, TN 37034
  (931)364-7819   <Marshall>
PA: Joe Wiggins   <M1>
  2734 US Highway 41A S
  Eagleville, TN 37060
  (615)274-2011
  jwigginz@aol.com

CL: Spence Walls
  4521 Polaris Drive
  Chapel Hill, TN 37034
  (931)364-2573
  walls.family95@yahoo.com

_____
Columbia   (4MWC)TNCO7110
  1106 Nashville Highway
  Columbia, TN 38401
  (931)388-9177   <Maury>
  pastor@fcpccolumbia.com
SS: Scott Yates   <M1>
  1632 Lindsey Drive
  Columbia, TN 38401
  (615)274-3000
  revscottyates@outlook.com
CL: Jimmy Upshaw
  1588 Fountain Heights Road
  Columbia, TN 38401
  (931)388-214   <Maury>
  jhupshaw@bellsouth.net

_____
Elora   (2C)TNCO7111
  69 Bear Wallow Road (mailing)
  Flintville, TN 37335
  Elora, TN 37328 (physical)
  ( )   <Lincoln>
SS: John Blair   <M1>
  108 Cliff Drive
  Lawrenceburg, TN 38464
  (931)762-2480
  jnbblair@charter.net
CL: Jim Ramsey
  69 Bear Wallow Road
  Flintville, TN 37335
  (931)937-8765
  jim.brenda.ramsey710@gmail.com

_____
Faith Fellowship   (4WC)TNCO7146
  920 Bear Creek Pike (mailing)
  1118 Nashville Highway (physical)
  Columbia, TN 38401
PA: Terry Kinnaman   <M1>
  2018 Spring Meadow Circle
  Spring Hill, TN 37174
  (615)302-3321
  kinnaman91@att.net
CL: Marcen Jeffiers
  1347 Mapleash Avenue
  Columbia, TN 38401

_____
Fayetteville   (4WC)TNCO7112
  1015 Lewisburg Highway
  Fayetteville, TN 37334
  (931)433-5441   <Lincoln>
  FAX: (931)433-0056
  cpc@fpunet.com
PA: Timothy Smith   <M1>
  214 Jeffrey Drive
  Fayetteville, TN 37334
  (931)438-2820
  FAX: (931)433-0056
  tims38@hotmail.com
CL: Andrea Gibson
  33 Hilldale Church Road
  Fayetteville, TN 37334
  (931)433-2666
  FAX: (931)433-0056

_____
Fiducia   (2EW C)TNCO7113
  108 Cliff Drive (mailing)
  Lawrenceburg, TN 38478
  1695 Fiducia Road (physical)
  Prospect, TN 38477
  ( )   <Giles>
PA: John Blair   <M1>
  108 W Cliff Drive
  Lawrenceburg, TN 38464
  (931)766-2480
  jnbblair@charter.net
CL: David Dison
  25661 Beulah Road
  Elkmontm AL 35620
  (256)296-1139
  dison25661@charter.net

_____
Flintville   (2C)TNCO7115
  35 Well Lee Road (mailing)
  9 Flintville School Road (physical)
  Flintville, TN 37335
  ( )   <Lincoln>
PA: John Blair   <M1>
  108 W Cliff Drive
  Lawrenceburg, TN 38464
  (931)766-2480
  jnbblair@charter.net
CL: Jimmie D Wicks
  35 Wells Lee Road
  Flintville, TN 37335
  (931)937-8562
  bfwicks@bellsouth.net

_____
Franklin   (4MC)TNCO7116
  PO Box 1134 (mailing)
  615 West Main Street (physical)
  Franklin, TN 37065
  (615)599-0029   <Williamson>
  FAX: (615)807-2959
  cp1876@hotmail.com
CL: Dorris Douglass
  1721 Old Hillsboro Road
  Franklin, TN 37069
  (615)794-7891
  FAX: (615)595-1247
  anscher@aol.com

_____
Green Hill   (3WC)TNCO7118
  1900 Unionville-Deason Road
  Bell Buckle, TN 37020
  (931)294-2040   <Bedford>
PA: Lisa Cook   <M1 M9>
  4101 Dalemere Court
  Nashville, TN 37207
  (615)830-6217
  sacredsparksministry@gmail.com
CL: Angela Burns
  328 Dunnaway Road
  Shelbyville, TN 37160
  (931)294-5105

_____
Harpeth Lick   (4C)TNCO7119
  6981 Arno Allisona Road
  College Grove, TN 37046
  ( )   <Williamson>
SS: Larry Guin   <M1>
  125 Glider Loop
  Eagleville, TN 37060
  (615)668-5236
  lguin43@hotmail.com

COLUMBIA PRESBYTERY CONTINUED

CL: Pam Waddey
6851 Arno Allisona Road
College Grove, TN 37046
(615)948-8560
pamwaddey.1951@gmail.com

_____

Hohenwald   (4MWC)TNCO7120
PO Box 456 (mailing)
201 Park Avenue S (physical)
Hohenwald, TN 38462
(931)796-3657   <Lewis>
CL: Sandra Burgdorf
750 Long Branch Road
Hohenwald, TN 38412
(931)796-5729
outdoor111@hughes.net

_____

Howell   (4MWC)TNCO7121
43 Brown Teal Road
Fayetteville, TN 37334
(931)433-0818   <Lincoln>
PA: Todd Gaskill   <M1>
47 Brown Teal Road
Fayetteville, TN 37334
(931)580-2708
revtgaskill@gmail.com
CL: Tim Porter
85 Icy Bank Road
Fayetteville, TN 37334
(931)433-8306

_____

Jenkins   (4MWC)TNCO7144
PO Box 518 (mailing)
2501 York Road (physical)
Nolensville, TN 37135
(615)776-2339   <Williamson>
FAX: (615)776-3520
jenkinspastor@gmail.com
PA: Jason Mikel   <M1>
410 Ramblewood Lane
Nolensville, TN 37135
(615)243-8938
jenkinspastor@gmail.com
CL: Johnny Crawford
PO Box 518
Nolensville, TN 37135
(615)776-2339
jmc300@att.net

_____

Kelso   (4MWC)TNCO7122
PO Box 28 (mailing)
16 Teal Hollow Road (physical)
Kelso, TN 37348
( )   <Lincoln>
PA: Tony Gaskin   <M1>
18 Teal Hollow Road
Kelso, TN 37348
Cullman, AL 35055
(256)338-7893
tgaskin46@yahoo.com
CL: Bill Dickey
1501 Swanson Boulevard
Fayetteville, TN 37334
(931)433-2462

_____

Kingdom   (4C)TNCO7123
4532 Barfield Crescent Road (mailing)
Murfreesboro, TN 37128
800 Kingdom Road (physical)
Unionville, TN 37180
( )   <Bedford>

SS: Larry Guin   <M1>
125 Glider Loop
Eagleville, TN 37060
(615)668-5236
lguin43@hotmail.com
CL: Thelma Shockey
4532 Barfield Crescent Road
Murfreesboro, TN 37128
(615)896-1890

_____

Lawrenceburg   (4MWC)TNCO7124
228 S Military Avenue
Lawrenceburg, TN 38464
(931)762-4343   <Lawrence>
cumberlandpresby@bellsouth.net
CL: Patricia Hudgins
PO Box 297
Lawrenceburg, TN 38464
(931)242-6628
patriciahudgins84@outlook.com

_____

Lewisburg 1st   (4MWC)TNCO7125
402 2nd Avenue N
Lewisburg, TN 37091
(931)359-3857   <Marshall>
FAX: (931)270-8624
fcpclewisburg@bellsouth.net
PA: Roger Reid   <M1>
637 Colburn Drive
Lewisburg, TN 37091
(931)637-4467
drrtr@yahoo.com
CL: Tammy Caneer
1850B Lowe Street
Lewisburg, TN 37091
(931)637-7374
FAX: (931)270-8624
cantam@bellsouth.net

_____

McCains   (4MWC)TNCO7126
PO Box 985 (mailing)
3532 McCains Lane (physical)
Columbia, TN 38402
(931)540-0160   <Maury>
PA: Tommy Clark   <M1>
124 Roberta Drive
Memphis, TN 38112
(931)703-7542
fattire77@gmail.com
CL: Tracy McGlocklin
3541 Neeley Hollow Road
Columbia, TN 38401
(615)969-1661
tracygmcglocklin@gmail.com

_____

Mt Carmel   (4C)TNCO7127
4810 Ash Hill Road (mailing)
Spring Hill, TN 37174
2300 Lewisburg Pike (physical)
Franklin, TN 37064
(615)591-3930   <Williamson>
CL: Peggy S Fisher
4810 Ash Hill Road
Spring Hill, TN 37174
(615)944-9300
fishpest@ymail.com

_____

Mt Joy   (4MWC)TNCO7129
8364 Mt Joy Road
Mount Pleasant, TN 38474
( )   <Maury>

PA: Mark King   <M1>
713 Baptist Branch Road
Hampshire, TN 38461
(931)379-7614
pastorking1963@gmail.com
CL: Ashlee King
393 Loggins Road
Burns, TN 37029
(931)374-0331
ashleemarieking@gmail.com

_____

Mt Lebanon   (4EC)TNCO7130
4497 Kedron Road
Spring Hill, TN 37174
( )   <Maury>
mortonco@bellsouth.net
PA: William Rolman, Jr   <M1>
602 Canyon Drive
Columbia, TN 38401
(931)388-2611
wlrolman@charter.net
CL: Judy L Morton
1272 John Sharp Road
Columbia, TN 38401
(931)381-1140
mortonco@bellsouth.net

_____

Mt Moriah   (4C)TNCO7131
485 Agnew Road (mailing)
463 Big Dry Creek Road (physical)
Pulaski, TN 38478
( )   <Giles>
PA: Steve Nave   <M1>
5172 Fall River Road
Leoma, TN 38468
(931)424-0020
stevemnave19@gmail.comt
CL: Dickson Marks
485 Agnew Road
Pulaski, TN 38478
(931)363-2432
jmarks0912@mindspring.com

_____

Mt Nebo   (4C)TNCO7132
84 S Old Military Road (mailing)
Saint Joseph, TN 38481
473 Mt Nebo Road (physical)
Iron City, TN 38463
( )   <Lawrence>
LS: Sean Richardson   <M6>
4227 Highway 43 N
Ethridge, TN 38456
(931)829-2094
sean@misterrichardson.com
CL: William B Gabel
104 Spring Street
Saint Joseph, TN 38481
(931)845-4203
stjoemerry@gmail.com

_____

Mt Pleasant   (4EWC)TNCO7133
PO Box 689 (mailing)
504 Florida Avenue (physical)
Mount Pleasant, TN 38474
(931)379-3662   <Maury>
SS: Jimmy Rochelle   <M1>
609 Woods Drive
Columbia, TN 38401
(931)698-6829
tnpappy53@yahoo.com

COLUMBIA PRESBYTERY CONTINUED

CL: Rickey Massey
609 Circle Drive
Mount Pleasant, TN 38474
(931)379-3617
rickeymassey@bellsouth.net

New Bethel   (2C)TNCO7134
5060 Reynolds Road
Columbia, TN 38401
(931)364-2378   <Marshall>
CL: James W Hood
1532 Lewisburg Pike
Franklin, TN 37064
(615)591-8689

Petersburg   (4MWC)TNCO7135
PO Box 82 (mailing)
303 Russell Street (physical)
Petersburg, TN 37144
(931)607-1859   <Lincoln>
petersburgpreacher@att.net
PA: Troy Green   <M1>
105 Cobb Hollow Lane
Petersburg, TN 37144
(931)659-6627
thegreens101@att.net
CL: Ann Hemphill
803 Washington Street W Apt B
Fayetteville, TN 37334
(931)433-8380
ahemphill@fpunet.com

Pleasant Mount   (4WC)TNCO7136
609 Woods Drive (mailing)
1620 Fountain Heights Road (physical)
Columbia, TN 38401
( )   <Maury>
PA: Byrd Broyles   <M1>
1856 Culleoka Highway
Culleoka, TN 38451
(931)224-5193
b3broyles@outlook.com
CL: Ryan Pilkinton
1676 Vaughn Road
Columbia, TN 38401
(931)374-2767
rpilkinton@maurycoop.com

Richland   (4C)TNCO7137
304 S Monte Murrey Road (mailing)
3452 Spring Place Road (physical)
Lewisburg, TN 37091
(931)270-6135   <Marshall>
CL: Douglas A Looney
3045 Monte Murrey Road
Lewisburg, TN 37091
(931)359-3781
ld.looney@yahoo.com

Santa Fe   (4WC)TNCO7138
PO Box 58 (mailing)
2630 Santa Fe Pike (physical)
Santa Fe, TN 38482
(931)682-3555   <Maury>
SS: Sherry Ladd   <M1>
4521 Turkey Creek Road
Williamsport, TN 38487
(931)682-2263
revsherryladd@gmail.com
CL: Whitney Seaton
111 W Hardin Drive
Columbia, TN 38401
(931)374-7273

Swan   (4C)TNCO7140
4521 Turkey Creek Road (mailing)
Williamsport, TN 38487
2250 Swan Creek Road (physical)
Centerville, TN 37033
(931)682-2263   <Hickman>
revsherryladd@gmail.com
PA: Sherry Ladd   <M1>
4521 Turkey Creek Road
Williamsport, TN 38487
(931)682-2263
revsherryladd@gmail.com
CL: George C Ladd
4521 Turkey Creek Road
Williamsport, TN 38487
(931)682-2263
gladd@hughes.net

Union Grove   (4C)TNCO7141
1452 Cliff White Road
Columbia, TN 38401
(931)486-2799   <Maury>
patricia.cates@att.net
PA: Scott Yates   <M1>
1632 Lindsey Drive
Columbia, TN 38401
(615)274-3000
revscottyates@outlook.com
CL: Patricia Cates
2409 Green Mills Road Lot 30
Columbia, TN 38401
(931)486-2799
patricia.cates@att.net

Waynesboro   (4MEWC)TNCO7142
PO Box 234 (mailing)
110 North High Street (physical)
Waynesboro, TN 38485
(931)722-5621   <Wayne>
PA:Patric Fife   <M1>
73 Jordan Road
Lawrenceburg, TN 38464
(931)629-8146
pnlfifernak@gmail.com
CL: Susan Myers
PO Box 234
Waynesboro, TN 38485
(931)722-5621
warden02@tds.net

West Point   (4MC)TNCO7143
1431 Spainwood Street (mailing)
1533 Theta Pike (physical)
Columbia, TN 38401
(931)388-7268   <Maury>
PA: Terry Peery   <M1>
1431 Spainwood Street
Columbia, TN 38401
(931)381-6871
coppreacher@gmail.com
CL: Mike McCord
4543 Snow Creek Road
Santa Fe, TN 38482
(931)682-2500
mmccord59@bellsouth.net

OTHERS ON MINISTERIAL ROLL:

Blair, Fonda   <M1 WC>
PO Box 11093
Murfreesboro, TN 37129
(615)605-9755
fblair4334@gmail.com
Cole, Dwayne   <M1 HR>
6460 Village Parkway
Anchorage, AK 99504
(907)854-5793
tadpolejr@aol.com
Heflin, Robert   <M1 DE>
4144 Meadow Court Drive
Bartlett, TN 38135
(901)382-8198
rheflin@cumberland.org
Hudson, Ellen Clark   <M1 WC>
301 N Royal Oaks Blvd Apt 2614
Franklin, TN 37067
(731)780-1004
ellen.hudson17@icloud.com
Hyden, John   <M1 WC>
6525 Peytonsville Arno Road
College Grove, TN 37046
(615)975-9584
john.hyden@wcs.edu
Liles, Dwight   <M1 WC>
8467 Joy Road
Mount Pleasant, TN 38474
(931)379-0326
dwightliles@att.net
Luttrell, Ben   <M1 WC>
608 County Road 992
Iuka, MS 38852
(931)332-1012
luttrellben993@gmail.com
Mullenix, Robert   <M1 RT>
122 Sunnyside Lane
Columbia, TN 38401
(931)364-4611
glonix@live.com
Trotter, Wendell   <M1 HR>
1516 Fell Avenue NE
Huntsville, AL 35811
(256)519-6571
wendelltrotter@knology.net

OTHER LICENTIATES ON ROLL:

Hone, Phillips   <M2>
301 S Walnut Street
Hohenwald, TN 38462
(931)306-8000
kaitiaki39@gmail.com

OTHER CANDIDATES ON ROLL:

Arnold, Dwight   <M3>
2925 Ragsdale Road
Santa Fe, Tennessee
(931)682-3237
Rogers, Steve   <M3>
101 Gillespie Drive Apt 13302
Franklin, TN 37067
(731)882-2229
srtn68@yahoo.com

Covenant Presbytery
MIDWEST SYNOD

	1.Church Number	2.Active	3.Total	4.Church School	5.Prof. of Faith	6.Gains	7.Losses	8.Children Baptized	9. OUR UNITED OUT-REACH	10. Total Out-Reach Giving	11. All Other Expenses	12. Total Income Received	13. Value Church Prop. 1=1000
	1	2	3	4	5	6	7	8	9	10	11	12	13
Bayou de Chien	3401	70	133	40	0	NRR	0	0	0	0	0	0	300
Benton	3403	15	40	15	0	NRR	0	0	0	0	0	0	215
Bethel	3404	184	363	95	1	4	3	0	20,380	52,554	263,151	315,705	2,500
Calvary	3405	23	52	25	0	NRR	0	0	0	0	0	0	332
Camp Ground	5103	16	53	17	0	2	1	0	1,406	6,534	26,495	19,811	972
Chandler*	5302	80	381	58	1	0	11	0	12,913	35,739	89,508	140,976	1,502
Ebenezer	5105	20	25	15	0	NRR	0	0	0	0	0	0	50
Ebenezer Hall	5106	1	11	5	0	NRR	0	0	643	0	0	0	38
Flat Lick	3606	26	92	16	0	NRR	0	0	6,027	0	0	0	400
Fredonia	3608	93	253	63	0	2	0	1	19,404	42,510	122,078	194,084	1,950
Gilead*	5110	30	35	15	0	0	12	0	2,657	22,791	66,713	108,567	1,250
Good Springs	3609	19	44	10	0	NRR	0	0	2,000	0	0	0	140
Grace Covenant	3415	83	113	20	0	NRR	0	0	3,638	0	0	0	750
Highland	3414	130	234	102	2	5	2	0	7,200	51,355	187,491	251,762	1,000
Hopewell	3610	100	100	10	2	1	2	0	720	720	59,551	52,476	120
Hopkinsville	3611	41	70	36	0	NRR	0	0	1,200	0	0	0	1,450
Liberty (ClC)	3406	97	107	55	0	NRR	0	0	0	0	0	0	720
Lisman	3613	21	49	21	0	6	0	0	1,245	6,061	63,041	41,455	225
Macedonia	3614	22	22	25	0	NRR	0	0	0	0	0	0	300
Madisonville	3615	40	150	25	0	NRR	0	0	0	0	0	0	355
Marion First	3616	44	137	20	0	NRR	0	0	0	0	0	0	353
Milburn Chapel	3416	71	247	28	2	8	0	0	0	8,969	115,334	136,243	1,800
Mt. Carmel	3617	35	134	6	0	0	0	0	0	987	26,788	16,515	600
Mt. Pleasant	3618	21	24	23	1	2	0	0	0	2,197	15,986	17,802	50
Mt. Sterling	5117	180	270	80	0	NRR	0	0	0	0	0	0	330
Mt. Zion	5118	10	10	5	0	0	1	0	2,400	7,225	17,303	23,540	35
New Hope	3410	108	215	50	0	2	21	0	16,200	34,936	132,191	192,158	3,200
No. Pleasant Gr	3411	23	53	31	0	NRR	0	0	0	0	0	0	200
Oak Grove	3412	60	98	40	0	NRR	0	0	0	0	0	0	400
Oak Grove Union**	3619	29	29	29	0	NRR	0	0	0	0	0	0	200
Oakland	3413	45	132	32	0	NRR	0	0	0	0	0	0	1,250
Piney Fork	3620	40	79	20	0	0	0	0	1,071	11,369	39,944	51,813	320
Pleasant Valley	3418	5	7	5	0	NRR	0	0	0	0	0	0	150
Providence 1st	3621	5	21	0	0	NRR	0	0	0	0	0	0	80
Rose Creek	3622	23	57	10	0	NRR	0	0	0	0	0	0	900
Rozzell Chapel	3419	58	96	53	0	0	2	0	3,500	17,244	54,521	144,585	380
Sturgis	3625	106	215	64	0	0	2	0	18,786	35,706	156,906	187,836	2,100
Sugar Grove	3626	71	145	39	0	NRR	0	0	3,000	0	0	0	700
Union Chapel	5123	33	54	19	0	NRR	0	0	0	0	0	0	150
Unity	3422	115	193	65	0	NRR	0	0	2,200	0	0	0	350
Vaughn's Chapel**	3423	14	20	9	0	NRR	0	0	3,233	0	0	0	300
Village	5125	8	8	8	0	NRR	0	0	0	0	0	0	10
Wheatcroft	3627	32	57	10	0	NRR	0	0	2,419	0	0	0	110
Woodlawn	3417	70	307	53	0	NRR	0	0	0	0	0	0	1,744
TOTALS	44	2,317	4,935	1,367	9	32	57	1	132,242	336,897	1,437,001	1,895,328	30,281

*Math error corrected. **Purged roll. NRR - No Report Received

COVENANT PRESBYTERY CONTINUED

CHURCHES, PASTORS, AND CLERKS:

Bayou de Chine   (4MWC)MICO3401
  2 Kingston Road
  Water Valley, KY 42085
  (270)355-2089   <Graves>
PA: Robert Goodman   <M1>
  756 Kingston Road
  Water Valley, KY 42085
  (580)756-4726
  rgoodman4gvn@hotmail.com
CL: Mark Crass
  1990 Kingston Road
  Water Valley, KY 42085
  (270)355-2381
  jimcrassauto10@bellsouth.net

Benton   (4WC)MICO3403
  2968 Aurora Highway (mailing)
  Hardin, KY 40248
  Kentucky Highway 58 (physical)
  Benton, KY 42025
  ( )   <Marshall>
CL: Michele Shearer
  2969 Aurora Highway
  Hardin, KY 42048
  (270)354-8656
  mshearer92858@hotmail.com

Bethel   (4WC)MICO3404
  12304 Wickliffe Road
  Kevil, KY 42053
  (270)876-7239   <Ballard>
  FAX: (270)876-7513
  bethelcpchurch@gmail.com
PA: Drew Gray   <M1>
  12304 Wickliffe Road
  Kevil, KY 42053
  (270)331-5569
  drewgray01@gmail.com
CL: Teresa Higdon
  230 Lake Point Drive
  Paducah, KY 42003
  (270)554-5003
  teresa@qservicesco.com

Calvary   (4MC)MICO3405
  98 Calvary Church Road
  Mayfield, KY 42066
  (270)376-5525   <Graves>
CL: Darla Jo Tucker
  665 McNutt Road
  Wingo, KY 42088
  (270)376-2065

Camp Ground   (4C)MICO5103
  2645 Lick Creek Road (mailing)
  70 Tunnel Lane (physical)
  Anna, IL 62906
  (618)833-9000   <Union>
PA: Dee Ann Thompson   <M1>
  1299 Mt Sterling Road
  Brookport, IL 62910
  (618)445-0310
  deethomp5@hotmail.com
CL: Sandra Boaz
  2645 Lick Creek Road
  Anna, IL 62906
  (618)697-0097
  skboaz@yahoo.com

Chandler   (4MWC)MICO5302
  338 S State Street
  Chandler, IN 47610
  (812)925-6175   <Warrick>
  FAX: (812)925-3628
  chandlercpc2@hotmail.com
CL: Robert Hooper
  PO Box 351
  Chandler, IN 47610
  (812)925-6965
  rwhooper@yahoo.com

Ebenezer   (C)MICO5105
  Thompsonville, IL 62890
  ( )   <Saline>
CL: Pat Fletcher
  24535 Kaskaskia Road
  Thompsonville, IL 62890
  (618)627-2288

Ebenezer Hall   (4WC)MICO5106
  9850 Lick Creek Road (mailing)
  750 Grand View (physical)
  Buncombe, IL 62912
  (618)833-8280   <Union>
CL: Carolyn Hammon
  9850 Lick Creek Road
  Buncombe, IL 62912
  (618)833-8280

Flat Lick   (4WC)MICO3606
  415 Bennetttown Street (mailing)
  Herndon, KY 42236
  9355 Lafayette Road (physical))
  Herndon, KY 42236
  (270)885-1350   <Christian>
  pastorsteve88@yahoo.com
PA: Jack (Nick) Ashley   <M1>
  12278 Herndon Oak Grove Road
  Herndon, KY 42236
  (812)204-1422
  edencarteringusa@aol.com
CL: Mike Barbee
  415 Bennetttown Street
  Herndon, KY 42236
  (270)498-3664

Fredonia   (4MEWC)MICO3608
  204 West Pierson Street (mailing)
  303 Cassidy Avenue (physical)
  Fredonia, KY 42411
  (270)545-3481   <Caldwell>
PA: Marc Bell   <M1>
  3467 State Route 175 N
  Bremen, KY 42325
  (270)846-4203
  marc.bell1@att.net
CL: Cindy Cruce
  46 Penn Drive
  Marion, KY 42064
  (270)965-4520
  ccruce@fredoniavalleybank.com

Gilead   (4EC)MICO5110
  3470 Gilead Church Road (mailing)
  4385 Gilead Church Road (physical)
  Simpson, IL 62985
  (618)695-2653   <Johnson>
  tim-arm@live.com

PA: Daniel Hopkins   <M1>
  1608 Oak Park Boulevard
  Calvert City, KY 42029
  (270)205-1847
  danielhopkins2469@yahoo.com
CL: Tim Armstrong
  745 Webb Town Road
  Tunnel Hill, IL 62972
  (618)559-7021
  tim-arm@live.com

Good Spring   (2WC)MICO3609
  1800 Old Fredonia Road (mailing)
  Princeton, KY 42445
  4142 Good Spring Road (physical)
  Fredonia, KY 42411
  ( )   <Caldwell>
CL: Mike Stephens
  1800 Old Fredonia Road
  Princeton, KY 42445
  (270)559-6032
  mwstephens1800@gmail.com

Grace Covenant   (4WC)MICO3415
  1526 Park Avenue
  Paducah, KY 42001
  (270)443-3689   <McCracken>
  holyday@vci.net
PA: Christopher Fleming   <M1>
  3745 Ramona Drive
  Paducah, KY 42001
  (615)424-8561
  holyday@vci.net
CL: Amy Fleming
  133 Minerva Place
  Paducah, KY 42001
  (270)443-3689
  holyday@vci.net

Highland   (4MWC)MICO3414
  3950 Lovelaceville Road
  Paducah, KY 42001
  (270)554-3572   <McCracken>
  hcpsec@highlandcpc.comcastbiz.net
PA: Olen (Bud) Russell   <M1>
  9595 Wickliffe Road
  Wickliffe, KY 42087
  olen552@aol.com
  (270)562-1096
AP: Douglas Hughes   <M1>
  5545 Hocker Road
  Paducah, KY 42001
  (270)488-2588
  milburnchapel@gmail.com
CL: Elaine S Overton
  3915 Lovelaceville Road
  Paducah, KY 42001
  (270)554-1259
  jred3915@bellsouth.net

Hopewell   (4C)MICO3610
  768 Lola Road (mailing)
  1235 Lola Road (physical)
  Salem, KY 42078
  (270)988-3859   <Livingston>
SS: Troy Newcomb   <M2>
  PO Box 858
  Salem, KY 42078
  (270)210-4902
  newcomb.troy@yahoo.com

COVENANT PRESBYTERY CONTINUED

SS: Larry Buchanan   \<M1>
  466 North County Line Road
  Calvert City, KY 42029
  (270)519-9292
  lbuchanan.tse@gmail.com
CL: Michael Heneisen
  1162 Hampton Road
  Salem, KY 42078
  (270)988-4856
  heneisen@tds.net

Hopkinsville   (4MWC)MICO3611
  2701 Faircourt
  Hopkinsville, KY 42240
  (270)886-1464   \<Christian>
  FAX: (270)885-1531
  cumberland1@bellsouth.net
PA: Robert T Spurling Jr   \<M1>
  305 Wayne Drive
  Hopkinsville, KY 42240
  (865)803-8582
CL: Doris Ann Russell
  1114 Walnut Court
  Hopkinsville, KY 42240
  (270)886-4045
  drussell161@wnconnect.com

Liberty   (4C)MICO3406
  510 Richardson Street (mailing)
  150 Liberty Road (physical)
  Murray, KY 42071
  ( )   \<Calloway>
PA: Gary Vacca   \<M1>
  2203 Creekwood Drive
  Murray, KY 42071
  (270)978-0818
  garyvacca@spiritualliving.com
CL: Brenda Lawson
  441 Old Shiloh Road
  Murray, KY 42071
  (270)227-5872
  bsnip10@hotmail.com

Lisman   (4EC)MICO3613
  153 Woodland Acres (mailing)
  Dixon, KY 42409
  2085 State Route 270 W (physical)
  Clay, KY 42404
  ( )   \<Webster>
CL: Nancy Burnett
  451 Jim Villines Road
  Dixon, KY 42409
  (270)639-6204

Macedonia   (4WC)MICO3614
  18030 Beulah Road (mailing)
  Princeton, KY 42445
  Highway 291 (physical)
  Dalton, KY
  ( )   \<Hopkins>
PA: Wayne Hopkins   \<M1>
  1413 E Unity Church Road
  Hardin, KY 42048
  (270)437-4481
CL: Narvin Darnall
  18030 Beulah Road
  Princeton, KY 42445
  (279)836-7089
  narvin-d@yahoo.com

Madisonville   (4MWC)MICO3615
  PO Box 392 (mailing)
  1540 Anton Road (physical)
  Madisonville, KY 42431
  (270)821-5970   \<Hopkins>
CL: Jean Duncan
  330 S Daves Street
  Madisonville, KY 42431
  (270)821-5138
  jduncan42431@att.net

Marion First   (4MEWC)MICO3616
  PO Box 323 (mailing)
  224 W Bellville Street (physical)
  Marion, KY 42064
  (270)965-4746   \<Crittenden>
  firstcpchurch@mchsi.com
PA: Dee Ann Thompson   \<M1>
  1299 Mt Sterling Road
  Brookport, IL 62910
  (618)445-0310
  deethomp5@hotmail.com
CL: Jo Ann McClure
  PO Box 92
  Marion, KY 42064
  (270)965-3323

Milburn Chapel   (4EC)MICO3416
  3760 Metropolis Lake Road
  West Paducah, KY 42086
  (270)488-2588   \<McCracken>
  milburnchapel@gmail.com
CL: Joe Neal Neftzger
  903 E 6th Street
  Metropolis, IL 62960
  (618)524-5349
  milburnchapel@gmail.com

Mt Carmel   (4MW C)MICO3617
  11504 Mt Carmel Road (mailing)
  11410 Mt Carmel Road (physical)
  White Plains, KY 42464
  (270)676-3563   \<Hopkins>
  bshoulta@bellsouth.net
CL: Larry Putman
  1319 Mt Carmel Pond River Road
  White Plains, KY 42464
  (270)676-3628

Mt Pleasant   (4 C)MICO3618
  16647 State Route 109
  Sullivan, KY 42460
  ( )   \<Union>
PA: Dale Williams   \<M1>
  3156 State Route 2837
  Clay, KY 42404
  (270)664-2044
CL: Richard White
  2465 State Route 270 E
  Sturgis, KY 42459
  (270)333-6109
  whitefarms1@att.net

Mt Sterling   (4MWC)MICO5117
  1780 Mt Sterling Road
  Brookport, IL 62910
  (618)564-2616   \<Massac>
  FAX: (618)564-2616
  mscpchurch@yahoo.com

PA: David LeNeave   \<M1>
  1403 Mt Zion Church Road
  Marion, KY 42064
  (731)414-8232
  mscpchurch_bd@yahoo.com
CL: Gary N Angelly
  8646 Independence Road
  Brookport, IL 62910
  (618)564-2874
  FAX: (618)564-2874
  angelly@djklink.net

Mt Zion   (4WC)MICO5118
  PO Box 383 (mailing)
  1159 Mt Zion Road (physical)
  Dongola, IL 62926
  (618)827-4463   \<Union>
  jsr487@frontier.com
SS: Donna Davenport   \<M1>
  PO Box 234
  Wingo, KY 42088
  chamberdonna@yahoo.com
  (270)376-5488
SS: Philip Brown   \<M1>
  540 Mt Pisgah Road
  Dongola, IL 62926
  (618)697-0972
  brownlp75@yahoo.com
CL: Sharon R. Resch
  PO Box 383
  Dongola, IL 62926
  (618)827-4463
  jsr487@frontier.com

New Hope   (4MWC)MICO3410
  7620 Cross Mill Road
  Paducah, KY 42001
  (270)554-0473   \<McCracken>
  newhopecpchurch@hotmail.com
PA: Curtis Franklin   \<M1>
  3394 Old Mayfield Road
  Paducah, KY 42003
  (270)625-1898
  brocurtis@fredonia.biz
AP: Dusty Luthy   \<M1>
  2900 Foxcroft Circle
  Denton, TX 76209
  (270)933-2722
  dustyluthy@gmail.com
CL: Glenda Barkley
  325 Gatewood Drive
  Paducah, KY 42001
  (270)554-2851
  troybarkley@comcast.net

North Pleasant Grove   (4WC)MICO3411
  Murray, KY 42071
  ( )   \<Calloway>
PA: April Watson   \<M1>
  529 W Bellville
  Marion, KY 42064
  (270)965-2850
  aprilwatson@hotmail.com
CL: Fred Kemp
  276 Airport Road
  Murray, KY 42071

Oak Grove   (4MWC)MICO3412
  2465 Magness Road
  Benton, KY 42025
  (270)437-4606   \<Calloway>

COVENANT PRESBYTERY CONTINUED

PA: Randy Lowe <M1>
222 McDougal Drive
Murray, KY 42071
(270)753-8255
loweshodle@aol.com
CL: Jeff Gordon
2465 Magness Road
Benton, KY 42025
(270)437-4613
jgordon@wk.net

_____

Oak Grove Union (4C)MICO3619
Highway 132
Clay, KY 42404
(270)664-0008 <Webster>
jvfulton@wk.net
CL: Daniel M Heady
2564 State Route 132 W
Dixon, KY 42409
(270)748-6848
danielheady@kycourts.net

_____

Oakland (4MWC)MICO3413
9104 US Highway 68 W
Calvert City, KY 42029
(270)898-2630 <Marshall>
PA: Danny York <M1>
5420 State Routh 902 W
Fredonia, KY 42411
(270)350-7262
nonnieyork@yahoo.com
CL: John Jenkins
1265 Elva Loop Road
Symsonia, KY 42082
(270)705-3229

_____

Piney Fork (4WC)MICO3620
4294 Coppers Spring Road
Marion, KY 42064
( ) <Crittenden>
PA: William E Martin, Jr <M1>
741 Chapel Hill Road
Marion, KY 42064
(870)270-3344
juniormartin@yahoo.com
CL: Sarah Ford
220 S Weldon Street
Marion, KY 42064
(270)965-3833

_____

Pleasant Valley (4C)MICO3418
111 College Drive
Kevil, KY 42053
(270)224-2497 <Ballard>
SS: April Watson <M1>
529 W Bellville
Marion, KY 42064
(270)965-2850
aprilwatson@hotmail.com
CL: William E Kilby
PO Box 413
La Center, KY 42056
(270)665-5405

_____

Providence 1st (4MEWC)MICO3621
305 Locust Street (mailing)
119 Locust Street (physical)
Providence, KY 42450
(270)667-2485 <Webster>
chalit@apex.net

CL: Paul Northern
317 N Broadway
Providence, KY 42450
(270)667-2636

_____

Rose Creek (4WC)MICO3622
7650 Island Ford Road (mailing)
Hanson, KY 42413
7220 Rose Creek Road (physical)
Nebo, KY 42441
( ) <Hopkins>
PA: Paul Stone <M1>
3490 State Route 2837
Clay, KY 42404
(270)664-6244
CL: Joseph E Peyton
7650 Island Ford Road
Hanson, KY 42413
(270)619-0636
jepeyton@madisonville.com

_____

Rozzell Chapel (4C)MICO3419
1258 Rozzell Church Road
Mayfield, KY 42066
(270)623-6866 <Graves>
PA: D Frederick (Fred) Fahl <M1>
500 3rd Street
Fulton, KY 42041
(270)472-1476
dffahl@gmail.com
CL: Donna Davenport <M1>
PO Box 234
Wingo, KY 42088
(270)804-3526
chamberdonna@yahoo.com

_____

Sturgis (4MWC)MICO3625
504 N Main Street
Sturgis, KY 42459
(270)333-2851 <Union>
FAX: (270)333-3118
sturgiscpc@att.net
PA: Victor Hassell <M1>
510 N Main Street
Sturgis, KY 42459
(270)333-9170
FAX: (270)333-3118
hassellvictor@hotmail.com
AP: Samantha Hassell <M1>
510 N Main Street
Sturgis, KY 42459
(270)333-9170
hassell_samantha@hotmail.com
CL: Barbara B Sutton
849 State Route 950
Morganfield, KY 42437
(270)333-4385

_____

Sugar Grove (4MWC)MICO3626
585 Sugar Grove Church Road
Marion, KY 42064
(270)965-4435 <Crittenden>
CL: Gladys Brown
423 N Main Steet
Marion, KY 42064
(270)965-2969
gbrown6781@live.com

Union Chapel (4C)MICO5123
313 E Illinois Street (mailing)
2210 Droit Road (physical)
Galatia, IL 62935
( ) <Saline>
CL: Session Clerk
313 E Illinois Street
Galatia, IL 62935

_____

Unity (4MWC)MICO3422
1503 Story Avenue (mailing)
Murray, KY 42071
1929 E Unity Church Road (physical)
Hardin, KY 42048
(270)354-8216 <Marshall>
cprevbhayes@gmail.com
PA: Brian Hayes <M1>
69 Cactus Drive
Benton, KY 42025
(270)210-8165
cprevbhayes@gmail.com
CL: Jonathan Whisman
5352 Murray Highway
Hardin, KY 42048
(270)437-3949
jwhisman@wk.net

_____

Vaughn's Chapel (4MWC)MICO3423
4775 Calvert City Road
Calvert City, KY 42029
(270)395-7318 <Marshall>
PA: Wendell Ordway <M1>
4775 Calvert City Road
Calvert City, KY 42029
(270)395-7318
CL: John P Case
93 W Second Avenue
Calvert City, KY 42029
(270)395-4203

_____

Village (4C)MICO5125
319 County Road 450 N
Norris City, IL 62869
(618)962-3256 <White>
PA: Bernice Belt <M1>
PO Box 8372
Paducah, KY 42002
(270)217-4623
haroldbelt@comcast.net
CL: Rose Spence
319 County Road 450 N
Norris City, IL 6286
(618)378-3852
rspencester6@gmail.com

_____

Wheatcroft (4WC)MICO3627
PO Box 7 (mailing)
47 Hammock Street E (physical)
Wheatcroft, KY 42463
( ) <Webster>
PA: Dale Williams <M1>
3156 State Route 2837
Clay, KY 42404
(270)664-2802
dalewilliams@roadrunner.com
CL: Jackie Gass
3394 State Route 147
Sebree, KY 42455
(270)664-9310

COVENANT PRESBYTERY CONTINUED

Woodlawn   (4MWC)MICO3417
3402 Old Benton Road
Paducah, KY 42002
(270)442-7713   <McCracken>
woodlawnchurch@live.com
CL: Todd Belt
3402 Old Benton Road
Paducah, KY 42002
(270)442-7713
woodlawnyouth@msn.com

OTHERS ON MINISTERIAL ROLL:

Barnett, Rudolph   <M1 WC>
3014 Mockingbird Lane
Evansville, IN 47710-3259
(618)643-3253
Facker, David   <M1 WC>
3409 Benton Road
Paducah, KY 42003
(270)442-7713
woodlawnpastor@live.com
Fulton, James V   <M1 HR>
1520 Oak Grove Road
Benton, KY 42025
(270)437-4320
Gerard, Eugene S   <M1 OM>
615 N 42nd Street
Paducah, KY 42001
(270)443-2889
Heidel, Jason   <M1 WC>
218 Morningside Drive
Hopkinsville, KY 42240
(270)498-7380
heidelj@hotmail.com
Lawson, James   <M1 OM>
1003 West 3rd Street
Fulton, KY 42041
(270)472-5272
ridgepointefarm@bellsouth.net
Mays, Ronald B   <M1 PR>
124 Summers Lane
Kevil, KY 42053
(270)247-0070
rbmays@wk.net
Potts, Danny   <M1 WC>
585 State Route 1125 S
Fulton, KY 42041
(270)376-2901
Rogers, John A   <M1 WC>
2349 Lynnwood Drive
Paducah, KY 42001
(270)534-1195
jrogers308@comcast.net
Rudolph, Allie D   <M1 WC>
855 Old Rosebower Church Road
Paducah, KY 42003
(270)898-4903
rallie307@aol.com
Shauf, Steve   <M1 WC>
4630 Mt Sharon Road
Greenbrier, TN 37073
(270)331-5247
theshaufs@hotmail.com
Shauf, Teresa   <M1 WC>
4630 Mt Sharon Road
Greenbrier, TN 37073
(270)331-5217
theshaufs@hotmail.com

Smith, James A   <M1 M9 WC>
309 Lutes Road
Paducah, KY 42001
(901)574-2345
james1493@att.net
Weaver, Dennis   <M1 WC>
2589 Magness Road
Benton, KY 42025
(731)592-9054
dsweaver@memphisseminary.edu
Wieland, Jack G, Jr   <M1 WC>
104 N Orchid
Skidmore, MO 64487
(217)823-4331
jgwieland@hotmail.com
Williams, David J   <M1 WC>
20 Acorn Drive
Harrisburg, IL 62946
(618)252-1851
Zahrte, Rebecca   <M1 WC>
1550 Anton Road
Madisonnville, TN 42431
(270)978-3328
rebecca.zahrte@gmail.com

OTHER LICENTIATES ON ROLL:

OTHER CANDIDATES ON ROLL:

Barkley, Kevin   <M3>
588 Contest Road
Paducah, KY 42001
(270)556-3924
kevbark5@yahoo.com
Cook, Douglas   <M3>
822 County Road 365 E
Norris City, IL 62869
(618)380-6112
dcookster2@gmail.com
Impastato, Paulino   <M3>
1547 Mt Zion Church Road
Marion, KY 42064
(270)965-9528
Kibler, Taylor   <M3>
1070 W Main Street Apt 1720
Hendersonville, TN 37075
(615)509-7114
taylorkibler@gmail.com
Marcott, Skyla   <M3>
1980 Mark Avenue
Clarksville, TN 37043
(513)907-6055
skylamarcott@yahoo.com
Mitchell, Cherry   <M3>
PO Box 64
Nebo, KY 42441
(270)836-6229
mitchell9620@bellsouth.net
Simmons, Dyllan   <M3>
203 Cambridge Drive
(270)534-1770
dyllansimmons121999@yahoo.com

Cumberland Presbytery
MIDWEST SYNOD

GENERAL		MEMBERSHIP			CHANGES				FINANCES				
	1.Church Number	2.Active 3.Total	4.Church School	5.Prof. of Faith	6.Gains	7.Losses 8.Children Baptized		9. OUR UNITED OUT- REACH	10. Total Out- Reach Giving	11. All Other Expenses	12. Total Income Received	13. Value Church Prop. 1=1000	
	1	2	3	4	5	6	7	8	9	10	11	12	13
Antioch	3101	30	30	16	0	NRR	0	0	0	0	0	0	300
Auburn	3301	57	100	30	0	NRR	0	0	0	0	0	0	405
Bald Knob	3302	5	5	4	0	NRR	0	0	0	0	0	0	60
Bethel	3102	61	61	28	0	0	1	0	0	5,149	26,207	29,795	0
Bethel #1	3103	13	71	11	0	NRR	0	0	0	0	0	0	200
Beulah*	3501	20	35	18	0	NRR	0	0	1,406	0	0	0	150
Boiling Springs	3303	16	19	14	0	NRR	0	0	0	0	0	0	27
Bowling Green	3304	140	230	77	0	NRR	0	0	16,812	0	0	0	1,400
Bridgeport 1st	3131	87	87	9	0	NRR	0	0	0	0	0	0	651
Brier Creek	3503	80	157	65	0	0	5	0	7,726	15,867	67,868	83,734	350
Campbellsville	3104	92	89	41	0	0	3	0	0	3,061	110,081	110,498	1,950
Caneyville	3201	3	3	15	0	NRR	0	0	0	0	0	0	175
Casey's Fork	3105	14	19	14	0	NRR	0	0	1,058	0	0	0	37
Cedar Flat	3106	14	53	20	0	NRR	0	0	0	0	0	0	90
Clear Point	3107	20	20	12	0	NRR	0	0	608	0	0	0	60
Clifton Mills	3202	17	39	45	0	0	1	0	0	1,892	21,847	24,780	275
Coyle	3203	37	40	24	0	0	1	0	0	1,735	24,570	37,175	200
Dukes	3204	8	32	6	0	0	4	0	0	900	7,820	9,276	300
Ephesus	3205	3	12	4	0	0	0	0	300	1,646	6,654	7,392	150
Fairview	3504	13	30	0	2	2	1	0	2,122	7,619	9,277	21,220	50
Freedom	3207	67	90	52	1	1	3	0	1,759	11,871	72,215	88,034	500
Garfield	3208	55	119	55	0	0	2	0	0	4,004	82,657	113,895	495
Gasper River	3306	36	49	20	0	NRR	0	0	0	0	0	0	105
Gill's Chapel	3307	7	23	0	0	NRR	0	0	0	0	0	0	34
Glasgow	3108	194	245	110	2	3	1	6	0	2,553	245,234	300,611	2,600
Good Hope	3109	32	32	32	0	0	0	0	0	0	18,771	27,508	50
Green Ridge	3308	32	57	15	1	1	1	0	3,000	3,400	35,173	51,711	440
Greensburg	3110	138	138	60	0	7	4	0	10,853	14,601	101,157	108,533	1,000
Greenville	3505	13	46	0	0	0	0	0	500	4,817	62,663	46,425	623
Harrodsburg	3111	16	128	7	0	0	1	0	0	1,235	14,028	11,845	526
Heartsong	3222	48	48	20	0	NRR	0	0	0	0	0	0	1,650
High Point	3314	19	19	13	0	2	2	0	0	1,500	13,980	17,945	500
Irvington*	3210	12	12	8	2	4	0	0	0	0	15,589	12,800	80
Leitchfield*	3211	53	83	32	0	1	3	2	0	3,010	77,898	80,698	525
Lewisburg	3309	22	62	20	0	NRR	0	0	1,250	0	0	0	300
Liberty	3116	29	61	10	0	1	1	0	0	2,182	53,097	57,383	750
Lick Branch	3117	64	191	38	0	NRR	0	0	0	0	0	0	90
Little Muddy	3310	19	19	10	0	NRR	0	0	2,531	0	0	0	119
Louisville 1st	3212	59	127	30	0	NRR	0	0	0	0	0	0	1,000
Louisville Japanese	3223				0	NRR	0	0	500	0	0	0	
Magnolia	3214	75	75	65	0	0	1	0	0	11,850	43,725	58,120	850

Cumberland Presbytery   (Continued)
MIDWEST SYNOD

	GENERAL	MEMBERSHIP			CHANGES				FINANCES			
	1.Church Number	2.Active 3.Total 4.Church School		5.Prof. of Faith 6.Gains 7.Losses 8.Children Baptized				9. OUR UNITED OUT-REACH	10. Total Out-Reach Giving	11. All Other Expenses	12. Total Income Received	13. Value Church Prop. 1=1000
	1	2	3	4	5	6	7	8	9	10	11	12	13
Monroe Chapel	3119	31	31	21	0	0	2	0	1,451	4,011	12,557	15,124	150
Morgantown	3311	21	21	6	0	NRR	0	0	0	0	0	0	80
Mt. Moriah	3120	10	32	10	0	NRR	0	0	0	0	0	0	75
Mt. Olive	3216	11	11	9	0	0	0	0	0	10,504	8,442	20,118	70
Mt. Olivet*	3312	32	43	15	0	1	1	0	0	406	31,700	23,850	1,121
Mt. Pleasant	3217	55	71	40	0	0	1	0	4,315	7,308	39,214	44,134	230
Mt. Vernon	3218	26	34	13	0	0	1	0	900	2,200	17,854	32,819	70
Mt. Zion (DC)	3507	15	61	10	0	0	0	0	6,480	9,300	35,300	106,900	255
Neal's Chapel	3122	10	40	5	0	0	1	0	1,727	16,695	18,422	150
Needham	3219	9	9	7	0	NRR	0	0	0	0	0	0	6
Oak Forest	3123	97	203	90	0	NRR	0	0	7,264	0	0	0	115
Owensboro	3509	118	116	66	0	5	6	2	4,462	17,091	153,916	116,753	1,646
Point Pleasant	3313	3	3	0	0	NRR	0	0	0	0	0	0	0
Poplar Grove*	3511	13	14	13	0	0	1	0	1,884	2,440	17,594	18,818	90
Radcliff+*	3220	22	22	10	0	0	1	0	760	91,971	98,668	600	237
Sacramento	3512	84	84	60	1	1	3	0	11,389	18,144	95,700	113,844	1,200
Salem	3127	9	32	0	0	NRR	0	0	0	0	0	0	35
Seven Springs	3128	16	35	18	0	NRR	0	0	0	0	0	0	267
Shiloh*	3129	32	36	16	0	0	18	0	5,539	6,464	38,227	52,156	568
Short Creek	3221	23	53	24	3	3	2	0	3,332	9,693	20,029	33,250	95
Wisdom	3130	7	28	10	0	0	0	0	0	552	1,410	5,269	75
TOTALS	**62**	**2,364**	**3,735**	**1,493**	**12**	**32**	**72**	**10**	**98,201**	**280,703**	**1,697,817**	**1,901,435**	**25,602**

*Math error corrected. **Purged roll. NRR - No Report Received

CHURCHES, PASTORS, AND CLERKS:

Antioch (4C)MICU3101
103 Clarksdale Circle (mailing)
Glasgow, KY 42141
68 Antioch Church Road (physical)
Knob Lick, KY 42154
( )   <Metcalfe>
SS: Michael E Fancher   <M3>
356 Breeding Road
Edmonton, KY 42129
(270)432-3138
princo1975@live.com
CL: Kathy B Nason
103 Clarksdale Circle
Glasgow, KY 42141
(270)670-4796

Auburn   (4MWC)MICU3301
695 Howlett Road (mailing)
Auburn, KY 42206
(270)542-4304   <Logan>
PA: Grant Minton   <M1>
PO Box 270
Auburn, KY 42206
(270)542-7991
FAX. (270)271-4603
gminton@logantele.com
CL: Ashley Engler
695 Howlett Road
Auburn, KY 42206
(270)542-6730

Bald Knob   (4C)MICU3302
102 Bald Knob Church Road
Russellville, KY 42276
( )   <Logan>
CL: Kathi Steenbergen
2940 Caney Fork Road
Lewisburg, KY 42268

Bethel   (2WC)MICU3102
454 Iron Mountain Road (mailing)
Center, KY 42214
( )   <Metcalfe>

SS: Keith G Atwell   <M1>
20 Dishman Cemetery Road
Canmer, KY 42722
(279)528-2521
oldpeacemaker38@live.com
CL: Mike Hough
1987 Perryville Road
Harrodsburg, BY 40330
(859)734-5634
mchough@mindspring.com

Bethel #1   (4MWC)MICU3103
1987 Perryville Road (mailing)
2586 Perryville Road (physical)
Harrodsburg, KY 40330
( )   <Mercer>
PA: John Contini   <M1>
4344 Poor Ridge Pike
Lancaster, KY 40444
(859)339-0747
john@hillsideheritagefarm.com
CL: Mike Hough
1987 Perryville Road
Harrodsburg, KY 40330
mehough@mindspring.com

CUMBERLAND PRESBYTERY CONTINUED

Beulah   (4WC)MICU3501
  2856 Beda Road (mailing)
  320 Beulah Church Road (physical)
  Hartford, KY 42347
  (270)298-3352   <Ohio>
  FAX: (270)298-7007
  cmwsaw2@bellsouth.net
SS: Wallace Renner   <M1>
  1648 Griffith Avenue
  Owensboro, KY 42303
  (270)685-4359
  pwrenner@adelphia.net
CL: Chuck Westerfield
  2856 Beda Road
  Hartford, KY 42347
  (270)298-3352
  smwsaw@connectgradd.net

Boiling Springs   (4C)MICU3303
  3360 Highway 259 (mailing)
  2412 Highway 259 (physical)
  Portland, TN 37148
  (615)325-2618   <Sumner>
CL: Pearl Kepley
  3380 Highway 259
  Portland, TN 37148
  (615)325-3645

Bowling Green   (4MWC)MICU3304
  807 Campbell Lane
  Bowling Green, KY 42104
  (270)781-3295   <Warren>
  FAX: (270)781-2368
  church@bgcpcoffice.com
PA: Steve Delashmit   <M1>
  2705 Garrett Drive
  Bowling Green, KY 42104
  (270)796-8822
  FAX: (270)781-2368
CL: Caroline Smith
  228 Pine Pointe
  Bowling Green, KY 42103
  (270)842-6623
  cns57@hotmail.com

Bridgeport 1st   (4C)MICU3131
  515 DeKalb Street
  Bridgeport, PA 19405
  (610)275-6942   <Philadelphi>
PA: Aaron Craig   <M1>
  325 Cherry Avenue
  McKenzie, TN 38201
  (731)352-6718
CL: William McLay
  9 E Brown Street
  Norristown, PA 19401
  (610)277-8295

Brier Creek   (4MWC)MICU3503
  3467 State Route 175 N
  Bremen, KY 42325
  (270)525-3611   <Muhlenberg>
PA: Marc Bell   <M1>
  3467 State Route 175 N
  Bremen, KY 42325
  (270)846-4203
  marc.bell1@att.net
CL: Sherry Skimehorn
  77 Jarvis Lane
  Central City, KY 42330
  (270)525-3472
  skimehor@bellsouth.net

Campbellsville   (4MWC)MICU3104
  500 Cumberland Way
  Campbellsville, KY 42718
  (270)465-4091   <Taylor>
  FAX: (270)469-9651
  firstcpchurch@windstream.net
PA: John Butler   <M1>
  501 Cherokee Drive
  Campbellsville, KY 42718
  (270)403-7602
  rev.butlerj8134@gmail.com
CL: Faye Adams
  902 Rosecrest Avenue
  Campbellsville, KY 42718
  (270)789-1791
  newlifeblessed@yahoo.com

Caneyville   (4EWC)MICU3201
  PO Box 264 (mailing)
  203 River Park Drive (physical)
  Caneyville, KY 42721
  (   )   <Grayson>
CL: Mary Alice Woosley-Logsdon
  PO Box 334
  Leitchfield, KY 42721
  (270)230-2818
  FAX: (270)879-9211
  alicewoosley71@yahoo.com

Casey's Fork   (1C)MICU3105
  PO Box 186 (mailing)
  Highway 90 (physical)
  Marrowbone, KY 42759
  (502)864-3129   <Cumberland>
SS: Barry Craddock   <M1dusty>
  147 Moss Way
  Glasgow, KY 42141
  (270)678-7615
  craddock.barry53@gmail.com
CL: Jimmy Mosby
  210 Bombshell Creek Road
  Burkesville, KY 42717

Cedar Flat   (C)MICU3106
  1444 Milam Clark Road (mailing)
  Summer Shade, KY 42166
  Cedar Flat - Curtis Road (physical)
  Edmonton, KY 42129
  (   )   <Metcalfe>
CL: Janet A Proffitt
  1444 Milam Clark Road
  Summer Shade, KY 42166
  (270)428-4379

Clear Point   (4MWEC)MICU3107
  113 Woods Drive (mailing)
  Glasgow, KY 42141
  Bowling Green, KY 42104
  (   )   <Hart>
PA: Darrell Pickett   <M1>
  113 Woods Drive
  Glasgow, KY 42141
  (270)834-6102
  dpickett@glasgow-ky.com
CL: Connie Pickett
  113 Woods Drive
  Glasgow, KY 42141
  dpickett@glasgow-ky.com

Clifton Mills   (4WC)MICU3202
  521 Butler Hobbs Road (mailing)
  Hardinsburg, KY 40143
  6406 W Highway 86 (physical)
  Irvington, KY 40146
  (270)547-5717   <Breckinridge>
CL: Edna M Hobbs
  521 Butler Hobbs Road
  Hardinsburg, KY 40143
  (270)756-2592
  tejthbs@att.net

Coyle   (4C)MICU3203
  1285 Centerview Rough River Lane
  Hudson, KY 40145
  (270)257-0851   <Breckinridge>
  tucker_rd@bellsouth.net
CL: Ralph D Tucker
  1285 Centerview Rough River Lane
  Hudson, KY 40145
  (270)257-0851
  tucker_rd@bellsouth.net

Dukes   (4C)MICU3204
  4743 Happy Hollow Road (mailing)
  7814 State Route 144 E (physical)
  Hawesville, KY 42348
  (270)927-9577   <Hancock>
CL: Joe Wilborn
  4743 Happy Hollow Road
  Hawesville, KY 42348
  (270)927-9577
  joeandkimwilborn@bellsouth.net

Ephesus   (4EC)MICU3205
  452 Ephesus Church Road (mailing)
  30 Ephesus Church Loop (physical)
  Harned, KY 40144
  (   )   <Breckinridge>
  bridget.keesee@ky.gov
CL: Nancy Macy
  452 Ephesus Church Road
  Harned, KY 40144
  namacy@bbtel.com

Fairview   (4C)MICU3504
  4141 Barrett Hill Road (mailing)
  Livermore, KY 42352
  Fairview Road (physical)
  Bremen, KY
  (270)736-5189   <Muhlenberg>
CL: Danny Markwell
  4141 Barrett Hill Road
  Livermore, KY 42352
  (270)736-5189
  danny_markwell@yahoo.com

Freedom   (4MWC)MICU3207
  224 John Drane Lane (mailing)
  394 John Drane Lane (physical)
  Harned, KY 40144
  (270)617-4016   <Breckinridge>
PA: Jeff McMichael   <M1>
  224 John Drane Lane
  Harned, KY 40144
  (270)617-4016
  revmcmichael@outlook.com
CL: Debbie Hendrick
  744 W Highway 86
  Harned, KY 40144
  (270)756-5284

CUMBERLAND PRESBYTERY CONTINUED

Garfield   (4MWC)MICU3208
6307 E Highway 60 (mailing)
90 W Highway 86 (physical)
Garfield, KY 40140
(270)580-4796   <Breckinridge>
mccallum@bbtel.com
CL: Greg Campbell
6307 E Highway 60
Garfield, KY 40140
270-756-7599
gregc40140@yahoo.com

Gasper River   (4C)MICU3306
3201 Bucksville Road (mailing)
3005 Bucksville Road (physical)
Auburn, KY 42206
(270)542-8998   <Logan>
CL: Sandy Tinsley
3201 Bucksville Road
Auburn, KY 42206
(270)542-7900
tinsley@logantele.com

Gill's Chapel   (4EC)MICU3307
955 Hermon Road
Guthrie, KY 42234
(270)755-4282   <Todd>
CL: Session Clerk
955 Hermon Road
Guthrie, KY 42234

Glasgow   (4MWC)MICU3108
101 Cumberland Street
Glasgow, KY 42141
(270)651-3308   <Barren>
gcpc@glasgow-ky.com
PA: Kenny Hardin   <M1>
606 Lexington Drive
Glasgow, KY 42141
CL: Bobby Carson
101 Cumberland Street
Glasgow, KY 42141
(270)590-4819
bcarson@glasgow-ky.com

Good Hope   (2C)MICU3109
700 Dutton Creek Road (mailing)
Lemon Bend Road (physical)
Campbellsville, KY 42718
(270)789-1482   <Taylor>
glwgaw@windstream.net
PA: Earl West   <M1>
246 Maple Avenue
Greensburg, KY 42743
(207)932-5010
west5010@windstream.net
CL: Gayle Whitley
700 Dutton Creek Road
Campbellsville, KY 42718
(270)789-1482
glwgaw@windstream.net

Green Ridge   (4MWC)MICU3308
7424 Highland Lick Road
Lewisburg, KY 42256
(270)726-8497   <Logan>
brojoe2@logantele.com
CL: Debbie Bilyeu
259 W Valley Drive
Russellville, KY 42276
(270)726-7986
dbilyeu1@yahoo.com

Greensburg   (4MEWC)MICU3110
699 Old Hodgenville Road
Greensburg, KY 42743
(270)932-4864   <Green>
greensburgcpc@windstream.net
CL: John David Pickett
1956 Greensburg Road
Campbellsville, KY 42718
(270)405-0201
johnpickett77@gmail.com

Greenville   (4WC)MICU3505
1335 Coventry Lane (mailing)
Owensboro, KY 42301
108 S Cherry Street (physical)
Greenville, KY 42345
(270)338-0882   <Muhlenberg>
PA: Arthur L Burrows, Jr   <M1>
PO Box 511
Hopkinsville, KY 42241
(270)886-1301
CL: Lori Cornett
517 Paradise Road
Greenville, KY 42345
loricornett63@gmail.com

Harrodsburg   (4MWC)MICU3111
1113 Louisville Road
Harrodsburg, KY 40330
( )   <Mercer>
PA: Chris Darland   <M1>
1111 Louisville Road
Harrodsburg, KY 40330
(859)325-6796
revchrisd@yahoo.com
CL: Heather Plum
750 Parkway Avenue
Harrodsburg, KY 40330
(859)619-9071
hdplum@gmail.com

Heartsong   (4C)MICU3222
6322 Labor Lane (mailing)
6104 Bardstown Road (physical)
Louisville, KY 40291
(502)635-8587   <Jefferson>
PA: Drew Hayes   <M1>
6322 Labor Lane
Louisville, KY 40291
(731)796-7076
dhayes72@gmail.com
CL: Susan Lawson
6322 Labor Lane
Louisville, KY 40291
(502)968-0006

High Point Community   (C)MICU3314
190 Longview Drive
West Somerset, KY 42503
(606)271-0842   <Pulaski>
highpointcpc@gmail.com
PA: Fred Michael (Mike) Adams   <M1>
42 Julies Way
Somerset, KY 42503
(606)451-9155
fma46@twc.com
CL: Ralph Ratliff
52 Janies Drive
Somerset, KY 42501
(606)219-9981
ralphratliff48@gmail.com

Irvington   (4MWC)MICU3210
4108 Highway 477 (mailing)
Webster, KY 40176
111 W Walnut Street (physical)
Irvington, KY 40146
( )   <Breckinridge>
CL: Ruby Bell
4108 Highway 477
Webster, KY 40176
(270)547-7455
rrbells@bbtel.com

Leitchfield   (4MC)MICU3211
501 W Chestnut Street
Leitchfield, KY 42754
(270)259-3835   <Grayson>
PA: Jim Butler   <M1>
507 W Chestnut Street
Leitchfield, KY 42754
(502)635-8587
jbutler3026@att.net
CL: Patricia Butler
507 W Chestnut Street
Leitchfield, KY 42754
(270)200-3583
jbutler3026@att.net

Lewisburg   (4MWC)MICU3309
178 Cardinal Street (mailing)
101 Church Street (physical)
Lewisburg, KY 42256
(270)755-4282   <Logan>
CL: Ralph Cropper
178 Cardinal Street
Lewisburg, KY 42256
(270)755-2357
ralph.cropper@novelis.com

Liberty   (4WC)MICU3116
PO Box 4105 (mailing)
4139 Old Columbia Road (physical)
Campbellsville, KY 42718
(270)849-7377   <Taylor>
PA: Earl West   <M1>
246 Maple Avenue
Greensburg, KY 42743
(207)932-5010
west5010@windstream.net
CL: Barbara Davenport
216 Happy Hill Drive
Campbellsville, KY 42718
(270)465-3633
teebdee@windstream.net

Lick Branch   (4C)MICU3117
50 B Jones Road (mailing)
7318 Lecta Kino Road (physical)
Glasgow, KY 42141
(270)670-6698   <Barren>
doncynem@gmail.com
OD: Jerry D Martin   <M5>
292 Bristletown Road
Glasgow, KY 42141
(270)678-2476
doncynem@glasgow-ky.com
CL: Nancy Jolly
2979 Kino Road
Glasgow, KY 42141
(270)428-5722
jollyfarms@scrtc.com

CUMBERLAND PRESBYTERY CONTINUED

Little Muddy   (4MC)MICU3310
1061 Sugar Grove Road (mailing)
170 Little Muddy Church Road (physical)
Morgantown, KY 42261
( )   \<Butler\>
SS: Michael Justice   \<M1\>
250 W 5th Street #B
Russellville, KY 42276
(270)726-6673
CL: William Gabe Keen
822 Sugar Grove Road
Morgantown, KY 42261
(270)526-5895

Louisville 1st   (4MWC)MICU3212
4610 Manslick Road
Louisville, KY 40216
(502)368-4709   \<Jefferson\>
FAX: (502)368-4709
firstcumberland@att.net
PA: Rodney E Harris   \<M1\>
7420 Conjar Court
Louisville, KY 40214
(502)724-7334
rodneypat@insightbb.com
CL: Laura Kaelin
6314 May Pen Road
Louisville, KY 40228
(502)368-4709
firstcumberland@att.net

Louisville Japanese   (4C)MICU3223
8710 Hickory Falls Lane
Pewee Valley, KY 40056
(502)657-9643
PA: Iwao Satoh
8710 Hickory Falls Lane
Pewee Valley, KY 40056
(502)657-9643
iwaosatoh@gmail.com
CL: Session Clerk
8710 Hickory Falls Lane
Pewee Valley, KY 40056
(502)657-9643

Magnolia   (4MWC)MICU3214
PO Box 1 (mailing)
235 Old L and N Turkpike (physical)
Magnolia, KY 42757
(270)324-3472   \<LaRue\>
magnoliacpchurch@gmail.com
SS: Richard Harrison   \<M3\>
158 Enlow Road
Hodgenville, KY 42748
(270)505-2102
sundaydrummer75@yahoo.com
CL: Charlotte Tucker
1080 Greensburg Road
Hodgenville, KY 42748
(270)358-3090
charlotte.tucker@larue.kyschools.ust

Monroe Chapel   (4C)MICU3119
2465 Possum Trot Road (mailing)
11392 Hardyville Road (physical)
Hardyville, KY 42746
(270)528-3667   \<Hart\>
jbuggforbis@hotmail.com
CL: Janie B Forbis
2465 Possum Trot Road
Hardyville, KY 42746
(270)528-3873
jbuggforbis@hotmail.com

Morgantown   (4MWC)MICU3311
308 Helm Lane (mailing)
118 W Ohio Street (physical)
Morgantown, KY 42261
( )   \<Butler\>
CL: Carolyn Henderson
308 Helm Lane
Morgantown, KY 42261
(270)526-3439

Mt Moriah   (2C)MICU3120
107 James Street (mailing)
Edmonton, KY 42129
2038 Mt Moriah Road (physical)
Summer Shade, KY 42166
( )   \<Metcalfe\>
CL: Sandy England
107 James Street
Edmonton, KY 42129
(270)432-3778
englandsim@scrtc.com

Mt Olive   (4WC)MICU3216
1295 Solway Meeting Road (mailing)
Mt Olive Church Road (physical)
Big Clifty, KY 42712
( )   \<Hardin\>
CL: Gayle Johnson
1295 Solway Meeting Road
Big Clifty, KY 42712
(270)862-4313
vonnie.g0000@yahoo.com

Mt Olivet   (4MEWC)MICU3312
2640 Mt Olivet Road
Bowling Green, KY 42101
(270)843-0223   \<Warren\>
PS: Danny Willis   \<M3\>
3328 E 6th Street
Owensboro, KY 42303
(270)993-0882
dwillis.cpc@gmail.com
CL: Betty Grammer
180 Sir Wilburn Way
Alvaton, KY 42122
(270)781-4435
thememaw02@walmartconnect.com

Mt Pleasant   (4C)MICU3217
364 E Big Reedy Road (mailing)
E Big Reedy Road (physical)
Caneyville, KY 42721
( )   \<Edmonson\>
SS: Greg Bowen   \<M2 ST\>
3241 South Fork Road
Glasgow, KY 42141
(270)576-8011
gbowen@commonwealthbroadcasting.com
CL: Gloria Slaughter
364 E Big Reedy Road
Caneyville, KY 42721
(270)286-9372
gslaughter@mtownbank.com

Mt Vernon   (4WC)MICU3218
1358 Ephesus Church Road (mailing)
Harned, KY 40144
2373 Brandenburg Road (physical)
Leitchfield, KY 42754
( )   \<Grayson\>

PA: William M Macy   \<M1\>
1358 Ephesus Church Road
Harned, KY 40144
(270)756-2775
CL: Shirley Macy
1358 Ephesus Church Road
Harned, KY 40144
(270)756-2775
slmacy@bbtel.com

Mt Zion (DC)   (4MWC)MICU3507
7447 Knottsville Mt Zion Rd (mailing)
8001 Knottsville Mt Zion Rd (physical)
Philpot, KY 42366
( )   \<Daviess\>
PA: Dennis J Preston   \<M1\>
7447 Knottsville Mount Zion Road
Philpot, KY 42366
(270)925-8144
dpreston@roadrunner.com
CL: Shirley L Bratcher
3815 Locust Hill Drive
Owensboro, KY 42303
(270)993-4056
slbratcher24@yahoo.com

Neal's Chapel   (4C)MICU3122
62 Oscar Gilpin Road (mailing)
860 Lecta Kino Road (physical)
Glasgow, KY 42141
( )   \<Barren\>
CL: Pam H Browning
62 Oscar Gilpin Road
Glasgow, KY 42141
(270)670-1047
pshbrowning@hotmail.com

Needham   (4WC)MICU3219
3179 Meeting Creek Road (mailing)
State Route 84 (physical)
Eastview, KY 42732
( )   \<Hardin\>
CL: Odelia Dewall
2548 Meeting Creek Road
Eastview, KY 42732
(270)862-4362

Oak Forest   (4MWC)MICU3123
170 Milby Rattliff Road
Summersville, KY 42782
(270)932-4685   \<Green\>
CL: Mike Durrett
170 Milby Rattliff Road
Summersville, KY 42782
(270)932-4685
thedurretts@windstream.net

Owensboro   (4C)MICU3509
910 Booth Avenue
Owensboro, KY 42301
(270)683-4479   \<Daviess\>
brotim.cpc@gmail.net
PA: Timothy McGuire   \<M1\>
PO Box 42
Mt Sherman, KY 42764
(270)766-9027
brotim.cpc@gmail.com
CL: Judy Mattingly
1125 W 11th Street
Owensboro, KY 42301
(270)929-1315
sec.ocpc@gmail.com

CUMBERLAND PRESBYTERY CONTINUED

Point Pleasant   (1C)MICU3313
  7030 State Route 269
  Beaver Dam, KY 42320
  ( )   <Butler>
CL: Kathy Pharris
  7030 State Route 269
  Beaver Dam, KY 42320
  (270)274-7418
  kathyspharris@yahoo.com

Poplar Grove   (4WC)MICU3511
  2929 Kentucky 254 W (mailing)
  5112 State Highway 1155 (physical)
  Sacramento, KY 42372
  ( )   <McLean>
CL: Gibson H Riggs
  PO Box 224
  Calhoun, KY 42327
  (270)273-3280
  FAX: (270)273-3280
  riggsg@bellsouth.net

Radcliff   (4U)MICU3220
  1751 S Logsdon Parkway
  Radcliff, KY 40159
  (270)351-6199   <Hardin>
  radpres@bbtel.com
OD: John Lentz   <M5>
  1876 Highway 44 E
  Shepherdsville, KY 40165
  (502)543-2659
  lentzhome@aol.com
CL: Patricia T. Crosby
  851 S Archer Street
  Radcliff, KY 40160
  (270)351-8548
  ptcrosby@bbtel.com

Sacramento   (4MWC)MICU3512
  PO Box 257 (mailing)
  40 Lyons Lane (physical)
  Sacramento, KY 42372
  (270)736-5176   <McLean>
PA: Kevin T Brantley   <M1>
  9801 State Route 81 South
  Island, KY 42350
  (270)405-2222
  ktbrantley1971@gmail.com
CL: Brenda Lee
  386 Dillahay Dame Loop
  Island, KY 42350
  (270)736-5160

Salem   (2C)MICU3127
  1570 Old Salem Church Road (mailing)
  291 Clay Wright Road (physical)
  Greensburg, KY 42743
  ( )   <Green>
CL: Joan Cook
  1570 Old Salem Church Road
  Greensburg, KY 42743
  (502)932-5717

Seven Springs   (2C)MICU3128
  1607 Seven Springs Church Road
  Center, KY 42214
  (270)565-4865   <Metcalfe>
PA: Randall Gray   <M1>
  1230 New Liberty Big Meadow Road
  Knob Lick, KY 42154
  (270)432-5322

CL: Louise London
  2466 Highway 1048
  Center, KY 42214
  (270)565-3015

Shiloh   (4MEWC)MICU3129
  PO Box 1193 (mailing)
  1186 Shiloh Road (physical)
  Campbellsville, KY 42719
  (270)789-2346   <Taylor>
CL: Tammy Stamp
  3320 Old Greensburg Road
  Campbellsville, KY 42718

Short Creek   (4WC)MICU3221
  9312 Owensboro Road (mailing)
  Hollow Church Road (physical)
  Falls of Rough, KY 40119
  ( )   <Grayson>
PA: Billy Ray Carter   <M1>
  33 Mockingbird Drive
  Leitchfield, KY 42754
  (270)259-3897
  cartercbc@windstream.net
CL: George Fentress
  11680 Owensboro Road
  Falls of Rough, KY 40119
  (270)879-8883

Wisdom   (2C)MICU3130
  254 Echo Road (mailing)
  State Route 640 (physical)
  Knob Lick, KY 42129
  ( )   <Metcalfe>
CL: Frances Royse
  491 Cave Ridge Road
  Knob Lick, KY 42154
  (270)432-0112
  froyse82@gmail.com

OTHERS ON MINISTERIAL ROLL:

Akai, Anum   <M1 WC>
  458 Dean Taylor Court
  Simpsonville, KY 40067
  (502)405-3120
  aakai@uwalumni.com
Barnhouse, Jr, Donald Grey   <M1 WC>
  51 Harristown Road
  Paradise, PA 17562
  (717)768-0048
  donaldbarnhouse@gmail.com
Barton, Robert   <M1 RT>
  22460 Klines Resort Road #290
  Three Rivers, MI 49093
  (859)613-2686
  csm2ndinfbde2002@yahoo.com
Bishop, Brenson   <M1 WC>
  12000 Hudson View Court
  Louisville, KY 40299
  (502)641-5925
  pappyvet@gmail.com
Blevins, Tom   <M1 WC>
  50 Blevins Road
  Center, KY 42214
  (270)565-1792
Boggs, Robert   <M1 WC>
  89 Maple Leaf Lane
  Leitchfield, KY 42754
  (270)259-5546
Bunnell, Robert (Bob)   <M1 RT>
  329 Lexington Drive
  Glasgow, KY 42141
  (270)629-6209
  bob_bunnell@yahoo.com

Byrd, James F   <M1 WC>
  1732 Cornishville Road
  Harrodsburg, KY 40330
  (859)734-0534
  jfbyrd@bluezoomwifi.com
Cottingim, Tom   <M1 WC>
  353 Atwood Drive
  Lexington, KY 40515
  (859)273-3800
  FAX: (859)272-4315
  t.cottingim@insightbb.com
Fortner, Terry   <M1 WC>
  118 W 5th Avenue
  Central City, KY 42330
  (270)836-3635
  terryfortner@outlook.com
Guarneros, Stephen H   <M1 WC>
  141 Angela Trail
  Nicholasville, KY 40356
  (270)869-7544
  pastorsteve88@yahoo.com
Love, James R   <M1 WC>
  14382 Sonora Hardin Springs Road
  Eastview, KY 42732
  (502)862-4119
Milby, Elizabeth L   <M1 WC>
  207 Summersville Road
  Greensburg, KY 42743
  (270)932-5659
McCallum, Frank   <M1 WC>
  1500 Coach Estates Road Lot E 16
  Murray, KY 42071
  (270)580-4796
  mccallum@bbtel.com
Norris, Freddie   <M1 WC>
  330 Lexington Drive
  Glasgow, KY 42141
  (270)651-7932
Phelps, John   <M1 M8>
  361 Chaco Road
  Yona, GUAM 96915
  (671)689-6764
  jbphelps75@yahoo.com
Ricketts, Roger   <M1 WC>
  205 Contantz Drive
  Canton, MO 63435
Romines, Sam   <M1 RT>
  299 Misty Lane
  Bowling Green, KY 42101
  (270)221-5856
  sam60romines@hotmail.com
Stefan, Gregory   <M1 WC>
  1917 Birchwood Street
  East Pearl, PA 17519
  (717)838-1171
  pastorstefan@att.net
Thompson, Eugene   <M1 WC>
  1244 S 4th Street Apt 522
  Louisville, KY 40203
Thompson, W Fay   <M1 RT>
  210 Macbeth Lane
  Glasgow, KY 42141
  (270)646-2218
Tucker, James D   <M1 WC>
  PO Box 34
  Mc Daniels, KY 40152
  (270)257-8971
Underwood, Jerrell M   <M1 RT>
  1157 E Highway 86
  Irvington, KY 40146
  (270)536-3706

CUMBERLAND PRESBYTERY CONTINUED

Wilson, Brenda　　　　　　　　　　　<M1 WC>
35 Collins Drive
Elizabethtown, KY 42701
(270)249-3835
susieq2007@windstream.net

OTHER LICENTIATES ON ROLL:
Lindsey, Tyler　　　　　　　　　　　<M2>
108 Patterson Street
Paris, TN 38242
(270)777-5760
alindsey87@bethelu.edu
Watts, Glenn David　　　　　　　　<M2 ST>
629 E High Street
Union City, TN 38261
(502)797-5685
hongkongbrother@hotmail.com

OTHER CANDIDATES ON ROLL:

Skipper, Steve　　　　　　　　　　　<M3>
312 E Market Street
Jeffersonville, IN 47130
samuel.skipper@jeffersonkyschools.us
(502)424-0022
Smith, Steven　　　　　　　　　　<M3 ST>
100 Valleyview Drive
Leitchfield, KY 42754
Stevenson, Mark
27 Scott Street
Leitchfield, KY 42754
(270)668-4183
markstevenson@windsteam.net

Vertrees, Matthew　　　　　　　　　<M3>
42 Herbert Carman Lane
Vine Grove, KY 40175
(270)734-2378
familylegacy2003@yahoo.com

Cumberland East Coast Presbytery
SOUTHEAST SYNOD

GENERAL		MEMBERSHIP			CHANGES					FINANCES			
1.Church Number	2.Active	3.Total	4.Church School	5.Prof. of Faith	6.Gains	7.Losses	8.Children Baptized	9. OUR UNITED OUT-REACH	10. Total Out-Reach Giving	11. All Other Expenses	12. Total Income Received	13. Value Church Prop. 1=1000
	1	2	3	4	5	6	7	8	9	10	11	12	13
Comeback	2446	10	10	0	0	NRR	0	0	0	0	0	0	0
Gil	2444	4	4	0	0	NRR	0	0	0	0	0	0	0
Hope Korean*	2131	21	26	0	0	10	3	0	500	10,400	81,915	92,315	0
One Way	2137	75	101	48	0	NRR	0	0	0	0	0	0	255
Outreach	2143				0	NRR	0	0	0	0	0	0	
Sharing	2141	20	20	4	0	NRR	0	0	0	0	0	0	0
Sunnyside					0	NRR	0	0	0	0	0	0	
True Love	2443	13	13	0	0	NRR	0	0	0	0	0	0	25
TOTALS	**7**	**143**	**174**	**52**	**0**	**10**	**3**	**0**	**500**	**10,400**	**81,915**	**92,315**	**280**

*Math error corrected. **Purged roll. NRR - No Report Received

CHURCHES, PASTORS, AND CLERKS:

Comeback　　　　　　　　　(C)SECE2446
316 Prospect Avenue Apt 6D (mailing)
Hackensack, NJ 07601
15 Wallington Avenue (physical)
Wallington, NJ 07057
PA: Ji Woo Park
316 Prospect Avenue Apt 6D
Hackensack, NJ 07601
(201)694-3005
jiwoos@gmail.com
CL: Session Clerk
316 Prospect Avenue Apt 6D
Hackensack, NJ 07601

Gil　　　　　　　　　　　　(C)SECE2444
139 A Grove Street
Tenafly, NJ 07670
PA: Si Chun Ryu
139 A Grove Street
Tenafly, NJ 07670
(201)410-3445
isaac9191@hotmail.com
CL: Session Clerk
139 A Grove Street
Tenafly, NJ 07670

Hope Korean　　　　　　　(C)SECE2131
1189 Hope Road
Tinton Falls, NJ 07724
(　)　　　　　　　　　　　<Monmouth>

PA: Buhwan Yang　　　　　　　　　<M1>
33 Rockingham Way
Manchester, NJ 08759
(732)456-2203
yangmoksa@gmail.com
CL: Session Clerk
1189 Hope Road
Tinton Falls, NJ 07724

One Way　　　　　　　　　(C)SECE2137
9 Carlton Avenue
Port Washington, NY 11050
(516)815-1164　　　　　　　<Queens>
FAX: (516)921-2821

CUMBERLAND EAST COAST PRESBYTERY CONTINUED

PA: Jin Soo Park   <M1>
  21155 45th Drive
  Bayside, NY 11361
  (516)558-7298
  jpkorea@daum.net
AP: Si Hoon Park   <M1>
  511 4th Street #B
  Palisades Park, NJ 07650
  (201)944-7913
CL: Session Clerk
  21155 45th Drive
  Bayside, NY 11361
  (516)558-7298
  jpkorea@daum.net

_____

Outreach   (C)SECE2143
  800 Silver Lane Room 205
  East Hartford, CT 06118
  (860)830-6808
PA: Sansook Cho   <M1>
  7 Falmouth Court
  Middletown, CT
  (860)830-6808
CL: Session Clerk
  800 Silver Lane Room 205
  East Hartford, CT 06118
  (860)830-6808

_____

Sharing   (C)SECE2141
  503 119 Street
  College Point, NY 11356
  (646)479-2305   <Queens>
  seungno@gmail.com
PA: Seungno Kim   <M1>
  503 119 Street
  College Point, NY 11356
  (646)479-2305
  seungno@gmail.com
CL: Session Clerk
  503 119 Street
  College Point, NY 11356
  (646)479-2305
  seungno@gmail.com

_____

Sunnyside   (C)SECE0000
  27-27 Bayside Lane
  Flushing, NY 11354
  (718)809-5191
PA: Kio Seob Kim   <M1>
  27-27 Baysied Lane
  Flushing, NY 11358
  (718)539-3476
  imkioseob@hotmail.com
CL: Session Clerk
  14430 35th Avenue Apt A62
  Flushing, NY 11354
  (718)539-3476
  imkioseob@hotmail.com

_____

True Love   (C)SECE2443
  42-40 208th Street
  Bayside, NY 11361
  (347)308-4333
  ingodswill@gmail.com
CL: Session Clerk
  42-40 208th Street
  Bayside, NY 11361

_____

OTHERS ON MINISTERIAL ROLL:

Ko, John Jae   <M1 RT>
  185 Old Ferris Farm Road
  Grand Gorge, NY 12434
  (718)460-1118
  spcko@hanmail.net
Lee, Choongmin   <M1 WC>
Lee, Paul   <M1 WC>
Ma, Choil   <M1 WC>
  105 Mandarin Drive
  Oak Grove, KY 42262
  (931)809-0725
  choilma@yahoo.com
Min, Kim   <M1 WC>
  55 Magnolia Avenue
  Tenafly, NJ 07670
Park, Sooyeol   <M1 WC>
Ryoo, Hwa Chang   <M1 WC>
  450 Island Road Unit 146
  Ramsey, NJ 07446
  (404)512-9147
Son, Woosuk   <M1 WC>

_____

OTHER LICENTIATES ON ROLL:

Chin, Kwang Sik   <M2>
  1168 Palisade Avenue
  Fort Lee, NJ 07024
  (201)220-3390
Sung, John   <M2>
  26 Old Orchard Road
  Cherry Hill, NJ 08003
  (856)751-0227

_____

OTHER CANDIDATES ON ROLL:

Kang, Eun Hee   <M3>
  14715 46th Avenue
  Flushing, NY 11355
  (718)762-0778

Presbytery del Cristo
MISSION SYNOD

GENERAL		MEMBERSHIP			CHANGES				FINANCES				
1.Church Number	2.Active	3.Total	4.Church School	5.Prof. of Faith	6.Gains	7.Losses	8.Children Baptized	9. OUR UNITED OUT-REACH	10. Total Out-Reach Giving	11. All Other Expenses	12. Total Income Received	13. Value Church Prop. 1=1000
	1	2	3	4	5	6	7	8	9	10	11	12	13
316 Fellowship	8710	8	12	3	0	0	4	0	0	1,200	27,070	23,873	0
Chinese	8501	439	439	180	0	0	102	0	30,936	73,061	877,728	1,201,819	7,600
Desert Gardens	8705	20	20	10	0	0	0	0	2,000	7,763	46,263	63,244	180
Grace Fellowship	8510	117	131	36	0	1	5	0	20,004	98,175	257,341	502,289	2,774
Heights	8701	283	2,493	15	0	0	13	2	8,500	141,154	867,345	942,386	2,851
Lubbock First	8702	82	82	30	0	0	5	0	2,500	33,671	233,571	222,245	4,000
Maranatha	8706	100	100	60	0	NRR	0	0	360	0	0	0	0
Redeemer	8512	57	71	60	2	0	0	2	4,000	28,136	283,827	339,914	0
St. Andrew	8703	95	194	58	0	NRR	0	0	6,738	0	0	0	1,645
Trona	8503	18	52	0	0	2	0	0	0	557	14,754	12,410	125
Westside	8709	40	40	17	0	0	9	0	600	9,191	137,264	146,612	250
TOTALS	**11**	**1,259**	**3,634**	**469**	**2**	**3**	**138**	**4**	**75,638**	**392,908**	**2,745,163**	**3,454,792**	**19,425**

*Math error corrected. **Purged roll. NRR - No Report Received

CHURCHES, PASTORS, AND CLERKS:

316 Fellowship (4C)MSDC8710
2200 E Dartmouth Circle
Englewood, CO 80113
PA: Jean Hess <M1>
2200 E Dartmouth Circle
Englewood, CO 80113
(303)504-0275
jeanhess@316denver.com
AP: Rick Hess <M1>
2200 E Dartmouth Circle
Englewood, CO 80113
(303)504-0275
rick@densem.edu
CL: Session Clerk
2200 E Dartmouth Circle
Englewood, CO 80113

Chinese (4C)MSDC8501
865 Jackson Street
San Francisco, CA 94133
(415)421-1624 <San Francisco>
FAX: (415)421-1874
church@cumberlandsf.org
PA: Walter Lau <M1>
865 Jackson Street
San Francisco, CA 94133
(415)421-1624
FAX: (415)421-1874
walter@cpccsf.org
AP: Steven Chen <M1>
865 Jackson Street
San Francisco, CA 94133
(415)421-1624
steven.chen@cpccsf.org

AP: Alexis Yu <M1>
1761 Willow Way
San Bruno, CA 94066
(415)421-1624
alexis.yu@cpccsf.org
CL: John Fang
2362 39th Avenue
San Francisco, CA 94116
(415)568-0805
johnfangtoo@gmail.com

Desert Gardens (4C)MSDC8705
10851 E Old Spanish Trail
Tucson, AZ 85748
(520)296-0703 <Pima>
PA: Gerald (Jerry) Hagelin <M1>
10851 E Old Spanish Trail
Tucson, AZ 85712
(520)275-8110
azcef@cs.com
CL: Cheryl Curtis
7131 E Kiva Way
Tucson, AZ 85750
clc@curtisplumbing.tuccoxmail.com

Grace Fellowship (4C)MSDC8510
3265 16th Street
San Francisco, CA 94103
(415)703-6090 <San Francisco>
office@gfccsf.org
PS: Paul Conti <M1 OD>
621 Callippe Court
Brisbanem, CA 94005
(415)713-2351
pconti@gfccsf.org
CL: Pamela Chen
3265 16th Streeete
San Francisco, CA 94103
(415)703-6090
stated-clerk@gfccsf.org

Heights (4WC)MSDC8701
8600 Academy Road NE
Albuquerque, NM 87111
(505)821-1993 <Bernalillo>
FAX: (505)797-8599
PA: Lyle Reece <M1>
8600 Academy Road NE
Albuquerque, NM 87111
(505)884-2952
lreece@heightscpc.org
AP: Jerry Smyrl <M1>
10617 Hagen NE
Albuquerque, NM 87111
(505)999-8852
gpasmyrl@gmail.com
AP: Marty Goehring <M1>
8600 Academy NE
Albuquerque, NM 87111
(505)821-3628
FAX: (505)797-8599
mmgoehring@heightscpc.org
AP: Justin Richter <M1>
8600 Academy Road NE
Albuquerque, NM 87111
(505)363-8738
jrichter@heightscpc.org
CL: Barbara J Cok
8600 Academy Road NE
Albuquerque, NM 87112
(505)275-0108
FAX: (866)280-0731
barbara@lobo.net

Lubbock First (4WC)MSDC8702
7702 Indiana Avenue
Lubbock, TX 79423
(806)792-3553 <Lubbock>

PRESBYTERY DEL CRISTO CONTINUED

PA: Nathaniel Mathews   `<M1>`
14314 Avenue U
Lubbock, TX 79423
(931)209-6645
pastor@cpclubbock.com
CL: Diana K Akins
4712 63rd Street
Lubbock, TX 79414
(806)797-5246
FAX: (806)744-0640
akinsarms@sbcglobal.net

_____

Maranatha   (4C)MSDC8706
PO Box 1040 (mailing)
San Elizario, TX 79849
11497 Socorro Road (physical)
Socorro, TX 79927
(915)851-8349   `<El Paso>`
hectoryliz@att.net
PA: Hector Mata   `<M1>`
PO Box 1040
San Elizario, TX 79849
(915)704-9930
hectoryliz@att.net
AP: Elizabeth Mata   `<M1>`
PO Box 1040
San Elizaro, TX 79849
(915)704-9930
hectoryliz@att.net
AP: Isaac Mata   `<M1>`
PO Box 1040
San Elizaro, TX 79849
(915)920-0897
isaacmata96@yahoo.com
CL: Miguel Flores
PO Box 1040
San Elizario, TX 79849
(915)346-2071
mr_titof@yahoo.com

_____

Redeemer   (4C)MSDC8512
1224 Fairfax Avenue
San Francisco, CA 94124
(415)671-2194   `<San Francisco>`
info@redeemersf.org
PA: Danny Fong   `<M1>`
1224 Fairfax Avenue
San Francisco, CA 94124
(415)671-2194
dfong@redeemersf.org
PA: Cindi Fong   `<M1>`
1835 Alemany Boulevard
San Francisco, CA 94112
(415)335-8067
cfong@redeemersf.org
CL: Peter Lu
1224 Fairfax Avenue
San Francisco, CA 94124
(415)632-9426
peterslu@gmail.com

_____

St Andrew   (4MEWC)MSDC8703
1415 N Grandview
Odessa, TX 79761
(432)367-8603   `<Ector>`
FAX: (432)367-8605
standrewcp@sbcglobal.net
SS: Larry Hood   `<M2>`
2825 E 17th Street
Odessa, TX 79761
(432)770-8307
l3lhood@yahoo.com

AP: Sharon Notley   `<M1>`
16500 S Grey Wolf Apt 5
Odessa, TX 79766
(432)210-9059
sharon_standrewcp@outlook.com
CL: Ryan McGuire
3405 Clearmont
Odessa, TX 79762
(432)208-4480
cytotn74@gmail.com

_____

Trona   (4C)MSDC8503
83456 Argus Avenue
Trona, CA 93592
(760)382-8636   `<San Bernardino>`
PA: Dennis Benadom   `<M1>`
13314 Sage Street
Trona, CA 93562
(760)372-4536
galerose91@msn.com
CL: Sean Johnson
82195 7th Street
Trona, CA 93562
(760)372-4078
shyloo85@gmail.com

_____

Westside   (4C)MSDC8709
PO Box 15209 (mailing)
4110 Sabana Grande Avenue (physical)
Rio Rancho, NM 87174
(505)620-2427   `<Sandoval>`
nancye320@aol.com
PA: Harry W Chapman   `<M1>`
4908 El Picador Court
Rio Rancho, NM 87124
(505)620-2427
wrightrev@gmail.com
CL: Melanie Corn
2809 Dallas NE
Albuquerque, NM 87110
(505)898-0087
mcorn08@gmail.com

_____

OTHERS ON MINISTERIAL ROLL:

Bondurant, Lee   `<M1 WC>`
PO Box 371137
El Paso, TX 79937
(915)309-7269
64lee.bondurant@gmail.com
Bower, Clay   `<M1 WC>`
1514 Donette Place NE
Albuquerque, NM 87112
(704)575-9497
cbrev.9497@gmail.com
Braswell, Jimmy   `<M1 WC>`
1514 E 10th Street
Odessa, TX 79761
(432)967-3765
jjcgbraz@cableone.net
Cho, Kun Ho   `<M1 WC>`
8362 Walker Street Apt 18
Buena Park, CA 90623
(949)241-6167
pkhch3@gmail.com
Collins, Paul   `<M1 RT>`
915 Warm Sands Drive SE
Albuquerque, NM 87123
(505)294-3842
FAX: (505)254-7707
preachtheword44@gmail.com

Estes, George R   `<M1 RT>`
7910 Cloverbrook Lane
Germantown, TN 38138
(901)275-4812
geoestes@gmail.com
Freund, Henry O   `<M1 RT>`
913 Sam Houston Drive
Dyersburg, TN 38024
(731)285-1744
freundly@att.net
Fung, David   `<M1 WC>`
19928 Bothell Everett Highway Apt 513
Bothell, WA 98012
Fung, Lawrence   `<M1 WC>`
367 Eldorado Drive
Daly City, CA 94015
(415)535-8754
revfung@gmail.com
Gonzales, Homer   `<M1 WC>`
8924 Armistice NE
Albuquerque, NM 87109
(505)235-0215
FAX: (505)841-4267
hgabq1985@gmail.com
Green, Paul   `<M1 RT>`
5228 Anchorage Avenue
El Paso, TX 79924
(915)751-7960
Headley, Daniel   `<M1 WC>`
9526 Academy Hills Drive NE
Albuquerque, NM 87111
(720)724-0961
danieliheadleyp@gmail.com
Huey, Sharon   `<M1 WC>`
1945 23rd Avenue
San Francisco, CA 94116
(415)568-7835
sharon_huey@yahoo.com
Kim, Byong Sam   `<M1 RT>`
2815 Le Bourget Lane
Lincoln, CA 95648
(916)253-7291
byongkim903@gmail.com
Knight, Melissa   `<M1 M9>`
3514 Westbrook Drive SE
Smyrna, GA 30082
(530)632-6472
revlissa@gmail.com
Lee, Douglas   `<M1 WC>`
70 Sanchez Street
San Francisco, CA 94114
(415)252-9698
dougblee643@gmail.com
Lui, Stephen   `<M1 RT>`
512 16th Avenue
San Francisco, CA 94118
(415)386-2302
FAX: (415)386-2302
Luo, Tian-en   `<M1 RT>`
87 Berta Circle
Daly City, CA 94015
(650)754-9885
FAX: (650)754-9885
tianenyang555@gmail.comt
McNeese, Michael C   `<M1 RT>`
16410 Wesley Evans Road
Prairieville, LA 70769
(225)715-6293
mcneesemc@cox.net

PRESBYTERY DEL CRISTO CONTINUED

Oh, Taeho   <M1 WC>
2470 Montrose Avenue #5
Montrose, CA 91020
(213)334-1506
ingodswill@gmail.com

O'Mara, Shelia   <M1 RT>
PO Box 170
Gadsden, TN 38337
(443)699-2321
chaplainshelia@aol.com

Rincon, Alfredo   <M1 OM>
12008 Fred Carter
El Paso, TX 79936
(915)857-1343
yaanaivitaly@yahoo.com

Rincon, Lyvia   <M1 OM>
12008 Fred Carter
El Paso, TX 79936
(915)857-1343
yaanaivitaly@yahoo.com

Saldana, Manuel (Alex)   <M1 WC>
536 Telop
El Paso, TX 79927
(915)329-9538
campe13@yahoo.com

Sze, Joseph   <M1 WC>
Rau Sao Joaquim, 382
Liberdale, Sao Paulo, SP
CEP 015068-000 Brazil
WeChat971507345761
pastorsze@yahoo.com

Tan, Pek Hua   <M1 WC>
7 Belhaven Avenue
Daly City, CA 94015
(415)515-0076
ptan27@yahoo.com

Terpstra, Tami   <M1 WC>
10 Rainbow Crest Drive
Evergreen, CO 80127
(303)396-3604
tami.terpstra@yahoo.com

Tsujimoto, Mark   <M1 WC>
88 S Broadway Unit 3210
Millbrae, CA 94030
(650)697-6901
mltsujimoto@gmail.com

Wan, Sonny   <M1 RT>
13 Wexford Place
Aladema, CA 94502
(510)847-2069
sonny.wan@gmail.com

Wilson, Don   <M1 M9 RT>
7300 Calle Montana NE
Albuquerque, NM 87113
(505)280-5822
don-wilson07@comcast.net

Wong, Bruce   <M1 WC>
716 Duncanville Court
Campbell, CA 95008
(415)290-1101
revbwong@gmail.com

Young, Timothy   <M1 WC>
501 7th Avenue
San Francisco, CA 94118
(415)350-8201
tdy223@gmail.com

Yu, Pyong San (Sonny)   <M1 WC>
139 Silverado Drive
Santa Teresa, NM 88008
(915)329-3451
pyongsanyu@hotmail.com

OTHER LICENTIATES ON ROLL:

Barricklow, Gary   <M2>
3012 Winston Meadows
Rio Rancho, NM 87144
(505)417-0331
garysr@barricklow.com

George, Thomas   <M2>
908 N Brown Avenue
Casa Grande, AZ 85222
(640)447-2676
tgeorge@aerogram.net

Gnewuch-Schmidt, Karen   <M2>
9555 Yukon Street
Westminster, CO 80021
(303)403-4538
chartreusemonk12@gmail.com

Kang, Myung   <M2>
4600 La Luz Avenue
El Paso, TX 79903
(915)305-9119
mkang3000@gmail.com

Pritchett, Huiling   <M2>
5562 S Yank Court
Littleton, CO 80127
(303)330-3929
whuiling88@yahoo.com

OTHER CANDIDATES ON ROLL:

Hom, Patti   <M3>
811 Faxon Avenue
San Francisco, CA 94112
(415)586-5998
pattihom@gmail.com

Presbytery of East Tennessee
SOUTHEAST SYNOD

GENERAL		MEMBERSHIP			CHANGES				FINANCES			
	1.Church Number	2.Active	3.Total	4.Church School	5.Prof. of Faith	6.Gains	7.Losses	8.Children Baptized	9. OUR UNITED OUT-REACH	10. Total Out-Reach Giving	11. All Other Expenses	12. Total Income Received	13. Value Church Prop. 1=1000
	1	2	3	4	5	6	7	8	9	10	11	12	13
Beaver Creek	2301	475	730	275	1	7	36	2	44,215	87,919	412,230	513,891	3,600
Bethesda	2201	48	48	40	0	0	2	0	4,339	21,907	37,708	72,796	170
Casa De Fe	2220	10	12	9	0	0	8	0	400	1,595	20,704	19,478	600
Cedar Hill	2202	49	172	38	1	2	7	0	9,540	17,800	87,724	95,815	850
Clark's Grove	2302	48	48	23	0	0	1	0	5,624	9,096	43,552	56,283	631
Corntassel	2304	28	35	17	0	3	4	0	3,636	10,477	33,731	33,731	200
Dover	2203	36	42	0	2	5	1	0	8,678	13,317	65,726	83,312	1,834
Fairview	2204	44	60	25	0	1	3	0	6,182	9,570	80,429	125,425	648
FaithFellowship	2319	52	65	25	0	1	4	0	3,660	7,869	200,461	262,928	2,843
Greeneville	2206	406	562	96	0	0	8	2	40,511	74,400	458,675	442,523	4,200
Heartland	2306	52	131	32	0	0	0	0	3,584	6,941	88,933	82,273	600
Knoxville	2305	100	269	60	2	4	0	1	7,417	19,864	393,359	459,885	2,500
Lebanon	2207	10	18	7	0	1	1	0	2,000	8,156	21,069	28,261	300
Loudon	2307	163	192	120	0	2	13	1	30,777	33,036	198,165	273,655	5,585
Marietta	2308	65	197	60	0	0	4	0	19,685	55,111	231,285	220,192	735
Maryville 1st	2309	54	215	45	0	1	2	0	2,400	7,669	106,784	115,055	1,561
Mercy	2320	11	11	10	0	2	3	1	200	500	500	5,525	5
Mohawk	2208	14	46	15	0	0	1	0	1,603	0	25,353	18,630	300
Mt. Carmel	2310	40	70	18	0	0	4	0	3,371	9,726	36,509	35,521	475
Mt. Pleasant	2209	30	67	22	0	0	0	0	4,358	6,859	33,802	43,584	300
New Bethel	2210	12	23	17	0	0	0	0	1,011	2,819	8,572	12,481	333
New Hope	2311	25	26	16	0	0	8	0	3,077	6,624	38,168	36,785	800
Oak Ridge	2313	104	115	20	0	5	8	0	17,916	35,280	179,248	230,616	1,650
Oakland*	2211	28	28	10	0	2	0	0	0	3,401	2,493	28,418	612
Oliver Springs	2314	4	4	0	0	0	0	0	1,276	1,086	4,078	6,710	175
Philadelphia	2212	22	22	22	0	0	0	0	660	600	26,049	18,645	300
Pilot Knob	2213	8	8	15	0	NRR	0	0	871	0	0	0	100
Pleasant Hill	2214	20	20	14	0	0	2	0	2,316	6,029	17,718	23,748	400
Pleasant Vale	2215	7	14	20	2	5	14	0	229	755	20,833	32,433	240
Salem	2216	22	22	40	0	NRR	0	0	0	0	0	0	100
Shiloh	2217	91	172	23	0	0	5	0	13,310	20,138	101,184	141,701	1,150
Talbott	2218	48	97	28	3	3	1	0	4,909	12,437	57,238	58,612	1,125
Union	2315	270	439	94	4	5	6	0	15,215	68,014	361,887	444,038	2,441
Virtue	2316	43	65	15	1	2	2	0	3,730	16,810	119,564	292,182	1,600
Walkertown	2222	11	11	11	0	NRR	0	0	0	0	0	0	220
Willoughby	2219	7	10	8	0	0	1	0	621	621	9,278	6,213	250
Young's Chapel	2317	71	93	47	1	2	2	0	18,113	28,933	124,458	181,740	1,000
TOTALS	37	2,528	4,159	1,337	17	53	151	7	285,434	605,359	3,647,467	4,503,085	40,433

*Math error corrected. **Purged roll.   NRR - No Report Received

PRESBYTERY OF EAST TENNESSEE CONTINUED

CHURCHES, PASTORS, AND CLERKS:

Beaver Creek (4WC)SEET2301
7225 Old Clinton Pike
Knoxville, TN 37921
(865)938-7245 <Knox>
FAX: (865)938-1465
tsweet1@comcast.net
PA: Thomas Sweet <M1>
7225 Old Clinton Pike
Powell, TN 37849
(865)938-7245
tsweet1@comcast.net
AP: Billy Price <M1>
12510 Buttermilk Road
Knoxville, TN 37932
(901)494-4851
beavercreekyouth@gmail.com
AP: Fran Vickers <M1>
7225 Old Clinton Pike
Knoxville, TN 37921
(865)859-0805
franv3@comcast.net
AP: Patrick Wilkerson <M1>
903 Park Crest Court
Mount Juliet, TN 37122
(865)236-7737
patrickwilkerson3@gmail.com
CL: John Todd
4912 Montmorency Drive
Powell, TN 37849
(865)938-7211
jtodd4912@comcast.net

Bethesda (4C)SEET2201
155 Old Shiloh Road (mailing)
Greeneville, TN 37745
16340 Kingsport Highway (physical)
Fall Branch, TN 37656
(423)620-7753 <Greene>
FAX: (423)798-2042
kcor_98@yahoo.com
OD: Wade McAmis <M5>
3010 Whitehouse Road
Greeneville, TN 37745
(423)639-7711
CL: Jeff H Hayes
155 Old Shiloh Road
Greeneville, TN 37745
(423)639-8404
mdlpilot@yahoo.com

Casa De Fe (PRESC)SEET2220
493 Main Street, 2nd Floor
Malden, MA 02148
(781)322-2685 <Middlesex>
casadefemalden@gmail.com
CL: Myriam Santizo
125 Pennsylvania Avenue
Somerville, MA 02145
(617)666-6763

Cedar Hill (4EWC)SEET2202
4170 Newport Highway
Greeneville, TN 37743
(423)639-0268 <Greene>
cedarhill@centurylink.net

PA: Andrew (Andy) Eppard <M1>
6 Sanford Circle
Greeneville, TN 37743
(417)770-1153
reformedminister@yahoo.com
CL: Carolyn Harmon
4435 Newport Highway
Greeneville, TN 37743
(423)639-3037
richardharmon09@comcast.net

Clark's Grove (4WC)SEET2302
1662 Peppertree Drive (mailing)
Alcoa, TN 37701
3137 Old Knoxville Highway (physical)
Maryville, TN 37802
(865)982-5280 <Blount>
FAX: (865)273-8726
lynn@lynnwaters.com
PA: Robert Nick Coker <M1>
112 Olympia Drive
Alcoa, TN 37701
(865)237-7616
nickcoker@bellsouth.net
CL: Lynn Waters
1662 Peppertree Drive
Alcoa, TN 37701
(865)982-9083
FAX: (865)379-0654
lynn@lynnwaters.com

Corntassel (4C)SEET2304
933 Kahite Trail (mailing)
Vonore, TN 37885
2100 Povo Road (physical)
Madisonville, TN 37354
(423)884-3909 <Monroe>
miriamf23@tds.net
PA: Don Winn <M1>
375 Cumberland Mountain Circle
Sunbright, TN 37872
(615)478-9910
dwinn_ky@yahoo.com
CL: Carolyn Swabe
2203 Povo Road
Madisonville, TN 37354
(423)442-4377
swabec@aol.com

Dover (4MEWC)SEET2203
1550 Dover Road
Morristown, TN 37813
(423)581-4719 <Hamblen>
dovercp@comcast.net
PA: Jerry Scott <M1>
1580 Dover Road
Morristown, TN 37813
(865)803-3669
dmjlscott@yahoo.com
CL: Carolyn McCarter
2550 Springvale Road
Morristown, TN 37813
(423)581-2553
jesus.singer@gmail.com

Fairview (4MWC)SEET2204
4720 Snapps Ferry Road
Afton, TN 37616
(423)639-9011 <Greene>
faircpafton@gmail.com

PA: Ronnie Duncan <M1>
146 Deseree Road
Chuckey, TN 37641
(423)552-0321
ronkduncan@icloud.com
CL: Rick Taylor
175 Stone Dam Road
Chuckey, TN 37641
(423)470-0216
gadgetrt@comcast.net

Faith Fellowship (4EWC)SEET2319
PO Box 24162 (mailing)
Knoxville, TN 37933
14025 Highway 70 E (physical)
Lenoir City, TN 37772
(865)988-8522 <Knox>
info@faithfellowshipcp.org
PA: Greg Tucker <M1>
170 Whitney Drive
Lenoir City, TN 37772
(865)242-4086
greg.tucker311@outlook.com
CL: Lori Rosenbloom
12532 Willow Cove Way
Knoxville, TN 37934
(865)256-3343
loribloom354@gmail.com

Greeneville (4MEWC)SEET2206
201 N Main Street
Greeneville, TN 37745
(423)638-4119 <Greene>
FAX: (423)636-1017
office@gcpchurch.org
PA: James W Lively <M1>
906 Lyle Circle
Greeneville, TN 37745
(423)798-1959
FAX: (423)636-1017
jlively@gcpchurch.org
AP: Abby Cole Keller <M1>
162 Owen Lane
Greeneville, TN 37745
(423)863-6565
abbycolekeller@gmail.com
CL: Lori Cornett
517 Paradise Road
Greeneville, KY 42345
jimmycornett@bellsouth.net

Heartland (4MWC)SEET2306
160 Harrison Road
Lenoir City, TN 37772
(865)986-3018 <Loudon>
lccpc@icx.net
PA: Kenneth P Phillips <M1>
6419 Town Creek Road East
Lenoir City, TN 37772
(865)986-7344
CL: Jennifer L Smith
1085 Crestview Circle
Lenoir City, TN 37772
(865)986-5099
jlleslie@chartertn.net

PRESBYTERY OF EAST TENNESSEE CONTINUED

Knoxville　　(4WC)SEET2305
6900 Nubbin Ridge Drive
Knoxville, TN 37919
(865)588-8581　　<Knox>
FAX: (865)588-8581
firstcpc@earthlink.net
PA: Michael Wilkinson　　<M1>
1174 Tanglewood Street
Memphis, TN 38114
(334)517-6568
pastormike@kfcpc.comcastbiz.net
CL: Dianne Pipkin
1725 Covey Rise Trail
Knoxville, TN 37922
(865)675-2872
pndpip@aol.com

Lebanon　　(4MEC)SEET2207
2117 Murray Street (mailing)
Morristown, TN 37814
714 Lebanon Road (physical)
Jefferson City, TN 37760
( )　　<Jefferson>
PA: Howard E Shipley　　<M1>
3800 Dan Drive
Morristown, TN 37814
(423)581-1092
hshipley@charter.net
CL: Mary McCarter
804 W Jefferson Street
Jefferson City, TN 37760
(865)475-6572
mccrtrmary@aol.com

Loudon　　(4MWC)SEET2307
PO Box 373 (mailing)
503 College Street (physical)
Loudon, TN 37774
(865)458-2270　　<Loudon>
loudoncp@gmail.com
PA: Mark S Hester　　<M1>
724 Brixworth Boulevard
Knoxville, TN 37934
(865)924-2732
markstephenhester@gmail.com
CL: Russ Newman
623 Mulberry Street
Loudon, TN 377747302
(865)282-1977
mulberry623@yahoo.com

Marietta　　(4MC)SEET2308
1922 Marietta Church Road
Knoxville, TN 37932
(865)693-0080　　<Knox>
mariettacpchurch@gmail.com
PA: Randall Mayfield　　<M1>
12470 Daisywood Drive
Knoxville, TN 37932
(865)769-4756
FAX: (865)769-4756
mayfield07@comcast.net
CL: Virgil R Hubbard
2122 Campbell Station Road
Knoxville, TN 37932
(865)740-4863
vrhubbard@comcast.net

Maryville First　　(4MWC)SEET2309
1301 E Broadway
Maryville, TN 37804
(865)982-7860　　<Blount>
firstcumberland@gmail.com
PA: Ronald L Longmire　　<M1>
2041 Eckles Drive
Maryville, TN 37804
(865)984-1647
ronaldlongmire@charter.net
CL: Tom Longmire
630 Garfield Street
Alcoa, TN 37701
(865)983-3604

Mercy　　(4C)SEET2320
634 Martel Road
Lenoir City, TN 37772
(865)660-7579　　<Knox>
iglesiapcmisericordia@gmail.com
PA: Alfonso Oscar Marquez　　<M1>
389 Bethel Drive
Lenoir City, TN 37772
(865)660-7579
amarquez61@bellsouth.net
AP: Martha Marquez　　<M1>
389 Bethel Drive
Lenoir City, TN 37772
(865)660-7579
amarquez61@bellsouth.net
AP: Miguel Gonzales　　<M1>
200 Bethel Drive
Lenoir City, TN 37772
(865)988-4238
CL: Miguel Angel Gonzalez
200 Bethel Drive
Lenor City, TN 37772
(865)227-2710
mgonzalez865@bellsouth.net

Mohawk　　(4MWC)SEET2208
2149 Phillipi Road (mailing)
50 Soville Loop (physical)
Mohawk, TN 37810
( )　　<Greene>
SS: Chris Franklin　　<M2>
310 Yellow Springs Road
Midway, TN 37809
(423)972-3609
chrisfranklin104@comcast.net
CL: Velta Rhea Riley
2149 Phillipi Road
Mohawk, TN 37810
(423)235-6179

Mt Carmel　　(4EC)SEET2310
PO Box 4 (mailing)
Coalfield, TN 37719
5515 Knoxville Highway (physical)
Oliver Springs, TN 37840
(865)435-9247　　<Morgan>
PA: Donald W Acton　　<M1>
1186 Jenkins Lane
Knoxville, TN 37922
(865)966-5132
CL: Lisa Layne
714 Back Valley Road
Oliver Springs, TN 37840
(865)382-8817
lalayne64@yahoo.com

Mt Pleasant　　(4MWC)SEET2209
3945 Babbs Mill Road
Afton, TN 37616
( )　　<Greene>
PA: James L Carter　　<M1>
6155 Hummingbird Lane
Whitesburg, TN 37891
(423)587-8423
jandjmt@comcast.net
CL: Louise Gass
1205A Price Lanet
Greeneville, TN 37745
(423)639-3731

New Bethel　　(3WC)SEET2210
2820 Blue Springs Parkway (mailing)
90 Cox Road (physical)
Greeneville, TN 37743
( )　　<Greene>
CL: Coriece Baxter
2820 Blue Springs Parkway
Greeneville, TN 37743
(423)638-4089

New Hope　　(4C)SEET2311
904 Acorn Gap Road
Madisonville, TN 37354
( )　　<Monroe>
CL: Brenda Leslie
853 Acorn Gap Road
Madisonville, TN 37354
(423)519-9430
bftayles@yahoo.com

Oak Ridge　　(4EWC)SEET2313
PO Box 4836 (mailing)
127 Lafayette (physical)
Oak Ridge, TN 37831
(865)483-8433　　<Anderson>
FAX: (865)483-8445
1stcpc@comcast.net
PA: Larry A Blakeburn　　<M1>
790 Emory Valley Road Apt 714
Oak Ridge, TN 37830
(731)676-2978
larry@1stcpc.org
PA: Carlton Harper　　<M1C>
255 Glenview Circle
Lenoir City, TN 37771
(865)317-1296
carltonharperone@gmail.com
CL: Linda Diggs
315 Laurel Hollow Road
Clinton, TN 37716
(865)457-5355
ldiggs06@comcast.net

Oakland　　(4C)SEET2211
694 Oakland Road
Telford, TN 37690
(423)257-2258　　<Washington>
OD: Dale Mitchell　　<M5>
370 Ebenezer Loop
Chuckey, TN 37641
(423)329-3044
CL: Freda Graham
959 Bowmantown Road
Limestone, TN 37681
(423)257-5050

PRESBYTERY OF EAST TENNESSEE CONTINUED

Oliver Springs   (4C)SEET2314
PO Box 175 (mailing)
400 Spring Street (physical)
Oliver Springs, TN 37840
firstcumberland@gmail.com
( )   <Roane>
PA: Ken Johnson   <M1>
122 Ridge Lane
Clinton, TN 37716
(865)463-7090
kenjoxav122@bellsouth.net
CL: Sid Thurmer
PO Box 175
Oliver Springs, TN 37840
(865)435-5438

Philadelphia   (4MWC)SEET2212
509 Snapp Bridge Road (mailing)
757 Snapp Bridge Road (physical)
Limestone, TN 37681
( )   <Washington>
CL: Greg Stafford
509 Snapp Bridge Road
Limestone, TN 37681
(423)257-3796
gregandlesa509@comcast.net

Pilot Knob   (2C)SEET2213
515 Marvin Mountain Road (mailing)
445 Gap Creek Road (physical)
Bulls Gap, TN 37711
( )   <Greene>
LS: Richard Snowden   <M6>
PO Box 6004
Morristown, TN 37815
(423)235-5914
FAX: (423)254-3206
richard.snowden@wallacehardware.com
CL: Joyce Lamb
4185 Gap Creek Road
Bulls Gap, TN 37711
(423)235-6858

Pleasant Hill   (4WC)SEET2214
13385 Kingsport Highway
Chuckey, TN 37641
( )   <Greene>
LS: Richard Snowden   <M6>
PO Box 6004
Morristown, TN 37815
(423)235-5914
FAX: (423)254-3206
richard.snowden@wallacehardware.com
CL: Genevieve M Bolton
15440 Kingsport Highway
Chuckey, TN 37641
(423)234-7942

Pleasant Vale   (4C)SEET2215
525 Pleasant Vale Road
Chuckey, TN 37641
( )   <Greene>
OD: Robert Charlton   <M5>
1722 West Pines Road
Afton, TN 37616
(423)620-8905
CL: Howard Collins
3750 Rheatown Road
Chuckey, TN 37641
(423)278-6072

Salem   (4C)SEET2216
695 West Pines Road (mailing)
Afton, TN 37616
1927 Lost Mountain Pike (physical)
Greeneville, TN 37745
( )   <Greene>
OD: Billy Moore   <M5>
880 Black Bear Road
Greeneville, TN 37745
(423)552-1594
CL: Helen Starnes
695 West Pines Road
Afton, TN 37616
(423)234-0281
cehwstarnes@comcast.net

Shiloh   (4WC)SEET2217
1121 Shiloh Road
Greeneville, TN 37745
(423)639-3763   <Greene>
shilohcumberland@gmail.com
PA: Tammy L Greene   <M1>
109 Armitage Drive
Greeneville, TN 37745
(423)972-5525
tg6386@aol.com
CL: Debbie Chapman
1121 Shiloh Road
Greeneville, TN 37745
(423)639-3763
shilohcumberland@gmail.com

Talbott   (4C)SEET2218
PO Box 116 (mailing)
7410 W Andrew Johnson Hwy (physical)
Talbott, TN 37877
(865)475-1221   <Hamblen>
FAX: (865)475-1221
talbottchurch@bellsouth.net
PA: Karen Borchert   <M1>
PO Box 116
Talbott, TN 37877
(865)696-8225
mborchert@cn.edu
PA: Mark Borchert   <M1>
PO Box 116
Talbott, TN 37877
(865)696-0489
mborchert@cn.edu
CL: Lon Barry Knight
950 Rocktown Road
Jefferson City, TN 37760
(865)548-8449
lonknight1@hughes.net

Union   (4WC)SEET2315
400 Everett Road
Knoxville, TN 37934
(865)966-9040   <Knox>
FAX: (865)675-3787
union@unioncpchurch.com
PA: Leonard E Turner, Jr   <M1>
12651 Wagon Wheel Circle
Knoxville, TN 37934
(865)966-9040
FAX: (865)675-3787
pastor@unioncpchurch.com

AP: Chris Caldwell   <M1>
829 Chateaugay Road
Knoxville, TN 37923
(865)599-1044
luke64345@gmail.com
CL: Bernie Fay
1208 Granada Drive
Lenoir City, TN 37772
(708)710-1575
fayb99@sbcglobal.net

Virtue   (4MWC)SEET2316
725 Virtue Road
Knoxville, TN 37934
(865)966-1491   <Knox>
FAX: (865)966-0558
virtuecpchurch@tds.net
CL: Dana Frasier
11113 Pleasant Forest Drive
Knoxville, TN 37934
(865)599-8926
dcfrasier61@yahoo.com

Walkertown   (4C)SEET2222
6885 Kingsport Highway
Afton, TN 37616
(423)639-1333   <Greene>
OD: Raymond Conklin   <M5>
6885 Kingsport Highway
Afton, TN 37616
(423)638-3671
CL: Debbie Smith
4833 Landon Court
Kingsport, TN 37664
(423)288-6396

Willoughby   (4C)SEET2219
240 Wheeler Road (mailing)
220 Willoughby Road (physical)
Bulls Gap, TN 37711
( )   <Greene>
SS: Chris Franklin   <M2>
310 Yellow Springs Road
Midway, TN 37809
(423)638-5600
chrisfranklin104@comcast.net
CL: Charles Clowers
240 Wheeler Road
Bulls Gap, TN 37711
(423)235-5249

Young's Chapel   (4WC)SEET2317
1705 Lawnville Road
Kingston, TN 37763
(865)376-2192   <Roane>
FAX: (865)376-2196
info@youngschapel.net
PA: Dale Watson   <M1>
1705 Lawnville Road
Kingston, TN 37763
(865)376-2192
revdwatson@comcast.net
CL: Paul McCallie
3340 Kingston Highway
Kingston, TN 37763
(865)376-9199
pt57466@bellsouth.net

PRESBYTERY OF EAST TENNESSEE CONTINUED

OTHERS ON MINISTERIAL ROLL:

Blackwelder, Andrew   <M1 WC>
43 E Ridgefield Court
Greeneville, TN 37745
(423)525-3818
ablackwelder@gcpchurch.org

Campbell, Thomas D   <M1 RT>
7437 Old Clinton Pike
Powell, TN 37849
(870)297-3931
tdcampbellar@gmail.com

Choi, Ezra   <M1 WC>
605 Arbor Hollow Circle #203
Cordova, TN 38018
(901)236-82635

Creamer, Jennifer   <M1 WC>
310 5th Street
Pacific Grove, CA 93950
(831)809-9890
jencreamer@gmail.com

Fly, William   <M1 OM>
2820 Old Sam's Creek Road
Pegram, TN 37143
(865)938-6273
billyfly3@gmail.com

Franco, Ricardo   <M1 WC>
35 Bayrd Terrace Apt 2
Malden, MA 02148
(781)605-5900
fsfamily64@gmail.comt

Freeman, A Daniel   <M1 WC>
210 Dogwood Drive
Greeneville, TN 37743
(423)638-5925

Graham, Steve   <M1 WC>
804 Sky Blue Drive
Knoxville, TN 37923
(865)206-0012
eve1ts@hotmail.com

Greenwell, James C   <M1 WC>
7165 Wind Whisper Boulevard
Knoxville, TN 37924
(865)742-1653
FAX: (865)742-1653
greenwelljc@comcast.net

Hartman, Gary   <M1 WC>
3001 Hines Valley Road
Lenoir City, TN 37771
(865)986-4949
g37771@att.net

Hubbard, Donald   <M1 RT>
2128 N Campbell Station Road
Knoxville, TN 37932
(865)693-0264
djhubbard@mindspring.com

Kelly, Patrick L   <M1 M9>
1449 Rainbow Road
Mountain City, TN 37681
(423)727-4067

Koopman, David L   <M1 WC>
5606 Brandon Park Drive
Maryville, TN 37804
(865)660-2440
racewthrev@aol.com

Malinoski, T J   <M1 DE>
9087 Fenmore Cove
Cordova, TN 38016
(901)276-4572
tmalinoski@cumberland.org

McBeth, David   <M1 WC>
109 Gloria Place
Jacksonville, NC 28540
(910)238-4279
dsj3mcbeth@gmail.com

McConnell, Donald R   <M1 RT>
147 Confederacy Circle
Knoxville, TN 37934
(865)288-0230
donjoyce515@hotmail.com

McGuire, James D   <M1 WC>
220 Southwind Circle #2
Greenville, TN 37745
(423)638-6380
jmcguire915@comcast.net

Nicholson, Casey   <M1 WC>
1020 Tusculum Boulevard
Greeneville, TN 37745
(423)639-0268
caseynicholson@mac.com

Ortiz, Milton   <M1 DE>
1257 Magilbra Street
Cordova, TN 38016
(901)486-6679
mortiz@cumberland.org

Peach, John   <M1 WC>
221 Geronimo Road
Knoxville, TN 37934
(865)675-5956

Peterson, Lisa   <M1 RT>
7778 Cedar Creek Road
Townsend, TN 37882
(901)604-0737
petersonli@aol.com

Pickard, Ronald   <M1 WC>
6292 Golden Drive
Morristown, TN 37814
(423)587-9735

Prenshaw, Rebecca   <M1 WC>
1100 Albemarie Lane
Knoxville, TN 37923
(865)531-1954
bprenshaw@yahoo.com

Sanchez, Josefina   <M1 WC>
2625 Benson Gardens Boulevard
Omaha, NE 68134
(479)970-8654
fsfamily64@gmail.com

Sledge, Jeff   <M1 WC>
241 Long Bow Road
Knoxville, TN 37934
(865)318-5565
jeffsledge@charter.net

West, Fred E, Jr   <M1 WC>
510 Cedaredge Drive
New Smyrna, FL 32168
(206)409-8321
jwest616@earthlink.net

OTHER LICENTIATES ON ROLL:

OTHER CANDIDATES ON ROLL:

Adair, Ed   <M3>
3028 Staffordshire Boulevard
Powell, TN 37849
(865)850-8785
edadair@gmail.com

Belizaire, Gama   <M3>
26 West Street
Stoughton, MA 02072
(857)349-5588
gamab2000@gmail.com

Brooks, Marcy   <M3>
220 W sevier Heights
Greeneville, TN 37745
(423)747-4500
marcybrooks52@hotmail.com

Johnson, Kris   <M3>
130 Essex Street Box 192B
South Hamilton, MA 01982
(808)741-3370
kris.johnson2198@gmail.com
peachroot@aol.com

Shelton, Duncan   <M3>
533 Carrington Boulevard
Lenoir City, TN 37771
865-635-1338
duncanshelton@charter.net

Smith, Griffen   <M3>
1801 Westchester Drive
Knoxville, TN 37918
(865)804-1571
gryffinder2644@gmail.com

Wood, Gina   <M3>
10919 Gillian Lane
Farragut, TN 37934
(865)679-4332
ginawood02@gmail.com

Emaus Presbytery
MISSION SYNOD

	GENERAL	MEMBERSHIP			CHANGES					FINANCES				
	1.Church Number	2.Active	3.Total	4.Church School	5.Prof. of Faith	6.Gains	7.Losses	8.Children Baptized	9. OUR UNITED OUT-REACH	10. Total Out-Reach Giving	11. All Other Expenses	12. Total Income Received	13. Value Church Prop. 1=1000	
	1	2	3	4	5	6	7	8	9	10	11	12	13	
El Rebano	8905	294	314	16	0	NRR	0	0	0	0	0	0	435	
Horeb-Central	8915	62	75	20	0	NRR	0	0	0	0	0	0	153	
La Rosa DeSaron*	8911	79	83	35	0	NRR	0	0	0	0	0	0	64	
Senda de Libertad	8919	52	53	15	0	NRR	0	0	0	0	0	0	50	
Zamora	8918	109	109	27	0	NRR	0	0	0	0	0	0	67	
Presbytery	A8900													
TOTALS	**5**	**596**	**634**	**113**	**0**	**0**	**0**	**0**	**0**	**0**	**0**	**0**	**769**	

*Math error corrected. **Purged roll.. NRR - No Report Received

---

CHURCHES, PASTORS, AND CLERKS:

El Rebano-Caldas (4WMCF)MSEM8905
Calle 128 Sur #48-13
barrio Central
Caldas, Antioquia
Colombia, South America
(574)278-0787   <S America>
FAX: (574)278-0787
rebcaldas@une.net.co
PA: Edilberto Daza   <M1 HR>
Cra 12 #8-47
Cartago, Valle
Colombia, South America
57(314)794-1905
presbicartago@gmail.com
AP: Zenobia Rivera   <M1 WC>
Cra 12 #8-47
Cartago, Valle
Colombia, South America
57(310)500-1791
zenobiadedaza@yahoo.com.mx
CL: Consuelo Pena
Calle 130 Sur #57-09, Int 301
Caldas, Antioquia
Colombia, South America
(574)338-6190
FAX: (574)278-0787
chelitopeco@hotmail.com

Horeb-Central (4WMC)MSAN8915
Carrera 50D #62-69, Prado Centro
Medellin, Antioquia
Colombia, South America
(574)263-2154   <S America>
ipchoreb@hotmail.com
SS: Rene Wilgen Porras   <M3>
Cra 50 D #62-69
Medellin
Colombia, South America
(321)637-3089
renewilgen@hotmail.com
CL: Johana Daza Rivera
Direccion Cra 50D #62-69
Colombia, South America
(312)834-7999
johadaza@gmail.com

La Rosa de Saron (4C)MSAN8911
Calle 100 #50C-09
Barrio Santa Cruz Sector La Rosa
Medellin, Antioquia
Colombia, South America
(574)236-6509   <S America>
SS: Andres Giraldo   <M2>
Calle 76 #87-14 Apto 202
Medellin, Antioquia
Colombia, South America
(574)422-6669
andresgiraldo@une.net.co
CL: Claudia Cordoba
Calle 100 #50C-35
Barrio Santa Cruz Sector La Rosa
Medellin, Antioquia
Colombia, South America
57(315)605-0011

Senda de Libertad (C)MSAN8919
Cra 120 #39 F-91
Medellin, Antioquia
Colombia, South America
(574)496-1681
ipcsaladomedellin@gmail.com
PA: Josue Guerrero   <M1>
Calle 76 #88-65
Medellin, Antioquia
Colombia, South America
(574)412-3504
josueggutierrez@yahoo.es
AP: Cruzana Guerrero   <M1>
Cra 120 #39 F-91
Medellin, Antioquia
Colombia, South America
(574)496-1681
ipcsaladomedellin@gmail.com
CL: Session Clerk
Cra 120 #39 F-91
Medellin, Antioquia
Colombia, South America
(574)496-1681
ipcsaladomedellin@gmail.com

Zamora (4WC)MSAN8918
Calle 20D #42C-56 (physical)
Cra 58 #32A-41 Apt 420 (mailing)
Bello, Antioquia
Colombia, South America
(574)461-0069   <S America>
ipczamora@gmail.com
PA: Alejandro Vasquez   <M1>
Cra 58 #32A-41 Apt 420
Bello, Antioquia
Colombia, South America
(574)451-4816
almaesda@une.net.co
CL: Cecilia Taborda
Direccion calle 20 #42c-56
Colombia, South America
(300)783-5638
chilalu1147@hotmail.com

OTHERS ON MINISTERIAL ROLL:

Correa, Juan David   <M1 WC>
Calle 78 #87014 Robledo Palenque
Medellin
Colombia, South America
(312)769-7711
juanda_519@hotmail.com
Daza, Johan   <M1 DE>
8148 Yellow Stone Drive
Cordova, TN 38016
(281)793-3869
jdaza@cumberland.org
Martinez, Dagoberto   <M1 RT>
Cra 62D #71-113
Bello, Antioquia
Colombia, South America
(574)452-3466
Morales, Juan Fernando   <M1 WC>
Calle 38 Sur #40-45
Envigado
Colombia, South America
(574)236-6509
juanpresbiteriano@hotmail.com
Varilla, Adan Manuel   <M1 WC>
Calle 44 94-68 Barrio La America
Medellin
Colombia, South America
(300)241-1896
adanvarilla@hotmail.com

EMAUS PRESBYTERY CONTINUED

Varilla, Lida Patricia Vargas   <M1 WC>
   Calle 44 94-68 Barrio La America
   Medellin
   Colombia, South America
   (301)657-4906
   lidapavargas@hotmail.com

Velez, Gloria Patricia   <M1>
   Cra 50D #62-69
   Medellin
   Colombia, South America
   (310)890-1655
   gloriapvelez14@gmail.com

OTHER CANDIDATES ON ROLL:
Lopez, Yeison   <M3>
   Barrio San Francisco
   Istmina (Choco)
   Colombia, South America
   (315)290-1817

Grace Presbytery
SOUTHEAST SYNOD

GENERAL	MEMBERSHIP				CHANGES				FINANCES				
1.Church Number	2.Active	3.Total	4.Church School	5.Prof. of Faith	6.Gains	7.Losses	8.Children Baptized	9. OUR UNITED OUT-REACH	10. Total Out-Reach Giving	11. All Other Expenses	12. Total Income Received	13. Value Church Prop. 1=1000
	1	2	3	4	5	6	7	8	9	10	11	12	13
Antioch	701	26	33	0	0	1	2	0	1,266	3,459	8,396	12,660	150
Beersheba	702	174	212	101	0	0	3	1	24,144	33,383	171,919	224,582	1,300
Branchville*	106	175	175	25	2	2	50	1	0	3,060	115,913	107,203	1,650
Cairo	704	10	22	6	0	0	1	0	0	2,770	13,072	15,702	150
Christ	303	21	34	7	0	0	16	0	1,850	1,900	81,007	76,956	800
Coker	705	0	69	4	0	0	17	0	100	811	24,120	20,488	1,936
Columbus	706	162	162	25	0	2	0	1	800	1,300	114,400	126,000	1,500
Crestline	102	31	31	19	0	0	3	0	6,000	9,032	84,889	112,382	1,500
El Camino	310	45	74	10	0	0	0	0	500	1,225	58,164	60,157	490
Enon	707	147	276	93	0	4	4	1	1,200	16,419	250,369	288,378	1,050
Erin	601	46	108	40	0	NRR	0	0	0	0	0	0	218
First Hispanic	307	76	76	39	0	NRR	0	0	0	0	0	0	175
Gadsden	402	97	155	49	0	0	5	0	10,076	15,424	125,006	163,363	800
Glencoe	404	85	247	70	0	NRR	0	0	0	0	0	0	2,000
Grace Community*	407	99	153	20	2	7	5	1	9,372	20,738	113,616	144,373	1,320
Greens Chapel	208	35	58	15	0	2	2	0	7,500	15,624	65,924	77,711	901
Groverton	602	13	13	13	0	0	2	0	0	367	2,813	3,180	0
Helena	108	59	59	40	0	NRR	0	0	2,324	0	0	0	700
Homewood	111	74	109	35	0	NRR	0	0	5,421	0	0	0	2,025
Hopewell	101	25	27	13	0	0	5	0	1,058	2,704	3,894	47,616	1,461
House of Prayer	214	112	112	54	0	NRR	0	0	0	0	0	0	400
HousePrayerCullman	116	48	48	15	0	NRR	0	0	0	0	0	0	0
McLeod's Chapel	708	15	20	10	0	NRR	0	0	0	0	0	0	350
Mt. Zion	709	16	16	10	0	0	2	0	3,519	10,379	17,203	35,253	812
New Hope	104	171	238	55	0	3	5	2	35,102	67,359	283,176	350,535	2,400
Piedmont	406	52	70	35	0	0	1	0	1,300	3,760	81,175	92,767	1,101
Pleasant Hill	710	8	8	7	0	0	4	1	0	0	0	0	160
Roca De Salvacion	115	46	74	15	0	8	6	6	0	14,100	26,650	64,182	14
Rocky Ridge	105	75	225	40	1	1	0	2	25,006	38,241	167,707	240,814	1,200
Salem	607	15	15	15	4	4	2	0	0	17,711	11,512	24,214	150
Spring Creek	113	121	177	77	0	0	4	0	4,400	35,300	237,600	301,600	1,400
Steam Mill	608	42	56	51	0	1	1	0	0	15,891	70,068	92,783	400
Union	114	40	40	37	0	NRR	0	0	70	0	0	0	500
TOTALS	33	2,161	3,192	1,045	9	35	140	16	141,008	330,957	2,128,593	2,682,899	29,013

*Math error corrected. **Purged roll.. +Union Church   NRR - No Report Received

GRACE PRESBYTERY CONTINUED

CHURCHES, PASTORS, AND CLERKS:

Antioch   (2C)SEGR0701
2994 Antioch Church Road
Reform, AL 35481
( )   <Pickens>
CL: Reba Carpenter
3951 County Road 45
Reform, AL 35481
(205)375-6042
rebcar0228@gmail.com

Beersheba   (4MEWC)SEGR0702
1736 Beersheba Road
Columbus, MS 39702
(662)327-9615   <Lowndes>
FAX: (662)324-8320
secretary@beershebachurch.com
PA: Timothy Daniel Lee   <M1>
186 Blasingame Drive
Columbus, MS 39702
(601)433-3714
pastor@beershebachurch.com
CL: Charles Studdard
95 Studdard Drive
Columbus, MS 39702
(662)251-2075
FAX: (662)327-8773
charliestuddard@outlook.com

Branchville   (4MWC)SEGR0106
80 Hurst Road
Odenville, AL 35120
(205)629-3258   <St Clair>
FAX: (205)629-3258
SS: Mickey Thomason   <M3>
50 Thomason Road
Odenville, AL 35120
(205)283-2225
mickeythomason@yahoo.com
CL: Ronnie Browning
790 Browning Road
Odenville, AL 35120
(205)229-5937
rbrowning@american-usa.com

Cairo   (4MC)SEGR0704
23225 Highway 50 W (mailing)
West Point, MS 39773
Cairo Road (physical)
Cedar Bluff, MS 39741
( )   <Clay>
CL: Judy Chrismond
23225 Highway 50 W
West Point, MS 39773
(662)494-7290
tjchrismond@gmail.com

Christ   (4EWC)SEGR0303
19501 Holly Lane
Lutz, FL 33548
(813)909-9789   <Hillsborough>
CL: Laura Reed   <M3>
3017 Banyan Hill Lane
Land O'Lakes, FL 34639
(813)401-2332
lola04@reagan.com

Coker   (4MEWC)SEGR0705
PO Box 262 (mailing)
14705 Romulus Road (physical)
Coker, AL 35452
(205)339-1178   <Tuscaloosa>
CL: Retha Channell
15535 Lisenba Drive
Coker, AL 35452
(205)339-8125
rcchannell@aol.com

Columbus   (4EWC)SEGR0706
2698 Ridge Road
Columbus, MS 39705
(662)328-2692   <Lowndes>
fcpcsecretary@att.net
PA: Luke Lawson   <M1>
270 N Ridgeland Circle
Columbus, MS 39705
(662)295-9322
luke_lawson03@hotmail.com
CL: Carol Carley
71 Little Tom Road
Columbus, MS 39705
(662)328-4589
carleyr@bellsouth.net

Crestline   (4MWC)SEGR0102
605 Hagood Street
Birmingham, AL 35213
(205)879-6001   <Jefferson>
FAX: (205)968-8105
jan@crestlinechurch.org
PA: Janice M Overton   <M1>
3320 Pipeline Road
Birmingham, AL 35243
(205)281-6819
FAX: (205)968-8105
jan@crestlinechurch.org
CL: Maggie Smith
124 Stoneview Road
Birmingham, AL 35210
(205)956-9243

El Camino   (C)SEGR0310
6248 SW 14th Street (mailing)
6790 SW 12th Street (physical)
West Miami, FL 33144
(305)261-6200   <Dade>
lucatha@aol.com
CL: Session Clerk
6248 SW 14th Street
West Miami, FL 33144
(305)261-6200

Enon   (4MWC)SEGR0707
PO Box 294 (mailing)
9000 Highway 12 (physical)
Ackerman, MS 39735
(662)285-3303   <Choctaw>
enoncpchurch@gmail.com
PA: Jerry L Lawson   <M1>
9187 MS Highway 12
Ackerman, MS 39735
(662)285-8295
lawson@dtcweb.net
CL: Raymond D Gillon Jr
PO Box 294
Ackerman, MS 39735
(601)916-3589
rgillon@gmail.com

Erin   (4WC)SEGR0601
c/o Steve Burton (mailing)
1391 Andrew Milling
Decatur, MS 39327
590 Pete Freeman Road (physical)
Union, MS 39051
( )   <Newton>
PA: Rodney McInnis   <M1>
6589 Harbor Place
Gadsden, AL 35907
(256)454-2399
mcinnisrodneyand@bellsouth.net
CL: Derek Burton
1496 Andrew Milling Road
Decatur, MS 39327
(601)562-5762
bbhauling07@yahoo.com

First Hispanic   (4MWU)SEGR0307
2828 W Kirby Street
Tampa, FL 33614
(813)932-9684   <Hillsborough>
FAX: (813)932-9700
PA: Alexandri Sosa   <M1>
2828 W Kirby Street
Tampa, FL 33614
(813)960-1473
FAX: (813)932-9700
sosapcus@gmail.com
CL: Jorge Troche
14909 Aire Place
Tampa, FL 33624
(727)280-3806
jorgei.troche@icloud.com

Gadsden   (4MWC)SEGR0402
PO Box 2055 (mailing)
1200 Piedmont Cutoff (physical)
Gadsden, AL 35903
(256)492-2556   <Etowah>
FAX: (256)492-2525
office@gadsdencp.com
PA: Daniel Barkley   <M1>
2732 Rexford Street
Hokes Bluff, AL 35903
daniel@gadsdencp.com
(256)478-0397
CL: Maureen Latronico
2240 Cypress Bend Circle
Hokes Bluff, AL 35903
(256)390-7630
nanalats@aol.com

Glencoe   (4WC)SEGR0404
200 N College Street
Glencoe, AL 35905
(256)492-1584   <Etowah>
FAX: (256)492-1584
CL: Scott Stewart
200 N College Street
Gadsden, AL 35905
(256)492-1584
stewie242@hotmail.com

Grace Community   (4C)SEGR0407
3515 Highway 14
Millbrook, AL 36054
(334)285-4655   < >
millbrookgcc@gmail.com

GRACE PRESBYTERY CONTINUED

PA: Albert Russell   <M1>
104 Weston Street
Prattville, AL 36066
(334)455-3690
chemistry.russell@gmail.com
CL: Elaine Moore
5911 Dogwood Circle
Millbrook, AL 36054
(334)717-7553
kandemoore@att.net

Greens Chapel   (4WC)SEGR0208
PO Box 729 (mailing)
811 Greens Chapel Road (physical)
Cleveland, AL 35049
(205)559-7671   <Blount>
PA: David Linski   <M1>
202 Green's Chapel Road
Cleveland, AL 35049
(205)240-0943
pastor@greenschapelcpc.org
CL: Mark Edwards
PO Box 729
Cleveland, AL 35049
(205)353-3462
clerk@greenschapelcpc.org

Groverton   (2C)SEGR0602
222 Leon Harrell Road
Morton, MS 39117
( )   <Scott>
CL: Joel Lingle
6266 Highway 481 N
Morton, MS 39117
(601)942-1927

Helena   (4MC)SEGR0108
PO Box 418 (mailing)
3396 Helena Road (physical)
Helena, AL 35080
(205)663-2174   <Shelby>
youareloved@helenacpchurch.net
SS: Mike Ensminger   <M2>
180 Breland Street
Wilsonville, AL 35186
(205)529-7878
me0573@att.com
CL:Tonya Brancato
4024 Kinross Lane
Birmingham, AL 35242
(205)718-0602
tonybrancato@yahoo.com

Homewood   (4WC)SEGR0111
513 Columbiana Road
Homewood, AL 35209
(205)942-3051   <Jefferson>
homewoodcpc@gmail.com
PA: Mathew Derek Jacks   <M1>
341 Shadeswood Drive
Hoover, AL 35226
(205)903-8469
pastorderek77@gmail.com
CL: Delores Moore
1006 Highland Road
Homewood, AL 35209
(205)879-6206
donhmoore@charter.net

Hopewell   (4MWC)SEGR0101
2139 Cumberland Drive SE
Bessemer, AL 35023
(205)425-2126   <Jefferson>
SS: James Scott Edwards   <M3>
226 Jasmine Drive
Alabaster, AL 35007
(205)837-4069
jedwards53163@bellsouth.net
CL: Beverly Edwards
226 Jasmine Drive
Alabaster, AL 35007
(205)830-4318
jedwards53163@bellsouth.net

House of Prayer   (4C)SEGR0214
405 E Moulton Street
Decatur, AL 35601
(256)355-0947   <Cullman>
FAX: (256)355-0947
nlajap@yahoo.com
PA: Neil Aguiar   <M1>
2005 8th Street SW
Decatur, AL 35601
(256)616-1318
nlajap@yahoo.com
CL: Andres Esteban
405 E Moulton Street
Decatur, AL 35601
(256)355-0947
FAX: (256)355-0947

House of Prayer Cullman (4C)SEGR0116
170 County Road 703
Cullman, AL 35055
(256)531-8193
PA: Antonio Mena Rojas   <M1>
1421 1st Street NW
Cullman, AL 35055
(256)531-8193
antoniomena614@gmail.com
CL: Guadalupe Gonzalez
170 County Road 703
Cullman, AL 35055
(256)708-7140

Immanuel   (4MC)SEGR0311
(CLOSED 3/13/2020)

McLeod Chapel   (4MC)SEGR0708
207 E Minor Street (mailing)
Macon-Lynn Creek Road (physical)
Macon, MS 39341
(662)726-4609   <Noxubee>
CL: James B Moore III
207 E Minor Street
Macon, MS 39341
(662)726-4609

Mt Zion   (4C)SEGR0709
3044 Wolfe Road
Columbus, MS 39705
(662)328-3778   <Lowndes>
mjmims@muw.edu
CL: Martha Jo Mims
3011 Wolfe Road
Columbus, MS 39705
(662)328-3778
mjmims@muw.edu

New Hope   (4EWC)SEGR0104
5521 Double Oak Lane
Birmingham, AL 35242
(205)991-5252   <Shelby>
jessie@newhopecpc.org
PA: Donny Acton   <M1>
5521 Double Oak Lane
Birmingham, AL 35242
(205)991-5252
donny@newhopecpc.org
AP: Mindy Acton   <M1>
1413 Oak Ridge Drive
Birmingham, AL 35242
(205)601-2454
mindy@newhopecpc.org
AP: Sherrlyn Frost   <M1>
5557 Surrey Lane
Birmingham, AL 35242
(205)408-0729
sherrlyn@newhopecpc.org
CL: Jessie R Dunnaway
120 Virginia Way
Birmingham, AL 35242
(205)937-3684
jessie@newhopecpc.org

Piedmont   (4MWC)SEGR0406
23746 AL Highway 9 N
Piedmont, AL 36272
(256)447-7275   <Calhoun>
PA: Ken Byford   <M1>
23716 AL Highway 9 N
Piedmont, AL 36272
(205)965-7111
kenabyford@gmail.com
CL: Charles Needham
537 County Road 176
Piedmont, AL 37282
(256)405-5661
cneedham537@gmail.com

Pleasant Hill   (4MC)SEGR0710
115 Westwood Drive SW (mailing)
7782 CR 181, Eutaw, AL (physical)
Bessemer, AL 35022
(205)515-8163   <Greene>
williambetts7177@gmail.com
LS: W Haven Betts   <M6>
115 Westwood Drive SW
Bessemer, AL 35022
(205)515-8163
williambetts7177@gmail.com
CL: Greg Espey
12034 County Road 60
Eutaw, AL 35462
(205)372-2260
gregandmichel@yahoo.com

Roca De Salvacion   (C)SEGR0115
2404 Altadena Road
Birmingham, AL 35243
(205)994-1978   <Jefferson>
cpcrocadesalvacion@gmail.com
PA: William Alas   <M1>
105 Waterford Cove Drive
Calera, AL 7655
(205)966-9411
alas3542085@yahoo.es

GRACE PRESBYTERY CONTINUED

CL: Arely Torres
1902 Chandalar Court
Pelham, AL 35124
(205)994-1978
arelimartinez07@live.com

_____

Rocky Ridge   (4WC)SEGR0105
2404 Altadena Road
Birmingham, AL 35243
(205)823-2719   <Jefferson>
rockyridgecpchurch@gmail.com
PA: James DuWayne Pounds   <M1>
364 Vincent Street
Alabaster, AL 35007
(205)253-3910
duwaynelbs50@gmail.com
CL: Jaclyn Tow
2241 Timberlane Drive
Bessemer, AL 35022
(205)910-3758
jackietow13@gmail.com

_____

Salem   (4WC)SEGR0607
PO Box 121 (mailing)
Sebastopol, MS 39359
1220 Highway 487 E (physical)
Walnut Grove, MS 39189
(601)253-2678   <Leake>
sondragould@att.net
PA: Rodney McInnis   <M1>
6589 Harbor Place
Gadsden, AL 35907
(256)454-2399
mcinnisrodneyand@bellsouth.net
CL: Virginia Gould
1231 Highway 487 E
Walnut Grove, MS 39189
(601)253-2678
sondragould@att.net

_____

Spring Creek   (4MWC)SEGR0113
3411 Spring Creek Road (mailing)
3455 Spring Creek Road (physical)
Montevallo, AL 35115
(205)665-4184   <Shelby>
sccpchurch@yahoo.com
PA: Scott Fowler   <M1>
1900 Alex Mill Road
Montevallo, AL 35115
(205)901-8478
springcreekchurch@aol.com
CL: Ben Ingram
15 Quincy Lane
Montevallo, AL 35115
(205)665-4145
ben_ingram@msn.com

_____

Steam Mill   (4WC)SEGR0608
6517 Highway 492 (mailing)
11551 Road 101 (physical)
Union, MS 39365
( )   <Neshoba>
CL: Myra Bankston
6517 Highway 492
Union, MS 39365
(601)616-0436
myrabankston@yahoo.com

_____

Union   (4MWC)SEGR0114
PO Box 64 (mailing)
11633 Bama Rock Garden Road (physical)
Vance, AL 35490

( )   <Tuscaloosa>
LS: Herbie Gray   <M6>
2554 A Rocky Ridge
Birmingham, AL 35226
(205)823-3209
CL: Clifford Odell
11491 Bama Rock Garden Road
Vance, AL 35490
cliffodell39@yahoo.com

_____

OTHERS ON MINISTERIAL ROLL:

Barrios, Janina   <M1 WC>
7766 Greenwich Court E
Jacksonville, FL 32227
(786)757-0366
janina83@hotmail.com
Black, Gary G   <M1 WC>
11376 AL Highway 21 N
Piedmont, AL 36272
(205)452-2038
Brasher, Karen   <M1 WC>
2931 Barker Cypress Road, Apt 415
Houston, TX 77084
(205)777-2420
ekb077@gmail.com
Carter, Patricia   <M1 RT>
2509 Decatur Stratton Road
Decatur, MS 39327
(601)604-3813
revtree@yahoo.com
Clark, J Don   <M1 RT>
400 University Park Drive Apt 111
Homewood, AL 35209
(205)902-5161
jdsjcl@charter.net
Davis, C Timothy   <M1 WC>
8880 Childress Road
West Paducah, KY 42086
(850)995-8383
FAX: (904)994-6003
charles0828@earthlink.net
Diego, Aida Melendez   <M1 WC>
412 SW 87 Place
Miami, FL 33174
(305)815-1197
revaidamd@yahoo.com
Edmonds, Wayne   <M1 RT>
112 Dogwood Trail
Eclectic, AL 36024
(334)857-2202
sweetpea@comlinkinc.net
Foreman, Samuel L   <M1 WC>
22 Weston Lane
Hattiesburg, MS 39402
(601)562-1415
samfcpc@gmail.com
Gaither, Randy   <M1 WC>
No 3 Pacific Street
Belmopan City
Belize, Central America
rgaither@valuelinx.net
Halford, Angela   <M1 WC>
1818 N Taylor Street B-168
Little Rock, AR 72207
(767)274-0224
angelahalford2000@gmail.com
Hartung, J Thomas   <M1 M9>
2291 Americus Boulevard W Apt 1
Clearwater, FL 33763
(727)797-2882
revtom6@aol.com

Hayes, Sherrad   <M1 WC>
1405 N 7th Avenue
Lanett, AL 36863
(706)773-5201
sherrad.hayes@gmail.com
Headrick, Anthony   <M1 M9>
625 Bakers Bridge Avenue
Suite 105 PMB 197
Frankline, TN 37067
(208)972-7602
anthony.headrick@va.gov
Headrick, Christopher   <M1 WC>
635 Kensington Manor Drive
Calera, AL 35040
(205)240-0979
bravespop@gmail.com
Headrick, Jerry   <M1 RT>
7642 Zeigler Boulevard Apt 106
Mobile, AL 36608
(251)295-0041
willjheadrick@gmail.com
Hunley, Jearl   <M1 RT>
2618 Canterbury Road
Columbus, MS 39705
(662)329-1516
jdhunley@cableone.net
Lathem, W Ray   <M1 WC>
452 County Road 1462
Cullman, AL 35055
(256)734-7146
lathemray@bellsouth.net
Lefavor, David   <M1 M9>
414 S Monroe Siding Road
Xenia, OH 45395
(937)262-3394
david.lefavor@va.gov
Lockmiller Jr, Lem   <M1 WC>
PO Box 348
Leesburg, AL 35983
(256)490-3021
McNair, Mark   <M1 WC>
13 Cedar Lane
Columbia, MS 39429
(901)605-5559
fryerbuck1385@gmail.com
Mora, Wilfredo   <M1 WC>
17512 SW 153rd Court
Miami, FL 33187
(786)554-1478
moraw68@gmail.com
Morrow, Charles   <M1 RT>
5032 Pine Grove Road
Union, MS 39365
(601)479-0288
morrowp7@yahoo.com
Munoz, Mardoqueo   <M1 WC>
816 NW 87th Avenue #101
Miami, FL 33172
(305)801-6424
tonymardo@comcast.net
Murray, Joshua   <M1 WC>
3875 Avalon Boulevard Apt 7
Milton, FL 32583
(980)723-3286
jdm4428@yahoo.com
Payne, Robert (Bob)   <M1 WC>
PO Box 11
Lauderdale, MS 39335
(205)856-2427
payne.bob.emmet@gmail.com

GRACE PRESBYTERY CONTINUED

Reed, Charles   <M1 WC>
36839 In, dian Lake Cemetary Road
Dade City, FL 33525
instchuck12@embarqmail.com
(352)567-7427

Ros, Ramiro   <M1 WC>
107 Bracken Lane
Brandon, FL 33511
(813)633-1548
bethel@gte.net

Rowlett, Ron   <M1 WC>
336 Alfred Ladd Road E
Franklin, TN 37064
(912)351-0736

Schultz, Don   <M1 RT>
708 Gateway Lane
Tampa, FL 33613
(813)960-1473

Sumerlin, Larkin   <M1 WC>
920 Dogwood Circle
Birmingham., AL 35124
(334)357-0007
larkin.sumerlin@gmail.com

Talley, Ed   <M1 WC>
404 Serenity Circle
Walland, TN 37886
(205)854-1886
dptalley@hotmail.com

Tejada, Jose   <M1 OM>
488 SW 126th Terrace
Davie, FL 33325
(786)817-0972
jtejadapastor@hotmail.com

Thomas, Don H   <M1 RT>
4829 Caldwell Mill Lane
Birmingham, AL 35242
(205)747-0785
dhtatn4ybc@cs.com

Thomas, Lynn   <M1 DE>
4833 Caldwell Mill Lane
Birmingham, AL 35242
(205)601-5770
lynndont@gmail.com

Tobler, Garth   <M1 WC>
1641 Pocota Drive Apt 205
Oneonta, AL 35121
(205)683-0298
gatobler@gmail.com

Travieso, Julio   <M1 WC>
15913 Countrybrook Street
Tampa, FL 33624
(813)963-3727
jutra98@aol.com

Weldon, Mark   <M1 WC>
2606 Acton Road
Birmingham, AL 35243
(205)913-3033
weldonm5@gmail.com

Yarce, Omar   <M1 WC>
3015 N Ocean Boulevard #6K
Fort Lauderdale, FL 33308
yarces@yahoo.com
(305)798-0849

OTHER LICENTIATES ON ROLL:

Castellanos, Sandra   <M2>
488 SW 126th Terrace
Davie, FL 33325
(754)442-4820
sandramcastellanosg@gmail.com

Dussan, Hedemarrie   <M2>
6248 SW 14th Street
West Miami, FL 33144
(305)812-0613
hedemarrie@gmail.com

Stough, Karen   <M2>
120 Hunters Hills Drive
Chelsea, AL 35043
(205)218-9781
raneyday54@aol.com

Yarce, Virginia   <M2>
3015 N Ocean Blvd Apt 6K
Fort Lauderdale, FL 33308
(954)213-9064
yarces@yahoo.com

OTHER CANDIDATES ON ROLL:

Acton, Avery   <M3>
222 Yellowhammer Drive
Alabaster, AL 35007
(205)441-9915
averyacton@gmail.com

Edwards, Scott   <M3>
226 Jasmine Drive
Alabaster, AL 35007
(205)358-7456
jedwards5316@bellsouth.net

Hernandez, Jhonathan   <M3>
7766 Greenwich Court E
Jacksonville, FL 32277
jhoto41@gmail.com
(786)508-8578

Marquez, Jose Ignacio   <M3>
8976 W Flagler Street
Miami, FL 33174
jimarquez.aviation@gmail.com

Nichols, Patrick   <M3>
508 Brook Highland Lane
Birmingham, AL 35242
(205)445-9238
patrick.nichols@dcial.com

Perez, Milagro   <M3>
923 SW 8th Court
Miami, FL 33130

Laura Reed   <M3>
3017 Banyan Hill Lane
Land O'Lakes, FL 34639
(813)401-2332
lola04@reagan.com

Seva, Judith   <M3>
7685 Tara Circle Apt 204
Naples, FL 34104
(239)269-3917
jclthgirl12@gmail.com

Straube, Edgar   <M3>
170 Stirrup Lane
Bonne, NC 28607
(828)719-8170
edgarstraube@aol.com

Straube, Iris   <M3>
170 Stirrup Lane
Boone, NC 28607
(828)719-8170
irisathala@yahoo.com

Thornton, Matt   <M3>
773 Cahaba Manor Trail
Pelham, AL 35124
(205)807-6795
mjamest47@gmail.com

Troyano, Sergio   <M3>
923 SW 8th Court
Miami, FL 33130

Hong Kong Presbytery
MISSION SYNOD

1.Church Number	2.Active	3.Total	4.Church School	5.Prof. of Faith	6.Gains	7.Losses	8.Children Baptized	9. OUR UNITED OUT-REACH	10. Total Out-Reach Giving	11. All Other Expenses	12. Total Income Received	13. Value Church Prop. 1=1000
1	2	3	4	5	6	7	8	9	10	11	12	13
Cheung-chau 8801	39	39	20	0	0	1	0	64	1,979	33,281	41,732	128
Kowloon Chapel 8803	78	297	20	0	1	5	0	769	28,568	238,524	267,766	513
Macau 8804	135	182	45	18	5	0	5	2,570	22,444	309,424	321,783	650
Mu Min 8810	310	459	30	5	11	4	3	595	10,014	397,502	421,792	0
N. Point Chapel 8805	45	114	39	0	0	0	0	2,855	1,071	137,226	189,788	100
Po Lam 8808	76	156	2	4	4	1	2	641	32,128	120,804	158,389	0
Shatin 8807	198	283	83	16	18	4	2	214	19,778	419,520	428,517	385
Tao Hsien 8806	300	559	100	0	0	5	0	2,563	157,918	930,772	998,637	2,881
Xi Lin 8809	90	169	0	0	1	1	0	256	6,579	83,978	189,242	0
Yao Dao 8811	105	231	45	19	1	0	0	1,666	45,086	268,340	382,963	0
TOTALS 10	1,376	2,489	384	62	41	21	12	12,193	325,565	2,939,371	3,400,609	4,657

CHURCHES, PASTORS, AND CLERKS:

Cheung Chau   (4C)MSHK8801
 11 On Wing Centre 2/F
 Pak She Back Street
 Cheung Chau, HONG KONG
 (852)2981-4933   <Hong Kong>
 cccpcmail@yahoo.com.hk
SS: Kelvin Ho   <M2>
 11 On Wing Centre 2/F
 Pak She Back Street
 Cheung Chau, HONG KONG
 (852)2981-4933
 kelvinskho@gmail.com
CL: Ho Sat Kit Kelvin
 11 On Wing Centre 2/F
 Pak She Back Street
 Cheung Chau, HONG KONG
 (852)2981-4933
 kelvinskho@gmail.com

Kowloon   (4WC)MSHK8803
 338-340 Castle Peak Road
 Flat D 2/FL
 Kowloon, HONG KONG
 (852)2386-6563   <Hong Kong>
 FAX: (852)3020-0365
 kcumber@cpckln.org
PA: Ting Bong Ha   <M1>
 338-340 Castle Peak Road
 Flat D 2/FL
 Kowloon, HONG KONG
 (852)2386-6563
 FAX: (852)3020-0365
 tingbongha@yahoo.com.hk
CL: Jesse Au
 338-340 Castle Peak Road
 Flat D 2/FL
 Kowloon, HONG KONG
 (852)2386-6563
 FAX: (852)3020-0365
 kcumber@cpckln.org

Macau   (4WC)MSHK8804
 258 Carlos D'Assumpcao
 Ed Kin Heng Long 4 Andar LMNP
 MACAU
 (853)2892-1702   <Macau>
 cpc_macau@yahoo.com.hk
PA: Jackson Tsui   <M1>
 258 Carlos D'Assumpcao
 Ed Kin Heng Long 4 Andar LMN
 MACAU
 tsuih@yahoo.com
 (853)2892-1702
CL: Mei Teng Lio
 258 Carlos D'Assumpcao
 Ed Kin Heng Long 4 Andar LMN
 MACAU
 (853)2892-1702
 cpc_macau@yahoo.com.hk

Mu Min   (C)MSHK8810
 2/F Fu Tung Shopping Center
 Tung Chung
 Lantau Island, HONG KONG
 (852)2109-1738   <Hong Kong>
 FAX: (852)2109-1737
 mmcpc@cumberland.org.hk
PA: So Tat Wing Patrick   <M1>
 2/F Fu Tung Shopping Center
 Tung Chung
 Lantau Island, HONG KONG
 (852)2109-1738
 FAX: (852)2109-1737
 cpctwso@yahoo.com.hk
CL: Kong Sing Chan
 2/F Fu Tung Shopping Center
 Tung Chung
 Lantau Island, HONG KONG
 (852)2109-1738
 FAX: (852)2109-1737
 mmcpc@cumberland.org.hk

North Point   (4WC)MSHK8805
 14-16 Tsat Tsz Mui Road
 1/Fl Block B
 North Point, HONG KONG
 (852)2562-2148   <Hong Kong>
 FAX: (852)2564-2898
 cpc.northpoint@gmail.com
PA: Li Chun Wai   <M1>
 1/Fl Block B
 14 TsatTsz Mui Road
 North Point, HONG KONG
 (852)2562-2148
 FAX: (852)2564-2898
 cwli2000hk@gmail.com
CL: Queenie Tang
 14-16 Tsat Tsz Mui Road
 1/Fl Block B
 North Point, HONG KONG
 (852)2562-2148
 FAX: (852)2564-2898
 cpc.northpoint@gmail.com

Po Lam   (ARC)MSHK8808
 Wing B&C, G/F, Ming Wik House
 Kin Ming Estate
 Tseung Kwan O NT, HONG KONG
 (852)2706-0111   <Hong Kong>
 FAX: (852)2706-0114
 polamcpc@yahoo.com.hk
SS: Sukie Tsui   <M2>
 Wing B & C
 G/F Ming Wik House
 Kin Ming Es
 (852)2706-0111
 FAX: (852)2706-0114
 sukiecpc@yahoo.com.hk
CL: Anna Wong
 Wing B&C G/F Ming Wik House
 Kin Ming Estate
 Tseung Kwan O NT, HONG KONG
 (852)2706-0111
 polamcpc@yahoo.com.hk

HONG KONG PRESBYTERY CONTINUED

Shatin (ARC)MSHK8807
  G/1F 251 Tin Sam Village
  Shatin NT, HONG KONG
  (852)2693-3444   <Hong Kong>
  FAX: (852)2607-2245
  cpcshatin@yahoo.com.hk
PA: Siu Chor Kong   <M1>
  G/1F 251 Tin Sam Village
  Shatin NT, HONG KONG
  (852)2693-3444
  FAX: (852)2607-2245
  cpccksiu@yahoo.com.hk
CL: Angelo Chui
  G/1F 251 Tin Sam Village
  Shatin NT, HONG KONG
  (852)2693-3444
  FAX: (852)2607-2245
  cpcshatin@yahoo.com.hk

Tao Hsien (4F)MSHK8806
  2/F Welland Plaza
  188 Nam Cheong Street
  Sham Shui Po, Kowloon, HONG KONG
  (852)2783-8923   <Hong Kong>
  FAX: (852)2771-2726
  thchurch@taohsien.org.hk
PA: Yuen Pui Chung Amos   <M1>
  2/F Welland Plaza
  188 Nam Cheong Street
  Sham Shui Po, Kowloon, HONG KONG
  (852)2783-8923
  FAX: (852)2771-2726
  revyuen@taohsien.org.hk
CL: Adays Lee
  2/F Welland Plaza
  188 Nam Cheong Street
  Sham Shui Po, Kowloon, HONG KONG
  (852)2783-8923
  FAX: (852)2771-2726
  thchurch@taohsien.org.hk

Xi Lin (4C)MSHK8809
  28 Hong Yip Street
  Yuen Long, HONG KONG
  (852)2639-9176   <Hong Kong>
  FAX: (853)2639-5620
  info@yuenlongchurch.org
PA: Siu Kei Hung Ella   <M>
  2/F Welland Plaza
  188 Nam Cheong Street
  Sham Shui Po, Kowloon, HONG KONG
  (852)2783-8923
  FAX: (852)2771-2726
  ellahung@gmail.com
CL: Loarinne Tang
  28 Hong Yip Street
  Yuen Long, HONG KONG
  (852)2639-9176
  FAX: (852)2639-5620
  loarinne@yuenlongchurch.org

Yao Dao (4C)MSHK8811
  CPC Yao Dao Primary School
  Tin Yuet Estate
  Tin Shui Wai, NT, HONG KONG
  (852)2617-7872   <Hong Kong>
  FAX: (852)2617-0287
  ydgrowth@gmail.com
PA: Samson Wong   <M>
  2/F Fu Tung Shopping Centre

Tung Chung
  Lantau Island NT, HONG KONG
  (852)2109-1738
  FAX: (852)2109-1737
  wongchishui@yahoo.com.hk
CL: Sum Lam
  CPC Yao Dao Primary School
  Tin Yuet Estate
  Tin Shui Wai, NT, HONG KONG
  (852)2617-7872
  FAX: (852)2617-0287
  ydgrowth@gmail.com

OTHERS ON MINISTERIAL ROLL:

Cheung, Luke   <M1 WC>
  2/F Welland Plaza
  188 Nam Cheong Street
  Sham Shui Po Kowloon, HONG KONG
  (852)3705-8390
  FAX: (852)3705-8901
  luke.cheung@gmail.com

Lee, Ted Shu Tak   <M1 WC>
  2/F Welland Plaza
  188 Nam Cheong Street
  Sham Shui Po, Kowloon, HONG KONG
  (852)2783-8923
  FAX: (852)2771-2726
  tedlee@taohsien.org.hk
Leung, Grace Siu Tim Yu   <M1 WC>
  2/F Welland Plaza
  188 Nam Cheong Street
  Sham Shui Po, Kowloon, HONG KONG
  (852)3705-8390
  FAX: (852)3705-8390
  yuleungsiutim@netvigator.com
Wong, So Li   <M1 WC>
  2/F Welland Plaza
  188 Nam Cheong Street
  Sham Shui Po, Kowloon, HONG KONG
  (852)3705-8390
  FAX: (852)3705-8390
  soliwong@gmail.com
Yeung, William   <M1 WC>
  2/F Welland Plaza
  188 Nam Cheong Street
  Sham Shui Po, Kowloon, HONG KONG
  (852)3705-8390
  FAX: (852)3705-8390
  williamyeung@gmail.com
Yu. Carver Tat Sum   <M1 WC>
  2/F Welland Plaza
  188 Nam Cheong Street
  Sham Shui Po, Kowloon, HONG KONG
  (852)3705-8390
  FAX: (852)3705-8390
  carver.yu@yahoo.com.hk

OTHER LICENTIATES ON ROLL:

Ho, Carmen   <M2>
  Tin Yuet Estate
  Tin Shui Wai NT, HONG KONG
  (852)2617-7872
  FAX: (852)2617-0287
  ho_carcar@yahoo.com.hk
Ho, Jessie   <M2>
  2/F Welland Plaza
  188 Nam Cheong Street
  Sam Shui Po

Kowloon, HONG KONG
  (852)2783-8923
  FAX: (852)2771-2726
  jesse@taoshien.org.hk
Lam, Janice   <M2>
  G/F & 1/F 251 Tin Sum Village
  Tai Wai, Shatin NT, HONG KONG
  (852)2693-3444
  FAX: (852)2607-2245
  janiceyeung929@gmail.com
Liu, Lai Yuet   <M2>
  2/F Fu Tung Shopping Centre
  Tung Chung
  Lantau Island NT, HONG KONG
  (852)2109-1738
  FAX: (852)2109-1737
  laiyuet0914@gmail.com
Mak, Daphne   <M2>
  28 Hong Uip Street
  Yuen Long. NT, HONG KONG
  (852)2639-9176
  daphne@yuenlongchurch.org
Sze, Yat Sung   <M2>
  Tin Yuet Estate
  Tin Shui Wai NT, HONG KONG
  (852)2617-7872
  FAX: (852)2617-0287
  yatsungs@yahoo.com.hk
Tang, Po Kau   <M2>
  G/1F, 251 Tin Sam Village
  Shatin, NT, HONG KONG
  (852)2693-3444
  FAX: (852)2607-2245
  cpc_pokau@yahoo.com.hk
Yuen, Susanna   <M2>
  2/F Welland Plaza
  188 Nam Cheong Street
  Sham Shui Po, Kowloon, HONG KONG
  (852)2783-8923
  FAX: (852)2771-2726
  susanna@yuenlongchurch.org
Yung, Karen Wing Man   <M2>
  Flat D 2/F
  338-340 Castle Peak Road
  Kowloon, HONG KONG
  (852)2386-6563
  FAX: (852)3020-0365
  yungyungmiss@yahoo.com.hk

OTHER CANDIDATES ON ROLL:

Cho, Ming Yan   <M3>
  Wing B & C, G/F, Ming Wik House
  Kin Ming Estate
  Tseung Kwan O, HONG KONG
  (852)2706-0111
  polamcpc@yahoo.com.hk
Chu, Jurice
  28 Hong Yip Street, Yuen Long,
  NT, HONG KONG
  (852)2639-9176
  jurice@yuenlongchurch.org
Fong, Kwok Fung   <M3>
  14-16 Tsat Tsz Mui Road
  1/F, Block B
  Northpoint, HONG KONG
  (852)2783-8923
  FAX: (852)2771-2726
  njrrr@icloud.com

HONG KONG PRESBYTERY CONTINUED

Fu, Pedro　　　　　　　　　　　<M3>
　258 Carlos D'Assumpcao Ed Kin Heng
　Log 4 A MACAU
　(852)2892-1702
　macaupedro@yahoo.com
Lam, Chris　　　　　　　　　　<M3>
　2/F Welland Plaza
　188 Nam Cheong Street
　Shamshuipo, Kowloon, HONG KONG
　(852)2783-8923
　FAX: (852)2771-2726
　chrislam@taohsien.org.hk
Lam, Dicky　　　　　　　　　　<M3>
　Flat D 2/F
　338-340 Castle Peak Road
　Kowloon, HONG KONG
　(852)2386-6563
　FAX (852)3020-0365
　lamdicky912@gmail.com
Lam, So Wah　　　　　　　　　<M3>
　G/F & 1/F, 251 Tin Sum Village
　Tai Wai, Shatin NT, HONG KONG
　(852)2693-3444
　FAX (852)2607-2245
　cpcshatin@yahoo.com.hk

Lee, Mei Wah　　　　　　　　　<M3>
　2/F Welland Plaza, 188 Nam Cheong St
　Sham Shui Po Kowloon HONG KONG
　(852)2783-8923
　FAX: (852)2771-2726
　vivianyuen@taohsien.org.hk
Lee, Siu Yee　　　　　　　　　<M3>
　258 Carlos D'Assumpcao Ed Kin Heng
　Log 4 A MACAU
　(852)2892-1702
　FAX: (852)2892-1702
　leisioi@yahoo.com.hk
Leung, Ho Wai　　　　　　　　<M3>
　G/F & 1/F, 251 Tin Sum Village
　Tai Wai, Shatin NT, HONG KONG
　(852)2693-3444
　FAX (852)2607-2245
　cpcshatin@yahoo.com.hk
So, Oldfield　　　　　　　　　<M3>
　2/F Welland Plaza
　188 Nam Cheong Street
　Shamshuipo, Kowloon, HONG KONG
　(852)2783-8923
　oldfield@taohsien.org.hk

Tam, Wai Sun　　　　　　　　　<M3>
　Wing B & C
　G/F Ming Wik House
　Kin Ming Es
　Tseung Kwan O, HONG KONG
　(852)2706-0111
　FAX: (852)2706-0114
　tsw428@gmail.com
Yan, Lok Yi　　　　　　　　　<M3>
　2/F Welland Plaza
　188 Nam Cheong Street
　Shamshuipo, Kowloon, HONG KONG
　(852)2783-8923
　foster@taohsien.org.hk

Hope Presbytery
SOUTHEAST SYNOD

GENERAL		MEMBERSHIP				CHANGES				FINANCES				
1.Church Number	2.Active	3.Total	4.Church School	5.Prof. of Faith	6.Gains	7.Losses	8.Children Baptized	9. OUR UNITED OUT-REACH	10. Total Out-Reach Giving	11. All Other Expenses	12. Total Income Received	13. Value Church Prop. 1=1000
	1	2	3	4	5	6	7	8	9	10	11	12	13
Allsboro	501	35	82	18	1	1	1	0	0	6,395	56,087	63,951	300
Baldwin Chapel	202	34	34	10	0	0	1	0	3,312	7,559	31,891	39,450	200
Faith	213	54	108	0	0	NRR	0	0	0	0	0	0	750
Florence, 1st	506	50	79	36	0	0	8	0	15,716	15,715	144,391	157,094	1,547
Hickory Grove	507	26	37	16	0	NRR	0	0	0	0	0	0	150
Hurricane	508	40	40	26	0	NRR	0	0	0	0	0	0	300
Maud	509	10	4	0	0	NRR	0	0	0	0	0	0	90
Mt. Hester	510	6	6	0	0	NRR	0	0	0	0	0	0	200
Mt. Pleasant	511	14	51	13	0	3	0	0	200	1,905	19,105	24,496	280
Nebo	512	28	35	10	0	1	2	0	0	1,317	27,890	42,924	1,250
Old Mt Bethel	513	32	34	29	0	NRR	0	0	0	0	0	0	60
Park Terrace	514	24	41	15	0	NRR	0	0	125	0	0	0	671
Rogersville 1st	517	112	286	77	1	1	5	0	12,000	117,519	290,906	190,729	1,131
Springfield	515	89	173	57	0	NRR	0	0	0	0	0	0	1,200
Union Hill	516	93	146	35	0	NRR	0	0	0	0	0	0	1,500
Welti	212	116	197	65	0	1	1	0	20,500	45,484	154,736	202,908	950
TOTALS	16	763	1,353	407	2	7	18	0	51,853	195,894	725,006	721,552	10,579

*Math error corrected. **Purged roll.　NRR - No Report Received

HOPE PRESBYTERY CONTINUED

CHURCHES, PASTORS, AND CLERKS:

Allsboro   (4MEWC)SEHO0501
  515 Iuka Road (mailing)
  1925 Allsboro Road (physical)
  Cherokee, AL 35616
  (256)360-2919   <Colbert>
SS: George Lee   <M1>
  314 Kingston Drive
  Florence, AL 35633
  (256)740-0809
  butchleeautos@yahoo.com
CL: Dale Johnson
  515 Iuka Road
  Cherokee, AL 35616
  (256)360-2973
  weplay97@aol.com

Baldwin Chapel   (4MEWC)SEHO0202
  381 County Road 404 (mailing)
  126 County Road 1153 (physical)
  Cullman, AL 35057
  (256)737-1850   <Cullman>
PA: Gary Carter   <M1>
  8311 County Road 1082
  Vinemont, AL 35179
  (256)443-8389
  garycarter51@gmail.com
CL: Bonnie Marty
  381 County Road 404
  Cullman, AL 35057
  (256)734-6399
  brmarty45@yahoo.com

Faith   (4WC)SEHO0213
  5821 County Road 1114 (mailing)
  Vinemont, AL 35179
  6880 AL Highway 157 (physical)
  Cullman, AL 35057
  (256)734-0893   <Cullman>
PA: Dudley Brock   <M1>
  490 County Road 1184
  Cullman, AL 35057
  (256)734-0893
  preacherbrock@att.net
CL: Philip Nickles
  5821 County Road 1114
  Vinemont, AL 35179
  (256)620-1977
  phillipnickles996@yahoo.com

Florence First   (4WC)SEHO0506
  PO Box 3297 (mailing)
  2422 Darby Drive (physical)
  Florence, AL 35630
  (256)766-0471   <Lauderdale>
  FAX: (256)766-0736
  fcpoffice@comcast.net
PA: Dwayne McDuff   <M1>
  9770 County Road 5
  Florence, AL 35633
  (256)764-6354
  FAX: (256)766-0736
  fcpdmcduff@comcast.net
CL: Jim Cassel
  1317 Cypress Mill Road
  Florence, AL 35630
  (256)760-1672
  jcassel1672@hotmail.com

Hickory Grove   (4MC)SEHO0507
  75 County Road 59
  Moulton, AL 35650
  (256)306-0025   <Lawrence>
  dhtatn4ybc@cs.com
SS: Andy Coffey   <M3>
  PO Box 88
  Bremen, AL 35033
  andycoffey3@gmail.com
  (259)590-4995
CL: Noah Williamson
  655 County Road 38
  Mount Hope, AL 35651
  (256)974-9413
  mwilliamson@lawrenceal.org

Hurricane   (4EWC)SEHO0508
  1331 County Road 86 (mailing)
  1000 County Road 156 (physical)
  Rogersville, AL 35652
  (256)247-7483   <Lauderdale>
PA: Jimmy R Cox   <M1>
  2250 County Road 156
  Anderson, AL 35610
  (256)710-1702
  dcox01@msn.com
CL: Bryan Belue
  1331 County Road 86
  Rogersville, AL 35652
  (256)247-7175
  rbeluebigboy@aol.com

Maud   (4MWC)SEHO0509
  2280 Maud Road (mailing)
  Gypsy Loop (physical)
  Cherokee, AL 35616
  (256)360-2811   <Colbert>
CL: Paula Pardue
  2280 Maud Road
  Cherokee, AL 35616
  (256)360-2811

Mt Hester   (4MEWC)SEHO0510
  PO Box 174 (mailing)
  14720 Mount Hester Road (physical)
  Cherokee, AL 35616
  ( )   <Colbert>
CL: Leigh Ann Malone
  2625 Sutton Hill Road
  Cherokee, AL 35616
  (256)359-6134
  leighmalone05@yahoo.com

Mt Pleasant   (4MC)SEHO0511
  30 Carolyn Road (mailing)
  13575 County Line Road (physical)
  Muscle Shoals, AL 35661
  (256)446-5397   <Colbert>
SS Frankie Raney   <M3>
  259 Ditto Lane
  Rogersville, AL 35652
  (256)284-8965
  franey@heavymachinesinc.com
CL: James Letsinger
  8285 2nd Street
  Leighton, AL 35646
  (256)446-9367

Nebo   (4MEWC)SEHO0512
  8630 Highway 101
  Lexington, AL 35648
  (256)577-5952   <Lauderdale>
  nebo9491@gmail.com
CL: Ronnie Barnett
  3686 Highway 101
  Rogersville, AL 35652
  (256)810-1807

Old Mt Bethel   (4C)SEHO0513
  County Road 51
  Rogersville, AL 35652
  ( )   <Lauderdale>
PA: Terry Herston   <M1>
  390 County Road 95
  Rogersville, AL 35652
  (256)247-3004
  tpaw51@gmail.com
CL: Tommy Word
  620 County Road 521
  Lexington, AL 35648
  (256)247-3182
  tword1956@gmail.com

Park Terrace   (4MEWC)SEHO0514
  100 E Wheeler Avenue
  Sheffield, AL 35660
  (256)383-8052   <Colbert>
  pastor@parkterracechurch.org
CL: Peggy Vickers
  112 Pasadena Avenue
  Muscle Shoals, AL 35661
  (256)383-1992
  pebobu95@mail.com

Rogersville First   (4WC)SEHO0517
  16751 Highway 72
  Rogersville, AL 35652
  (256)247-3339   <Lauderdale>
SS: James P Driskell   <M1 RT>
  16751 Highway 72
  Rogersville, AL 35652
  (256)648-6758
  patprespax@yahoo.com
CL: Suzanne Christopher
  16751 Highway 72
  Rogersville, AL 35652
  (256)710-7432
  19scd59@gmail.com

Springfield   (4MWC)SEHO0515
  5400 Highway 101
  Rogersville, AL 35652
  (256)247-1424   <Lauderdale>
  FAX: (256)247-1424
  kennymorgan330@hotmail.com
PA: Kenneth P Morgan   <M1>
  5400 Highway 101
  Rogersville, AL 35652
  (256)247-3890
  FAX: (256)247-1424
  kennymorgan330@hotmail.com
CL: Charles G Lash
  170 Meadow Ridge Lane
  Rogersville, AL 35652
  (256)247-0040

HOPE PRESBYTERY CONTINUED

Union Hill   (4MEWC)SEHO0516
6535 Bailey Road
Anderson, AL 35610
(256)233-1841   <Limestone>
PA: Charles Hood   <M1>
1200 County Road 519
Anderson, AL 35610
(256)229-6251
hooddad11@gmail.com
CL: Curtis Usery
28341 Easter Ferry Road
Lester, AL 35647
(256)232-9237

Welti   (4MWC)SEHO0212
8817 County Road 747
Cullman, AL 35055
(256)737-9138   <Cullman>
weltipastor@welticpchurch.com

PA: James L Peyton   <M1>
1455 County Road 643
Cullman, AL 35055
(256)735-3620
jakjpeyton@att.net
AP: Abigail Prevost   <M1>
9111 County Road 747
Cullman, AL 35055
(270)889-1985
abbyprevost@gmail.com
CL: Lee Holder
6589 County Road 747
Cullman, AL 35055
(256)962-3700
holder4bama@yahoo.com

OTHERS ON MINISTERIAL ROLL:

Deaton, John   <M1 WC>
277 School Lane
Springfield, PA 19064
(215)906-7067
deatonjr11@gmail.com

Malone, John W   <M1 RT>
3693 Highway 67 South
Sommerville, AL 35670
(256)778-8237
Parker, Susan   <M1 WC>
655 York Drive
Rogersville, AL 35652
(256)247-3877
park9301@bellsouth.net
Rodgers, Howard   <M1 RT>
336 County Road 1216
Vinemont, AL 35179
(256)739-6296
djbr421@yahoo.com

Japan Presbytery
MISSION SYNOD

GENERAL	MEMBERSHIP			CHANGES				FINANCES				
1.Church Number	2.Active	3.Total	4.Church School	5.Prof. of Faith	6.Gains	7.Losses	8.Children Baptized	9. OUR UNITED OUT-REACH	10. Total Out-Reach Giving	11. All Other Expenses	12. Total Income Received	13. Value Church Prop. 1=1000
	1	2	3	4	5	6	7	8	9	10	11	12	13
Asahi	8315	30	31	5	0	1	1	1	130	2,485	7,775	38,484	63
Den-en Mission	8310	14	35	2	0	0	0	0	36	31,129	516	51,212	70
EbinaShionNoOka	8311	103	162	40	0	1	4	3	373	10,342	90,523	10,086	74
Higashi Koganei	8301	35	33	4	0	1	3	0	144	2,990	57,625	45,752	130
Ichikawa Grace Mission Point	8314	20	28	5	0	0	0	0	71	928	54,512	34,661	45
Izumi	8312	34	47	8	2	2	4	0	68	904	31,812	32,323	39
Kibougaoka	8302	169	343	60	1	2	6	0	664	44,943	138,144	183,087	501
Koza	8303	400	1,119	200	20	25	22	0	2,219	123,718	593,589	717,306	1,536
KunitachiNozomi	8306	49	104	84	0	2	1	0	274	4,875	80,821	87,208	170
Megumi	8309	38	54	4	0	0	1	0	219	3,378	56,152	48,109	71
Naruse	8305	33	113	4	0	0	5	0	283	6,141	63,238	68,129	99
Sagamino	8304	27	52	8	0	0	1	0	169	3,290	54,487	53,414	63
Shibusawa	8307	32	100	10	0	1	0	0	339	8,345	65,608	65,223	255
TOTALS	13	984	2,221	434	23	35	48	4	4,989	243,468	1,294,802	1,434,994	3,116

*Math error corrected. **Purged roll.

CHURCHES, PASTORS, AND CLERKS:

Asahi Mission   (4C)MSJA8315
Uchida-Bldg
1-34-10 Honcho Tsurugamine
Asahi-ku Yokohama, Kanagawa-Ken
241-0826 JAPAN
(045)489-3721   <Japan>
FAX: (045)953-2588
info@asahi-ch.com

PA: Atsushi Suzuki   <M1>
53-17 Higashi Kibogaoka Asahi-ku
Yokohama, Kanagawa-ken
241-0826 JAPAN
(045)362-2603
FAX: (045)362-2603
asyuwa98@m10.alpha-net.ne.jp
CL: Yayoi Uchida
4-13-30 Seya
Seya-ky Yokohama-shi, Kanagawa-ken
241-0031 JAPAN

Den-en Mission   (4MC)MSJA8310
9-41-2 Kamitsuruma-honcho
Sagamihara-Shi, Kanagawa-Ken
252-0318 JAPAN
(042)744-6804   <Japan>
FAX: (042)744-6804
den-en.church@pc5.so-net.ne.jp

JAPAN PRESBYTERY CONTINUED

PA: Kazuhiko Furuhata   <M1>
9-41-15-310 Kamitsuruma-honcho
Sagamihara-shi, Kanagawa-ken
252-0318 JAPAN
(042)814-7802
FAX: (042)814-7802
cpc.furuhata@gmail.com
CL: Kazuhiko Furuhata
9-41-15-310 Kamitsuruma-honcho
Sagamihara-shi, Kanagawa-ken
252-0318 JAPAN
(042)814-7802
FAX: (042)814-7802
cpc.furuhata@gmail.com

Ebina Shion No Oka (4MWC)MSJA8311
3-17-57 Nakashinden
Ebina-shi, Kanagawa-ken
243-0422 JAPAN
(046)234-3426   <Japan>
ebinazion@gmail.com
PA: Yukio Tamai   <M1>
3-17-35-4 Nakashinden
Ebina-shi, Kanagawa-ken
243-0422 JAPAN
(046)234-3426
yukiotamai@icloud.com
CL: Eizo Matsura
5-6-11 Minamidai Minami-ky
Sagamihara, Kanagawa-ken
252-0314 JAPAN
(042)742-6315

Higashi Koganei   (4MWC)MSJA8301
2-14-16 Higashi-cho
Koganei-shi, Tokyo
184-0011 JAPAN
(042)231-1279   <Japan>
FAX: (042)231-1279
PA: Nobuko Seki   <M1>
2-14-16 Higashi-cho Koganei-Shi
Tokyo
184-0011 JAPAN
(042)231-1279
nobukoseki866@gmail.com
CL: Jyunko Kuchiki
4-15-20 Kajinocho
Koganei-shi, Tokyo
184-0002 JAPAN
(042)251-7781
FAX: (042)251-7781
kazenifukarete.j_k@docomo.ne.jp

Ichikawa Grace Mission (4MF)MSJA8314
1-11-20 Kokubu
Ichikawa-shi, Chiba-ken
272-0834 JAPAN
(047)369-7540   <Japan>
FAX: (047)369-7540
ichikawa-grace@mbi.nifty.com
PA: Yasuo Masuda   <M1>
1-11-20 Kokubu
Ichikawa-shi, Chiba-ken
272-0834 JAPAN
(047)369-7540
FAX: (047)369-7540
fwgc6854@mb.infoweb.ne.jp

CL: Yasuo Masuda
1-11-20 Kokubu
Ichikawa-shi, Chiba-ken
272-0834 JAPAN
(047)369-7540
FAX: (047)369-7540
fwgc6854@mb.infoweb.ne.jp

Izumi Mission   (4WC)MSJA8312
3-43-15 Izumi-cho Kita Izumi-ku
Yokohama, Kanagawa-ken
245-0024 JAPAN
(045)803-1749   <Japan>
FAX: (045)361-4351
izumi@kyokai.org
PA: Kenji Ushioda   <M1>
2-47-3 Akuwa-higashi Seya-ku
Yokohama, Kanagawa-ken
243-0023 JAPAN
(046)361-4351
ushioda@jc.ejnet.ne.jp
CL: Yukie Suzuki
22-3-2-203 Yayoidai Izumi-ku
Yokohama, Kanagawa-ken
245-0008 JAPAN
(045)392-9755
ykesuzuki@jasmine.ocn.ne.jp

Kibogaoka   (4WMC)MSJA8302
72-2 Naka Kibogaoka
Asahi-ku Yokohama, Kanagawa-ken
241-0825 JAPAN
(045)391-6038   <Japan>
FAX: (045)391-6653
PA: Ryuzo Matsuya   <M1>
72-2 Naka Kibogaoka Asahi-ku
Yokohama, Kanagawa-ken
241-0825 JAPAN
(045)364-8297
matuyar@yahoo.co.jp
CL: Kobun Kawamura
W-218 171 Naka Kibogaoka Asahi-ku
Yokohama, Kanagawa-ken
241-0825 JAPAN
(045)391-4299
ponicher@gmail.com

Koza   (4MWC)MSJA8303
2-14-1 Minami Rinkan
Yamato-shi, Kanagawa-ken
242-0006 JAPAN
(046)274-1370   <Japan>
FAX: (046)276-9685
cpckoza@koza-church.jp
PA: Masahiro Matsumoto   <M1>
2-14-1 Minami Rinkan
Yamato-shi, Kanagawa-ken
242-0006 JAPAN
(046)274-1370
matsumoto@koza-church.jp
AP: Ichiro Wada   <M1>
2-14-21 Minami Rinkan Yakmato-shi
Kanagawa-ken
242-0006 JAPAN
(046)275-9616
wada@koza-church.jp

AP: Ken Miyagi   <M2>
9-41-2 Kamitsuruma-honcho
Sagamihara-shi, Kanagawa-ken
252-0318 JAPAN
(080)4947-0026
miyagi@koza-church.jp
CL: Yutaka Shibata
1-18-3 Rinkan Yamato-shi
Kanagawa-ken
242-0003 JAPAN
(046)272-0579
shibata@koza-church.jp

Kunitachi Nozomi   (4MWC)MSJA8306
3-15-9 Higashi
Kunitachi-shi, Tokyo
186-0002 JAPAN
(042)572-7616   <Japan>
FAX: (042)572-7616
nozomi-ch@ceres.ocn.ne.jp
PA: Kenta Karasawa   <M1>
3-15-10 Higashi
Kunitachi-shi, Tokyo
186-0002 JAPAN
(042)575-5549
FAX: (042)575-5549
smbno6@gmail.com
CL: Shunji Kokubu
5-30-36 Kumegawa-cho
Higashimurayama-shi, Tokyo
189-0003 JAPAN
(042)208-7819
shunkodamo@yahoo.co.jp

Megumi   (4MWC)MSJA8309
3-355-4 Kami Kitadai Higashi
Yamato-shi, Tokyo
207-0023 JAPAN
(042)564-0593   <Japan>
megumikyokai@gmail.com
SS: Keishi Ishitsuka   <M1 RT>
6-13-31 NishiOizumi
Nerima-ky, Tokyo
178-0065 JAPAN
(080)5896-1139
keishi@gmail.com
CL: Shigeru Yanagawa
2-68-25 Sunagawa-cho
Tachikawa-shi, Tokyo
190-003 JAPAN
(042)536-5332
punisumo33noa@tbz.t-com.ne.jp

Naruse   (4WC)MSJA8305
7-20-12 Tamagawa Gakuen
Machida-shi, Tokyo
194-0041 JAPAN
(042)725-9909
FAX: (042)725-9909   <Japan>
cpc-naruse@nifty.com
PA: Masanori Taira   <M1>
1-11-13 Higashi Tamagawagakuen
Machida-shi, Tokyo
194-0042 JAPAN
(042)813-0997
non.slope@gmail.com

JAPAN PRESBYTERY CONTINUED

CL: Kazuyuki Yamaguchi
  7-61 Sumiyoshidai Aoba-ku
  Yokohama-shi, Kanagawa-ken
  227-0035 JAPAN
  (045)963-5278
  kazuyamaguchi1@gmail.com

_____

Sagamino   (4MWC)MSJA8304
  4-13-24 Higashihara
  Zama-shi, Kanagawa-ken
  252-0004 JAPAN
  (046)255-6441   <Japan>
  FAX: (046)255-6441
  sagamino.church@gmail.com
PA: Takehiko Miyai   <M1>
  4-13-24 Higashihara Zama-shi
  Kanagawa-ken
  252-0004 JAPAN
  (046)255-6441
  FAX: (046)255-6441
  tacke.m@gmail.com
CL: Akimasa Nakano
  6222-16 Izumicho Izumi-ku
  Yokohama-shi Kanagawa-ken
  245-0016 JAPAN
  (046)884-3093
  nakano.a.ipt@gmail.com

_____

Shibusawa   (4MWC)MSJA8307
  1-8-50 Magarimatsu
  Hadano-shi, Kanagawa-ken
  259-1321 JAPAN
  (046)387-1203   <Japan>
  FAX: (046)387-1203
  keitaro_o@hotmail.com

PA: Keitaro Ohi   <M1>
  1-8-50 Magarimatsu
  Hadano-shi, Kanagawa-ken
  259-1321 JAPAN
  (046)387-1203
  FAX: (046)387-1203
  keitaro_o@hotmail.com
CL: Shinobu Araki
  313 Daia Paresu Hontsugi Dai2
  779-1 Mita Atsugi-shi, Kanagawa-ken
  243-0211 JAPAN
  araki_shinobu@yahoo.co.jp

_____

OTHERS ON MINISTERIAL ROLL:

Arase, Makihiko   <M1 PR>
  1-350-13 Ogawamachi
  Kodaira-shi, Tokyo
  187-0032 JAPAN
  (080)6636-1960
  viator@cb3.so-net.ne.jp
Asayama, Masaharu   <M1 RT>
  6-3-2-308 Toyogaoka
  Tama-shi, Tokyo
  206-0031 JAPAN
  (042)373-2710
  asa@ipcc-21.com
Hamazaki, Takashi   <M1 RT>
  1551-1-202 Inokuchi
  Nakai-cho Ashigarakami-gun
  Kanagawa-ken
  259-0151 JAPAN
  (046)543-8550
  gen22-14@qf7.so-net.ne.jp

Ikushima, Michinobu   <M1 RT>
  2074 Nakashinden
  Ebina-Shi, Kanagawa-Ken
  243-0422 JAPAN
  (046)232-9888
  m.ikushima@tbz.t-com.ne.jp
Katsuki, Shigeru   <M1 RT>
  3-8-77 Fujimicho Hihgashimurayami-shi
  189-0024 JAPAN
  (042)315-5382
  shigeru.katsuki@nifty.com

_____

OTHER LICENTIATES ON ROLL:

_____

OTHER CANDIDATES ON ROLL:

Yohena, Takeshi   <M3>
  7-7-44 Ryokuen Izumi-ku
  Yokohama-shi
  245-0002 JAPAN
  (045)814-4537
  tyohena@uc.catv-yokohama.ne.jp

Korean Presbytery of the Southeast
SYNOD OF THE SOUTHEAST

GENERAL		MEMBERSHIP			CHANGES					FINANCES			
1.Church Number	2.Active	3.Total	4.Church School	5.Prof. of Faith	6.Gains	7.Losses	8.Children Baptized	9. OUR UNITED OUT-REACH		10. Total Out-Reach Giving	11. All Other Expenses	12. Total Income Received	13. Value Church Prop. 1=1000
1	2	3	4	5	6	7	8	9		10	11	12	13
Agape	2127	38	43	5	0	0	1	0	0	2,400	17,600	23,000	0
Walking w/God	2125	112	126	14	0	23	20	0	0	10,500	138,000	149,000	2
TOTALS	**2**	**150**	**169**	**19**	**0**	**23**	**21**	**0**	**0**	**12,900**	**155,600**	**172,000**	**2**

CHURCHES, PASTORS, AND CLERKS:

_____

Agape   (4C)SEKP2127
  11575 Jones Bridge Road
  Johns Creek, GA 30022
  (678)462-7526
PA: Jin Koo Kang   <M1>
  2310 His Way
  Lawrenceville, GA 30044
  (678)462-7526
  agatopia@hanmail.net
CL: Kwan Soo Kim
  805 Mount Royal Cove
  Lawrenceville, GA 30043
  (678)779-2692
  airworldservicellc@gmail.com

_____

Walking with God   (4WC)SEKP2125
  3299 Highway 120
  Duluth, GA 30096
  (678)600-2787
PA: Enoch Jaehyung Yu   <M1>
  2012 Shenley Park Lane
  Duluth, GA 30097
  (678)600-2787
  jaeyu117@yahoo.com
CL: Seungho Chung
  2040 Noblin Ridge Trail NW
  Duluth, GA 30097
  (678)799-0403

_____

OTHERS ON MINISTERIAL ROLL:

Choi, Sean   <M1 WC>
  1284 New Liberty Way
  Braselton, GA 30517
  (901)826-2993
  esloveh2@hotmail.com
Kim, Yoong S   <M1 WC>
  2770 Farmstead Way
  Suwanee, GA 30024
  (901)490-8973
  yoongkim1934@yahoo.com

OTHER CANDIDATES ON ROLL:

Park, Young Kwang   \<M3\>
3340 Bentbill Crossing
Cummings, GA 30041
(770)912-8477
barkmogun@gmail.com

Park, Young Jin   \<M3\>
3340 Bentbill Crossing
Cummings, GA 30041
(731)845-3173
084657@gmail.com

Missouri Presbytery
GREAT RIVERS SYNOD

GENERAL		MEMBERSHIP			CHANGES				FINANCES			
1.Church Number	2.Active	3.Total	4.Church School	5.Prof. of Faith	6.Gains	7.Losses	8.Children Baptized	9. OUR UNITED OUT-REACH	10. Total Out-Reach Giving	11. All Other Expenses	12. Total Income Received	13. Value Church Prop. 1=1000
	1	2	3	4	5	6	7	8	9	10	11	12	13
Bethel	4102	6	7	7	0	0	0	0	0	4,866	7,873	11,879	10
Elk Creek	4304	19	19	11	0	NRR	0	0	0	0	0	0	75
God's Grace	4104	25	28	0	0	NRR	0	0	0	0	0	0	100
Happy Home	4306	15	22	0	0	0	0	0	0	2,204	16,983	17,852	175
Harmony	4203	14	43	6	0	NRR	0	0	0	0	0	0	80
Hopewell	4105	28	34	15	0	NRR	0	0	3,000	0	0	0	310
Korean	4316	25	46	23	0	7	5	0	500	8,487	40,178	48,666	0
Mansfield	4308	54	73	30	0	NRR	0	0	0	0	0	0	75
Marshall	4210	82	209	21	0	2	4	0	10,328	49,203	90,327	103,282	1,100
New Hope (DeC)	4309	17	17	9	0	NRR	0	0	0	0	0	0	60
Orange	4108	50	50	50	0	0	2	0	8,400	24,905	54,223	90,174	826
Phillipsburg	4311	9	13	6	0	NRR	0	0	0	0	0	0	150
Pierson	4312	8	12	6	0	NRR	0	0	1,684	0	0	0	150
Pleasant Grove	4109	10	55	0	0	NRR	0	0	0	0	0	0	30
Salem	4216	9	12	0	0	NRR	0	0	0	0	0	0	150
Seymour	4313	15	29	6	0	NRR	0	0	0	0	0	0	50
Shawnee Mound	4111	3	35	4	0	0	1	0	870	1,447	5,971	8,705	60
Spring Creek*	4113	24	38	8	0	0	4	0	4,450	11,949	16,728	31,722	200
Springfield 1st	4314	24	36	28	0	0	2	0	0	7,222	34,981	44,423	1,500
Warrensburg	4115	26	40	10	0	0	1	0	1,500	2,030	22,901	25,885	500
White Oak Pond**	4315	108	128	60	0	0	3	2	18,278	35,800	125,396	182,776	2,438
TOTALS	21	571	946	300	0	9	22	2	49,010	148,113	415,561	565,364	8,039

*Math error corrected. **Purged roll. NRR - No Report Received

---

CHURCHES, PASTORS, AND CLERKS:

Bethel   (2C)GRMI4102
  14621 Lawrence 1032 (mailing)
  Sarcoxie, MO 64862
  Crossroads Lawrence 1030 & Lawrence 2170 (physical)
  Wentworth, MO
  (417)285-6571   \<Lawrence\>
PA: Tim Steeley   \<M1\>
  PO Box 281
  Mt Vernon, MO 65712
  (417)466-4345
  timsteeley99@gmail.com

CL: Lana Moore
  14621 Lawrence 1032
  Sarcoxie, MO 64862
  (417)285-6571
  lanajeanmoore@hotmail.com

Elk Creek   (4MEC)GRMI4304
  7423 County Road 3730 (mailing)
  Peace Valley, MO 65788
  US Highway 160 E (physical)
  West Plains, MO 65775
  (417)257-0983   \<Howell\>
OD: Dale Kester   \<M5\>
CL: Cindy Rasor
  7423 County Road 3730
  Peace Valley, MO 65788
  (417)256-7353
  rrasor@centurytel.net

God's Grace   (4MC)GRMI4104
  415 Water Street (mailing)
  417 W Water Street (physical)
  Greenfield, MO 65661
  ( )   \<Dade\>
CL: Debra Kay Bartlett
  423 Water Street
  Greenfield, MO 65661
  (417)637-5678
  debrakaybartlett@gmail.com

Happy Home   (4C)GRMI4306
  510 S Newport Avenue (mailing)
  5604 State Highway ZZ (physical)
  Conway, MO 65632
  ( )   \<Webster\>

MISSOURI PRESBYTERY CONTINUED

CL: Rex Luallin
510 S Newport Avenue
Conway, MO 65632
(417)589-3804

_____

Harmony (4WC)GRMI4203
3508 Scott Street (mailing)
Saint Joseph, MO 64507
SE State Road Z (physical)
San Antonio, MO 64443
(816)279-0733 <Buchanan>
orvalschafer@aol.com
OD: Marion Cannon <M5>
110 Ausman Drive Apt 25
Maysville, MO 64469
(816)449-2437
orvalschafer@aol.com
CL: Viola Schafer
3508 Scott Street
Saint Joseph, MO 64507
(816)279-0733
orvalschafer@aol.com

_____

Hopewell (4EWC)GRMI4105
248 NE 50th Road (mailing)
273 NE 50th Road (physical)
Lamar, MO 64759
(417)682-2396 <Barton>
FAX: (417)682-3514
parrishron@att.net
OD: George Haag <M5>
301 Gulf Street
Lamar, MO 64759
(417)682-3876
CL: Peggy Phipps
248 NE 50th Road
Lamar, MO 64759
(417)682-5909

_____

Korean (4C)GRMI4316
4216 Charleston Avenue
Springfield, MO 65408
(417)888-0442
hesed-park@hanmail.net
PA: Sang Hoon Park <M1>
2980 W Melbourne Street
Springfield, MO 65810
(417)888-0442
hesed-park@hanmail.net
CL: Session Clerk Korean
4216 Charleston Avenue
Springfield, MO 65408

_____

Mansfield (4MEC)GRMI4308
PO Box 673 (mailing)
307 S Phelps Avenue (physical)
Mansfield, MO 65704
( ) <Wright>
CL: Leon Veenstra
4680 Highway F
Hartville, MO 65667
(417)741-7408
veenstra@getgoin.net

_____

Marshall (4MWC)GRMI4210
1000 S Miami
Marshall, MO 65340
(660)886-2402 <Saline>
pastor_randy_shannon@yahoo.com

PA: Randy Shannon <M1>
30282 Highway H
Marshall, MO 65340
(660)886-9454
pastor_randy.shannon@yahoo.com
CL: Karen Guthrie
1506 Broadmoor Lane
Marshall, MO 65340
(660)886-5797
kguthrie7878@gmail.com

_____

New Hope (DeC) (4WC)GRMI4309
230 County Road 2630 (mailing)
Dent County Road 6200 (physical)
Salem, MO 65560
( ) <Dent>
PA: Michael Reno <M1>
52 Rolla Gardens
Rolla, MO 65401
(573)578-5321
rollarenomike@gmail.com
CL: Kim Moser
1862 Highway BB
Jadwin, MO 65501
(573)729-2780

_____

Orange (4WC)GRMI4108
18540 Lawrence 1247 (mailing)
Marionville, MO 65705
15743 Highway K (physical)
Aurora, MO 65605
(417)678-5220 <Lawrence>
PA: D Kevin Vanderlaan <M1>
17246 Highway K
Aurora, MO 65605
(217)620-2723
pastorkevin2@gmail.com
CL: Leah Estes
18540 Lawrence 1247
Marionville, MO 65705
(417)723-8033
lestesx5@centurytel.net

_____

Phillipsburg (4WC)GRMI4311
16889 Miller Drive (mailing)
Grover Street (physical)
Phillipsburg, MO 65722
( ) <Laclede>
OD: Chris Wilson <M5>
745 Birchwood
Marshfield, MO 65706
(417)425-0863
chris@springfieldbsu.org
CL: Linda House
16889 Miller Drive
Phillipsburg, MO 65722
(417)425-4806
l.burdhouse@gmail.com

_____

Pierson (4C)GRMI4312
12754 State Highway M (mailing)
Billings, MO 65610
45129 State Highway 413 (physical)
Billings, MO 65610
(417)369-2104 <Stone>
CL: Kary Crumpley
1513 Crumpley Drive
Marionville, MO 65705
(417)839-3552
karycrumpley@gmail.com

_____

Pleasant Grove (4C)GRMI4109
836 SE Y Highway (mailing)
891 SE Y Highway (physical)
Knob Noster, MO 65336
( ) <Johnson>
CL: Dana Smith
836 Southeast Y Highway
Knob Noster, MO 65536
(660)563-9739
dsmith@knobnoster.k12.mo.us

_____

Salem (4WC)GRMI4216
211 NW County Road OO (mailing)
382 NW County Road H (physical)
Warrensburg, MO 64093
( ) <Johnson>
OD: Lenny Carver <M5>
Box 852
Marshall, MO 65340
CL: Anne Patrick
211 NW County Road OO
Warrensburg, MO 64093
(660)747-8902
apatrick52@hotmail.com

_____

Seymour (4C)GRMI4313
PO Box 40 (mailing)
222 Main Street (physical)
Seymour, MO 65746
(417)935-2235 <Webster>
OD: Sam Burt <M5>
102 E Summit Avenue
Seymour, MO 65746
(417)735-2759
CL: Denise Burt
102 E Summit Avenue
Seymour, MO 65746
(417)300-6451
gerrydburt@gmail.com

_____

Shawnee Mound (4WC)GRMI4111
30 NW 1150 Road
Chilhowee, MO 64733
( ) <Henry>
PA: Mary Anna Townsend <M1>
1123 Tyler Avenue
Warrensburg, MO 64093
(660)909-5966
wrenhse1123@gmail.com
CL: Doris Hunter
18 NW 1150 Road
Chilhowee, MO 64733
(660)885-3709
dfhunter@embarqmail.com

_____

Spring Creek (4EWC)GRMI4113
PO Box 281 (mailing)
Stockton, MO 65785
Hwy 123 & Hwy A Junction (physical)
Dunnegan, MO 65640
( ) <Polk>
OD: Scott Garner <M5>
1403 E Primrose Lane
Republic, MO 65738
(417)732-4218
scottygarner@gmail.com
CL: Larry Nottingham
PO Box 281
Stockton, MO 65785
(417)276-3792
mopresbyterycpc2@yahoo.com

MISSOURI PRESBYTERY CONTINUED

_____
Springfield First   (4MWC)GRMI4314
   4216 S Charleston Avenue
   Springfield, MO 65804
   (417)883-4248
   reformedminister@yahoo.com
SS: Eddie Cintron   <M3>
   5695 S Franklin
   Springfield, MO 65810
   (417)894-1480
   eddiecintron7@gmail.com
CL: Carol Fare
   302 N Market Street
   Nixa, MO 65714
   (417)725-2775
   cjfare52@sbcglobal.net

_____
Warrensburg   (4WC)GRMI4115
   201 Grover Street
   Warrensburg, MO 64093
   (660)747-3021   <Johnson>
CL: Julie Montgomery
   48 NE 500th Road
   Warrensburg, MO 64093
   (660)441-5270
   mjmontgomery@embarqmail.com

_____
White Oak Pond   (4MWC)GRMI4315
   16551 Highway 5
   Lebanon, MO 65536
   (417)532-5049   <Laclede>
   wopcpc@whiteoakpond.org
PA: Neal Wilkinson   <M1>
   296 Sunset Drive
   Lebanon, MO 65536
   (615)934-7342
   nwilkinson@whiteoakpond.org
AP: Jill Carr   <M1>
   1601 Arbour Drive
   Lebanon, MO 65536
   (417)532-6760
   dig.micah.6.8@gmail.com
CL: Nancy Stokes
   16549 Highway 5
   Lebanon, MO 65536
   (417)532-5049

_____
OTHERS ON MINISTERIAL ROLL:

Ang, John   <M1 HR>
   5843 S Farm Road 157
   Springfield, MO 65810
   (417)886-3487
   pastorcares@yahoo.com
Appling, John   <M1 WC>
   1722 S Fairway Avenue
   Springfield, MO 65804
   (417)877-4643
   pegblessings@sbcglobal.net
Appling, Peggy   <M1 WC>
   1722 S Fairway
   Springfield, MO 65804
   (417)877-4643
   pegblessings@sbcglobal.net

Brown, Dale M   <M1 HR>
   714 W Leyda Street
   West Plains, MO 65775
   (417)257-0983
   pastorbrown44@yahoo.com
Crawshaw, Randy   <M1 WC>
   136 NE 1271 Road
   Knob Noster, MO 65336
   (660)563-5149
   randy_crawshaw@yahoo.com
Hansen, Terry   <M1 HR>
   319 Forest Drive
   Humboldt, TN 38343
   (417)533-8106
   thansen@whiteoakpond.org
Harris, Edward   <M1 HR>
   10000 Wornall Road Apt 2315
   Kansas City, MO 64114
   (816)214-8977
   ed121@kcrr.com
Ostrander, Shirley   <M1 WC>
   24069 New Willow Drive #5
   Lebanon, MO 65536
   (901)827-4830
Plachte, Richard   <M1 HR>
   615 Grover Street
   Warrensburg, MO 64093
   (660)441-4427
   rap@aerobiz.org
Rodden, Linda   <M1 WC>
   PO Box 582
   Phillipsburg, MO 65536
   (417)588-2207
   lindaleerodden@centurylink.net
Roedder, Unhui Grace   <M1 WC>
   419 S Jonathan Avenue
   Springfield, MO 65802
   (417)494-6491
   kimroedder@hotmail.com
Scott, Lisa   <M1 WC>
   ADDRESS ON FILE
   (816)332-0604
   lascott1979@att.net

_____
OTHER LICENTIATES ON ROLL:
_____
OTHER CANDIDATES ON ROLL:

Hudson, Jennifer   <M3>
   716 Apache Drive
   Marshall, MO 65340
   (660)631-3893

Murfreesboro Presbytery
TENNESSEE SYNOD

	GENERAL	MEMBERSHIP			CHANGES				FINANCES				
	1.Church Number	2.Active	3.Total	4.Church School	5.Prof. of Faith	6.Gains	7.Losses	8.Children Baptized	9. OUR UNITED OUT-REACH	10. Total Out-Reach Giving	11. All Other Expenses	12. Total Income Received	13. Value Church Prop. |1=1000
	1	2	3	4	5	6	7	8	9	10	11	12	13
Algood	7201	25	27	0	0	2	0	0	0	3,647	37,739	86,745	410
Banks	7202	8	17	7	0	3	0	0	1,000	1,175	30,270	22,044	344
Bates Hill	7203	52	77	30	0	0	0	0	8,328	14,449	63,404	84,467	325
Beech Grove	7204	26	26	12	0	NRR	0	0	0	0	0	0	597
Belvidere	7205	4	5	4	0	0	0	0	0	312	4,970	5,379	60
Blues Hill	7207	11	15	11	0	0	2	0	2,809	5,394	27,218	28,089	80
Cloyd's	7208	107	107	48	0	NRR	0	0	5,400	0	0	0	2,500
Commerce*	7209	50	50	50	2	0	2	3	3,000	6,800	47,200	54,000	750
Cookeville 1st	7210	552	632	230	4	11	14	0	44,707	90,383	346,087	453,447	4,600
Cowan	7211	73	98	55	0	2	1	0	6,018	17,700	75,223	108,383	1,880
Dibrell	7212	10	10	11	0	0	1	0	0	0	10,926	11,443	40
Dry Valley	7213	6	9	7	0	0	0	0	0	3,900	11,788	10,323	10
Goshen	7214	49	82	26	0	0	2	0	3,500	5,502	57,230	51,305	874
Gum Creek	7215	20	20	10	0	NRR	0	0	0	0	0	0	130
Harmony	7216	58	93	34	1	3	1	0	10,391	16,034	86,958	132,959	1,041
Hickory Valley	7251	9	9	21	0	NRR	0	0	0	0	0	0	0
Hillsboro	7217	16	18	6	0	NRR	0	0	0	0	0	0	250
Jerusalem	7218	39	39	26	0	0	1	0	8,811	30,105	72,370	88,185	275
LaGuardo	7219	25	25	3	0	NRR	0	0	0	0	0	0	150
Lebanon	7220	225	277	145	1	7	11	0	27,950	44,158	383,399	497,505	4,000
Liberty**	7222	69	90	25	0	8	40	0	10,761	22,351	66,258	107,614	989
Livingston 1st	7223	12	15	0	0	NRR	0	0	0	0	0	0	80
LuzD.L.Naciones	7252	19	26	19	0	NRR	0	0	0	0	0	0	85
Manchester	7224	63	206	40	0	0	5	0	19,617	29,582	140,858	196,171	1,338
McMinnville	7225	8	8	5	0	NRR	0	0	1,363	0	0	0	45
Monteagle*	7227	8	8	0	0	3	0	0	0	1,770	49,557	28,132	144
Mt. Carmel	7228	7	7	0	0	NRR	0	0	1,508	0	0	0	250
Mt. Tabor	7230	28	28	12	0	NRR	0	0	4,221	0	0	0	138
Mt. Vernon	7231	32	37	26	0	NRR	0	0	0	0	0	0	410
Murfreesboro	7232	91	329	87	0	0	16	1	10,633	35,664	207,072	240,029	2,928
New Hope	7233	51	81	14	0	NRR	0	0	1,200	0	0	0	1,022
Old Zion	7234	11	11	11	0	0	0	0	4,347	4,930	28,990	43,400	300
Owens Chapel	7235	38	64	14	0	0	3	0	1,000	5,485	88,408	83,976	230
Providence	7238	14	14	38	0	NRR	0	0	0	0	0	0	150
Rock Island	7274	14	14	0	0	0	1	0	0	1,941	36,283	41,793	250
Rockvale	7239	64	135	30	2	2	7	0	4,000	8,015	87,873	93,688	1,401
Rocky Glade	7240	62	71	55	0	7	7	3	3,500	17,300	45,500	65,000	600
Ruth Chapel	7241	2	2	0	0	NRR	0	0	0	0	0	0	100
Sewanee	7242	23	29	13	0	NRR	0	0	2,625	0	0	0	245
Smithville	7243	123	123	100	0	0	9	0	21,000	56,377	168,384	219,634	2,600
Suggs Creek	7244	6	6	0	0	0	3	0	3,748	3,747	27,748	34,317	120
Union Hill	7246	36	36	36	0	0	1	0	0	10,475	45,641	65,036	250
Watertown	7247	18	18	13	0	NRR	0	0	1,000	0	0	0	479

Murfreesboro Presbytery   (Continued)
TENNESSEE SYNOD

GENERAL	MEMBERSHIP			CHANGES				FINANCES				
1.Church Number	2.Active	3.Total	4.Church School	5.Prof. of Faith	6.Gains	7.Losses	8.Children Baptized	9. OUR UNITED OUT-REACH	10. Total Out-Reach Giving	11. All Other Expenses	12. Total Income Received	13. Value Church Prop. 1=1000
1	2	3	4	5	6	7	8	9	10	11	12	13
Winchester 1st	7249	566	998	400	1	22	9	2	64,009	110,764	527,173	646,054	3,500
TOTALS	44	2,730	3,992	1,674	11	70	136	9	276,446	547,960	2,774,527	3,499,118	35,970

*Math error corrected. **Purged roll.   NRR - No Report Received

---

CHURCHES, PASTORS, AND CLERKS:

Algood   (4WC)TNMU7201
 3617 Burton Cove Road (mailing)
 Cookeville, TN 38506
 Corner Harp & Main Street (physical)
 Algood, TN 38506
 ( )   <Putnam>
PA: Richard Bond   <M1>
 136 N 2nd Avenue
 Algood, TN 38506
 (931)319-4399
 erbond@frontier.net
CL: E Burton
 3617 Burton Cove Road
 Cookeville, TN 38506
 (931)537-6661
 e_burton@frontier.com

Banks   (4MWC)TNMU7202
 846 Avenue (mailing)
 2933 Banks Pisgah Road (physical)
 Smithville, TN 37166
 ( )   <DeKalb>
SS: Greg Whaley   <M2>
 4970 Comstock Road
 Chapel Hill, TN 37034
 (931)364-7637
 grewha@mail.com
CL: John Slickmeyer
 3041 Banks Pisgah Road
 Smithville, TN 37166
 jslickjr@gmail.com

Bates Hill   (4MEWC)TNMU7203
 308 W Greenhll Road (mailing)
 6111 Old Nashville Highway (physical)
 Mc Minnville, TN 37110
 (931)939-3235   <Warren>
 cavecrew1979@gmail.com
SS Robby Black   <M5>
 9957 Nashville Highway
 Mc Minnville, TN 37110
CL: William R Black
 9980 Nashville Highway
 Mc Minnville, TN 37110
 (931)743-9809
 cavecrew1979@gmail.com

Beech Grove   (4MC)TNMU7204
 PO Box 26 (mailing)
 471 Oscar Crowell Road (physical)
 Beechgrove, TN 37018
 (931)394-2387   <Coffee>

CL: Crystal B Brandon
 269 French Brantley Road
 Wartrace, TN 37183
 (931)394-2387
 no_tenn@hotmail.com

Belvidere   (4WC)TNMU7205
 Walnut Hill Road
 Belvidere, TN 37306
 ( )   <Franklin>
PA: Joseph H Butler   <M1>
 56 Cline Ridge Road
 Winchester, TN 37398
 (931)224-8423
 jhbu737@bellsouth.net
CL: Alton Smith
 123 Post Oak Road
 Belvidere, TN 37306
 starsmith53@hotmail.com

Blues Hill   (4MWC)TNMU7207
 7292 Short Mountain Road
 Mc Minnville, TN 37110
 ( )   <Warren>
CL: Naomi Smith
 522 Smith Town Road
 Mc Minnville, TN 37110
 (931)939-2435
 memesmith@blomand.net

Cloyd's   (4WC)TNMU7208
 PO Box 277 (mailing)
 595 West Division (physical)
 Mt Juliet, TN 37121
 (615)758-7434   <Wilson>
PA: Michael Reese   <M1>
 114 Palmer Road
 Lebanon, TN 37090
 (615)443-0457
 michaelhreese@bellsouth.net
AP: Kenny Butcher   <M1>
 403 Kalye Court
 Mt Juliet, TN 37122
 (615)719-1887
 butcherkenny@yahoo.com
CL: Vickie Hibdon
 7141 Lebanon Road
 Mount Juliet, TN 37122
 (615)444-6498

Commerce   (4WC)TNMU7209
 351 Borum Road (mailing)
 4260 S Commerce Road (physical)
 Watertown, TN 37184
 (615)237-9409   <Wilson>
 crutchmckinwater@aol.com

SS: Denny C Shepard   <M1>
 8514 Newsom Station Road
 Nashville, TN 37221
 (615)662-1114
CL: Jacki Crutcher
 351 Borum Road
 Watertown, TN 37184
 (615)237-3310
 crutchmckinwater@aol.com

Cookeville First   (4WC)TNMU7210
 565 E 10th Street
 Cookeville, TN 38501
 (931)526-6585   <Putnam>
 FAX: (931)528-2270
 charles@cookevillecpchurch.org
PA: Christian Smith   <M1>
 1094 Tanglewood Drive
 Cookeville, TN 38501
 (931)265-8896
 csmith2490@gmail.com
CL: Stacey Byers
 1713 Tyler Drive
 Cookeville, TN 38501
 (931)2650715
 snlbyers@gmail.com

Cowan   (4MC)TNMU7211
 PO Box 277 (mailing)
 206 Cowan Street W (physical)
 Cowan, TN 37318
 (931)967-7431   <Franklin>
 cowancpchurch@bellsouth.net
PA: Ronnie M Pittenger   <M1>
 207 Cowan Street W
 Cowan, TN 37318
 (615)832-8832
 cspronnie@gmail.com
CL: Cindy Henn
 PO Box 277
 Cowan, TN 37318
 (931)967-7431
 cowancpchurch@bellsouth.net

Dibrell   (4C)TNMU7212
 128 Mitchell Road (mailing)
 Mike Muncey Road (physical)
 McMinnville, TN 37110
 ( )   <Warren>
SS Robby Black   <M5>
 9957 Nashville Highway
 Mc Minnville, TN 37110
CL: Jacqulyn S Boyd
 128 Mitchell Road
 McMinnville, TN 37110
 (931)934-2088
 jackie.boyd@e-farmcredit.com

MURFREESBORO PRESBYTERY CONTINUED

Dry Valley　　　　　(4C)TNMU7213
5196 Shady Lane (mailing)
4415 Highway 70 N (physical)
Cookeville, TN 38506
(　)　　　　　<Putnam>
PA: Richard Bond　　　　　<M1>
136 N 2nd Avenue
Algood, TN 38506
(931)319-4399
CL: Janice F Bohannon
5196 Shady Lane
Cookeville, TN 38506
(931)528-7894
jandan80@gmail.com

Goshen　　　　　(4MWC)TNMU7214
PO Box 881 (mailing)
1262 Williams Cove Road (physical)
Winchester, TN 37398
(931)967-0245　　　　　<Franklin>
PA: Richard Morgan　　　　　<M1>
1468 Williams Cove Road
Winchester, TN 37398
(931)349-4474
icthuse3@gmail.com
CL: Betsy Grant
97 Hilton Street
Monteagle, TN 37356
(423)774-6055
bgrant@sewanee.edu

Gum Creek　　　　　(4C)TNMU7215
1063 Franklin Heights Drive
Winchester, TN 37398
(931)967-6539　　　　　<Franklin>
CL: Molly Perry
1063 Franklin Heights Drive
Winchester, TN 37398
(931)967-6539

Harmony　　　　　(4MWC)TNMU7216
8891 Lynchburg Road
Winchester, TN 37398
(931)962-0842　　　　　<Franklin>
PA: Joseph H Butler, Jr　　　　　<M1>
261 Ridgefield Drive
Winchester, TN 37398
(931)224-8423
jhbu737@live.com
CL: Mary Ann Morrison
971 Dripping Springs Road
Winchester, TN 37398
(716)713-5153
maryamore@hotmail.com

Hickory Valley　　　　　(4U)TNMU7251
Sparta, TN 38583
(931)738-5812　　　　　<White>
PA: Richard Bond　　　　　<M1>
1528 Eastlake Drive
Cookeville, TN 38506
(931)526-7610
CL: Kathryn Adcock
1450 Oak Grove Road
Sparta, TN 38583
(931)761-5858
kadcock@blomand.net

Hillsboro　　　　　(4EC)TNMU7217
PO Box 4
Hillsboro, TN 37342
(931)394-2415　　　　　<Coffee>

CL: Robert L Jenkins
68 Hillsboro Viola Road
Hillsboro, TN 37342
(931)596-2745

Jerusalem　　　　　(4MWC)TNMU7218
7192 Mona Road
Murfreesboro, TN 37129
(615)895-8118　　　　　<Rutherford>
PA: Brent Wills　　　　　<M1>
4607 E Richmond Shop Road
Lebanon, TN 37090
(615)449-3258
bwills9185@yahoo.com
CL: Jimmy C Francis
4657 W Jefferson Pike
Murfreesboro, TN 37129
(615)893-8311
jcfjimmy@aol.com

LaGuardo　　　　　(4WC)TNMU7219
7320 Highway 109 N
Lebanon, TN 37087
(615)444-0419　　　　　<Wilson>
OD: Gary Mraz　　　　　<M5>
8630 Highway 109 N
Lebanon, TN 37087
CL: Nancy Voight
500 Woods Ferry Pike
Lebanon, TN 37087

Lebanon　　　　　(4MWC)TNMU7220
522 Castle Heights Avenue
Lebanon, TN 37087
(615)444-7453　　　　　<Wilson>
FAX: (615)444-6671
lcpsecretary@hotmail.com
PA: Kevin Medlin　　　　　<M1>
316 Dandelion Drive
Lebanon, TN 37087
(615)444-7453
FAX: (615)444-6671
kmedlin12@hotmail.com
AP: Kevin Twilla　　　　　<M1>
731 Taylorsville Road
Lebanon,TN 37087
CL: Kelly Hendricks
464 Locust Grove Road
Watertown, TN 37184
(615)443-0226
FAX: (615)444-6671

Liberty　　　　　(4MWC)TNMU7222
317 Liberty Lane
McMinnville, TN 37110
(931)473-3813　　　　　<Warren>
libertycpc@gmail.com
SS: Larry Green　　　　　<M1>
525 Dearman Street
Smithville, TN 37166
(615)406-5547
larrylgreen24@aol.com
CL: Jeana Boyd
5208 W Greenhill Road
McMinnville, TN 37110
(931)273-1221
youth@libertycpc.org

Livingston First　　　　　(4WC)TNMU7223
PO Box 393 (mailing)
110 Byrdstown Highway (physical)
Livingston, TN 38570
(931)823-5115　　　　　<Overton>

SS: Donald Ray Fossey, II　　　　　<M3>
328 Waterloo Road
Cookeville, TN 38506
(931)498-2149
dfossey@twlakes.net
CL: Janice Ledbetter
311 Garrett Mills Road
Livingston, TN 38570

Luz D L Naciones　　　　　(4F)TNMU7252
114 Northwood Lane
Mc Minnville, TN 37110
(　)　　　　　<Warren>
PA: Jose Perez　　　　　<M1>
89 Northwood Lane Apt A102
Mc Minnville, TN 37110
(931)743-5585
CL: Session Clerk
114 Northwood Lane
Mc Minnville, TN 37110
(931)815-9502

Manchester　　　　　(4MWEC)TNMU7224
838 McArthur Street
Manchester, TN 37355
(931)728-2975　　　　　<Coffee>
FAX: (931)728-2975
mancp@cafes.net
PA: Mark Barron　　　　　<M1>
836 McArthur Street
Manchester, TN 37355
(931)728-2975
FAX: (931)728-2975
mbarron@cafes.net
CL: Debbie Shelton
1255 MG England Road
Manchester, TN 37355
(931)580-9493
dshelton@bushins.com

McMinnville　　　　　(4MWC)TNMU7225
115 Peers Street
McMinnville, TN 37110
(　)　　　　　<Warren>
SS: Andrew Rogers　　　　　<M2>
541 Talpha Drive
Doweltown, TN 37059
(615)597-7963
awrogers21@gmail.com
CL: Leota Watson
804 W Main Street
Mc Minnville, TN 37110
(931)473-7561
leotaw@blomand.net

Monteagle　　　　　(4C)TNMU7227
PO Bos 125 (mailing)
343 College Street (physical)
Monteagle, TN 37356
(　)　　　　　<Grundy>
staff@moncpchurch.org
CL: Billie Faye Terrill
PO Box 243
Monteagle, TN 37356
(931)924-2787

Mt Carmel　　　　　(4MEWC)TNMU7228
1484 Elora Road
Huntland, TN 37345
(931)469-7394　　　　　<Franklin>
PA: Richard, "Rocky" Whray　　　　　<M1>
201 8th Avenue SE
Winchester, TN 37398
(931)636-4844
rocklex1017@att.net

MURFREESBORO PRESBYTERY CONTINUED

CL: Tina M Morrow
714 Baxter Hollow Road
Belvidere, TN 37306
(931)967-3853
ramtmm@netzero.net

Mt Tabor   (4EC)TNMU7230
3122 Donard Court (mailing)
6000 Manchester Highway (physical)
Murfreesboro, TN 37127
(615)545-4695   <Rutherford>
sheila.mcclain4695@gmail.com
PA: Lisa Oliver   <M1 M9 OM>
110 Allen Drive
Hendersonville, TN 37075
(615)474-3954
lisa.oliver316@gmail.com
CL: Sheila McClain
3122 Donard Court
Murfreesboro, TN 37128
(615)545-4695
sheila.mcclain4695@gmail.com

Mt Vernon   (4C)TNMU7231
131 Hickory Hills Drive (mailing)
Murfreesboro, TN 37128)
11915 Mt Vernon Road (physical)
Rockvale, TN 37153
(615)890-9125   <Rutherford>
PA: Judy Taylor Sides   <M1>
534 Bethany Circle
Murfreesboro, TN 37128
(615)895-1627
CL: Gregory L Sides
534 Bethany Circle
Murfreesboro, TN 37128
(615)895-1627

Murfreesboro   (4MEWC)TNMU7232
907 E Main Street
Murfreesboro, TN 37130
(615)893-6755   <Rutherford>
FAX: (615)893-4553
firstcp@comcast.net
PA: Christopher Warren   <M1>
906 Prince Lane
Murfreesboro, TN 37129
(615)828-8719
chris@murfreesborocpc.org
AP: Joy Warren   <M1>
906 Prince Lane
Murfreesboro, TN 37129
(615)828-0407
revjoywarren@gmail.com
CL: Margaret Barlow
4965 Steeplechase Road
Christiana, TN 37037
(615)895-4918
margaret.barlow2085@gmail.com

New Hope   (4EWC)TNMU7233
PO Box 1215 (mailing)
7845 Coles Ferry Pike (physical)
Lebanon, TN 37087
(615)449-7020   <Wilson>
PA: Paul Hancock   <M1>
106 Mallard Point
Lebanon, TN 37087
(615)429-4331
pah4331@gmail.com
CL: Mary Ann Smith
423 Stonegate Drive
Lebanon, TN 37090
(615)444-0102
nwhpchrch0@gmail.com

Old Zion   (4C)TNMU7234
c/o Linda Ingram (mailing)
PO Box 576
7489 Old Kentucky Road (physical)
Sparta, TN 38583
( )   <White>
PA:Barry Boggs   <M1>
1039 Johnnie Bud Lane
Cookeville, TN 38501
(931)979-1701
boggsone@hotmail.com
CL: Linda Ingram
PO Box 576
Sparta, TN 38583
(615)406-3976

Owens Chapel   (4C)TNMU7235
1310 Liberty Road (mailing)
3058 Liberty Road (physical)
Winchester, TN 37398
(931)308-7335   <Franklin>
ferguea9@gmail.com
PA: Blake Stephens   <M1>
2559 Holders Cove Road
Winchester, TN 37398
(931)308-7335
blsteph@edge.net
CL: Steve Arnold
45 Catherines Court
Winchester, TN 37398
(931)636-1443
sandkarnold@comcast.net

Providence   (3C)TNMU7238
c/o Pierce Dodson(mailing)
106 Bartonwood Drive
Lebanon, TN 37087
Providence Road (physical)
Hartsville, TN 37074
( )   <Trousdale>
CL: Session Clerk
c/o Pierce Dodson(mailing)
106 Bartonwood Drive
Lebanon, TN 37087

Rock Island   (4C)TNMU7274
PO Box 146
Rock Island, TN 38581
(931)979-1701
PA:Barry Boggs   <M1>
1039 Johnnie Bud Lane
Cookeville, TN 38501
(931)979-1701
boggsone@hotmail.com
CL: Mike Cornett
125 Great Oak Drive
Rock Island, TN 38581

Rockvale   (4MEWC)TNMU7239
PO Box 67 (mailing)
8769 Rockvale Road (physical)
Rockvale, TN 37153
(615)274-3143   <Rutherford>
PA: Jonathan Watson   <M1>
4017 Claude Drive
Smyrna, TN 37167
watsonjonathan@bellsouth.net
(615)630-9153
CL: Lynn Smith
11911 New Zion Road
Christiana, TN 37037
(615)995-5466
lynnsmith@cityschools.net

Rocky Glade   (4C)TNMU7240
PO Box 8 (mailing)
2017 Rocky Glade Road (physical)
Eagleville, TN 37060
( )   <Rutherford>
PA: J. Tommy Jobe   <M1>
807 Rockwood Drive
Nolensville, TN 37135
(615)776-7755
cppreacher@united.net
CL: Bill Lamb
425 River Eagleville Road
Eagleville, TN 37060
(615)274-2275
billlamb1@bellsouth.net

Ruth Chapel   (2C)TNMU7241
347 Windle Community Road (mailing)
146 Windle Community Road (physical)
Livingston, TN 38570
( )   <Overton>
SS: Donald Fossey II   <M3>
328 Waterloo Road
Cookeville, TN 38506
(931)498-2149
dfossey@twlakes.net
CL: Jo K Smith
347 Windle Community Road
Livingston, TN 38570
(931)823-5916

Sewanee   (4WC)TNMU7242
161 Kentucky Avenue (mailing)
Sewanee, TN 37375
(931)598-0766   <Franklin>
smdiam@hotmail.com
CL: Paul E Mooney
161 Kentucky Avenue
Sewanee, TN 37375
(931)598-0766

Smithville   (4MWC)TNMU7243
201 S College Street
Smithville, TN 37166
(615)597-4197   <DeKalb>
FAX: (615)597-4397
office@smithvillecpc.com
PA: Isaac Gray   <M1>
512 Ed Taft Drive
Smithville, TN 37166
(870)373-4731
revgray08@gmail.com
CL: Teresa Brown
PO Box 835
Smithville, TN 37166

Suggs Creek   (4MWC)TNMU7244
405 Corinth Road
Mount Juliet, TN 37122
( )   <Wilson>
OD: Eddie Smith   <M5>
405 Corinth Road
Mount Juliet, TN 37122
CL: Dianna Huff
167 Eakes Thompson Road
Mount Juliet, TN 37122
dhuff1983@bellsouth.net

Union Hill   (4MWC)TNMU7246
235 Sykes Road
Brush Creek, TN 38547
(615)683-8327   <Smith>
brotherperry@msn.com

MURFREESBORO PRESBYTERY CONTINUED

PA: Dennis Croslin   <M1>
165 Maple Street
Gordonsville, TN 38563
(615)934-2383
CL: Robin L Nixon
237 Temperance Hall Highway
Hickman, TN 38567
(615)418-5074
robinlpn@hotmail.com

Watertown   (4WC)TNMU7247
510 W Main Street
Watertown, TN 37184
( )   <Wilson>
OD: Rodger McCann   <M5>
352 Winding River Lane
Sparta, TN 38563
(931)738-0352
CL: Emily Nix
305 Cornwell Avenue
Watertown, TN 37184
(615)237-3488
samnix0421@att.net

Winchester First   (4WC)TNMU7249
PO Box 176 (mailing)
200 2nd Avenue NW (physical)
Winchester, TN 37398
(931)967-2121   <Franklin>
FAX: (931)967-8444
wintncp@bellsouth.net
PA: Michael Clark   <M1>
2353 Blue Springs Road
Decherd, TN 37324
(931)967-2121
mclark37398@gmail.com
AP: Amber Clark   <M1>
2353 Blue Springs Road
Decherd, TN 37324
(931)967-2121
amber.clark@winchestercp.org
AP: Anna Sweet-Brockman   <M1>
635 Country Estates Drive
Winchester, TN 37398
(931)967-2121
aannasweetbrockman@gmail.com
CL: Karen Zarecor
260 Harris Chapel Road
Estill Springs, TN 37330
(931)962-4465
zarecor@bellsouth.net

OTHERS ON MINISTERIAL ROLL:

Burrow, Vernon   <M1 RT>
603 Saratoga Drive
Murfreesboro, TN 37130
(615)406-6385
vernonburrow@comcast.net
DeBerry, Martha Jacqueline   <M1 WC>
2681 Roosevelt Boulevard Apt 3209
Clearwater, FL 33760
(931)304-8832
1spiritualdirector@earthlink.net
Estep, William   <M1 RT>
239 Skyline Drive
Harriman, TN 37748
(865)882-5114
Ferry, Aaron   <M1 WC>
3137 Glenbrook Drive
Twinsburg, OH 44087
(615)946-3078
amferry815@gmail.com

Green, Harry   <M1 WC>
45 Wood Way
McMinnville, TN 37110
(931)815-9190
Hackman-Truhan, Deborah   <M1 WC>
7314 N Miramar Drive
Peoria, IL 61614
(931)537-9040
cprevdeb@hotmail.com
Johnson, Lanny   <M1 RT>
74 Flagstone Drive
Rossville, GA 30741
(931)212-1658
ljohnson37357@gmail.com
Kerner, Leanne   <M1 WC>
9236 Church Road Apt 2041
Dallas, TX 752311
(270)851-9709
cooldoll@bellsouth.net
Labrada, Hector   <M1 WC>
74 Cumberland Drive
McMinnville, TN 37110
Logan, Jason   <M1 M8>
709 Cavalier Drive
Clarksville, TN 37040
(609)556-3128
jason.b.logan.mil@mail.mil
Matlock, Robert   <M1 RT>
156 Dovenshire Drive
Fairfield Glade, TN 38558
(931)210-0614
revbobm@msn.com
McCaskey, Charles   <M1 RT>
679 Canter Lane
Cookeville, TN 38501
(931)526-4885
charles@cookevillecpchurch.org
McCaskey, Mary   <M1 WC>
218 Downton Avenue
Cookeville, TN 38501
(931)260-1422
marykat_61@hotmail.com McGill,
James A   <M1 WC>
433 S Walnut Avenue
Cookeville, TN 38501
(931)526-6936
jam7235@frontiernet.net
Merritt, Joyce   <M1 WC>
3929 Snail Shell Cave Road
Rockvale, TN 37153
(615)574-3047
Nye, John   <M1 WC>
210 Crestview Drive
Mount Juliet, TN 37122
Parks, Sam   <M1 WC>
10 Lila Way
Cartersville, GA 60120
(615)529-2465
wsamparks@aol.com
Salisbury, Rebecca   <M1 WC>
1033 Twin Oaks Drive
Murfreesboro, TN 37130
(615)410-7801
Watson, Micah   <M1 WC>
2529 Middle Tennessee Boulevard
Murfreesboro, TN 37130
(615)692-2742
mwatson4289@gmail.com

OTHER LICENTIATES ON ROLL:

Norris, Caleb   <M2>
565 E 10th Street
Cookeville, TN 38501
caleb@cookeville, TN 38501
Ramiriz, Araceli   <M2>
234 Vinewood Road Apt DG
McMinnville, TN 37110
White, Mack   <M2>
408 W Main Street
Smithville, TN 37166
(615)318-9863
gmax408@yahoo.coM
Young, Ryan   <M2>
1925 Allsoboro Road
Cherokee, AL 35616
dennis.ryan.young@gmail.com

OTHER CANDIDATES ON ROLL:

Morgan, Leigh Ann   <M3>
PO Box 881
Winchester, TN 37398
Quevedo, Mariano   <M3>
289 Golf Club Lane
McMinnville, TN 37110
Slickmeyer, Kim   <M3>
431 Riley Avenue
Smithville, TN 37166
(931)650-1330
krslickmeyer@gmail.com
Stephens, Evan   <M3>
559 Holders Cove Road
Winchester, TN 37398
Thompson, D J   <M3>
808 Gentry Avenue
Smithville, TN 37166
(615)318-2743
djthompson272@gmail.com
Wills, Robin   <M3>
4607 E Richmond Shop Road
Lebanon, TN 37090
(615)870-4773
robinrush24@aol.com

Nashville Presbytery
TENNESSEE SYNOD

GENERAL		MEMBERSHIP			CHANGES				FINANCES				
	1.Church Number	2.Active	3.Total	4.Church School	5.Prof. of Faith	6.Gains	7.Losses	8.Children Baptized	9. OUR UNITED OUT-REACH	10. Total Out-Reach Giving	11. All Other Expenses	12. Total Income Received	13. Value Church Prop. 1=1000
	1	2	3	4	5	6	7	8	9	10	11	12	13
Arlington	7311	16	35	9	0	0	1	0	0	4,278	37,190	42,452	450
Beech	7301	140	197	50	1	3	5	0	13,348	45,160	280,084	416,659	3,233
Bethel	7302	58	61	22	0	0	20	0	0	7,700	107,689	104,392	725
Brenthaven	7331	226	312	140	0	0	6	0	30,114	83,000	367,451	444,462	7,000
Brush Hill	7325	113	161	54	0	0	19	0	6,000	13,439	166,020	216,228	1,899
Camp Ground	7312	14	14	10	0	0	3	0	0	2,100	38,223	42,188	450
Cane Ridge	7326	18	18	5	0	0	1	0	0	511	19,660	21,320	275
Charlotte+	7303	30	62	20	0	0	2	0	5,225	12,155	34,096	54,991	620
Clarksville	7304	252	250	180	0	4	26	2	40,438	55,236	248,510	414,350	5,633
Concord	7306	16	27	15	0	0	1	0	0	3,965	22,258	28,394	224
Cristo Vive	7314				0	NRR	0	0	0	0	0	0	0
Cumb. Valley	7307	22	39	12	0	0	0	0	2,213	4,463	15,027	22,134	250
Dickson	7308	334	415	107	3	3	3	1	11,000	37,960	202,544	230,153	1,500
Donelson	7327	34	54	42	0	0	3	0	1,400	6,416	73,907	76,564	1,650
Dry Fork	7309	15	24	0	0	0	1	0	1,000	3,759	13,513	21,286	125
Goodlettsville	7328	310	310	321	11	11	13	0	0	32,620	677,219	709,839	3,500
Halls Creek	7313	37	36	30	0	1	0	1	0	1,035	33,466	33,688	350
Hendersonville	7340	19	19	15	0	0	1	0	600	2,285	37,259	49,522	500
Liberty	7315	47	47	47	0	7	2	0	4,213	11,262	105,525	106,241	600
Locust Grove	7316	20	40	9	0	1	4	0	4,755	10,063	31,239	47,457	313
Madison 1st	7329	16	49	11	0	0	1	0	4,300	4,881	41,258	42,803	340
Mariah	7317	32	32	0	0	0	1	0	0	951	31,183	39,361	150
McAdoo	7318	35	35	21	2	2	0	0	6,408	6,408	75,721	118,923	646
Mt. Denson	7319	31	39	18	0	0	2	0	1,658	2,259	58,339	60,935	730
Mt. Liberty	7320	66	146	15	0	0	3	1	9,900	16,800	66,200	123,762	1,300
Mt. Sharon	7321	52	197	47	0	0	2	0	10,000	15,620	94,306	135,228	1,750
Mt. Sinai	7330	8	8	0	0	1	2	0	0	150	3,127	488	266
Mt. View	7322	43	77	31	8	8	2	0	1,200	13,638	66,936	103,397	475
New Hope	7337	5	6	6	0	NRR	0	0	0	0	0	0	20
New Providence	7305	19	19	10	0	0	5	0	3,000	4,500	35,796	39,852	900
Shiloh	7338	15	26	4	1	1	8	2	0	1,025	18,922	26,368	850
St. Luke	7332	111	297	42	3	5	5	0	18,944	18,647	230,140	168,411	1,703
Sudanese	7341	20	20	5	0	NRR	0	0	75	0	0	0	24
Tusculum	7333	131	230	103	0	0	4	0	0	26,573	247,280	252,836	7,510
Waverly	7339	31	31	5	0	NRR	0	0	0	0	0	0	592
West Nashville	7334	72	144	37	0	1	256	0	3,316	7,566	255,979	324,925	4,574
TOTALS	**36**	**2,408**	**3,477**	**1,443**	**29**	**48**	**402**	**7**	**179,107**	**456,425**	**3,736,067**	**4,519,609**	**51,127**

*Math error corrected. **Purged roll. +Union Church   NRR - No Report Received

NASHVILLE PRESBYTERY CONTINUED

CHURCHES, PASTORS, AND CLERKS:

Arlington   (4WC)TNNA7311
PO Box 624 (mailing)
7 Knight Street (physical)
Erin, TN 37061
(931)289-3597   <Houston>
CL: Andrea Dillard
85 Victor Lane
Erin, TN 37061
(931)289-4004
adillard@workforceessentials.com

Beech   (4MWC)TNNA7301
3216 Long Hollow Pike
Hendersonville, TN 37075
(615)824-3990   <Sumner>
FAX: (615)824-6507
office@beechcp.com
PA: Jeff DeWees   <M1>
116 Lancaster Court
Gallatin, TN 37066
(931)209-3331
pastorjeff@beechcp.com
CL: Roxanne Martindale
187 Mark Circle
Gallatin, TN 37066
(615)480-7250
roxannemartindale51@gmail.com

Bethel   (4MC)TNNA7302
3375 Sango Road
Clarksville, TN 37043
(931)358-3295   <Montgomery>
PA: Stewart Salyer   <M1>
2211 Foxfire Road
Clarksville, TN 37043
(931)980-2829
stewart.salyer@gmail.com
CL: Cathy Dyer
3375 Sango Road
Clarksville, TN 37043
(931)302-3539
cathylynndyer@hotmail.com

Brenthaven   (4C)TNNA7331
516 Franklin Road
Brentwood, TN 37027
(615)373-4826   <Williamson>
FAX: (615)373-4869
secretary@brenthaven.org
PA: Kip J Rush   <M1>
513 Meadowlark Lane
Brentwood, TN 37027
(615)714-6365
pastor@brenthaven.org
AP: Sandra Shepherd   <M1>
1432 Wexford Downs Lane
Nashville, TN 37211
(615)772-5358
woolywagon@gmail.com
CL: Christi Peppers
5008 Woodland Hills Drive
Brentwood, TN 37027
(615)376-9977
christi.peppers@gmail.com

Brush Hill   (4MEWC)TNNA7325
3705 Brush Hill Road
Nashville, TN 37216
(615)227-2504   <Davidson>
FAX: (615)227-0039
bhcpc@birch.net
AP: Paul Tucker   <M1>
3801 Brush Hill Pike
Nashville, TN 37216
(615)430-9158
paultucker@gmail.com
CL: Sylvia Slack
3705 Brush Hill Road
Nashville, TN 37214
(615)227-2504
sessionclerk@brushhillchurch.org

Camp Ground   (4MWC)TNNA7312
88 Campground Road
Erin, TN 37061
(931)289-4605   <Houston>
LS: Terry Mathis   <M6>
88 Campground Road
Erin, TN 37061
(931)289-3602
ttmathis@peoplestel.net
CL: Tammy Simmons
5970 Highway 13
Erin, TN 37061
(931)289-3727
tsimmons3658@yahoo.com

Cane Ridge   (4EC)TNNA7326
6867 Burkitt Road (mailing)
13412 Old Hickory Boulevard (physical)
Cane Ridge, TN 37013
(615)941-8317   <Davidson>
FAX: (615)941-2985
gdunn6867@comcast.net
LS: Gregory (Greg) Dunn   <M6>
6867 Burkitt Road
Cane Ridge, TN 37013
(615)941-8317
FAX: (615)941-2985
gdunn6867@comast.net
CL: Eleanor Willett
145 Greenwood Drive
La Vergne, TN 37086
(615)793-5016
tuffyw9@comcast.net

Charlotte   (4WC)TNNA7303
515 Mt Hebron Road (mailing)
3 Court Square (physical)
Charlotte, TN 37036
( )   <Dickson>
PA: Steve Jones   <M1>
PO Box 368
Burns, TN 37029
(615)441-6159
stevenejones@bellsouth.net
CL: Eloise Jones
515 Mount Hebron Road
Charlotte, TN 37036
(615)789-5353
joneseloise515@bellsouth.net

Clarksville   (4WC)TNNA7304
1410 Golf Club Lane
Clarksville, TN 37040
(931)648-0817   <Montgomery>
office@clarksvillecpc.com
PA: Jimmy Byrd   <M1 OP>
3810 Lake Road
Woodlawn, TN 37191
(615)289-3347
revjimmybyrd@hotmail.com
AP: Taylor Young   <M1>
903 W Old Hickory Boulevard
Madison, TN 37115
(615)830-3344
taylor@clarksvillecpc.com
CL: Sallie Noel
216 Alfred Drive
Clarksville, TN 37043
enoel3165@charter.net

Concord   (4MC)TNNA7306
63 Gander Branch Road
Waverly, TN 37185
( )   <Humphreys>
CL: Phyllis Webb
3571 Fire Tower Road
Erin, TN 37061
(931)289-4601

Cristo Vive   (4C)TNNA7314
611 Cheron Road
Madison, TN 37115
( )   <Davidson>
PA: Carlos Cinco   <M1>
611 Cheron Road
Madison, TN 37115
(615)586-1269
pastorcinco2020@gmail.com
CL: Session Clerk
611 Cheron Road
Madison, TN 37115

Cumberland Valley   (4WC)TNNA7307
285 Cumberland Valley Road
Mc Ewen, TN 37101
(931)582-8050   <Houston>
PA: Jesse L Freeman, Jr   <M1>
270 Eastside Road
Burns, TN 37029
(615)202-4594
mptc@bellsouth.net
CL: June R Hicks
1339 Highway 13 S
Waverly, TN 37185
(931)296-4284

Dickson   (4WC)TNNA7308
500 Highway 70 E
Dickson, TN 37055
(615)446-8511   <Dickson>
FAX: (615)446-7827
office@cumberlandpresbyterian.org
PA: Robert D Truitt   <M1>
1238 Old East Side Road
Burns, TN 37029
(615)740-9180
FAX: (615)446-7827
rdtjct@aol.com

NASHVILLE PRESBYTERY CONTINUED

AP: Dean Guye <M1>
2759 Highway 70 E
Dickson, TN 37055
(615)446-7687
deanjoy@att.net
CL: Mark Denney
2116 Maysville Road
Dickson, TN 37055
(615)319-5807
dmdenney@aol.com

_____
Donelson (4WC)TNNA7327
2914 Lebanon Road
Nashville, TN 37214
(615)516-9427 <Davidson>
email@donelsoncpchurch.com
PA: Michael Bertsch <M1>
204 Buckleigh Point
Gallatin, TN 37066
(423)763-8314
mikebertsch14@gmail.com
CL: Keith C Vanstone
3803 Plantation Drive
Hermitage, TN 37076
(615)454-1600
keithv@bellsouth.net

_____
Dry Fork (4C)TNNA7309
174 Dry Fork Creek Road (mailing)
1050 Dry Fork Creek Road (physical)
Bethpage, TN 37022
(615)841-3169 <Sumner>
CL: Sue Carr
174 Dry Fork Creek Road
Bethpage, TN 37022
(615)841-3169
suekencarr@nctc.com

_____
Goodlettsville (4MWC)TNNA7328
226 South Main Street
Goodlettsville, TN 37072
(615)859-5888 <Davidson>
FAX: (615)859-8820
gcpc@goodlettsvillechurch.com
PA: Tim Stutler <M1>
1044 Mansker Farm Boulevard
Hendersonville, TN 37075
(615)859-5888
tim@goodletttsvillechurch.com
CL: Dillard Tutor
292 Lake Terrace Drive
Hendersonville, TN 37075
dillardtutor@msn.com

_____
Halls Creek (4EC)TNNA7313
2803 Halls Creek Road
Waverly, TN 37185
(931)296-7758 <Humphreys>
CL: Jeremy Tolene
3631 Turkey Creek Road
Waverly, TN 37185
tolenej@hcss.com

_____
Hendersonville (4WC)TNNA7340
453 Walton Ferry Road
Hendersonville, TN 37075
(615)822-6091 <Sumner>
PA: Gregory Jones <M1>
4728 Reischa Drive
Nashville, TN 37211
(931)249-9512
greg1013@aol.com

CL: Susan Wyatt
115 Elissa Drive
Hendersonville, TN 37075
(615)948-8242
FAX: (615)824-0195
susandwyatt@comcast.net

_____
Liberty (4MWC)TNNA7315
725 S Liberty Church Road
Clarksville, TN 37042
( ) <Montgomery>
PA: Rocky Johnson <M1>
1208 Redwood Drive
Clarksville, TN 37042
(423)620-7753
rockyj1960@gmail.com
CL: Bob Del Giorno
1510 S Freestone Court
Clarksville, TN 37042
(931)647-1086
bodeno@charter.net

_____
Locust Grove (4WC)TNNA7316
3449 Locust Church Road
Cunningham, TN 37052
( ) <Montgomery>
SS: Timothy W Ferrell <M1>
1850 Dunbar Road
Woodlawn, TN 37191
(931)920-2662
ferrelltw@aol.com
CL: Lawanda Black
3192 Budds Creek Road
Palmyra, TN 37142
(931)326-5298
jobee39@hughes.net

_____
Madison First (4MWC)TNNA7329
735 Argyle Avenue
Madison, TN 37115
(615)868-2888 <Davidson>
FAX: (615)868-2888
madisonfirst@yahoo.com
CL: Edith Marlin
112 Becker Avenue
Old Hickory, TN 37138
(615)847-4148
edithmarlin@outlook.com

_____
Mariah (4MWC)TNNA7317
43 Mariah Church Lane
Waverly, TN 37185
(931)296-5546 <Humphreys>
CL: Anita Gehring
65 Warden Road
Waverly, TN 37185
(931)296-8059

_____
McAdoo (4WC)TNNA7318
3724 Ashland City Road
Clarksville, TN 37043
(931)362-3091 <Montgomery>
CL: Nancy Rhinehart
1601 Harville Road
Clarksville, TN 37043
(931)362-3105
rhinehart.nancy@yahoo.com

_____
Mt Denson (4MWC)TNNA7319
4558 Highway 161
Springfield, TN 37172
(615)384-3613 <Robertson>
SS: Nathan Barnes <M3>
1139 Kimberlty Drive
Goodlettsville, TN 37072
(615)429-0887
nathanwbarnes@gmail.com
CL: Joyce Munda
4747 N Old Highway 41
Springfield, TN 37172
(615)504-4814
joyce.munda@tn.gov

_____
Mt Liberty (4MWC)TNNA7320
3655 Highway 49 E
Charlotte, TN 37036
(615)789-5916 <Dickson>
SS: Patricia Shropshire <M2>
PO Box 330404
Nashville, TN 37203
(517)256-7454
patricia.a.shropshire@vumc.org
CL: Cindy Simpson
3378 Highway 49 E
Charlotte, TN 37036
(615)945-0010
cindyrsimpson@hotmail.com

_____
Mt Sharon (4MWC)TNNA7321
4634 Mount Sharon Road
Greenbrier, TN 37073
(615)384-8569 <Robertson>
pastor@mtsharoncpchurch.org
PA: Kimberly Moore <M1>
1025 Three Island Ford Road
Charlotte, TN 37036
(615)545-1595
reverend.kim.moore@gmail.com
CL: James D Jordan
2100 W End Avenue Ste 1150
Nashville, TN 37203
(615)329-2100
FAX: (615)329-2187
jdjordan@gjplaw.com

_____
Mt Sinai (4WC)TNNA7330
3738 Hydes Ferry Road
Nashville, TN 37218
(615)586-7886 <Davidson>
SS: David Lomax <M3>
1501 Robert Cartwright Drive
Goodlettsville, TN 37072
(615)753-2493
lomaxdavid53@yahoo.com
CL: Katherine B Pleas
555 Church Street #801
Nashville, TN 37219
(615)251-4037
pleas5@hotmail.com

_____
Mt View (4C)TNNA7322
2359 Leatherwood Road (mailing)
Stewart, TN 37175
282 Hickman Creek Road (physical)
Dover, TN 37058
(931)217-0893 <Stewart>
mvcpchurch@gmail.com

NASHVILLE PRESBYTERY CONTINUED

PA: Ronald D Burgess   \<M1\>
116 Harris Ridge Road
Dover, TN 37058
(931)232-5151
revron4@bellsouth.net

CL: Michelle Sills
126 Ralls Road
Dover, TN 37058
(931)305-8893
michellesills@gmail.com

New Hope   (4C)TNNA7337
c/o Sharon Cook (mailing)
8009 White Oak Road
Stewart, TN 37175
60 New Hope Road (physical)
Stewart, TN 37175
( )   \<Houston\>

LS: G Ray Mayo
3019 Lights Chapel Road
Clarksville, TN 37040

CL: Sharon E Cook
8009 White Oak Road
Stewart, TN 37175
(931)721-2513
ricsha55@yahoo.com

New Providence   (4MWC)TNNA7305
1307 Fort Campbell Boulevard
Clarksville, TN 37042
(931)647-4455   \<Montgomery\>

PA: Elizabeth Daniel   \<M1\>
1818 Memorial Drive
Clarksville, TN 37043
(931)645-6956
lizzy37@juno.com

CL: Linda Durrwachter
951 Dotsonville Road
Clarksville, TN 37042
(931)552-6657
lindadurr@charter.net

Shiloh   (4C)TNNA7338
4812 Shiloh-Canaan Road
Palmyra, TN 37142
(931)387-4198   \<Montgomery\>
greg1013@aol.com

SS: Rick Purcell   \<M3\>
895 Branch Road
Clarksville, TN 37043
(269)277-7277
rickkpurcell@sbcglobal.net

CL: Dianne Harris
400 Attaway Road
Clarksville, TN 37040
(931)206-8415
dharrisx2@acepipe.net

St Luke   (4MWC)TNNA7332
901 W Old Hickory Boulevard
Madison, TN 37115
(615)868-1982   \<Davidson\>
stlukecpchurch@gmail.com

IP: Stephen L Louder   \<M1 RT\>
98 Gallant Court
Clarksville, TN 37043
(931)217-0369
slouder81@gmail.com

CL: Angie Pinson
901 W Old Hickory Boulevard
Madison, TN 37115
(615)337-7311
stlukecpchurch@gmail.com

Sudanese   (F)TNNA7341
c/o John Tiaang Ping (mailing)
331 Plus Park Boulevard Apt 307
Nashville, TN 37217
(615)585-2842   \<Sumner\>

CL: John Tiang Ping
331 Plus Park Boulevard Apt 307
Nashville, TN 37217
(615)365-3274

Tusculum   (4MWC)TNNA7333
477 McMurray Drive
Nashville, TN 37211
(615)833-0742   \<Davidson\>
tusculumchurch@gmail.com

PA: Clifton Barna   \<M1\>
1012 Adam Court
Cottontown, TN 37066
(352)598-3246
cliff.barna@gmail.com

CL: Dawn Gannon
3417 County Hill Road
Antioch, TN 37013
(615)399-2782
dawngannon0317@yahoo.com

Waverly   (4MWC)TNNA7339
109 N Church Street
Waverly, TN 37185
(931)296-3232   \<Humphreys\>
FAX: (931)296-3232
waverlycpc@att.net

PS: Jerry Davis   \<M2\>
604 Nesbitt Hollow Road
McEwen, TN 37101
drjisin@yahoo.com

CL: Charles Stanton
1551 Baptist Branch Road
McEwen, TN 37101
(931)582-8449
cstanton@bellsouth.net

West Nashville   (4MWC)TNNA7334
6849 Charlotte Pike
Nashville, TN 37209
(615)352-2800   \<Davidson\>
FAX: (615)352-2801
info@wncp.org

PA: Tommy Clark   \<M1\>
924 Bresslyn Road
Nashville, TN 37205
(931)703-7542
tommy@wncp.org

IP: Jeff Stovall   \<M1\>
2829 Trelawny Drive
Clarksville, TN 37043
(931)993-6104
jeffstovall@juno.com

PA: CJ Cassell   \<M1\>
825 Aimes Court
Nashville, TN 37221
(615)594-2693
n4cjc@comcast.net

CL: Nancy Crowell
707 Newberry Road
Nashville, TN 37205
nancydcrowell@gmail.com

OTHERS ON MINISTERIAL ROLL:

Acuff, David   \<M1 RT\>
4969 Quail Lane
Columbia, SC 29206
(803)727-3910
theoldguard1957@gmail.com

Bane, Ted   \<M1 RT\>
123 Melanie Drive
Hendersonville, TN 37075
(615)975-9343
tedjan95@aol.com

Bourque, Leo   \<M1 WC\>
1620 Sarahs Cove
Hermitage, TN 37076
(615)767-2428
bourque120@gmail.com

Carlton, Gary   \<M1 RT\>
108 Greenbrier Street
Dickson, TN 37055
(615)441-8963
gwcarlton@yahoo.com

Chall-Hutchinson, Deborah   \<M1 M9\>
190 Ussery Road
Clarksville, TN 37043
(931)905-1671
challhut@gmail.com

Corbin, William   \<M1 HR\>
7300 N Lamar Road
Mount Juliet, TN 37122
(615)459-8998
raven.rest@comcast.net

De Vries, Raymond   \<M1 WC\>
2080 Stanford Village Drive
Antioch, TN 37013
(615)332-3587
raydevries3216@att.net

Duke, Michael E   \<M1 WC\>
106 Friar Tuck Drive
Dickson, TN 37055
(615)446-6515

Dumas, Byron   \<M1 OM\>
1775 Theresa Drive
Clarksville, TN 37043
(931)552-8772
bdumas7346@aol.com

Ferguson, E Blant   \<M1 RT\>
80 Smoky Mountain Lane Unit 305
Clayton, GA 30525
(706)896-9296
blantferg@yahoo.com

Goodwill, James L   \<M1 RT\>
9232 Duckhorn Drive
Charlotte, NC 28277
(704)526-8729
jim@jimgoodwill.com

Gough, Ernest E   \<M1 WC\>
8366 Highway 70
Nashville, TN 37221
(615)646-4372
eegough@bellsouth.net

Hurley, E C   \<M1 HR\>
#2 Killard Road, Killard
Doonbeg, County Clare
IRELAND
(931)551-6173
hurleyec@gmail.com

NASHVILLE PRESBYTERY CONTINUED

Louder, Paula   <M1 RT>
  98 Gallant Court
  Clarksville, TN 37043
  (615)804-4809
  plouder223@gmail.com
Miller, Carol   <M1 WC>
  101 Park Avenue
  Dickson, TN 37055
  (615)441-6656
  lcarolmiller@comcast.net
Norton, Kitty   <M1 WC>
  251 Westchase Drive
  Nashville, TN 37205
  (615)584-1464
  kitty.a.norton@vanderbilt.edu
Page, Rickey   <M1 RT>
  1369 Black River Drive
  Mt Pleasant, SC 29466
  (615)353-7850
  rickey.page59@gmail.com
Parrish, Steven   <M1 RT>
  4610 Dunn Avenue
  Memphis, TN 38117
  (901)743-9545
  sparrish@memphisseminary.edu
Patton, Malcolm   <M1 RT>
  921 Harris Drive
  Gallatin, TN 37066
  (615)452-5557
  FAX: (615)824-6507
  bpatton11@comcast.net
Pickett, Patricia (Pat)   <M1 M9>
  1460 Cheatham Dam Road
  Ashland City, TN 37015
  (615)792-4973
  tovahtoo@aol.com
Polacek, Fred E   <M1 WC>
  907 Graham Drive
  Old Hickory, TN 37138
  (615)754-5328
  revfredp@gmail.com
Rippy, James G   <M1 WC>
  442 Trina Street
  Gallatin, TN 37066
  (615)681-7086
  lrippy@live.com
Roddy, Lowell G   <M1 HR>
  628 Mannington Place
  Lexington,, KY 40503
  (931)249-1047
  lgroddy@yahoo.com
Sims, Edward G   <M1 HR>
  1176 Warfield Boulevard #410
  Clarksville, TN 37043
  (931)206-5759
  simseg@bellsouth.net
Tabor, Don M   <M1 RT>
  9611 Mitchell Place
  Brentwood, TN 37027
  (615)776-7292
  FAX: (615)373-3356
  dontabor@comcast.net
Tyus, Dwayne   <M1 RT>
  901 W Old Hickory Boulevard
  Madison, TN 37115
  (615)720-2564
  dwayne.tyus@gmail.com

Vick, Joe   <M1 HR>
  6064 Old Hickory Boulevard
  Whites Creek, TN 37189
  (615)519-5249
  joervick@gmail.com
Ward, Andrew   <M1 WC>
  407 Rose Hill Court
  Goodlettsville, TN 37072
  (615)456-9136
  andrewbward@aol.com
West, David   <M1 M9 RT>
  2027 Lucille Street
  Lebanon, TN 37087
  (615)427-8371
  drdavidlwest@aol.com
Whitworth, Gary W   <M1 RT>
  1706 Old Hickory Boulevard
  Brentwood, TN 37027
  (615)915-4180

_____

OTHER LICENTIATES ON ROLL:

Lomax, David   <M2>
  1501 Robert Cartwright Drive
  Goodlettsville, TN 37072
  (615)753-2493
  lomaxdavid53@yahoo.com

_____

OTHER CANDIDATES ON ROLL:

Edwards, Jimmie   <M3>
  3527 Hinton Road
  Clarksville, TN 37043
  (931)980-2802
  jimmieedwards@me.com
Evans, Daniel   <M3>
  126 Chesapeake Harbor
  Hendersonville, TN 37075
  (731)613-1806
  gcpcdaniel@comcast.net
Norris, Dakota   <M3>
  4456 Clarence Murphy Road
  Springfield, TN 37172
  (615)681-6346
  volsfan2011@gmail.com
Stutler, Ken   <M3>
  1044 Mansker Farms Boulevard
  Hendersonville, TN 37075
  (270)576-8367
  cpkenstutler@gmail.com
Taylor, Thomas (Ean)   <M3>
  437 Peach Creek Crescent
  Nashville, TN 37214
  (615)585-4158
  tetaylor91@gmail.com
Thomas, Dwight   <M3>
  1010 Gill Hodges Road
  Portland, TN 37148
  (615)906-2224
  dwiight21@gmail.com
Tiangping, John   <M3>
  331 Plus Park Boulevard #307
  Nashville, TN 37217
  (615)243-7101

North Central Presbytery
MIDWEST SYNOD

GENERAL		MEMBERSHIP			CHANGES				FINANCES				
	1.Church Number	2.Active	3.Total	4.Church School	5.Prof. of Faith	6.Gains	7.Losses	8.Children Baptized	9. OUR UNITED OUT-REACH	10. Total Out-Reach Giving	11. All Other Expenses	12. Total Income Received	13. Value Church Prop. 1=1000
	1	2	3	4	5	6	7	8	9	10	11	12	13
Bethany	5401	46	309	20	0	0	3	0	8,980	35,117	53,901	89,858	560
Burnt Prairie	5102	16	34	6	0	NRR	0	0	0	0	0	0	63
Campground	5402	13	15	15	0	NRR	0	0	536	0	0	0	50
Casey	5201	11	21	8	0	0	0	0	2,314	5,125	17,668	20,296	50
Christ	5305	8	11	7	0	NRR	0	0	0	0	0	0	150
Cumb. Chapel	5104	6	6	5	0	0	1	0	0	12,500	11,937	21,102	6
Ebenezer	5203	38	38	38	0	7	2	0	4,800	7,885	43,580	32,697	1,200
Elm River	5107	42	42	35	0	0	0	0	6,720	15,020	59,800	70,080	250
Fairfield	5108	141	222	75	0	1	7	0	0	11,868	224,849	211,199	1,000
Faith	5501	4	10	2	0	0	0	0	2,706	5,077	39,691	60,962	500
Fullerton	5404	24	24	17	0	0	1	0	1,911	4,135	21,085	20,191	50
Georgetown	5204	15	39	6	0	15	1	0	3,180	6,609	46,226	39,192	113
Good Prospect	5205	83	83	106	0	NRR	0	0	7,529	0	0	0	1,200
Grace	5502	12	29	16	0	NRR	0	0	0	0	0	0	245
Knights Chapel	5306	29	36	38	0	NRR	0	0	0	0	0	0	100
Lebanon North	5113	56	94	61	0	0	0	0	0	3,135	58,992	66,135	250
Lebanon South	5114				0	NRR	0	0	0	0	0	0	
Lincoln 1st	5405	39	91	12	0	NRR	0	0	5,133	0	0	0	575
Monroe City	5307	8	8	0	0	NRR	0	0	0	0	0	0	200
Morningside	5304	32	32	14	0	0	23	0	1,250	11,790	98,315	110,050	1,600
Mt. Gilead	5406	24	63	20	0	NRR	0	0	1,200	0	0	0	195
Mt. Olivet	5308	11	26	22	0	0	0	0	241	4,651	25,362	52,182	75
New Hope	5208	47	107	40	0	0	0	0	7,604	14,086	76,858	76,708	450
Pleasant Grove	5210	21	24	10	0	0	1	0	1,000	15,097	11,326	36,753	140
Shiloh	5409	22	76	31	0	0	2	0	3,500	17,612	27,173	49,687	310
Shinar**	5410	9	13	0	0	0	25	0	0	37,143	35,515	88	237
Spring Hill	5411	5	5	3	0	NRR	0	0	0	0	0	0	379
Union North	5124	35	75	19	1	3	0	0	0	14,825	32,066	46,060	120
United	5119	51	72	30	0	NRR	0	0	1,000	0	0	0	820
Willow Creek	5211	63	90	75	0	0	3	0	11,515	22,105	75,655	115,148	1,000
TOTALS	30	911	1,695	731	1	26	69	0	71,119	243,780	959,999	1,118,388	11,888

*Math error corrected. **Purged roll. NRR - No Report Received

NORTH CENTRAL PRESBYTERY CONTINUED

CHURCHES, PASTORS, AND CLERKS:

_____

Bethany   (4MWC)MINC5401
  PO Box 384 (mailing)
  219 S Lincoln Street (physical)
  Bethany, IL 61914
  (217)665-3034   <Moultrie>
CL: Dean McReynolds
  399 County Road 1600 N
  Bethany, IL 61914
  (217)665-3420
  wdeanmcreynolds@yahoo.com

_____

Burnt Prairie   (4MWC)MINC5102
  1621 County Road 950 N (mailing)
  Fairfield, IL 62837
  Church Street (physical)
  Burnt Prairie, IL 62820
  (618)925-1185   <White>
LS: Scott D Smothers   <M6>
  RR 5 Box 573
  Fairfield, IL 62837
  (618)842-6009
  lsmothers@myfrontiermail.com
CL: Andy Pottorff
  1621 County Road 950 N
  Fairfield, IL 62837
  (618)925-1185
  andypottorff@yahoo.com

_____

Campground   (4WEC)MINC5402
  1497 Hookdale Avenue (mailing)
  Route 4 (physical)
  Greenville, IL 62246
  (618)664-1547   <Bond>
CL: Rodney Reavis
  1497 Hookdale Avenue
  Greenville, IL 62246
  (618)664-1547
  rcreavis@yahoo.com

_____

Casey   (4C)MINC5201
  PO Box 21 (mailing)
  16 N Central (physical)
  Casey, IL 62420
  (217)932-5404   <Clark>
CL: Mary Gard
  7810 N 400th Street
  Casey, IL 62420
  (217)932-2971
  thetoymaker@wildblue.net

_____

Christ   (4MC)MINC5305
  6140 S Meridian
  Indianapolis, IN 46217
  (317)787-9585   <Marion>
CLOSED 2020

_____

Cumberland Chapel   (4C)MINC5104
  1075 County Road 2400E (mailing)
  Route 2 CR 1300 N, CR 1200 E (physical)
  Fairfield, IL 62837
  ( )   <Wayne>
PA: J B Gates   <M1>
  PO Box 289
  Enfield, IL 62835
  (618)963-2306
  rjjbgate@hamiltoncom.net

CL: Ronald E Huffman
  1075 County Road 2400E
  Fairfield, IL 62837
  (618)842-9518
  huffmanrj@hotmail.com

_____

Ebenezer   (4WF)MINC5203
  1941 W Belmont Avenue
  Chicago, IL 60657
  (773)528-8218   <Cook>
PA: Eduardo Montoya   <M1>
  2436 Anna Way
  Elgin, AL 60124
  (630)980-1577
  edmontoya@hotmail.com
CL: Esther Serna
  5648 Kimball Avenue
  Chicago, IL 60659
  (773)251-0606
  familiaserna@live.com

_____

Elm River   (4EC)MINC5107
  2250 County Highway 2
  Cisne, IL 62823
  ( )   <Wayne>
SS: Ralph Blevins   <M1>
  1623 County Road 2375 E
  Geff, IL 62842
  (618)854-2494
  pastorreblevins@gmail.com
CL: Cathy Barnfield
  1703 County Road 2300 E
  Geff, IL 62842

_____

Fairfield   (4MEWC)MINC5108
  1700 W Delaware
  Fairfield, IL 62837
  (618)847-5281   <Wayne>
  FAX: (618)842-2608
PA: Jeff Biggs   <M1>
  1504 Cumberland Drive
  Fairfield, IL 62837
  (618)842-2219
  jeffbiggsonline@gmail.com
CL: Kevan Stum
  15 Brock Lane
  Fairfield, IL 62837
  (618)842-2705

_____

Faith   (4C)MINC5501
  20301 E Ten Mile Road
  St Clair Shores, MI 48080
  (586)775-1524   <Macomb>
CL: Christopher D McMacken
  20396 Erben Street
  St Clair Shores, MI 48081
  (586)771-7855
  cmcmacken@itctransco.com

_____

Fullerton   (4WC)MINC5404
  1105 E Allen Street (mailing)
  Route 48 (physical)
  Farmer City, IL 61848
  ( )   <DeWitt>
CL: Duane Runyon
  1105 E Allen Street
  Farmer City, IL 61848
  (309)825-3324
  dprunyon@yahoo.com

Georgetown   (4EWC)MINC5204
  201 Frazier Street
  Georgetown, IL 61846
  (217)662-6988   <Vermilion>
CL: Stephen K Hughes
  1011 E 14th Street
  Georgetown, IL 61846
  (217)662-6988
  hughesst@sbcglobal.net

_____

Good Prospect   (4MWC)MINC5205
  PO Box 5 (mailing)
  301 E Trilla Road (physical)
  Trilla, IL 62469
  (217)234-8529   <Coles>
CL: Jedd Tolen
  PO Box 8
  Trilla, IL 62469
  trillatolens@gmail.com

_____

Grace   (4C)MINC5502
  1122 Harrison Boulevard
  Lincoln Park, MI 48146
  (313)381-3456   <Wayne>
CL: Dorinda Boyer
  21625 Knights Lane
  Brownstown, MI 48183
  (734)675-7322

_____

Knights Chapel   (4WC)MINC5306
  1285 S County Road 375 W
  Petersburg, IN 47567
  ( )   <Pike>
CL: Janet Church
  5541 W County Road 100 S
  Petersburg, IN 47567
  (812)749-3242

_____

Lebanon North   (4C)MINC5113
  1985 County Road 1070 N
  Fairfield, IL 62837
  (618)842-5205
  FAX: (618)842-5205   <Wayne>
PA: J C McDuffie   <M1>
  1985 County Road 1070 N
  Fairfield, IL 62837
  (618)842-5624
  mactrapper4@frontier.com
CL: De Young
  107 W King Street
  Fairfield, IL 62837
  (618)516-1736

_____

Lebanon South   (4C)MINC5114
  Route 3
  Galatia, IL 62935
  ( )   <Saline>
OD: Robert D Craig   <M5>
  46030 Sunset Drive
  Bay Minette, AL 36507
CL: James Patterson
  RR 2
  Galatia, IL 62935
  (618)268-4471

_____

Lincoln First   (4MEWC)MINC5405
  PO Box 596 (mailing)
  110 Broadway (physical)
  Lincoln, IL 62656
  (217)732-7568   <Logan>
  cumberland@frontier.com

NORTH CENTRAL PRESBYTERY CONTINUED

PA: Steven Blaum   <M1>
184 900 Street
Middletown, IL 62666
(217)871-3339
strab2010@yahoo.com
CL: Janet Brosamer
1402 1500th Street
Lincoln, IL 62656
(217)737-9125

_____

Monroe City   (4MWC)MINC5307
1278 S Welton Chapel Road (mailing)
Monroe City, IN 47591
8th & Cleveland Streets (physical)
Monroe City, IN 47557
(812)890-8408   <Knox>
FAX: (812)743-5171
PA: David Parman   <M1>
5034 S Monroe School Road
Monroe City, IN 47557
(812)743-2646
FAX: (812)743-5171
CL: Mary Welton
1278 S Welton Chapel Road
Vicennes, IN 47591
(812)890-8408

_____

Morningside   (4WC)MINC5304
8419 Newburgh Road
Evansville, IN 47715
(812)473-4700   <Vanderburgh>
FAX: (812)473-4765
morningsidechurch@sbcglobal.net
PA: James Messer   <M1 M8>
3653 Old Madisonville Road
Henderson, KY 42420
(270)827-0711
jcmess@hotmail.com
CL: Karen Gossman
5077 Kenosha Drive
Newburgh, IN 47630
(812)490-6522
km56gossman@yahoo.com

_____

Mt Gilead   (4C)MINC5406
PO Box 494 (mailing)
1077 Mt Gilead Road (physical)
Greenville, IL 62246
(   )   <Bond>
CL: Elizabeth File
547 IL Route 140
Pocahontas, IL 62275
(618)664-3216

_____

Mt Olivet   (4C)MINC5308
3153 S State Road 257 (mailing)
4299 S State Road 57 (physical)
Washington, IN 47501
(812)254-4077   <Daviess>
g9barnard@yahoo.com
OD: Rocky Wrye   <M5>
123 E 4th Street
Mt Carmel, IL 62863
(812)219-4563
mgwrye@hotmail.com
CL: Karen Barnard
3153 S State Road 257
Washington, IN 47501
(812)254-4077
g9barnard@yahoo.com

_____

New Hope   (4EC)MINC5208
3997 N 100th Street (mailing)
Casey, IL 62420
20955 E 2100th Avenue (physical)
Yale, IL 62481
(   )   <Jasper>
royndebbie@hotmail.com
PA: Kevin Jenkins   <M1>
411 E Main Street
Casey, IL 62420
(217)609-1120
newhoperevkev@gmail.com
CL: Roy Shanks
3997 N 100th Street
Casey, IL 62420
(217)932-2995
royndebbie@hotmail.com

_____

Pleasant Grove   (4EC)MINC5210
6360 E 2100th Avenue (mailing)
Martinsville, IL 62442
4125 E 200th Avenue (physical)
Annapolis, IL 62413
(618)569-4588   <Crawford>
donnie.bailey62@yahoo.com
LS: Bill Ulery   <M6>
10725 E 1500th Road
Marshall, IL 62441
(217)382-4593
CL: Donnie B Bailey
7970 E 1625th Avenue
Robinson, IL 62454
(618)569-4588
donnie.bailey62@yahoo.com

_____

Shiloh   (4MWC)MINC5409
7722 Shiloh Road
Virginia, IL 62691
(217)452-3802   <Cass>
CL: Anna Ruth Long
6614 IL Route 78
Virginia, IL 62691
(217)883-2654
hjlong@casscomm.com

_____

Shinar   (4WC)MINC5410
11383 147th Avenue (mailing)
West Burlington, IA 52655
19705 185th Avenue (physical)
New London, IA 52645
(319)457-2652   <Des Moines>
OD: Shane McCampbell   <M5>
109 Indian Terrace
Burlington, IA 52601
(319)457-2652
CL: Joyce Fischer
19250 - 250th Street
Morning Sun, IA 52640
joyfisch@hotmail.com

_____

Spring Hill   (4C)MINC5411
690 E 1800th Avenue (mailing)
9 miles SW of Beecher City (physical)
Beecher City, IL 62414
(   )   <Fayette>
OD: Donald Ray Miller   <M5>
Route 2 Box 136C
Beecher City, IL 62414
(618)487-5648

CL: Nelda Kline
690 E 1800th Avenue
Beecher City, IL 62414
(618)487-5363

_____

Union North   (4C)MINC5124
506 Lakeview Drive (mailing)
635 County Road 2400 E (physical)
Fairfield, IL 62837
(618)847-4061   <Wayne>
PA: Durant Axton   <M1>
2441 SE Browning Road
Evansville, IN 47725
(812)459-0089
revpeck@me.com
CL: Sandra Beckel
506 W Lakeview Drive
Fairfield, IL 62837
(618)842-6400
leesan409@outlook.com

_____

United   (4MC)MINC5119
204 S Powell Street
Norris City, IL 62869
(618)378-3341   <White>
FAX: (618)378-3064
tc_5854@yahoo.com
CL: Nellie Shepard
206 E Eubanks Street
Norris City, IL 62869
(618)378-3997

_____

Willow Creek   (4MWC)MINC5211
6492 E 400th Road
Martinsville, IL 62442
(618)569-4955   <Clark>
PA: Kevin Small   <M1>
6492 E 400th Road
Martinsville, IL 62442
(618)562-1463
revkev61@gmail.com
CL: Sarah Wilhoit
8652 E 700th Road
Martinsville, IL 62442
(217)382-5263
typtyp1@yahoo.com

_____

OTHERS ON MINISTERIAL ROLL:

Allen, Gail   <M1 WC>
488 County Road 1650 N
Bethany, IL 61914
(217)665-3387
kallen1_61914@yahoo.com
Aros, Jeremias   <M1 RT>
5649 W Roscoe Street
Chicago, IL 60634
(773)685-4395
jeremiasaros@sbcglobal.net
Bunting, Geoff   <M1 WC>
9229 Hedgewood Court
Evansville, IN 47725
(812)925-6630
geoff.bunting@yahoo.com
Dallwig, Roger   <M1 RT>
1661 Hickory Lane
Corydon, IN 47112
(812)705-5071
rcd129@hotmail.com

NORTH CENTRAL PRESBYTERY CONTINUED

Fell, Ron   <M1 WC>
  PO Box 285
  Fairfield, IL 62837
  (618)638-3744
  r.fell80@gmail.com
Furr, Wayne   <M1 WC>
  706 E 6th Street
  Coal Valley, IL 61240
  (309)756-9476
  prespreacher@gmail.com
Nichols, Oscar Lee   <M1 RT>
  1035 N County Road 650E
  Trilla, IL 62469
  (217)234-6551
Oliveira, Jose   <M1 WC>
  7310 Jasmine Drive
  Hanover Park, IL 60133
  (630)855-0870
  valdirsoares@yahoo.com
Richards, Carroll R   <M1 RT M9>
  210 Allison Drive
  Lincoln, IL 62656
  (217)732-7894
  FAX: (217)732-7894
  dr_cr@comcast.net
Thornton, Jesse   <M1 WC MY>
  2518 IL Highway 15 E
  Fairfield, IL 62837
  (618)200-0884
  jessedalethornton@gmail.com
Shirley, Betty L   <M1 RT>
  811 Rotherham Drive
  Ballwin, MO 63011
  (636)386-3174
  therevbls@prodigy.net
Watkins, Robert B   <M1 RT DE>
  5405 Kacena Avenue
  Marion, IA 52302
  (319)431-0990
  watkr@mac.com

OTHER LICENTIATES ON ROLL:

Sandiford, Holton   <M2>
  4227 E 300th Road
  Casey, IL 62420
  (217)259-3773
Stephenson, Joseph   <M2>
  326 S State Street
  Chandler, IN 47610
  (812)746-3123

OTHER CANDIDATES ON ROLL:

Lash, Colten   <M3>
  511 W North Water Street
  Bethany, IL 61914
  (217)620-1976
  coltenlash@gmail.com

Red River Presbytery
MISSION SYNOD

GENERAL	MEMBERSHIP			CHANGES				FINANCES				
1.Church Number	2.Active	3.Total	4.Church School	5.Prof. of Faith	6.Gains	7.Losses	8.Children Baptized	9. OUR UNITED OUT-REACH	10. Total Out-Reach Giving	11. All Other Expenses	12. Total Income Received	13. Value Church Prop. 1=1000
	1	2	3	4	5	6	7	8	9	10	11	12	13
Burns Flat	6301	91	91	50	0	0	1	1	3,700	13,197	945,220	107,765	1,600
Clinton	6302	59	80	10	1	4	2	0	6,994	13,089	92,716	116,453	1,047
Covenant	6304	92	119	59	1	2	1	0	6,000	15,503	169,691	153,167	1,500
Denton	8404	44	44	9	0	3	0	0	6,471	12,719	49,984	64,621	2,500
Eastlake	6205	41	138	12	0	0	9	0	6,634	8,054	94,277	97,042	1,300
Faith	6201	23	23	6	0	0	0	0	0	106	52,745	70,650	450
Lake Highlands+*	8411	93	93	24	0	2	3	0	2,700	24,096	298,879	276,861	3,606
Marlow	6305	53	73	31	0	3	1	0	9,455	18,100	76,708	106,020	690
Mesquite	8412	35	35	7	3	3	7	0	0	4,184	73,242	72,845	1,000
Mt. Zion	8414	5	7	10	0	0	2	0	2,782	0	17,722	13,698	100
Newberry	8415	26	28	0	0	0	0	0	800	6,700	33,787	35,537	466
Olney	8416	31	90	20	0	NRR	0	0	6,407	0	0	0	600
Pathway	8418	1,627	2,768	883	28	92	20	5	0	320,888	3,349,354	3,732,974	9,600
Sandy Springs	8420	26	26	1	0	NRR	0	0	2,060	0	0	0	200
Shiloh	8421	70	211	56	0	2	4	0	17,344	74,540	108,245	193,077	950
St. John	8413	50	57	11	4	4	1	0	8,432	14,160	117,495	94,136	1,032
St. Luke	8407	65	71	36	4	2	2	1	3,000	14,500	186,452	219,160	2,824
St. Mark (TX)	8408	19	18	5	0	NRR	0	0	0	0	0	0	1,048
St. Timothy	8419	77	146	20	0	1	1	0	27,481	60,037	0	1,013,208	3,000
Stonegate	6307	50	50	15	0	0	1	0	8,912	7,876	83,287	78,740	833
Trinity	8409	69	69	20	0	NRR	0	0	2,083	0	0	0	1,500
Zion Valley	8425	17	17	1	0	0	0	0	0	4,276	21,583	25,078	180
TOTALS	22	2,663	4,254	1,286	41	118	55	7	121,255	612,025	5,771,387	6,471,032	36,026

*Math error corrected. **Purged roll. +Union church NRR - No Report Received

CHURCHES, PASTORS, AND CLERKS:

Burns Flat (4WMC)MSRR6301
  PO Box 8 (mailing)
  205 Highway 44 (physical)
  Burns Flat, OK 73624
  (580)562-4706 <Washita>
  burnsflatcpc@windstream.net
PA: Thomas R Spence <M1>
  PO Box 802
  Burns Flat, OK 73624
  (580)562-4531
  tomspence0302@gmail.com
CL: Pat Stuart
  PO Box 304
  Burns Flat, OK 73624
  patience909@yahoo.com

Clinton (4WMC)MSRR6302
  500 S 30th Street
  Clinton, OK 73601
  (580)323-3440 <Custer>
SS: Bowman Vowell <M3>
  773 Heather Terrace
  Yukon, OK 73099
  (580)309-1563
  bowman.s.vowell@gmail.com
CL: Karen Murray
  4 Sandra Road
  Clinton, OK 73601
  (580)515-1327
  kmurray@bar-s.com

Covenant (4MEWC)MSRR6304
  15791 State Highway 1W
  Ada, OK 74820
  (580)332-0799 <Pontotoc>
PA: Duawn Mearns <M1>
  311 Chickasaw Drive
  Ada, OK 74820
  (580)332-0799
  duawn@covenantcpc.org
CL: Denna Gordon
  15738 County Road 3540
  Ada, OK 74820
  (580)310-0120
  dkbgordon@yahoo.com

Denton (4MWC)MSRR8404
  PO Box 236 (mailing)
  Denton, TX 76202
  1424 Stuart Road (physical)
  Denton, TX 76209
  (940)387-6811 <Denton>
  gacakee12@verizon.net
CL: Judy Thomason
  PO Box 236
  Denton, TX 76202
  (940)382-6809
  tobyjudy@hotmail.com

Eastlake (4C)MSRR6205
  700 SW 134th Street
  Oklahoma City, OK 73170
  (405)799-8987 <Oklahoma>
  eastlakecpc@eastlakechurch.org
PA: Leslie A Johnson <M1>
  11716 Price Drive
  Oklahoma City, OK 73170
  (405)248-4232
  pastorlesliej@gmail.com

RED RIVER PRESBYTERY CONTINUED

CL: Barbara Poppe
9916 Hefner Village Place
Oklahoma City, OK 73162
(405)831-5343
bpoppe1953@gmail.com

_____

Faith   (4WC)MSRR6201
PO Box 690715 (mailing)
2801 S 129th East Avenue (physical)
Tulsa, OK 74169
(918)437-2190   <Tulsa>
FAX: (918)437-2199
faithchurchcp@gmail.com
CL: Edwin Averill
19880 E Fox Run Circle
Owasso, OK 74055
(918)376-9648
elaverill3@yahoo.com

_____

Lake Highlands   (4WU)MSRR8411
8525 Audelia Road
Dallas, TX 75238
(214)348-2133   <Dallas>
lhpc@lhpres.org
PA: Perryn Rice   <M4>
2122 Auburn Drive
Richardson, TX 75081
(931)526-6585
perryn@lhpres.org
CL: Maureen Ramsay
8935 Larchwood Drive
Dallas, TX 75238
(214)542-6173
FAX: (214)348-2408
msramsay@hotmail.com

_____

Marlow   (4MWC)MSRR6305
202 N Sixth
Marlow, OK 73055
(580)658-2892   <Stephens>
PA: Terra Sisco   <M1>
811 W Cheyenne Street
Marlow, OK 73055
(618)384-6126
terrasisco@hotmail.com
CL: Kim Whaley
3010 Stagestand
Duncan, OK 73533
(405)779-6380
kimbra.whaley@duncanregional.com

_____

Mesquite   (4C)MSRR8412
819 N Town East Boulevard
Mesquite, TX 75150
(972)270-6923   <Dallas>
FAX: (972)270-6923
mcpchurch@gmail.com
SS: William (Eddie) Jenkins   <M1 RT>
10309 Tammaron Trail
Fort Worth, TX 76140
(813)579-8994
webkjl@verison.net
CL: Leecy Moore
1936 S Lakeshore Drive
Rockwall, TX 75087
(214)533-4472
locket0806@hotmail.com

_____

Mt Zion   (2C)MSRR8414
14366 State Highway 11 W (mailing)
Cumby, TX 75433
15175 Texas Highway 11 W (physical)
Cumby, TX 75433
(903)454-3444   <Hopkins>
bvwood10@yahoo.com
CL: Brenda McDaniel
14366 State Highway 11 W
Cumby, TX 75433
(903)886-2503
brendamcdaniel49@yahoo.com

_____

Newberry   (2C)MSRR8415
PO Box 253 (mailing)
1301 Newberry Road (physical)
Millsap, TX 76066
(   )   <Parker>
PA: Duane A Dougherty, Jr   <M1 RT>
4713 Lake Havasu
Fort Worth, TX 76103
(903)842-4745
revdad.duane@gmail.com
CL: Joel Young
2902 Old Milsap Road
Weatherford, TX 76088
(817)341-0800
joeleyoung@aol.com

_____

Olney   (4MEWC)MSRR8416
PO Box 756 (mailing)
210 S Avenue M (physical)
Olney, TX 76374
(940)564-2882   <Young>
olneycpc@brazosnet.comt
PA: David Carpenter   <M1>
909 W Elm Street
Olney, TX 76374
(940)564-2339
olneycpc@brazosnet.com
CL: Clifton W Key
PO Box 615
Olney, TX 76374
(940)564-2979
barkey8@brazosnet.com

_____

Pathway   (4EC)MSRR8418
(previously named St Matthew)
PO Box 182 (mailing)
325 NW Renfro(physical)
Burleson, TX 76097
(817)295-5832   <Johnson>
FAX: (817)295-2576
info@pathway.church
PA: Rick Owen   <M1>
3305 Wild Oaks Court
Burleson, TX 76028
(817)295-5832
FAX: (817)295-2576
rowen@pathway.church
AP: Jeffrey A Gehle   <M1>
PO Box 182
Burleson, TX 76097
(817)295-5832
jeff@pathway.church
AP: Judith Ellen Madden   <M1>
100 SW Brushy Mound
Burleson, TX 76028
(817)295-5832
jmadden@pathway.church

_____

AP: R Allan Mink   <M1>
1113 Hidden Glen Court
Burleson, TX 76028
(817)295-5832
FAX: (817)295-2576
alan.mink@pathway.church
AP: Chris Bohon   <M1>
505 Edgehill Road
Joshua, TX 76058
(817)228-9494
cbohon@pathway.church
CL: Kim Perkey
2600 Embry Lane
Burleson, TX 76028
(817)235-9061
jkjjperkey@sbcglobal.net

_____

Sandy Springs   (4C)MSRR8420
1865 Bones Chapel Road (mailing)
Rease Road (physical)
Whitesboro, TX 76273
(   )   <Grayson>
CL: Eddie Vidrine
1865 Bones Chapel Road
Whitesboro, TX 76273
(902)584-5148
eddievid@gmail.com

_____

Shiloh   (4MEWC)MSRR8421
7810 Shiloh Road
Midlothian, TX 76065
(972)723-3758   <Ellis>
CL: Linda Norton
8620 Mattie Lane
Waxahachie, TX 75167
(214)284-3255
lindaknorton@sbcglobal.net

_____

St John   (4WC)MSRR8413
6007 W Pleasant Ridge Road
Arlington, TX 76016
(817)478-6219   <Tarrant>
FAX: (817)478-8684
stjohncpc@att.net
PA: Adrian Scott   <M1>
7204 Johnstone Lane
Fort Worth, TX 76133
(817)205-7760
scott.adrian@zoho.com
CL: Barbara Harrell
6207 W Poly Webb Road
Arlington, TX 76016
(817)229-1796
baharrell@tx.rr.com

_____

St Luke   (4C)MSRR8407
1404 Sycamore School Road
Fort Worth, TX 76134
(817)293-3778   <Tarrant>
FAX: (817)293-2750
office@stlukecpc.org
CL: Pat Huff
249 Rancho Drive
Saginaw, TX 76179
(817)232-1558
phuff@rocketmail.com

_____

St Mark (TX)   (4MWC)MSRR8408
4101 Hardeman Street
Fort Worth, TX 76119
(817)536-1315   <Tarrant>

RED RIVER PRESBYTERY CONTINUED

PA: Roosevelt Baugh   <M1>
    4101 Hardeman Street
    Fort Worth, TX 76119
    (817)536-1315
    gmf1220@charter.net
CL: Hazel F Wilson
    2801 Sarah Jane Lane
    Fort Worth, TX 76119
    (817)536-4892
    jesseewilson@charter.net

_____
St Timothy   (4WC)MSRR8419
    PO Box 210338 (mailing)
    3001 Forest Ridge Drive (physical)
    Bedford, TX 76095
    (817)571-7474   <Tarrant>
    FAX: (817)571-7714
CL: Danny Washmon
    PO Box 210338
    Bedford, TX 76095
    (817)571-7474
    danwashmon@mail.com

_____
Stonegate   (ARC)MSRR6307
    17101 North Western Avenue
    Edmond, OK 73012
    (405)340-7281   <Oklahoma>
    stonegatecpc@gmail.com
PA: Marian Sontowski   <M1>
    17101 North Western Avenue
    Edmond, OK 73012
    (405)340-7281
    stonegatecpc@gmail.com
CL: Jacque Wilson
    17101 North Western Avenue
    Edmond, OK 73012
    (405)627-8947
    stonegate.clerk@gmail.com

_____
Trinity   (4MEWC)MSRR8409
    7120 W Cleburne Road
    Fort Worth, TX 76133
    (817)292-6149   <Tarrant>
    trinitycpc@sbcglobal.net
PA: Randy L Hardisty   <M1>
    4908 Redondo Street
    Fort Worth, TX 76180
    (817)428-3513
    rhardisty@sbcglobal.net
CL: Betty Jean Cooper
    3401 Amador Drive Apt 4304
    Fort Worth, TX 76177
    (817)741-9888
    bjjacoop@sbcglobal.net

_____
Zion Valley   (4C)MSRR8425
    2684 South FM 1655
    Chico, TX 76431
    ( )   <Wise>
PA: Barney Hudson   <M1>
    10541 Fossil Hill Drive
    Fort Worth, TX 76131
    (817)851-2960
    barneyrev@gmail.com
CL: Session Clerk

_____
OTHERS ON MINISTERIAL ROLL:

Aden, Marty   <M1 M9>
    202 Bennington Place
    Wilmington, NC 28412
    (910)274-8465
    maadretny@gmail.com
Baltimore, Claud G   <M1 RT>
    PO Box 1358
    1430 Lakehurst Drive
    Ada, OK 74821
    (580)332-2679
    baltimorejb@earthlink.net
Brown, Chuck   <M1 WC>
    2277 Union Avenue Unit 407
    Memphis, TN 38104
    (901)246-5837
Brown, Stephanie S   <M1 M9>
    475 N Highland Street 6B
    Memphis, TN 38122
    (817)915-1317
    scrudderbrown7@gmail.com
Burdick, Cynthia Maddux   <M1 WC>
    16501 SE 113th Street
    Newalla, OK 74857
    (405)395-8056
    cynthiaburdick02@gmail.com
Condon, Jr, Thomas W   <M1 RT>
    6508 Victoria Avenue
    N Richland Hills, TX 76180
    (817)656-9334
Ferrol, Ruben   <M1 M9 RT>
    13018 E 28th Street
    Tulsa, OK 74134
    (610)966-7289
    rubeferrol@msn.com
Fortney, Josh   <M1 WC>
    1614 Woodoak Drive
    Richardson, TX 75082
    (214)794-9912
    jfortney@pathway.church
Gardner, Charles   <M1 RT>
    PO Box 1035
    Elephant Butte, NM 87935
    (719)784-7744
Harris, Wendell   <M1 WC>
    329 N Louis Tittle Avenue
    Mangum, OK 73554
    (580)782-2142
    wendellharris@itlnet.net
Hayes, Jennifer   <M1 M9>
    7005 Woodmoor Road
    Fort Worth, TX 76133
    (205)533-1018
    hayesj712@gmail.com
Hayes, Marcus   <M1 WC>
    7005 Woodmoor Road
    Fort Worth, TX 76133
    (270)841-7576
    marcus.hayes@att.net
Henson, Kevin R   <M1 WC>
    8461 McDaniel Road
    Fort Worth, TX 76126
    (817)354-1182
    kevin.r.henson@gmail.com
Hong, Soon Gab   <M1 WC>
    13600 Doty Avenue Apt 4
    Hawthorne, CA 90250
    (972)446-0350
    lemuelhong@hotmail.com

Howell, Linda   <M1 WC>
    PO Box 80050
    Keller, TX 76244
    (817)564-2236
    sunnylindatrue@gmail.com
Johnson, Wesley   <M1 WC>
    6222 Crestmoore Lane
    Sachse, TX 75048
    (972)467-3571
    wes3131@icloud.com
Lain, Judy   <M1 WC>
    1928 Pine Ridge Drive
    Bedford, TX 76021
    (817)909-6702
    judylaine5@gmail.com
Lewis, Emily Fowler   <M1 M9>
    5225 Maple Avenue Apt 5309
    Dallas, TX 75235
    (817)9853-3559
    emilykaye.fowler@gmail.com
Lounsbury, Kristi   <M1 DE>
    902 Clearview
    Krum, TX 76249
    (940)435-5077
    klounsbury@cumberland.org
Martinez, Soledad   <M1 WC>
    2801 Biway Street
    Fort Worth, TX 76114
    (817)812-8247
    shirleymartinez1252@gmail.com
McGee, Charles Randall   <M1 WC>
    9037 Groveland Drive
    Dallas, TX 75218
    (214)328-2488
    randallmcgee@sbcglobal.net
Neese Dale   <M1 WC>
    415 59th Street
    Clinton, OK 73601
    (580)323-7557
Nelson, Charles E   <M1 WC>
    209 Classic Court
    Springtown, TX 76082
    (903)641-5466
    dundeal10@aol.com
Petty, Linda Lee   <M1 WC>
    8601 S Mingo Road Apt 3115
    Tulsa, OK 74133
    (918)252-4741
    linda.petty47@yahoo.com
Rice, Keith   <M1 HR>
    PO Box 582
    Itasca, TX 76055
    (254)087-2418
    rsvkeith@yahoo.com
Ruggia, Mario (Bud)   <M1 RT>
    603 Rumsey Street
    Kiowa, KS 67070
    (620)825-4076
    ruggia@aol.com
Sanders, Thomas R   <M1 DE>
    8480 N 69th East Avenue
    Owasso, OK 74055
    (918)269-0043
    FAX: (918)437-2199
    trsncf@msn.com
Sansom, Vernon   <M1 WC>
    7425 Northampton Boulevard
    Knoxville, TN 37931
    (865)556-4107
    vernon@sansom.us

RED RIVER PRESBYTERY CONTINUED

Schmoyer, Donna Marie   <M1 M9>
613 Mound Street
Monongahela, PA 15063
(817)266-6572
schmoyerdm@yahoo.com

Scrudder, Norlan   <M1 RT>
1514 Irene Lane
Fort Gibson, OK 74434
(918)949-1326
ndscrudder@gmail.com

Sharpe, Michael G   <M1 DE>
3423 Summerdale Drive
Bartlett, TN 38133
(901)276-4572

Smith, Robert H   <M1 WC>
5055 S 76th East Avenue Apt D
Tulsa, OK 74145
(918)671-5520
rhsmith@sstelco.com

Snelling, Linda   <M1 M9>
240 Dakota Drive
Waxahachie, TX 75167
(469)550-9074
lsnelling50@gmail.com

Topar, Shirley   <M1 WC>
628 Landershire Lane
Plano, TX 75023
(616)245-0625
s_j_topar@yahoo.com

Wagner, Hugh   <M1 RT>
12556 Timberline Drive
Garfield, AR 72732
(479)359-0021
hughawagner@gmail.com

Webb, Lonnie, Sr   <M1 WC>
618 N E Street
Duncan, OK 73533
(580)786-8840
lgwebb.sr@gmail.com

Webb, William G   <M1 OM>
7926 S 78th East Avenue
Tulsa, OK 74133
(918)294-9117

Youngman, Betty   <M1 RT>
1471 Creekview Court
Fort Worth, TX 76112
(817)492-4100
bettyy@swbell.net

Zumbrunnen, Craig H   <M1 WC>
1970 W Old Magee Trail Apt 14105
Tucson, AZ 85704
(580)471-0308
craigzum1@yahoo.com

OTHER LICENIATES ON ROLL:

Butler, Alan   <M2>
510 City House Court Apt 406
Memphis, TN 38103
(817)937-8488
abutler@cumberland.org

Carwheel, Greg   <M2>
12908 Smokey Ranch Drive
Haslet, TX 76052
(682)215-4516
gcarwheel@gmail.com

King, Keith   <M2 ST>
3341 S 137th East Avenue
Tulsa, OK 74134
(918)437-5464
cpkking@yahoo.com

Lofton, Kathy   <M2>
10636 County Road 1500
Ada, OK 74820
(580)332-0898
kdnlofton@gmail.com

Tucker, Dave   <M2>
3901 South Drive
Burleson, TX 76028
(817)506-9197
kc5cp@gmail.com

Westfall, Justin   <M2>
1604 Wickham Drive
Burleson, TX 76028
(832)628-7094
westfall0@gmail.com

OTHER CANDIDATES ON ROLL:

Brown, Houston   <M3>
866 N McLean
Memphis, TN 38107
(817)915-9090
hpbrown95@gmail.com

Bulgarelli, Kevin   <M3>
208 Silver Rose Boulevard
Burleson, TX 76028
(410)262-4140
kevinbulgarelli@mac.com

Davis, Cheyanne   <M3>
812 Valley Ridge Road
Burleson, TX 76028
(817)781-5155
cheyanne@pathway.church

Robert Donnell Presbytery
SOUTHEAST SYNOD

GENERAL	MEMBERSHIP			CHANGES					FINANCES				
1.Church Number	2.Active	3.Total	4.Church School	5.Prof. of Faith	6.Gains	7.Losses	8.Children Baptized	9. OUR UNITED OUT-REACH	10. Total Out-Reach Giving	11. All Other Expenses	12. Total Income Received	13. Value Church Prop. 1=1000
1	2	3	4	5	6	7	8	9	10	11	12	13
Alabaster	107	137	280	50	0	0	0	0	1,587	27,119	139,715	177,526	2,300
Big Cove	801	5	17	4	0	0	0	0	0	0	17,457	19,590	330
Christ Church	814	77	112	10	0	0	0	0	279	0	73,539	86,944	700
Concord	802	26	83	16	0	0	0	0	785	3,142	22,444	18,403	286
East Point	206	22	22	19	0	4	0	0	650	1,550	21,868	26,987	902
Edgefield	813	3	3	3	0	0	0	0	0	0	125	0	127
Goosepond	803	21	22	6	0	0	0	0	1,800	7,065	22,077	24,347	250
Gurley	804	56	56	25	0	2	2	0	1,200	20,335	76,420	112,187	751
Hope	812	22	22	8	0	0	2	0	2,050	3,775	51,605	55,380	600
Huntsville, 1st	806	35	117	20	0	0	1	0	1,700	7,878	72,769	68,108	1,670
Meridianville	808	24	34	12	0	0	2	0	0	0	55,427	51,424	1,350
Scottsboro	809	279	478	74	0	4	1	3	49,956	80,455	337,339	416,947	2,500
Stevenson	810	20	157	6	0	0	4	0	5,969	13,528	51,427	58,717	1,200
Walnut Grove	811	8	10	4	0	0	0	0	0	0	500	15,000	15
TOTALS	14	735	1,413	257	0	10	12	3	65,976	164,847	942,712	1,131,560	12,981

*Math error corrected. **Purged roll.   +Union church   NRR - No Report Received

---

CHURCHES, PASTORS, AND CLERKS:

Alabaster   (4WC)SERD0107
PO Box 650 (mailing address)
8828 Highway 119 (physical address)
Alabaster, AL 35007
(205)663-3152   \<Shelby>
FAX: (205)663-8323
fpcalabaster@bellsouth.net
PA: Matthew Ingram   \<M1>
333 Union Station Circle
Calera, AL 35040
(205)663-3123
matthew.ingram@fpcalabaster.org
CL: Margaret Russo
PO Box 650
Alabaster, AL 35007
(205)663-3152
russom@att.net

Big Cove   (4MWC)SERD0801
5984 Highway 431 S
Brownsboro, AL 35741
(256)518-9657   \<Madison>
CL: Kay Tidwell
730 Old Big Cove Road
Owens Cross Roads, AL 35763
(256)288-6651
greenthumbkt@gmail.com

Christ Church   (4WC)SERD0814
1580 Jeff Road
Huntsville, AL 35806
(256)837-6014   \<Madison>
christchurch@knology.net

PA: Cardelia Howell Diamond   \<M1>
1580 Jeff Road
Huntsville, AL 35806
(256)837-6014
cpclergymama@gmail.com
CL: Frances Dawson
PO Box 904
Scottsboro, AL 35768
(256)244-0554
francescdawson@gmail.com

Concord   (4MWC)SERD0802
1827 Joe Quick Road
New Market, AL 35761
(256)828-4503   \<Madison>
alverson354@mediacombb.net
CL: Richard Dixon
626 Briar Fork Road
Hazel Green, AL 35761
(256)828-0002
\ dixonelec16@gmail.com

East Point   (4WC)SERD0206
1441 US Highway 278 E
Cullman, AL 35055
(256)734-0900   \<Cullman>
SS: Philip Nickles   \<M1 OP>
5821 County Road 1114
Vinemont, AL 35179
(256)734-9847
phillipnickles996@yahoo.com
CL: Karen Munger
PO Box 1773
Cullman, AL 35056
(256)739-0746
karenamunger@bellsouth.net

Edgefield   (4UC)SERD0813
411 McMahan Cove Road (mailing)
Stevenson, AL 35772
311 County Road 158 (physical)
Stevenson, AL 35772
( )   \<Jackson>
CL: Christie Nunley
411 McMahan Cove Road
Stevenson, AL 35772
(256)437-9011

Goosepond   (4MWC)SERD0803
1155 East Hancock Drive
Scottsboro, AL 35769
(256)259-4386   \<Jackson>
betrich76@gmail.com
CL: Cathy Cowley
452 County Road 77
Scottsboro, AL 35769
(256)259-8335
cthycowley@icloud.com

Gurley   (4MEWC)SERD0804
223 Section Line Road
Gurley, AL 35748
(256)776-2331   \<Madison>
PA: Toy E Brindley   \<M1>
149 Joplin Street
Gurley, AL 35748
(256)776-2331
gurleycpc@gmail.com

ROBERT DONNELL PRESBYTERY CONTINUED

CL: Becky Arnold
423 Sharps Cove Road
Gurley, AL 35748
(256)776-6950
bailey@darnold.net
_____

Hope   (4WU)SERD0812
10001 Bailey Cove Road SE
Huntsville, AL 35803
(256)881-4673   <Madison>
hopepresby@comcast.net
OD: Christie Ashton   <M5>
10001 Bailey Cove Road SE
Huntsville, AL 35803
(256)881-4673\3
pastor@hopehuntsville.org
CL: Joanna Sterling-Clutts
10001 Bailey Cove Road SE
Huntsville, AL 35803
(256)479-9899
alabamahoosier@gmail.com
_____

Huntsville First   (4EWC)SERD0806
PO Box 777 (mailing)
1802 Bankhead Parkway (physical)
Huntsville, AL 35804
(256)536-9371   <Madison>
hsvfcpc@att.net
PA: Richard W Hughes   <M1>
2954 Bob Wade Lane
Harvest, AL 35749
(256)859-3178
hughesrichard23@gmail.com
CL: Steve Rowley
PO Box 777
2012 Brandy Court
Huntsville, AL 35811
(256)683-9784
rowley35@gmail.com
_____

Meridianville   (4MWC)SERD0808
PO Box 188 (mailing)
11696 Highway 231/431 N (physical)
Meridianville, AL 35759
(256)828-0160   <Madison>
dptalley@hotmail.com
PA: Keith Lorick   <M1>
127 Chesapeake Boulevard
Madison, AL 35757
(256)325-3865
keithlorick@knology.net
CL: Donna Talley
360 Monroe Road
Meridianville, AL 35759
(256)683-6111
dptalley@hotmail.com
_____

Scottsboro   (4WC)SERD0809
PO Box 639 (mailing)
315 S Kyle Street (physical)
Scottsboro, AL 35768
FAX: (256)259-2809
cumberland@scottsboro.org
(256)574-2575   <Jackson>
PA: Micaiah Thomas Tanck   <M1>
3218 Scenic Drive
Scottsboro, AL 35769
(205)478-5985
micaiah.thomas@gmail.com

CL: Gene Gossett
1707 Brandon Street
Scottsboro, AL 35769
256)574-6334
ggossett@scottsboro.org
_____

Stevenson   (4MEWC)SERD0810
112 College Street
Stevenson, AL 35772
(256)437-8632   <Jackson>
CL: Jen Stewart
112 College Street
Stevenson, AL 35772
(256)437-3116
jstewart306@hotmail.com
_____

Walnut Grove   (4WC)SERD0811
PO Box 403 (mailing)
711 New Hope/Cedar Point Road (physical)
New Hope, AL 35760
(   )   <Madison>
CL: Kathy Pegues
211 Butler Lane
New Hope, AL 35760
(256)723-8740
mcwoodpeg@nehp.net
_____

OTHERS ON MINISTERIAL ROLL:

Alverson, Elmer L   <M1 HR>
354 Roy Davis Road
New Market, AL 35761
(256)828-4503
1941buddy@att.net
Babcock, Edward S, Jr   <M1 HR>
200 River Vista Drive Unit 306
Sandy Springs, GA 30339
(256)882-9339
ejsb1@aol.com
Gillis, Aubrey Thomas   <M1 WC>
110 Blue Sky Lane
Alabaster, AL 35007
(251)947-1638
FAX: (205)664-8323
tomgillis63@hotmail.com
Goodwin, Earl   <M1 WC>
1255 Stevens Road
Bessemer, AL 35022
(205)222-1741
FAX: (205)664-8323
earlgoodwin@yahoo.com
Hall, Brad   <M1 WC>
1602 Toll Gate Road SE
Huntsville, AL 35801
(256)533-4845
Hall, Roy W   <M1 RT>
1713 Lookout Mountain Drive
Scottsboro, AL 35769
(256)259-9340
royhall@scottsboro.org
Herring, C E (Ed) Jr   <M1 RT>
969 Campground Circle
Scottsboro, AL 35769
(256)259-2721
edherring@scottsboro.org
Howell-Diamond, Steven   <M1 WC>
106 Ultimate Court
Madison, AL 35757
smdiam@hotmail.com
(931)636-7336

Howton, Orvie Ray   <M1 RT>
4928 Montauk Trail SE
Owens Cross Road, AL 35763
(256)533-9224
orphowton@yahoo.com
Hughes, Charles   <M1 HR>
114 Gaul Street
Estill Springs, TN 37330
(931)649-5189
cphugs@cafes.net
Kennemer, Darren   <M1 WC>
8828 Highway 119
Alabaster, AL 35007
(205)663-3152
FAX: (205)663-8323
dlkennemer@gmail.com
Livingston, Ronald L   <M1 HR>
11314 Maplecrest Drive
Huntsville, AL 35803
hairy404@outlook.com
Matthews, James N   <M1 HR>
241 Morning Star Drive
Huntsville, AL 35811
(256)337-2765
brojim10@att.net
Murphree, Hughlen   <M1 HR>
4298 County Road 1719
Holly Pond, AL 35083
(256)796-5352
hmurph@hiwaay.net
Phillips-Burk, Pam   <M1 DE>
3325 Bailey Creek Cove N
Collierville, TN 38017
(256)684-5247
pam@cumberland.org
Reeves, Donald   <M1 HR>
PO Box 528
Rainsville, AL 35986
(256)228-4057
reevesd@nacc.edu
Smith, James   <M1 WC>
1949 Little Cove Road
Owens Cross Roads, AL 35763
dr.james.smith42@gmail.com
Tanck, Brian   <M1 WC>
3218 Scenic Drive
Scottsboro, AL 35769
(630)730-1577
brian.tanck@gmail.com
_____

OTHER LICENTIATES ON ROLL:
_____

OTHER CANDIDATES ON ROLL:

Anderson, Angela   <M3>
128 Horse Pin Place
Harvest, AL 35749
divineanderson75@yahoo.com
Young, Lacey Grace   <M3>
1211 Michael Drive
Alabaster, AL 35007
laceygrace1918@gmail.com

Tennessee-Georgia Presbytery
SOUTHEAST SYNOD

GENERAL	MEMBERSHIP			CHANGES				FINANCES				
1.Church Number	2.Active	3.Total	4.Church School	5.Prof. of Faith	6.Gains	7.Losses	8.Children Baptized	9. OUR UNITED OUT-REACH	10. Total Out-Reach Giving	11. All Other Expenses	12. Total Income Received	13. Value Church Prop. 1=1000
	1	2	3	4	5	6	7	8	9	10	11	12	13

	1	2	3	4	5	6	7	8	9	10	11	12	13
Bartow	2101	95	163	27	2	11	6	2	0	18,326	122,142	137,687	1,307
Cedar Springs	2119	6	15	0	0	0	0	0	0	31	7,766	10,019	344
Charleston	2102	43	49	15	0	0	0	0	0	11,931	49,555	54,763	800
Chattanooga 1st*	2104	263	730	109	3	220	11	4	0	33,539	547,809	612,877	1,275
Cleveland	2108	102	183	60	0	NRR	0	0	7,313	0	0	0	2,500
Cornerstone Com	2107	12	42	9	0	NRR	0	0	0	0	0	0	675
Ebenezer	2110	5	6	0	0	NRR	0	0	200	0	0	0	75
El Redill	2149	39	42	35	0	0	5	0	5,608	8,954	39,400	46,352	780
Falling Water	2111	53	68	28	1	1	3	0	1,000	19,127	93,957	107,650	820
Flint Springs	2112	22	22	0	0	0	2	0	0	0	0	17,392	150
Jasper	2113	14	26	5	0	0	2	0	3,000	3,100	32,969	39,955	800
Kelly's Chapel	2120	10	10	10	0	NRR	0	0	0	0	0	0	100
New Hope	2115	55	92	30	3	3	5	0	1,431	6,454	100,263	100,206	1,000
Oak Grove	2121	12	29	0	0	NRR	0	0	0	0	0	0	110
Pikeville	2153	9	7	9	0	0	6	0	0	200	10,139	10,812	n/a
Prospect United	2116	36	36	11	0	0	0	0	1,300	2,090	46,492	60,947	1,400
Red Bank	2105	159	172	62	0	0	5	3	0	4,603	226,942	189,563	2,100
Richard City	2118	20	59	13	0	1	1	0	900	2,496	63,815	76,717	600
Silverdale	2106	127	161	45	0	2	2	1	9,983	20,602	130,696	165,161	1,800
South Pittsburg	2123	15	60	4	0	0	0	0	100	350	24,113	22,542	1,318
Sumach	2124	120	230	68	1	3	4	0	1,250	18,930	174,404	175,878	775
Whitwell	2122	8	9	10	0	NRR	0	0	0	0	0	0	25
TOTALS	22	1,225	2,211	550	10	241	52	10	32,085	150,733	1,670,462	1,828,521	18,754

*Math error corrected. **Purged roll. NRR - No Report Received PROV - Provisional Church

CHURCHES, PASTORS, AND CLERKS:

Bartow   (4MWEC)SETG2101
  1078 Cassville White Road (mailing)
  Cartersville, GA 30121
  2851 Highway 140 NE (physical)
  Rydal, GA 30171
  (770)382-3896   <Bartow>
  pastormarkbcpcga@gmail.com
PA: Mark Rackley   <M1>
  3060 Highway 140 NE
  Rydal, GA 30171
  (770)382-3790
  pastormarkbcpcga@gmail.com
CL: Susan Turner
  1129 Richards Road
  Rydal, GA 30171
  (770)547-0266
  susan.turner318@gmail.com

Cedar Springs   (4C)SETG2119
  495 Cedar Springs Loop (mailing)
  6665 Old Dunlap Road (physical)
  Whitwell, TN 37397
  ( )   <Marion>
PA: Kriss McGowan   <M1>
  885 Mount Calvary Road
  Whitwell, TN 37397
  (423)463-8609
  krissmcg658@gmail.com
CL: Sarah Way
  4595 Old Dunlap Road
  Whitwell, TN 37397
  (423)637-3616
  sarahway1958@aol.com

Charleston   (4MEWC)SETG2102
  PO Box 476 (mailing)
  Charleston, TN 37310
  8267 N Lee Highway (physical)
  Cleveland, TN 37312
  (423)336-5004   <Bradley>

PA: Bill Bond   <M1>
  205 Windmere Drive
  Chattanooga, TN 37411
  (423)316-0867
  bill@wcbj.net
CL: Vivian McCormack
  5502 Mouse Creek Road NW
  Cleveland, TN 37312
  (423)479-8230
  mcco6868@bellsouth.net

Chattanooga First   (4WC)SETG2104
  1505 N Moore Road
  Chattanooga, TN 37411
  (423)698-2556   <Hamilton>
  FAX: (423)629-6683
  office@firstcumberland.com
PA: Courtney Krueger   <M1>
  1505 N Moore Road
  Chattanooga, TN 37411
  (864)933-4912
  ck@firstcumberland.com

TENNESSEE-GEORGIA PRESBYTERY CONTINUED

CL: Tim McDonald
4533 East Ravenwood Drive
Chattanooga, TN 37415
(423)877-0999
scot4533@gmail.com

Cleveland   (4WC)SETG2108
PO Box 694 (mailing)
200 Church Street NE (physical)
Cleveland, TN 37364
(423)476-6751   <Bradley>
FAX: (423)476-6423
PA: Jennifer Newell   <M1>
2322 Maraco Circle
Chattanooga, TN 37421
(423)892-5834
FAX: (423)476-6423
newelljennifer3@gmail.com
CL: Tommy Newman
1231 Brymer Creek Road
McDonald, TN 37353
(423)472-8763

Cornerstone Com   (4MWC)SETG2107
9632 E Brainerd Road
Chattanooga, TN 37421
(423)892-3027   <Hamilton>
cornerstone3cp@gmail.com
SS: Jerry (Butch) Hullander   <M1>
767 Rifle Range Road
Ringgold, GA 30736
(423)802-6156
jerryihs@catt.com
CL: Connie O'Hare
9632 E Brainerd Road
Chattanooga, TN 37421
(423)827-5148
cornerstone3cp@gmail.com

Ebenezer   (4C)SETG2110
10699 Griffith Highway (mailing)
2400 Highway 108(physical)
Whitwell, TN 37397
(423)942-1939   <Marion>
cprevinsv@bellsouth.net
PA: Phillip Layne   <M1>
10699 Griffith Highway
Whitwell, TN 37397
(423)658-5849
44philliplayne@gmail.com
CL: Carol Renfro
PO Box 434
Sequatchie, TN 37374
(423)942-3191

El Redill   (C)SETG2149
875 Scenic Highway
Lawrenceville, GA 30045
(678)698-7971   <Monmouth>
FAX: (678)225-0127
mabega@juno.com
PA: Maria (Mabe) Garcia   <M1>
875 Scenic Highway
Lawrenceville, GA 30045
(678)698-7971
pastoramabegarcia@gmail.com
AP: Lucas Garcia   <M1>
875 Scenic Highway
Lawrenceville, GA 30045
(678)698-7971
lucasgarcia924@gmail.com

CL: Ana Valdez
112 Amelia Creek Way
Lawrenceville, GA 30045
(678)373-1226
ann valdez15@hotmail.com

Falling Water   (4WC)SETG2111
PO Box 2027 (mailing)
6534 Old Dayton Pike (physical)
Hixson, TN 37343
(423)843-3050   <Hamilton>
PA: Perry Whitaker   <M1>
1133 Forest Plaza Circle
Hixson, TN 37343
(615)691-2933
brotherperry@msn.com
CL: Gayle Hixson
6200 Fairview Road
Hixson, TN 37343
(423)842-8429
hixsongayle@gmail.com

Flint Springs   (4WC)SETG2112
2225 North East Road SE (mailing)
Flint Springs Road (physical)
Cleveland, TN 37311
( )   <Bradley>
PA: Kevin Wilson   <M1>
2225 North East Road SE
Cleveland, TN 37311
(423)284-6397
revkev1000@hotmail.com
CL: James F Mitchell, Jr
517 Mitchell Road SE
Cleveland, TN 37323
(423)479-7649

Jasper   (4MWC)SETG2113
PO Box 877 (mailing)
148 College Street (physical)
Jasper, TN 37347
(423)942-2188   <Marion>
FAX: (423)942-2188
PS: Mark Craven   <M2>
21 Kingston Street
Chattanooga, TN 37415
(4230618-0169
craven.ma@gmail.com
CL: Dorris G Ross
214 Hancock Road
Jasper, TN 37347
(423)942-5224
FAX: (423)942-2188
ross37347@charter.net

Kelly's Chapel   (4MC)SETG2120
3748 Alvin York Highway (mailing)
470 Highway 27 (physical)
Whitwell, TN 37397
( )   <Marion>
carolb8667@bellsouth.net
OD: Anthony Tucker   <M5>
209 Rock City Trail
Lookout Mountain, GA 30750
(423)595-1585
hos@hvcs.org
CL: Carol Brown
3748 Alvin York Highway
Whitwell, TN 37397
carolb8667@bellsouth.net

New Hope   (4MWC)SETG2115
196 E Valley Road (physical)
Whitwell, TN 37397
(423)949-3951   <Sequatchie>

CL: James Condra
PO Box 1001
Dunlap, TN 37327
(423)447-8126
jwcondra@bledsoe.net

Oak Grove   (4C)SETG2121
872 Alvin York Highway (mailing)
8150 Griffith Highway (physical)
Whitwell, TN 37397
( )   <Marion>
PA: Phillip H Layne   <M1>
10699 Griffith Highway
Whitwell, TN 37397
(423)658-6421
44philliplayne@gmail.com
CL: Martha S Layne
872 Alvin York Highway
Whitwell, TN 37397
(423)658-6421
mllayne09@gmail.com

Pikeville   (4C)SETG2153
PO Box 1001 (mailing)
Dunlap, TN 37327
544 Sequatchee Road (physical)
Pikeville, TN 37367
(423)447-6897
PA: Rhonda McGowan   <M1>
885 Mount Calvary Road
Whitwell, TN 37397
(423)619-5679
rhondam658@gmail.com
CL: Linda Jordan
735 Panter Bottom Road
Pikeville, TN 37367
(423)881-3042
marinemoi@hotmail.com

Prospect United   (4MC)SETG2116
310 New Murraytown Road NW
Cleveland, TN 37312
(423)476-6181   <Bradley>
prospectucpc@att.net
PA: Philip (Phil) Sumrall   <M1>
107 Barnhardt Circle
Fort Oglethorpe, GA 30742
(423)903-1938
phil.sumrall@gmail.com
CL: Patricia Stonecipher
607 Davis Road NW
Cleveland, TN 37312
(423)336-2295
pcstonecipher@gmail.comt

Red Bank   (4WC)SETG2105
115 Morrison Springs Road
Chattanooga, TN 37415
(423)877-1383   <Hamilton>
rbcpchurch@gmail.com
CL: Dee Clark
649 O Sage Drive
Soddy-Daisy, TN 37379

Richard City   (4MWC)SETG2118
1706 Marion Avenue
South Pittsburg, TN 37380
(423)837-6533   <Marion>
PA: Bruce Potter   <M1>
1712 Marion Avenue
South Pittsburg, TN 37380
(423)228-4485
brucepotter@charter.net

TENNESSEE-GEORGIA PRESBYTERY CONTINUED

CL: Bill Norman
624 19th Street
South Pittsburg, TN 37380
(423)837-6693
FAX: (423)837-8903
billnorman@catcore.com

Silverdale (4MEWC)SETG2106
7407 Bonny Oaks Drive
Chattanooga, TN 37421
(423)892-8710 <Hamilton>
FAX: (423)892-7751
PA: George Cliff Hudson <M1 DE>
4782 Waverly Court
Ooltewah, TN 37363
(423)645-7563
gchudson3@gmail.com
CL: Dotty Manis
7939 Clara Chase Drive
Ooltewah, TN 37363
(423)238-4021
dottmae@centurylink.net

South Pittsburg (4MWC)SETG2123
PO Box 327 (mailing)
400 Elm Avenue (physical)
South Pittsburg, TN 37380
(423)837-6488 <Marion>
spcpc1@yahoo.com
PA: Kriss McGowan <M1>
885 Mount Calvary Road
Whitwell, TN 37397
(423)463-8609
krissmcg658@gmail.com
CL: George Holland
214 Dixie Avenue
South Pittsburg, TN 37380
(423)837-7113
georgehollandsp@att.net

Sumach (4MWC)SETG2124
PO Box 804 (mailing)
9203 Highway 225 N (physical)
Chatsworth, GA 30705
(706)695-4773 <Murray>
FAX: (706)695-4773
sumachcpchurch@windstream.net
PA: Tom Clark <M1>
2089 Sumach Church Road
Chatsworth, GA 30705
(270)469-4377
tom402135@hotmail.com
CL: Carolyn Luffman
926 Long Avenue
Chatsworth, GA 30705
(706)695-4346
cizzle44@hotmail.com

Whitwell (4C)SETG2122
7390 Highway 108
Whitwell, TN 37397
(423)658-5849 <Marion>
PA: Phillip Layne <M1>
10699 Griffith Highway
Whitwell, TN 37397
(423)658-5849
44philliplayne@gmail.com
CL: Sue Caldwell
7390 Highway 108
Whitwell, TN 37397
(423)658-6463

OTHERS ON MINISTERIAL ROLL:

Barry, James C <M1 WC>
2912 Roy Road
Tyler, TX 75707
(903)315-7998
james_barry@bellsouth.net
Brister, Glenn <M1 WC>
3004 Deleware Avenue
McComb, MS 39648
(706)934-8629
bearmountainpenworks@gmail.com
Buttram, Jim <M1 RT>
5385 Bungalow Circle
Hixson, TN 37343
(423)260-1805
littlejimb@gmail.com
Carver, Gary <M1 HR>
2810 Cabin Road
Chattanooga, TN 37404
(423)698-2556
FAX: (423)629-6683
sandgatthecabin@epbfi.com
Hollingshed, Lee <M1 WC>
3612 Harmony Church Grove Road
Dallas, GA 30132
(770)548-0152
leearmstrong@bellsouth.net
Jackson, Lamar <M1 HR>
280 Deer Ridge Drive Apt D
Dayton, TN 37321
(423)570-9348
hljaxn@charter.net
Jones, Harold <M1 RT>
650 College Drive
Dalton, GA 30720
(478)320-4222
harold@personalcharacter.com
Lee, David <M1 WC>
Lee, Sarah <M1 WC>
Martin, Theresa <M1 WC>
116 Crisman Street
Chattanooga, TN 37415
(423)903-7260 (cell)
choochootm@usa.net
Martin, Tom <M1 WC>
116 Crisman Street
Chattanooga, TN 37415
(423)903-7260 (cell)
choochootm@usa.net
Patterson, James H. <M1 HR>
6705 Ballard Drive #211
Chattanooga, TN 37421
(423)267-8568
FAX: (423)942-2188
Prosser, Forest <M1 RT>
1157 Mountain Creek Road
Chattanooga, TN 37405
(423)877-4114
forestprosser@comcast.net
Tolley, Robert (Butch) <M1 WC>
975 6th Street
Cleveland, TN 37311
(423)837-6488
butchtolley@hotmail.com
Turner, Glyn <M1 M8>
601 Wynfal Drive
Holly Ridge, NC 28455
(585)307-7715
glynturner@hotmail.com

OTHER LICENTIATES ON ROLL:

Kennedy, Jim <M2>
613 English Ivy Way
Aberdeen, MD 21001
jpkak@comcast.net

OTHER CANDIDATES ON ROLL:
Jordan, Matthew <M3>
735 Painter Bottom Road
Pikeville, TN 37367
matthew.jordan3009@hotmail.com
Lollar, Jeff
154 Pathfinder Way
Dalton, GA 30721
(706)218-3379
jrlollar1873@gmail.com

Trinity Presbytery
MISSION SYNOD

	1.Church Number	2.Active	3.Total	4.Church School	5.Prof. of Faith	6.Gains	7.Losses	8.Children Baptized	9. OUR UNITED OUT-REACH	10. Total Out-Reach Giving	11. All Other Expenses	12. Total Income Received	13. Value Church Prop. 1=1000
	1	2	3	4	5	6	7	8	9	10	11	12	13
Antioch	8101	10	10	8	0	NRR	0	0	1,600	0	0	0	325
Bertram	8605	19	163	14	0	0	2	0	1,000	10,629	29,473	34,829	1,036
Concord	8104	51	51	40	0	0	1	0	9,893	9,200	82,799	91,999	805
Daingerfield	8106	4	6	2	0	0	0	0	0	2,361	24,282	22,734	122
Elmira Chapel*	8111	50	90	10	0	2	3	0	1,200	36,890	170,114	133,223	3,000
Freeport	8103	16	17	4	0	0	3	0	1,200	1,200	53,895	48,590	933
Houston, 1st	8606	61	126	120	0	0	1	0	44,900	95,271	392,762	448,982	3,000
Jefferson	8109	33	33	11	2	3	2	1	0	9,179	66,552	49,577	900
Marshall	8115	146	326	93	8	13	4	3	34,882	60,491	323,379	327,535	5,700
Mt. Hope	8117	1	1	6	0	NRR	0	0	0	0	0	0	178
New Journey	8112	15	120	10	0	0	0	0	0	6,890	61,963	53,030	440
Northminster+	8610	226	226	70	0	NRR	0	0	0	0	0	0	3,628
Nueva Vida	8612	75	94	45	0	NRR	0	0	0	0	0	0	516
Oak Grove*	8607	3	9	2	0	1	0	0	360	1,854	2,363	4,533	200
Pine Hill	8122	17	54	15	0	NRR	0	0	550	0	0	0	85
Pine Tree	8113	21	27	3	1	1	0	0	3,419	5,531	53,239	41,426	250
Progress	8123	6	7	6	0	NRR	0	0	0	0	0	0	0
Round Rock	8611	137	137	31	0	4	15	0	0	5,507	147,183	158,651	1,445
Shepherd/Hills	8604	103	103	19	1	2	9	0	0	46,411	192,334	236,873	843
Shiloh	8125	8	39	0	0	4	0	0	0	700	16,250	17,282	66
Stone Oak	8608	83	83	22	3	4	16	1	0	0	256,419	275,683	2,500
TOTALS	**21**	**1,085**	**1,722**	**531**	**15**	**34**	**56**	**5**	**99,004**	**292,114**	**1,873,007**	**1,944,947**	**25,972**

*Math error corrected. **Purged roll. +Union Church   NRR - No Report Received

---

CHURCHES, PASTORS, AND CLERKS:

Antioch   (4MWC)MSTR8101
  PO Box 42 (mailing)
  518 N Antioch Road (physical)
  Quitman, LA 71268
  (318)259-7069   <Jackson>
CL: Jerry L Hanes
  5104 Beech Springs Road
  Quitman, LA 71268
  (318)259-4246
  lindaameme@hotmail.com

Bertram   (4MEWC)MSTR8605
  PO Box 242 (mailing)
  430 Highway 29 (physical)
  Bertram, TX 78605
  (512)355-2182   <Burnet>
CL: Sam Hamilton
  8906 N FM 1174
  Burnet, TX 78611
  (512)788-2020
  samandlindaham@yahoo.com

Concord   (4MWC)MSTR8104
  212 County Road 4705
  Troup, TX 75789
  (903)842-4745   <Cherokee>
  FAX: (903)842-4745
PA: David Kurtz   <M1>
  244 County Road 4705
  Troup, TX 75789
  (817)683-4783
  davidk36@yahoo.com
CL: Sandy Mager
  356 County Road 4629
  Troup, TX 75789
  (903)842-3844
  stmager@yahoo.com

Daingerfield   (4MC)MSTR8106
  PO Box 645 (mailing)
  307 Broadnak (physical)
  Daingerfield, TX 75638
  (903)645-2183   <Morris>
  sharjohn@windstream.net
PA: John C Lawson   <M1>
  PO Box 645
  Daingerfield, TX 75638
  (903)645-2183
  sharjohn@windstream.net

CL: John C Lawson
  PO Box 645
  Daingerfield, TX 75638
  (903)645-2183
  sharjohn@windstream.net

Elmira Chapel   (4MWC)MSTR8111
  3501 Elmira Drive
  Longview, TX 75605
  (903)759-2069   <Gregg>
  elmirachapel@aol.com
PA: James M Cantey   <M1>
  3505 Elmira Drive
  Longview, TX 75605
  (903)452-6049
CL: Sherry Poteet
  3501 Elmira Drive
  Longview, TX 75605
  (903)759-2069
  elmirachapel@aol.com

Freeport   (4C)MSTR8103
  1402 W Broad Street
  Freeport, TX 77541

TRINITY PRESBYTERY CONTINUED

CL: Cathy Bettoney
1149 Ash Street
Clute, TX 77531
(979)265-7630
gbettoney@sbcglobal.net

Houston First   (4EWC)MSTR8606
2119 Avalon Place
Houston, TX 77019
(713)522-7821   <Harris>
FAX: (713)522-8869
firstcp@cphouston.org
PA: J Geoffrey Knight   <M1>
2119 Avalon Place
Houston, TX 77019
(713)522-7821
FAX: (713)522-8869
geoff@family.net
AP: Freddy Diaz   <M1>
2425 Holly Hall Apt B42
Houston, TX 77054
(832)305-2379
fredglobeus@yahoo.com
CL: Linda Trajo
2119 Avalon Place
Houston, TX 77019
(713)522-7821
FAX: (713)522-8869
firstcp@cphouston.org

Jefferson   (4EC)MSTR8109
PO Box 825 (mailing)
501 E Jefferson Street (physical)
Jefferson, TX 75657
(903)665-2883   <Marion>
office@jeffersonpresbyterian.org
PA: Mary Kathryn Kirkpatrick   <M1>
502 S Alley Street
Jefferson, TX 75657
(903)930-6236
mkkirkpatrick@gmail.com
CL: Sharon Davis
521 Houston Street
Jefferson, TX 75657
(903)601-2149
dav49@att.net

Marshall   (4EWC)MSTR8115
PO Box 1303 (mailing)
501 Indian Spring Road (physical)
Marshall, TX 75671
(903)935-3787   <Harrison>
FAX: (903)935-3193
info@cumberlandofmarshall.org
CL: Session Clerk
PO Box 1303
Marshall, TX 75671

Mt Hope   (4MC)MSTR8117
Box 66
Joinerville, TX 75658
(903)847-3451   <Rusk>
CL: Anna J Holman
PO Box 115
Joinerville, TX 75658
(903)847-3801

New Journey   (4WC)MSTR8112
(formerly Longview First)
PO Box 2349 (mailing)
2401 Alpine Street (physical)
Longview, TX 75601
(903)758-5184   <Gregg>
FAX: (903)757-2572
fcpclongview@sbcglobal.net

PA: Gary Schwitz   <M1>
PO Box 92
Longview, TX 75606
(903)359-5983
revschwitz@gmail.com
CL: Mollie Benson
567 Hidden Forest
Longview, TX 75601
(903)663-0443
FAX: (903)757-2572
fcpclongview@sbcglobal.net

Northminster   (4U)MSTR8610
6800 Tezel Road
San Antonio, TX 78250
(210)680-4825   <Bexar>
FAX: (210)680-4826
npcoffice@npcsatx.org
PA: Elise Renee Neal   <M1>
6800 Tezel Road
San Antonio, TX 78250
(210)680-4825
pastor@npcsatx.org
CL: Marsha Schendel
8730 Prince Heights
San Antonio, TX 78254
(210)681-4231

Nueva Vida   (F)MSTR8612
18060 Keith Harrow Road
Houston, TX 77084
(281)797-9797   <Harris>
PA: Ruben D Albarracin   <M1>
7411 Magnolia Shadows Lane
Houston, TX 77095
(281)797-9797
confiaendios@hotmail.com
CL: Patricia Nunez
7303 Hollow Field W
Cypress, TX 77433
(281)855-1881
FAX: (713)533-9735

Oak Grove   (4C)MSTR8607
12951 Ranch Road 2338
Georgetown, TX 78633
(   )   <Williamson>
CL: Wanda Shelton
2355 County Road 226
Florence, TX 76527
(512)579-1325

Pine Hill   (4C)MSTR8122
933 County Road 3369 (mailing)
Satillo,TX 75478
FM 3019 County Road 3281 (physical)
Winnsboro, TX 75494
(   )   <Hopkins>
CL: Kim Moore
933 County Road 3369
Satillo,TX 75478
(903)
kmoore@etmc.org

Pine Tree   (4MWC)MSTR8113
PO Box 5340 (mailing)
1805 Pine Tree Road (physical)
Longview, TX 75608
(903)759-2685   <Gregg>
ptcpc@sbcglobal.net
PA: Cindy Barton   <M1>
600 Green Lane
Tyler, TX 75701
(442)235-1393
cbarton53@hotmail.com

PA: John V Lindsay   <M1>
401 Greenwood Avenue
Marshall, TX 75670
(940)391-1213
CL: Darlynn Jones
1819 Flagstone Drive
Longview, TX 75605
(903)236-7310
darlynnj@att.net

Progress   (4C)MSTR8123
722 Gewin Lane (mailing)
3643 Progress Church Road (physical)
Pleasant Hill, LA 71065
(318)796-3725   <Sabine>
mamacgewin@yahoo.com
CL: Carolyn W Gewin
722 Gewin Lane
Pleasant Hill, LA 71065
(318)796-3703
mamacgewin@yahoo.com

Round Rock   (4U)MSTR8611
4010 Sam Bass Road
Round Rock, TX 78681
(512)544-2152   <Travis>
rrpc_info@roundrockpresbyterian.org
OD: Roland Perdue III   <M5>
4010 Sam Bass Road
Round Rock, TX 78681
CL: Elaine B Dodd
1805 Castleguard Way
Cedar Park, TX 78613
(512)260-0310
doddeb@sbcglobal.net

Shepherd of the Hills   (4U)MSTR8604
5226 W William Cannon Drive
Austin, TX 78749
(512)892-3580   <Travis>
FAX: (512)892-6307
church@shpc.org
OD: Jim Capps   <M5>
5226 W William Cannon Drive
Austin, TX 78749
(512)892-3580
FAX: (512)358-0879
jim@shpc.org
AP: Britta Dukes   <M1>
5226 W William Cannon Drive
Austin, TX 78749
(512)892-3580
FAX: (512)358-0879
britta@shpc.org
CL: Clift Bowman
5226 W William Cannon Drive
Austin, TX 78749
(512)288-5839
FAX: (512)358-0879
cbowman24@austin.rr.com

Shiloh   (4C)MSTR8125
4928 County Road 3275 (mailing)
2467 County Road 3205 (physical)
Clarksville, TX 75426
(903)427-3785   <Red River>
PA: Billy Jack Holt   <M1>
5039 Highway 37 N
Clarksville, TX 75426
(903)428-9909
jackdora@windstream.net
CL: Mary Jo McGill
4928 County Road 3275
Clarksville, TX 75426
(903)427-3785
hoopnmj@yahoo.com

TRINITY PRESBYTERY CONTINUED

Stone Oak (4C)MSTR8608
  20024 Crescent Oaks
  San Antonio, TX 78258
  (210)497-7974 <Bexar>
  FAX: (210)497-8724
  officemanager@satx.rr.com
CL: (none)

OTHERS ON MINISTERIAL ROLL:

Attema, Lee <M1 WC>
  PO Box 138
  San Ignacio Town, Cayo District
  BELIZE
  (281)728-6263
  lattema@icloud.com
Attema, Leslie <M1 WC>
  PO Box 138
  San Ignacio Town, Cayo District
  BELIZE
  (281)728-6263
  leslieattema@icloud.com
Bone, W Harold <M1 RT>
  28103 Cooperleaf Drive
  Bourne, TX 78015
  (210)859-5560
  revdocbone@yahoo.com
Bowers, Sharon G <M1 WC>
  1011 Wonder World Drive Apt 1911
  San Marcos, TX 78666
  (512)361-8471
  sharon.bowers@gmail.com
Bozeman, Robert <M1 HR>
  582 Bozeman Loop
  Belmont, LA 71406
  (318)256-5781
  bo@bozemanengineering.com
Chancellor, Hilton <M1 HR>
  11905 Preserve Vista
  Austin, TX 78738
  (512)382-1972
  hiltontex@aol.com
Colvard, Kevin <M1 RT>
  806 23rd Street NW
  Cleveland, TN 37311
  (205)267-9372
  rev_kev@satx.rr.com
Davenport, Mark A <M1 WC>
  1804 Stacie Street
  Mt Pleasant, TX 75455
  (205)427-4941
  hoginbama@yahoo.com
Diaz, Gloria Villa <M1 WC>
  2425 Holly Hall Apt B42
  Houston, TX 77054
  (832)758-5871
  gloria@newdayinchrist.org
Gonzalez, Nora <M1 OM>
  2515 Blueberry Lane
  Pasadena, TX 77502
  (832)202-5572
Hannah, Hugh <M1 HR>
  217 Mitchell Road SE
  Cleveland, TN 37323
  (423)473-7852
  pjhannah23@hotmail.com
Hoke, Walter <M1 RT>
  215 Navajo Trail
  Georgetown, TX 78633
  (512)869-1948
Jarnagin, Mary <M1 RT>
  1026 Clayton Lane Apt 6202
  Austin, TX 78723
  (512)709-4787
  marjar@yahoo.com

Kessie, John Paul <M1 HR>
  138 Pony Grass Lane
  Bastrop, TX 78602
  (512)585-1617
  jplmkessie@verizon.com
Killeen, Michael <M1 WC>
  5211 McCarty Lne
  Austin, TX 78749
  (512)892-3580
  mike@shpc.org
Magrill Jr, J Richard <M1 HR>
  500 Miller Drive
  Marshall, TX 75672
  (901)685-9454
  richardmagrill@att.net
McCarty, John <M1 M9 HR>
  305 W Martindale Drive
  Marshall, TX 75672
  (423)650-8788
  mtsjohn@gmail.com
McNeese, Mark <M1 HR>
  3306 Greenlawn Parkway
  Austin, TX 78757
  (512)517-1042
  2mam53@gmail.com
Park, Sung In <M1 OM>
  10109 Loxley Lane
  Austin, TX 78717
Peters, David J <M1 IT>
  4010 Sam Bass Road
  Round Rock, TX 78681
  (512)244-2152
Rush, Robert D <M1 OM>
  12935 Quail Park Drive
  Cypress, TX 77429
  (832)843-6124
  robertrush832@gmail.com
Rustenhaven III, William <M1 WC>
  PO Box 1303
  Marshall, TX 75671
  (903)935-7275
  FAX: (903)935-3193
  rusty@cumberlandofmarshall.org
Santillano, Ray Paul <M1 M8>
  10515 Lupine Canyon
  Helotes, TX 78023
  (210)425-1789
  ramon.p.santillano.mil@mail.mil
Smith, David R <M1 HR>
  PO Box 892
  Rosepine, LA 70659
  (903)297-6074
  ogreyfox@att.net
Wayman, Sam <M1 HR OM>
  707 High Hill Creek Road
  LaGrange, TX 78945
  (979)968-3734
  samndonnawayman@gmail.com
Weston, Robert E <M1 HR>
  9526 Antoine Forest Drive
  San Antonio, TX 78254
  (210)347-0232
  FAX: (210)680-4826
  rjaweston@gmail.com

OTHER LICENTIATES ON ROLL

OTHER CANDIDATES ON ROLL

Montoya, David <M3>
  20900 FM 1093 Apt 11208
  Richmond, TX 77407
  (823)366-6897
  davinay@hotmail.com

West Tennessee Presbytery
GREAT RIVERS SYNOD

	GENERAL	MEMBERSHIP			CHANGES				FINANCES				
	1.Church Number	2.Active	3.Total	4.Church School	5.Prof. of Faith	6.Gains	7.Losses	8.Children Baptized	9. OUR UNITED OUT-REACH	10. Total Out-Reach Giving	11. All Other Expenses	12. Total Income Received	13. Value Church Prop. 1=1000
	1	2	3	4	5	6	7	8	9	10	11	12	13
ACTS Korean	9436	115	125	25	40	0	15	4	500	42,000	189,014	222,392	1,200
Antioch Union	9401	26	27	21	0	NRR	0	0	0	0	0	0	343
Atwood*	9101	4	5	4	0	0	0	0	166	482	5,369	5,398	200
Beech	9402	82	82	31	0	NRR	0	0	2,247	0	0	0	400
Bells Chapel	9403	16	54	0	0	NRR	0	0	0	0	0	0	500
Bethel (TC)	9301	28	36	8	0	0	1	0	1,200	3,000	33,200	59,525	671
Bethesda	9404	20	35	10	0	NRR	0	0	1,000	0	0	0	360
Bolivar	9202	21	25	0	0	NRR	0	0	0	0	0	0	389
Bradford	9104	35	120	25	0	NRR	0	0	2,233	0	0	0	491
Brunswick	9302	16	54	0	0	NRR	0	0	1,346	0	0	0	418
Camden	9105	55	117	40	0	NRR	0	0	450	0	0	0	875
Camp Ground	9204	16	29	30	0	NRR	0	0	0	0	0	0	175
Claybrook	9205	8	8	8	0	NRR	0	0	0	0	0	0	10
Colonial**	9305	66	66	4	0	0	40	0	6,477	11,945	65,425	80,410	625
Concord	9106	42	53	20	2	2	3	1	0	3,925	56,860	62,107	500
Cool Springs CC	9107	63	75	40	4	4	2	0	1,321	6,189	27,884	42,708	200
Cool Springs GC	9408	62	62	36	0	0	4	0	6,971	14,735	46,942	82,967	300
Cristo Salva	9196	78	75	30	0	NRR	0	0	800	0	0	0	0
Davidson Chapel	9108	43	151	41	0	0	0	0	480	5,458	60,208	59,665	450
Double Springs	9109	36	62	23	0	0	2	0	3,322	7,004	22,256	38,060	565
Dresden	9110	25	31	12	0	0	1	0	4,390	6,804	43,101	43,898	315
Dyer	9409	111	111	50	1	1	2	0	13,939	22,504	93,416	139,387	1,085
Dyersburg, 1st	9410	303	328	120	0	0	3	0	43,000	103,600	514,676	714,392	6,627
Ebenezer (MC)	9206	6	6	7	0	NRR	0	0	0	0	0	0	50
Ebenezer (TC)	9303	128	128	60	0	NRR	0	0	3,600	0	0	0	380
Faith	9308	103	274	70	0	2	5	0	26,000	33,220	233,648	266,868	2,575
Fulton	9412	75	174	50	0	NRR	0	0	0	0	0	0	1,000
Germantown	9310	98	128	62	0	4	38	1	20,000	34,601	240,603	250,878	1,000
Gleason	9111	19	24	12	0	0	4	0	0	148	19,120	18,371	400
Good Springs*	9112	17	23	6	0	6	0	0	0	2,902	16,766	30,273	266
Holly Grove**	9304	403	420	157	4	4	401	5	0	35,252	352,406	433,689	2,236
Hopewell (BC)	9207	22	22	22	0	2	0	0	1,322	2,328	13,598	13,723	30
Hopewell (WC)	9115	20	22	15	0	7	0	0	2,300	4,900	18,644	26,468	90
Humboldt	9116	74	117	34	0	2	0	0	0	26,387	84,500	107,456	1,000
Hurricane Hill	9413	25	52	12	0	NRR	0	0	0	0	0	0	130
Jackson, 1st*	9208	273	420	75	0	5	0	1	8,487	16,975	278,474	347,020	3,500
Kenton	9414	15	31	17	0	0	4	0	3,829	7,866	24,404	38,294	475
Korean	9322	38	38	12	0	5	2	0	0	4,000	58,110	70,378	500
Lexington First	9209	53	122	14	0	0	2	0	4,000	6,565	44,297	50,863	900
Maple Springs	9210	81	104	0	1	1	1	1	0	0	0	0	485
Martin	9117	38	38	38	0	0	2	0	2,371	7,026	48,852	48,009	875
Mason Hall	9415	7	20	4	0	NRR	0	0	0	0	0	0	100
McKenzie	9118	262	353	160	0	0	4	0	28,022	45,072	260,145	287,686	5,000
Medina*	9119	17	35	16	0	3	1	0	3,361	12,677	25,762	44,213	161

West Tennessee Presbytery   (Continued)
GREAT RIVERS SYNOD

	1.Church Number	2.Active	3.Total	4.Church School	5.Prof. of Faith	6.Gains	7.Losses	8.Children Baptized	9. OUR UNITED OUT-REACH	10. Total Out-Reach Giving	11. All Other Expenses	12. Total Income Received	13. Value Church Prop. 1=1000
	1	2	3	4	5	6	7	8	9	10	11	12	13
Meridian	9120	65	141	35	0	NRR	0	0	0	0	0	0	175
Milan	9121	216	330	80	2	3	13	0	0	7,155	241,760	315,163	2,500
Mill Creek	9122	26	30	10	0	2	0	0	1,800	7,600	15,524	19,755	50
Morella	9416	6	26	6	0	NRR	0	0	0	0	0	0	125
Morning Sun	9314	30	35	11	0	0	3	0	3,422	8,454	37,348	55,006	750
Mt. Ararat	9417	54	159	38	2	6	6	0	0	21,825	58,637	80,456	500
Mt. Carmel	9315	14	39	8	0	0	3	0	1,771	4,330	10,349	17,712	150
Mt. Olive**	9418	8	8	6	2	2	19	0	0	0	22,157	19,200	201
Mt. Vernon	9213	9	19	0	2	2	2	1	1,346	2,256	18,737	16,638	380
Mt. Zion	9214	80	198	65	0	4	1	0	14,531	43,763	182,884	210,027	2,000
New Beginning	9306	68	186	14	0	NRR	0	0	600	0	0	0	124
New Bethel	9215	41	41	20	0	NRR	0	0	0	0	0	0	90
New Bethlehem	9420	4	4	4	0	NRR	0	0	4,578	0	0	0	8
New Ebenezer	9422	70	70	55	0	NRR	0	0	0	0	0	0	450
New Salem (MC)	9216	8	8	3	0	NRR	0	0	0	0	0	0	95
New Salem (SC)	9316	54	80	21	0	1	0	0	0	2,532	72,033	75,048	98
New Salem (WC)	9124	17	17	23	0	NRR	0	0	4,843	0	0	0	100
Newbern	9419	27	55	15	0	0	3	0	6,426	14,413	47,047	67,837	709
North Union	9423	68	75	40	0	NRR	0	0	0	0	0	0	360
Nuevo Empezar	9324	23	25	17	0	NRR	0	0	3,758	0	0	0	0
Oak Grove	9217	8	158	0	0	NRR	0	0	0	0	0	0	255
Oak Hill	9125	9	9	42	0	0	0	0	431	1,155	3,766	4,349	0
Olive Branch	9312	166	228	104	0	NRR	0	0	1,362	0	0	0	1,350
Oliver's Chapel	9127	30	74	30	0	NRR	0	0	0	0	0	0	314
Olivet	9220	198	333	100	2	3	16	0	6,188	33,284	305,862	339,147	2,108
Palestine (DC)	9424	5	5	7	0	NRR	0	0	0	0	0	0	50
Palestine (HC)	9221	44	107	20	0	0	0	0	3,976	7,545	31,323	40,181	300
Parsons, First	9222	28	49	8	0	0	2	1	0	0	29,496	32,668	550
Pleasant Green	9129	10	20	8	0	NRR	0	0	0	0	0	0	100
Pleasant Grove	9317	10	22		0	NRR	0	0	0	0	0	0	32
Pleasant Union	9318	100	100	20	0	NRR	0	0	0	0	0	0	305
Poplar Grove	9425	54	69	14	0	0	3	0	8,401	14,222	53,258	84,013	350
Protemus	9426	45	51	53	1	1	1	0	6,451	16,041	48,370	64,411	125
Ramer	9223	16	16	12	0	NRR	0	0	0	0	0	0	100
Roellen	9428	6	6	6	0	0	0	0	500	1,877	9,112	8,880	60
Rutherford	9429	11	21	9	0	NRR	0	0	2,269	0	0	0	300
Salem	9430	8	17	16	0	NRR	0	0	0	0	0	0	135
Savannah, 1st	9224	98	145	55	0	1	1	1	7,140	11,282	129,483	140,005	2,800
Selmer, Ct. Ave.	9225	61	82	16	0	NRR	0	0	800	0	0	0	550
Sharon	9130	13	24	17	0	NRR	0	0	500	0	0	0	589
Shiloh (AC)	9226	34	34	24	0	NRR	0	0	1,728	0	0	0	95
Shiloh (CC)	9131	31	46	0	0	NRR	0	0	2,213	0	0	0	175
Trezevant	9132	8	8	8	0	NRR	0	0	1,200	0	0	0	150
Troy	9432	17	24	15	0	NRR	0	0	80	0	0	0	100

West Tennessee Presbytery (Continued)
GREAT RIVERS SYNOD

	GENERAL	MEMBERSHIP			CHANGES				FINANCES				
	1.Church Number	2.Active	3.Total	4.Church School	5.Prof. of Faith	6.Gains	7.Losses	8.Children Baptized	9. OUR UNITED OUT-REACH	10. Total Out-Reach Giving	11. All Other Expenses	12. Total Income Received	13. Value Church Prop. 1=1000
	1	2	3	4	5	6	7	8	9	10	11	12	13
Union City	9433	115	224	74	0	NRR	0	0	0	0	0	0	2,000
West Union*	9321	91	223	39	0	0	4	0	800	4,800	126,102	128,400	2,500
Woodward's Chapel	9434	12	12	20	0	NRR	0	0	0	0	0	0	30
Yorkville	9435	26	59	22	0	NRR	0	0	0	0	0	0	575
Zion	9133	4	14	5	0	NRR	0	0	0	0	0	0	98
TOTALS	93	5,191	8,008	2,636	63	73	614	16	280,248	670,099	4,320,928	5,303,994	62,813

*Math error corrected. **Purged roll. NRR - No Report Received

CHURCHES, PASTORS, AND CLERKS:

ACTS Korean   (Provisional)GRWT9436
6524 Summer Avenue
Memphis, TN 38134
(901)381-4790
usyoun61@hotmail.com
PA: Daniel Youn   <M1>
6524 Summer Avenue
Memphis, TN 38134
(901)381-4790
usyoun61@hotmail.com
AP: Jennifer Muraya   <M1>
1261 Peabody Avenue Apt 10
Memphis, TN 38104
(469)230-5064
jmmuraya@memphisseminary..edu
CL: Session Clerk
6524 Summer Avenue
Memphis, TN 38134
(901)381-4790
usyoun61@hotmail.com

Antioch Union   (4C)GRWT9401
5765 Mount Olive Road (mailing)
486 W Newman Glover Road (physical)
Union City, TN 38261
(731)885-6435   <Obion>
CL: Sharon Barnes
5765 Mount Olive Road
Union City, TN 38261
(731)885-2521

Atwood   (4MWC)GRWT9101
PO Box 203 (mailing)
14010 Church Street (physical)
Atwood, TN 38220
(731)662-7692   <Carroll>
rickylong@tennesseetel.net
SS: Richard Reed   <M2>
236 Madison Street
Dyer, TN 38330
(731)692-3604

CL: Ricky Long
230 Brooks Road
Atwood, TN 38220
(731)662-7692
rickylong@tennesseetel.net

Beech   (4MEC)GRWT9402
PO Box 553 (mailing)
880 Beech Chapel Road (physical)
Union City, TN 38261
(731)885-1710   <Obion>
esw4454@hotmail.com
CL: Beth Williams
844 W Highway 22
Union City, TN 38281
(731)885-1710
bethcooks54@hotmail.com

Bells Chapel   (2WC)GRWT9403
309 Bells Chapel Road
Dyer, TN 38330
(731)643-6729   <Gibson>
LS: Dennis Emerson   <M6>
137 Midway Road 25
Dyer, TN 38330
(731)643-6539
dennied53@hotmail.com
CL: Dennis Emerson
137 Midway Road 25
Dyer, TN 38330
(731)643-6539
dennied53@hotmail.com

Bethel (TC)   (1WC)GRWT9301
512 J E Blaydes Parkway (mailing)
Atoka, TN 38004
3406 Tracy Road (physical)
Atoka, TN 38004
(901)837-0343   <Tipton>
PA: Melissa Reid Goodloe   <M1
3741 Highway 59W
Covington, TN 38019
(731)412-9657
rev.mgoodloe73@gmail.com

CL: Linda Drylie
512 J E Blaydes Parkway
Atoka, TN 38004
(901)837-1627
lindadrylie01@gmail.com

Bethesda   (4MWC)GRWT9404
10755 State Highway 188 (mailing)
9651 State Highway 188 (physical)
Friendship, TN 38034
( )   <Crockett>
jirvin527@yahoo.com
CL: Jim Irvin
10755 State Highway 188
Friendship, TN 38034
(731)414-7180
jirvin527@yahoo.com

Bolivar   (4MWC)GRWT9202
PO Box 413 (mailing)
448 Nuckolls Road (physical)
Bolivar, TN 38008
(731)658-5459   <Hardeman>
CL: Faye Cromwell
2995 Naylor Road
Toone, TN 38381
(731)658-5329
cromwellr@bellsouth.net

Bradford   (4MWC)GRWT9104
PO Box 186 (mailing)
117 Highway 45 S (physical)
Bradford, TN 38316
(731)742-3397   <Gibson>
CL: Donna Gibson
201 Bradford Acres
Bradford, TN 38316
(731)513-3323
donnasuegibson@hotmail.com

Brunswick   (4MWC)GRWT9302
PO Box 67 (mailing)
4976 Brunswick Road (physical)
Brunswick, TN 38014
(901)386-0105   <Shelby>
SS: Tiffany McClung   <M1 M9>
919 Dickinson Street
Memphis, TN 38107
(901)606-6615
thmcclung@att.net

WEST TENNESSEE PRESBYTERY CONTINUED

CL: Mary Ellen Starks
PO Box 142
Brunswick, TN 38014
(901)388-9862
mstarks9@att.net

_____

Camden   (4MWC)GRWT9105
239 W Main Street
Camden, TN 38320
(731)584-7598   \<Benton\>
FAX: (731)584-7598
camdencpoffice@bellsouth.net
SS: Carey Womack   \<M1\>
114 Doris Street
Camden, TN 38320
(731)220-3900
FAX: (731)584-7598
camdencppastor@bellsouth.net
CL: June Cox
239 W Main Street
Camden, TN 38320
(731)584-6691
FAX: (731)584-7598
june@camdencp.com

_____

Camp Ground   (4C)GRWT9204
2535 Middleburg Road
Decaturville, TN 38329
( )   \<Decatur\>
SS: David Hawley   \<M1\>
235 Florida Avenue N
Parsons, TN 38363
(731)427-7284
dhpreach@aol.com
CL: Fred Brasher
771 Middleburg Road
Decaturville, TN 38329
(731)852-4400

_____

Claybrook   (C)GRWT9205
1300 US Highway 412 E (mailing)
1364 US Highway 412 E (physical)
Jackson, TN 38305
( )   \<Madison\>
CL: Martha Wolfe
1300 US Highway 412 E
Jackson, TN 38305
(731)424-4979
jergensmith@aol.com

_____

Colonial   (4MWC)GRWT9305
1500 S Perkins Road
Memphis, TN 38117
(901)682-4747   \<Shelby\>
SS: Lisa Anderson   \<M1 M9\>
1790 Faxon Avenue
Memphis, TN 38112
(901)246-8052
anderli90@gmail.com
AP: Emily Trapp Young   \<M1\>
1925 Allsboro Road
Cherokee, AL 35616
(901)674-2342
ectrapp44@gmail.com
CL: George R Marston
1042 LaRue Place
Memphis, TN 38122
(901)685-1488
put11599@bellsouth.net

_____

Concord   (3MWC)GRWT9106
153 Herd Law Road
Trenton, TN 38382
( )   \<Gibson\>
CL: Don Gibson
4225 Christmasville Road
Medina, TN 38355
(731)783-0992

_____

Cool Springs CC   (4C)GRWT9107
240 Little Grove Road
Lavinia, TN 38348
( )   \<Carroll\>
LS: Robert Barger   \<M6\>
7127 Highway 104 W
Lavinia, TN 38348
(731)987-2477
rbarger104@att.net
CL: Ann Hammett
8725 US Highway 70
Cedar Grove, TN 38321
(731)987-2516

_____

Cool Springs GC   (4MWC)GRWT9408
37 Cool Spring Road
Trimble, TN 38259
(731)643-6153   \<Gibson\>
PA: Jamie Adams   \<M1\>
403 W Washington
Union City, TN 38261
(731)796-1814
adamsjamie@charter.net
CL: Mike Pruett
13 Harry King Road
Kenton, TN 38233
(731)697-4345
mikepruett1960@gmail.com

_____

Cristo Salva   (4C)GRWT9196
3442 Tutwiler
Memphis, TN 38122
diannwhite12@yahoo.com
PA: Carlos Solito   \<M1\>
3151 Pleasant Hill Road
Nesbit, MS 38651
(205)329-8514
fcg9700@gmail.com
CL: Session Clerk
3442 Tutwiler
Memphis, TN 38122

_____

Davidson Chapel   (4MWC)GRWT9108
399 Laneview Concord Road
Trenton, TN 38382
(731)618-1521
FAX: (731)664-3735
dale.cavaness@horne-llp.com \<Gibson\>
PA: Corey Cummings   \<M1\>
399 Laneview Concord Road
Trenton, TN 38382
(731)845-3173
cummings.corey@gmail.com
CL: Dale Cavaness
2093 Brentwood Drive
Milan, TN 38358
(731)618-1521
FAX: (731)664-3735
dale.cavaness@horne-llp.com

_____

Double Springs   (4WC)GRWT9109
18 Double Springs Road
Humboldt, TN 38343
(731)787-6422   \<Gibson\>

PA: Russell Little   \<M1\>
29 Cotton Row
Medina, TN 38355
(731)783-3565
russelllittle@bellsouth.net
CL: Susan Fitzgerald
PO Box 5
Milan, TN 38358
(731)414-2974
susanfitzgerald13@yahoo.com

_____

Dresden   (4MWC)GRWT9110
PO Box 131 (mailing)
121 S Wilson Street (physical)
Dresden, TN 38225
( )   \<Weakley\>
CL: Martha Killebrew
PO Box 131
Dresden, TN 38225
(731)364-3294
FAX: (731)364-3500
killebrewm@frontiernet.net

_____

Dyer   (4MEWC)GRWT9409
PO Box 181 (mailing)
256 E College Street (physical)
Dyer, TN 38330
(731)692-2594   \<Gibson\>
dyercpchurch@gmail.com
PA: Robert A Smith   \<M1\>
PO Box 501
Newbern, TN 38059
(731)627-3332
ras1957@bellsouth.net
CL: Johnny Ward
46 Old Dyer Trenton Road
Dyer, TN 38330
(731)692-2594
ward3363@bellsouth.net

_____

Dyersburg First   (4WC)GRWT9410
2280 Parr Avenue
Dyersburg, TN 38024
(731)285-5703   \<Dyer\>
FAX: (731)285-5792
cpoffice@cumberlandchurch.com
PA: Cory Williams   \<M1\>
585 Tater Hill Road
Newbern, TN 38059
(901)486-5981
coromis@hotmail.com
AP: Annetta Camp   \<M1\>
2303 Mill Creek Road
Halls, TN 38040
(731)285-5703
FAX: (731)285-5792
annetta@cumberlandchurch.com
CL: Robb Kerr
1840 Okeena Drive
Dyersburg, TN 38024

_____

Ebenezer (MC)   (2EWC)GRWT9206
Main Street
Mercer, TN 38392
(731)935-2391   \<Madison\>
CL: Pope Mulherin
8 Prestwick Drive
Jackson, TN 38305
(731)427-3113

_____

Ebenezer (TC)   (4WC)GRWT9303
70 Witherington Road
Mason, TN 38049
( )   \<Tipton\>

WEST TENNESEE PRESBYTERY CONTINUED

CL: Beth Witherington
295 Country Club Road
Covington, TN 38019
bethwitherington@yahoo.com

_____

Faith   (4WC)GRWT9308
3427 Appling Road
Bartlett, TN 38133
(901)377-0526   <Shelby>
FAX: (901)382-2600
faithcumberlandp@bellsouth.net
PA: Daniel J Earheart-Brown   <M1>
475 N Highland Street Apt 9L
Memphis, TN 38122
jearheartbrown@gmail.com
(901)463-0007
CL: Karen Patten
5728 North Street
Bartlett, TN 38134
(901)237-0535
mkpatten@outlook.com

_____

Fulton   (4MWC)GRWT9412
PO Box 5343 (mailing)
1159 Parker Road (physical)
South Fulton, TN 38257
(731)479-9912   <Obion>
CL: Donald R Moore
155 Cox Road
Fulton, KY 42041
(270)436-2723
donaldmoore9@aol.com

_____

Germantown   (4EWC)GRWT9310
2385 Riverdale
Germantown, TN 38138
(901)755-3884   <Shelby>
FAX: (901)759-3653
PA: Peggy Jean Craig   <M1>
113 Harbor Town Square #304
Memphis, TN 38103
(256)277-1147
peggy.jean.craig@cpcg.org
CL: Iva McCutchen
1240 Bristol Drive
Memphis, TN 38119
(901)761-0575
ivesmc@att.net

_____

Gleason   (4MC)GRWT9111
190 David Court (mailing)
McKenzie, TN 38201
171 Smyth Lane (physical)
Gleason, TN 38229
(731)648-5343   <Weakley>
CL: Donald Ray Stephens
190 David Court
McKenzie, TN 38201
(731)352-5852
tuvart@charter.net

_____

Good Springs   (4WC)GRWT9112
180 Barham Road (mailing)
Good Springs Road (physical)
Dukedom, TN 38226
( )   <Weakley>
OD: Johnnie Dalton   <M5>
949 Bill Nanney Circle
Dukedom, TN 38226

CL: Loretta Barham
180 Barham Road
Dukedom, TN 38226
(731)469-9555

_____

Holly Grove   (4MWC)GRWT9304
4538 Holly Grove Road
Brighton, TN 38011
(901)476-8379   <Tipton>
FAX: (901)476-3324
hollygrovecpchurch@att.net
PA: Peter Jeffrey   <M1>
4510 Holly Grove Road
Brighton, TN 38011
McKenzie, TN 38201
(615)417-0131
jeffreyp@hollygrovechurch.com
AP: Debbie Marshall   <M1>
1494 Bucksnort Road
Covington, TN 38019
(901)494-1251
dsmarshall05@att.net
CL: Shannon Leach
1911 Garland Drive
Covington, TN 38019
(901)491-4853
leachs@hollygrovechurch.com

_____

Hopewell (BC)   (2EWC)GRWT9207
2309 Saulsbury Road (mailing)
289 Hopewell Road (physical)
Walnut, MS 38683
( )   <Benton>
OD: LaMar Chamblee   <M5>
3755 Lake Village Cove
Olive Branch, MS 38654
CL: Kathy D Wilburn
2309 Saulsbury Road
Walnut, MS 38683
(662)223-6447
kwilburn@fareselaw.com

_____

Hopewell (WC)   (2WC)GRWT9115
1061 Gaylord Road (mailing)
Route 1 Box 91 (physical)
Sharon, TN 38255
( )   <Weakley>
CL: Lonnie Hazlewood
1061 Gaylord Road
Sharon, TN 38255
(731)973-2426
lonminh@citlink.net

_____

Humboldt   (4MEWC)GRWT9116
2375 E Mitchell Street
Humboldt, TN 38343
(731)784-2703   <Gibson>
pastor@humboldtcpc.org
PA: Robert Harris   <M1>
3441 Clinton Street
Humboldt, TN 38343
(731)420-6067
pastor@humboldtcpc.org
CL: Karen Clark
442 State Route 187
Medina, TN 38355
(731)234-0101
kleehc2@gmail.com

_____

Hurricane Hill   (4C)GRWT9413
Newbern, TN 38059
( )   <Dyer>
CL: Anna Frances Myers
220 Salem Road
Dyersburg, TN 38024
(731)225-1185
anna_myers@hotmail.com

_____

Jackson First   (4WC)GRWT9208
1730 US Highway 45 Bypass
Jackson, TN 38305
(731)664-1632   <Madison>
FAX: (731)664-1633
jfcpc1730@gmail.com
PA: Terry M Hunley   <M1>
48 Charleston Square
Jackson, TN 38305
(731)660-5685
thunley1@charter.net
CL: Glenn Fesmire
7 Broadfield Drive
Jackson, TN 38301
(731)234-9959
glennfes@aol.com

_____

Kenton   (4MEWC)GRWT9414
301 W College Street
Kenton, TN 38233
( )   <Obion>
LS: Charles McCall   <M6>
549 Mason Hall Road
Trimble, TN 38259
(731)297-3288
cmccall@ycinet.net
CL: Paul E Williams
206 Hillside Street
Kenton, TN 38233
(731)749-5656

_____

Korean   (P)GRWT9322
7565 Macon Road
Cordova, TN 38018
(901)755-9101   <Shelby>
kcomemphis@gmail.com
PA: Ho-Jin Lee   <M1>
7565 Macon Road
Cordova, TN 38018
(901)754-7070
hojin.lee70@gmail.com
CL: Gong Dickens
7565 Macon Road
Cordova, TN 38018
(901)758-1130

_____

Lexington First   (4MWC)GRWT9209
PO Box 11 (mailing)
931 N Broad Street (physical)
Lexington, TN 38351
(731)968-7176   <Henderson>
patfreelandjones@yahoo.com
PA: C William Jones Jr   <M1>
109 Lakewood Drive
Lexington, TN 38351
(731)967-7618
patfreelandjones@yahoo.com
CL: Teresa Ferguson
7747 Middleburg Road
Scotts Hill, TN 38374
(731)968-9079

WEST TENNESSEE PRESBYTERY CONTINUED

Maple Springs   (4MWC)GRWT9210
2005 Beech Bluff Road (physical)
Beech Bluff, TN 38313
(731)424-4065   <Henderson>
PA: Justin Griffin   <M1>
2625 Beech Bluff Road
Beech Bluff, TN 38313
(615)969-2426
jjjjgriff@gmail.com
CL: Tammy Gilliam
547 Fowler Road
Beech Bluff, TN 38313
tgilliam@jacksontn.gannett.com

Martin   (4MWC)GRWT9117
142 Rolling Meadows (mailing)
312 E Main Street (physical)
Martin, TN 38237
(731)587-3222   <Weakley>
FAX: (731)487-6484
cathyjahr@charter.net
PA: Michael T Lavender   (M1)
308 Main Street
Martin, TN 38237
(731)431-9127
mike_lavender@yahoo.com
CL: Cathy Jahr
142 Rolling Meadows
Martin, TN 38237
(731)587-6484
cathyjahr@charter.net

Mason Hall   (2EWC)GRWT9415
549 Mason Hall Road (mailing)
Trimble, TN 38259
1861 CP Church Road (physical)
Kenton, TN 38233
( )   <Obion>
mccall.cmccall@gmail.com
CL: Charles McCall
549 Mason Hall Road
Trimble, TN 38259
(731)431-8195
mccall.cmccall@gmail.com

McKenzie   (4WC)GRWT9118
PO Box 133 (mailing)
16835 Highland Drive (physical)
McKenzie, TN 38201
(731)352-2440   <Carroll>
FAX: (731)352-3101
church@mckenziecpc.org
PA: Kevin L Wood   <M1>
339 David Street
McKenzie, TN 38201
(865)228-0710
FAX: (865)588-8581
revkevbuford1972@gmail.com
CL: June Perritt
PO Box 133
McKenzie, TN 38201
(731)352-2440
FAX: (731)352-3101
church@mckenziecpc.org

Medina   (4EC)GRWT9119
104 Cumberland Street
Medina, TN 38355
(731)618-0192
          <Gibson>

PA: Linda H Glenn   <M1>
49 Mason Road
Threeway, TN 38343
(731)618-0192
lindahglenn@click1.net
CL: Kiara Castleman
307 W Main Street
Greenfield, TN 38230
(731)487-3363
kiascham@gmail.com

Meridian   (4C)GRWT9120
1099 Adams Road (mailing)
2590 Meridian Road (physical)
Greenfield, TN 38230
( )   <Weakley>
CL: David McBride
1099 Adams Road
Greenfield, TN 38230
(731)235-3058

Milan   (4WC)GRWT9121
6083 S First Street
Milan, TN 38358
(731)686-1851   <Gibson>
office@milancp.org
PA: Doy L Daniels Jr   <M1>
1095 Crestview Drive
Milan, TN 38358
(731)686-1851
FAX: (731)723-9324
revdrdoy@gmail.com
AP: Will Arnold   <M1>
6095 Ellington Cove
Milan, TN 38358
(731)335-3187
willarnold3187@gmail.com
CL: Bruce Niven
8 Seavers Road
Milan, TN 38358
(731)686-9511
bniven@charter.net

Mill Creek   (4C)GRWT9122
239 Smith Street (mailing)
434 Mill Creek Road (physical)
Puryear, TN 38251
( )   <Henry>
PA: Anne Hames   <M1 M9>
118 Paris Street
McKenzie, TN 38201
(731)352-4066
FAX: (731)352-4069
hamesa@bethelu.edu
CL: Robert Newcomb
376 Paschall Lane
Puryear, TN 38251
(731)336-2097
rdnewc@gmail.com

Morella   (2EWC)GRWT9416
51 Morella Road
Kenton, TN 38233
( )   <Gibson>
CL: J C Reed
121 Tull Road
Kenton, TN 38233
(731)749-5545

Morning Sun   (4MC)GRWT9314
2682 Morning Sun Road
Cordova, TN 38016
(901)382-3439   <Shelby>
mscpc13@gmail.com
SS: Andy McClung   <M1 DE>
919 Dickinson Street
Memphis, TN 38107
(901)606-6615
amcclung@cumberland.org
CL: Mary Smith
2682 Morning Sun Road
Cordova, TN 38016
(901)382-3439
mscpc13@gmail.com

Mt Ararat   (4WC)GRWT9417
1465 Troy-Hickman Road
Union City, TN 38261
(731)536-5406   <Obion>
CL: Bobby Hall
664 Mill Creek Road
Troy, TN 38260
(731)536-4798

Mt Carmel   (4C)GRWT9315
403 Charleston Street (mailing)
2355 Union Drive (physical)
Somerville, TN 38068
( )   <Fayette>
CL: Harry N Wiles
403 Charleston Street
Somerville, TN 38068
(901)465-9733

Mt Olive   (4MEC)GRWT9418
57 Yorkville Highway (mailing)
42 Mt Olive Road (physical)
Dyer, TN 38330
( )   <Gibson>
PA: Charles Fike   <M1>
2070 N 1st Street
Milan, TN 38358
(731)686-0224
CL: Session Clerk
57 Yorkville Highway
Dyer, TN 38330

Mt Vernon   (4MC)GRWT9213
3101 Mt Vernon Road
Ramer, TN 38367
(731)645-6420   <McNairy>
SS: David Sprenkle   <M1>
5733 Stone Street
Olive Branch, MS 38654
(901)604-8707
dsprenkle@memphisseminary.edu
CL: Larry Gage
130 Shiloh Terrace Drive
Selmer, TN 38375
(731)645-6828
lgage6828@charter.net

Mt Zion   (4MWC)GRWT9214
480 County Road 401
Falkner, MS 38629
(662)837-7013   <Tippah>
FAX: (662)837-7969
info@mtzioncpc.org

WEST TENNESSEE PRESBYTERY CONTINUED

PA: Thomas Richie Lockhart   <M1>
700 County Road 343
Falkner, MS 38629
(662)837-4281
nmsdiamonddawgs@yahoo.com
CL: Dennis Bogue
105 Gowdy Drive
Ripley, MS 38663
(662)837-0265
dennis.bogue@yahoo.com

New Beginning   (4C)GRWT9306
777 Stateline Road East
Southaven, MS 38671
(901)353-4011
PA: Craig Wilson   <M1>
777 Stateline Road East
Southaven, MS 38671
(901)277-4066
craigwilson2300@yahoo.com
SC: Elnora McKinzie
1111 Holmes Street
Memphis, TN 38122
(870)377-2174

New Bethel   (4C)GRWT9215
3708 New Bethel Road
Selmer, TN 38375
(   )   <McNairy>
PA: Jeff Powell   <M1>
694 White Avenue
Henderson, TN 38340
(731)608-2040
jfpowell2003@yahoo.com
CL:Session Clerk
3708 New Bethel Road
Selmer, TN 38375
(731)645-3150
kingpreston2828@yahoo.com

New Bethlehem   (2EWC)GRWT9420
1585 Bethlehem Road (mailing)
825 Bethlehem Road (physical)
Newbern, TN 38059
(   )   <Dyer>
CL: Mary Bell Murray
1585 Bethlehem Road
Newbern, TN 38059
(731)627-2332
murrayc2@juno.com

New Ebenezer   (4MEWC)GRWT9422
PO Box 364 (mailing)
1606 Ebenezer Road (physical)
Troy, TN 38260
(731)536-4936   <Obion>
PA: John Lowrance   <M1>
PO Box 871
Dyersburg, TN 38025
(731)676-4360
jclowrance1@gmail.com
CL: Lisa Hamm
656 Ebenezer Road
Troy, TN 38260
lhamm-newebenezer@hotmail.com

New Salem (MC)   (4C)GRWT9216
453 New Salem Road
Bethel Springs, TN 38315
(   )   <McNairy>

CL: Malcolm Dickson
153 Harris Road
Bethel Springs, TN 38315
(731)934-7282
FAX: (731)934-0736
robert.dickson@aol.com

New Salem (SC)   (4MWC)GRWT9316
6813 Salem Road
Lakeland, TN 38002
(901)829-3241   <Shelby>
FAX: (901)829-3241
ptcriss@hotmail.com
PA: Paul T Criss   <M1>
6831 Salem Road
Lakeland, TN 38002
(901)626-8462
ptcriss@hotmail.com
CL: Patty Butler Little
6909 Salem Road
Lakeland, TN 38002
(901)829-3218

New Salem (WC)   (3C)GRWT9124
3220 Sharon Highway 89 (mailing)
Highway 89 (physical)
Sharon, TN 38255
(   )   <Weakley>
SS: Kermit Travis   <M1>
3220 Sharon Highway 89
Dresden, TN 38225
(731)364-2315
CL: John C Clark
215 Rambo Road
Sharon, TN 38255
(731)364-3921
jcjclark@frontiernet.net

Newbern   (4MWC)GRWT9419
310 E Main
Newbern, TN 38059
(731)627-3646   <Dyer>
PA: Byron Forester   <M1>
2376 Eastwood Place
Memphis, TN 38112
(901)324-1707
bforester@bellsouth.net
CL: Jamie Kay Berkley
403 E Main Street
Newbern, TN 38059
(731)676-8626
jamiekayb@hotmail.com

North Union   (4EC)GRWT9423
15 Cardwell Road (mailing)
Dyer, TN 38330
78 Preacher Dowland Road (physical)
Kenton, TN 38233
(731)673-4122   <Gibson>
OD: Chris Marks   <M5>
78 Preacher Dowland Road
Kenton, TN 38322
CL: William Sims
126 Old Dyer-Rutherford Road
Dyer, TN 38330
wwsimssavedbygrace@hotmail.com

Nuevo Empezar   (4EC)GRWT9324
3442 Tutwiler
Memphis, TN 38122
(901)644-0513

PA: Bertha Davis   <M1>
2242 Slocum Avenue
Memphis, TN 38127
(901)644-0513
CL: Lydia Langbein
4675 Glenmore Lane
Millington, TN 38053
(901)487-6336
lile@rittermail.com

Oak Grove   (4MC)GRWT9217
PO Box 442 (mailing)
3655 Talley Store Road (physical)
Henderson, TN 38340
(731)989-3825   <Chester>
PA: Laura Todd   <M1>
3303 Decker Street
Bartlett, TN 38134
(901)496-1443
littlelaurarose@yahoo.com
CL: Mark Plunk
PO Box 442
Henderson, TN 38340
markplunk@gmail.com

Oak Hill   (1C)GRWT9125
5820 Highway 69 N (mailing)
5135 Highway 59 N (physical)
Paris, TN 38242
(   )   <Henry>
CL: Theresa Rushing
5820 Highway 69 N
Paris, TN 38242
(731)642-3499
theresarushing33@gmail.com

Olive Branch   (4MWC)GRWT9312
8161 Germantown Road
Olive Branch, MS 38654
(662)893-7347   <Desoto>
FAX: (901)893-7347
sandi@firstcpchurch.org
PA: Paul Earheart-Brown   <M1>
510 City House Court Apt 406
Memphis, TN 38103
(901)483-0018
paul.earheartbrown@gmail.com
CL: Charlie Trapp
4750 Harvest Knoll Cove N
Memphis, TN 38125
(901)626-2952
charliebethtrapp@bellsouth.net

Oliver's Chapel   (4WC)GRWT9127
91 Olivers Chapel Road (mailing)
22 Olivers Chapel Road (physical)
Bradford, TN 38316
(731)742-3559   <Gibson>
FAX: (731)742-3994
mpybas@yahoo.com
PA: Sam Harwell   <M1>
350 Freemont Street
Dyer, TN 38330
(731)414-2153
sambharl@yahoo.com
CL: Marcy Tahmazian
91 Olivers Chapel Road
Bradford, TN 38316
(731)742-3097
FAX: (731)742-3994
mpybas@yahoo.com

WEST TENNESSEE PRESBYTERY CONTINUED

Olivet (4MWC)GRWT9220
6095 Highway 226
Savannah, TN 38372
(731)925-2685 <Hardin>
olivetcp@bellsouth.net
PA: Mitch Boulton <M1>
80 Topsy Lane
Savannah, TN 38372
(731)487-2318
steelermitch@gmail.com
CL: Walton Williams
10875 Highway 64
Savannah, TN 38372
(731)412-7569

Palestine (DC) (4C)GRWT9424
985 Palestine Road (mailing)
Route 2 (physical)
Newbern, TN 38059
( ) <Dyer>
SS: Donnie Ragsdale <M1>
915 S Olive Street
Union City, TN 38261
(731)885-0014
CL: Session Clerk Palestine CP Church
985 Palestine Road
Newbern, TN 38059
(731)627-9227

Palestine (HC) (4MWC)GRWT9221
1010 Nobles Road (mailing)
6835 Highway 22A (physical)
Lexington, TN 38351
( ) <Henderson>
mcadamsjc@bellsouth.net
CL: Catherine Slate
85 N Helms Streer
Lexington, TN 38351
(731)845-6239
pcpcsessionclerk@gmail.com

Parsons First (4MEWC)GRWT9222
PO Box 141 (mailing)
114 Virginia Avenue N (physical)
Parsons, TN 38363
(731)847-7148 <Decatur>
PA: David Hawley <M1>
235 Florida Avenue N
Parsons, TN 38363
(731)427-7284
haw177@aol.com
CL: Tony Collett
6636 Rockhouse Road
Linden, TN 37096
(931)589-5103
tacollett@wildblue.net

Pleasant Green (4C)GRWT9129
c/o Helen Watkins (mailing)
2776 Highway 105
Trezevant, TN 38258
712 Idlewild-Holly Leaf (physical)
Atwood, TN 38220
( ) <Gibson>
OD: Keith Pence <M5>
PO Box 703
Gleason, TN 38229
(731)819-2553

CL: Helen Watkins
2776 Highway 105
Trezevant, TN 38258
(731)669-1601
hjoy1@charter.net

Pleasant Grove (2C)GRWT9317
2625 Pleasant Grove Road (mailing)
2320 Pleasant Grove Road (physical)
Moscow, TN 38057
(901)877-3287 <Fayette>
CL: Jack Joyner
2625 Pleasant Grove Road
Moscow, TN 38057
(901)877-3287

Pleasant Union (4MWC)GRWT9318
9251 Brunswick Road
Millington, TN 38053
(901)829-3262 <Shelby>
PA: Matthew Dean Cunningham <M1>
1646 Brighton-Clopton Road
Brighton, TN 38011
(901)475-4252
mcunningham0528@comcast.net
CL: Mike Wood
707 Bethel Road
Atoka, TN 38004
(901)840-2345
mwood864@gmail.com

Poplar Grove (4C)GRWT9425
492 Church Road
Halls, TN 38040
(731)627-2445 <Lauderdale>
2Orrs.mn@charter.net
PA: Johnnie Welch <M1>
PO Box 1506
Dyersburg, TN 38025
(731)287-9008
johnniewelch@msn.com
CL: Shea Harris
232 W Main Street
Halls, TN 38040

Protemus (4EWC)GRWT9426
2372 W Shawtown Road (mailing)
2033 W Shawtown Road (physical)
Troy, TN 38260
( ) <Obion>
LS: James R Gunter <M6>
6997 Bud Barker Road
Obion, TN 38240
(731)538-9252
CL: Betty Rhamy
2372 W Shawtown Road
Troy, TN 38260
(731)538-9458

Ramer (4MEWC)GRWT9223
4096 Highway 57 W
Ramer, TN 38367
( ) <McNairy>
OD: Albert Brown <M5>
1772 Buena Vista Road
Bethel Springs, TN 38315
(731)934-7349
CL: George Armstrong
216 Ballpark Road E
Ramer, TN 38367
(731)645-3987

Roellen (2C)GRWT9428
1810 Linden Road (mailing)
Highway 104 E (physical)
Dyersburg, TN 38024
(731)285-0300 <Dyer>
krector@cableone.net
SS: Byron Forester <M1>
2376 Eastwood Place
Memphis, TN 38112
(901)324-1707
bforester@bellsouth.net
CL: Betsy Jones
1810 Linden Road
Dyersburg, TN 38024

Rutherford (4MEWC)GRWT9429
945 S Trenton Street (mailing)
113 N Trenton Street (physical)
Rutherford, TN 38369
(731)665-6487 <Gibson>
PA: Hobert Walker <M1>
PO Box 66
Rutherford, TN 38369
(731)665-7236
rutherfordcpchurch@gmail.com
CL: Lila Browning
PO Box 413
Rutherford, TN 38369
(731)665-7377
lbrowning@twc.com

Salem (4MC)GRWT9430
189 Franklin Street (mailing)
961 Salem Road(physical)
Gadsden, TN 38337
( ) <Crockett>
CL: Ann Davis
189 Franklin Street
Gadsden, TN 38337
(731)784-4713
cloud31@bellsouth.net

Savannah First (4WC)GRWT9224
300 Tennessee Street
Savannah, TN 38372
(731)925-4493 <Hardin>
savannah1stcp@hotmail.com
LS: Helen Hamilton <M6>
245 Elm Street
Savannah, TN 38372
(731)925-7338
helmackham@aol.com
CL: Levin Edwards
300 Tennessee Street
Savannah, TN 38372
(731)925-4493
levinedwards@gmail.com

Selmer Court Ave (4MWC)GRWT9225
PO Box 741 (mailing)
234 Court Avenue (physical)
Selmer, TN 38375
(731)645-5257 <McNairy>
CL: Gwelda W Treece
299 Country Club Lane
Selmer, TN 38375
(731)645-5519
gweldat@bellsouth.net

WEST TENNESSEE PRESBYTERY CONTINUED

Sharon   (4MEC)GRWT9130
PO Box 588 (mailing)
5414 US Highway 45 (physical)
Sharon, TN 38255
( )   <Weakley>
SS: David Lancaster   <M1 PR>
426 Fugua Road
Martin, TN 38237
(731)588-5895
lancasterd@bethelu.edu
CL: Patricia Elam
2275 Mount Vernon Road
Sharon, TN 38255
(731)456-2882
jimelam@frontiernet.net

Shiloh (AC)   (4WC)GRWT9226
c/o Scott Coleman (mailing)
5 County Road 617A
164 County Road 634 (physical)
Corinth, MS 38834
( )   <Alcorn>
OD: LaMar Chamblee   <M5>
3755 Lake Village Cove
Olive Branch, MS 38654
CL: Carolyn James
31 Waukomis Lake Road
Corinth, MS 38834
(662)286-7901
carolyn.wild15@yahoo.com

Shiloh (CC)   (4C)GRWT9131
2880 Highway 423
McKenzie, TN 38201
( )   <Carroll>
church@shilohcp.org
CL: Vickie Summers
2880 Highway 423
McKenzie, TN 38201
(731)225-6714
vsum1956@gmail.com

Trezevant   (3EC)GRWT9132
PO Box 160 (mailing)
98 Church Street (physical)
Trezevant, TN 38258
(731)669-4525   <Carroll>
CL: Bobby Argo
PO Box 160
Trezevant, TN 38258
(731)669-6926

Troy   (4WC)GRWT9432
PO Box 454 (mailing)
308 Main Street (physical)
Troy, TN 38260
( )   <Obion>
CL: Alan Thompson
171 Country Valley Drive
Troy, TN 38260
(731)445-3061
art32265@gmail.com

Union City   (4MW C)GRWT9433
631 E Church Street
Union City, TN 38261
(731)885-9773   <Obion>
FAX: (731)885-9766
uccpc@yahoo.com

CL: Session Clerk
631 E Church Street
Union City, TN 38261
(731)885-9773   <Obion>
FAX: (731)885-9766
uccpc@yahoo.com

West Union   (4MWC)GRWT9321
3099 W Union Road
Millington, TN 38053
(901)876-5757   <Shelby>
westunionoffice@bigriver.net
PA: James R Hamblin   <M1>
60 Rolling Meadow Drive
Drummonds, TN 38023
(901)840-4747
brojim391@gmail.com
CL: Bobbie Roberts
8931 Bass Road
Millington, TN 38053
bobbiemroberts@gmail.com

Woodward's Chapel   (2C)GRWT9434
1357 Webster Street (mailing)
Union City, TN 38261
3054 Bud O Yates Road (physical)
Obion, TN 38240
(731)431-9127   <Obion>
FAX: (731)623-4226
SS: Mike Lavender   <M3 ST>
308 Main Street
Martin, TN 38237
(731)253-7308
FAX: (731)623-4226
mikelavender@alumni.vanderbilt.edu
CL: Alvin Minnick
1357 Webster Street
Union City, TN 38261
(731)442-1130
alviniraq2004@yahoo.com

Yorkville   (4MEC)GRWT9435
PO Box 156 (mailing)
17 Newbern Highway (physical)
Yorkville, TN 38389
(731)643-6594   <Gibson>
CL: Barbara Turner
447 Bells Chapel Road
Dyer, TN 38330
(731)487-7495
jimturner2007@yahoo.com

Zion   (4C)GRWT9133
8670 Highway 436 (mailing)
3890 New Zion Road (physical)
McKenzie, TN 38201
( )   <Carroll>
SS: Jon T Carlock   <M1>
248 Cherry Avenue
McKenzie, TN 38201
(731)693-0003
carlockj@bethelu.edu
SS: Richard Reed   <M2>
236 Madison Street
Dyer, TN 38330
(731)692-3604
CL: Stan Welch
3670 New Zion Road
McKenzie, TN 38201
(731)358-2238

OTHERS ON MINISTERIAL ROLL:

Akin, Hershel W   <M1 WC>
388 Mysen Drive
Cordova, TN 38018
(901)744-8980
Alexander, Merlyn A   <M1 HR>
80 N Hampton Lane
Jackson, TN 38305
m_j_alexander@eplus.net
(731)668-8185
Anderson, Barry L   <M1 DE>
1790 Faxon Avenue
Memphis, TN 38112
(901)458-8232
wa4mff@aol.com
Brown, Elinor   <M1 DE>
350 N Perkinst
Memphis, TN 38117
(901)274-1474
esb@cumberland.org
Brown, Mark   <M1 M9>
752 Hawthorne Street
Memphis, TN 38107
(901)274-1474
dmbrown@utmem.edu
Buck, Clinton   <M1 HR>
4912 Essexshire Avenue
Memphis, TN 38117
(901)409-7432
clintonbuck@aol.com
Burns, Garrett   <M1 WC>
387 Forrest Avenue
McKenzie. TN 38201
(731)535-3126
burnsg@bethelu.edu
Burns, J B, Jr   <M1 WC>
1020 Maud Road
Cherokee, AL 35616
(256)360-2252
Christoff, Whitney Brown   <M1 OM>
28 S Merton Street
Memphis, TN 38112
(865)387-0002
whitneymbrown@gmail.com
Condron, Dudley   <M1 RT>
1360 Harbert Avenue
Memphis, TN 38104
(901)726-1488
dudleywcondron@aol.com
Crisp, Gregory W   <M1 WC>
635 Eden Brook Lane
Cordova, TN 38018
(901)266-0406
Dyer, Stuart   <M1 WC>
3574 Foxfield Trail
Bartlett, TN 38135
(901)388-0612
Eddleman, Keith   <M1 WC>
2787 Stage Park Drive
Memphis, TN 38134
(901)388-9885
Edwards, Joey   <M1 WC>
5526 Highbury
Arlington, TN 38002
(901)867-7271
edwardsjoey@bellsouth.net
Gam, John   <M1 WC>
123 Riviera Road
Birmingham, AL 35209

WEST TENNESSEE PRESBYTERY CONTINUED

Gillock, Ed <M1 WC>
810 Rusell Road
Bolivar, TN 38008
(731)609-6744

Grimsley, Roger <M1 WC>
215 N Oak Street
Springfield, TN 37172

Harper, Josh <M1 WC>
227 LaCroix Drive #1
Collierville, TN 38017
(615)934-7940
jdharperministry@hotmail.com

Harwell, Keith <M1 WC>
11387 Highway 88
Halls, TN 38040
(731)613-3780

Heflin, Donna S <M1 HR>
4144 Meadow Court Drive
Bartlett, TN 38135
(901)382-8198
rdheflin@bellsouth.net

Holmes, Aaron G <M1 HR>
7240 Ellington Cove
Milan, TN 38358
(731)662-7595
agholmes@charter.net

Howe, Francis <M1 HR>
129 Manley Street
McKenzie, TN 38201
(731)352-5551

Hubbard, Pratt <M1 WC>
1565 Eli Brown Road
McKenzie, TN 38201
(731)352-9178

Jackson, Terry <M1 M9>
1461 Mount Pleasant Road
Hernando, MS 38632
(662)429-9741

James, William F <M1 WC>
4090 Meadow Field Lane
Bartlett, TN 38135
(615)653-1396
sparkbill54@gmail.com

Kleinjan, Lori <M1 WC>
6631 Millgrove Park Drive
Bartlett, TN 38135
(901)372-8413
lkleinj@prodigy.net

Latimer, James M <M1 WC>
3381 Moss Rose Drive
Memphis, TN 38115
(901)359-9201
sumnerbacon@me.com

Laurence, Brenda <M1 WC>
2823 Nine Mile Road
Enville, TN 38332
(731)687-2022
southernmoma@hotmail.com

Magliolo, Sam <M1 WC>
113 Hampstead Drive
Madison, MS 39110
(901)486-3527
smagliolo@comcast.net

Malinoski, Melissa <M1 WC>
9087 Fenmore Cove
Cordova, TN 38016
(420)620-0089
FAX: (423)636-1017
melissalmalinoski@gmail.com

Maynard, Geoffery <M1 WC>
1356 Marcia Road
Memphis, TN 38117
(901)409-5269

McClanahan, Jo Ann <M1 HR>
215 White Brothers Road
Humboldt, TN 38343
(731)784-1176
joannmcclanahan@hughes.net

McCurley, Don <M1 WC>
4036 McAllister Street
Milan, TN 38358
(731)723-3623
dcmccurley@hotmail.com

McMillan, L Ronald <M1 WC>
675 Kimberly Drive
Atoka, TN 38004
(901)837-1101
mcmillanron675@yahoo.com

Meeks, Brittany <M1 WC>
710 N Avalon Street
Memphis, TN 38107
(901)319-3474
brittany.meeke@garrett.edu

Minor, Mitzi <M1 PR>
875 S Cox
Memphis, TN 38104
(901)278-6115

Ndoro, Wonder <M1 WC>
111 Roberta Avenue
Memphis, TN 38112
(901)334-5861
gusungo@yahoo.com

Norton, Thomas H <M1 RT>
1049 Lakemont Circle
Winter Park, FL 32792
tomnorton33@gmail.com
(270)505-5218

Orr, Melvin <M1 HR>
806 Washington Street
Newbern, TN 38059
(731)627-2445
2Orrs.mn@charter.net

Perkins, Ed <M1 RT>
721 E Paris Avenue
McKenzie, TN 38201
(731)352-2754

Pinion, Phillip <M1 WC>
PO Box 87
Union City, TN 38281
(731)885-9175
ppinion.tn@gmail.com

Prosser, Robert <M1 RT>
1021 Old State Route 76
Henry, TN 38231
(731)243-4467

Qualls, Michael <M1 DE>
5355 June Cove
Horn Lake, MS 38637
(901)377-0526
FAX: (901)382-2600
mqualls1@yahoo.com

Quinton, Noah <M1 WC>
1617 Faxon Avenue
Memphis, TN 38112
(270)952-3875
noah.quinton@gmail.com

Ratliff, James L <M1 WC>
13 Hernando Drive
Cherokee Village, AR 72529
(901)758-0125
kudzu8161@yahoo.com

Ridgely, Michael <M1 WC>
5195 Broad Street
Trezevant, TN 38258
mdr26347@outlook.com
(731)669-3767

Scrivener, Carol <M1 WC>
746 Willowsprings Boulevard
Franklin, TN 37064
(731)660-6469
csscriv@juno.com

Searcy, James M <M1 HR>
1307 Lucy Way
Knoxville, TN 37912
(817)293-6132
gsearcy@earthlink.net

Shelton, Steven <M1 DE>
7886 Farmhill Cove
Bartlett, TN 38135
(901)377-0526
sshelton@cumberland.org

Smith, Jerald D <M1 WC>
502 Blackpatch Drive Apt A102
Springfield, TN 37172
(731)427-9316
jergensmith@aol.com

Thomas, Don F <M1 WC>
743 Rain Dance Way
Cordova, TN 38018
(901)412-3695
thomas63981@comcast.net

Thompson, Tommy <M1 WC>
9160 Tchulahoma Road
Southaven, MS 38671
(662)393-2552

Truax, Robert Lee, Jr <M1 HR>
2989 Champions Drive Apt 204
Lakeland, TN 38002
(901)266-5927

Todd, Christopher <M1 WC>
3303 Decker Street
Bartlett, TN 38134
(901)848-9*913
catodd1964@gmail.com

Turner, O Gene <M1 WC>
5160 McSpadden Road
Rives, TN 38253
(731)536-0189

Vance, Dennis <M1 WC>
22 Burnette Chapel Road
Sedalia, KY 42079
(731)644-3627
rvdvance@hotmail.com

Walker, Michael C <M1 WC>
177 Washington Avenue
Camden, TN 38320
(423)438-5650
mworator@gmail.com

Ward, Frank <M1 WC>
46 Henderson Cove
Atoka, TN 38004
(901)268-6067
fdward68@gmail.com

Warren, William <M1 RT>
7139 Toro Cove
Germantown, TN 38138
(901)755-8058
cpcgww@aol.com

Watson, Johnny E <M1 HR>
7 Hickory Lane
Metropolis, IL 62960
(731)414-3065
jewatson01@gmail.com

Westbrook, James <M1 RT>
1717 Wedgewood Drive
Union City, TN 38261
(731)884-0918
westbrook731@bellsouth.net

WEST TENNESSEE PRESBYTERY CONTINUED

Wheeler, Nathan   <M1 DE>
  2084 Linden Avenue
  Memphis, TN 38104
  (901)606-9535
  nwheeler@cumberland.org
White, Diann   <M1 WC>
  9394 Alex Dickson Cove
  Bartlett, TN 38133
  (901)377-7776
  diannwhite12@yahoo.com
Wilson, Thomas   <M1 HR>
  4543 Lake Vista
  Memphis, TN 38128
  (901)382-6190
  tomjw217@gmail.com

OTHER LICENTIATES ON ROLL:

Davison, Travis   <M2>
  5940 Highway 412 N
  Friendshp, TN 38034
  (731)499-3698
  travis.edgar.davison@gmail.com
Douglas, Dwight   <M2>
  3152 Dothan Street
  Memphis, TN 38118
  (901)826-7080
  dddouglas@memphisseminary.edu
Gibson, Brian   <M2>
  10002 Woodland Ash Drive
  Lakeland, TN 38002
  (901)674-2162
  briangibson64@gmail.com
Jett-Rand, Dana   <M2>
  78 Lester Lane
  Martin, TN 38237
  (731)587-0805
  msdanajett@yahoo.com

OTHER CANDIDATES ON ROLL:

Calheiros, Carolina   <M3>
  6858 Birch Lake Drive
  Memphis, TN 38119
  jonykaro@gmail.com
Calheios, Jonathan   <M3>
  6858 Bich Lake Drive
  memphis, TN 38119
  jonkkaro@gmail.com
Criswell, Bradley   <M3>
  2088 Baird Street
  Milan, TN 38358
  (731)487-6564
  criswellbj@gmail.com
Exley, Cliff   <M3>
  PSC 333 Box 985
  FPO, AP 96251-00
  gtmodawg@gmail.com
Ford, John   <M3>
  202 Greenfield Drive
  Greenwood, MS 38930
  (601)512-5003
  trueshepherdjohn@gmail.com
Keenan, Joshua   <M3
  6095 Highway 226
  Savannah, TN 38372
  (731)393-3125
  joshua.keenan16@gmail.com
Little, Claire   <M3>
  1736 N Reid Hooker Road
  Eads, TN 38028
  (901)734-8569
  j.claire.little@gmail.com
Puluc, Paul   <M3>
  1421 Greentree Valley Court Apt 5
  Memphis, TN 38119
  paul-tuba@hotmail.com
  (830)872-6090

ALPHABETICAL ROLL OF MINISTERS

Symbols in this roll:

(M0) - Mentored Minister
(M1) - Ordained Minister
(M2) - Licentiate
(M3) - Candidate
(M4) - Minister of another denomination who through reciprocal agreement is enrolled as a member of presbytery and has temporarily the rights and privileges of such membership according to the Constitution, Article 5.3.

--==<< A >>==--

Acton, Avery (M3)
222 Yellowhammer Drive
Alabaster, AL 35007
averyacton@gmail.com
(205)441-9915   SEGR#0100

Acton, Donald W (M1)
1186 Jenkins Lane
Knoxville, TN 37922
(865)966-5132   SEET#2310

Acton, Donny (M1)
1413 Oak Ridge Drive
Birmingham, AL 35242
donny@newhopecpc.org
(205)991-3204   SEGR#0104

Acton, Mindy (M1)
1413 Oak Ridge Drive
Birmingham, AL 35242
mindy@newhopecpc.org
(205)601-2454   SEGR#0104

Acuff, David (M1)
4969 Quail Lane
Columbia, SC 29206
david.acuff@us.army.mil
(803)727-3910   TNNA#7300

Adair, Ed (M3)
3028 Staffordshire Boulevard
Powell, TN 37849
edadair@gmail.com
(865)850-8785   SEET#2200

Adams, Fred Michael (M1)
42 Julies Way
Somerset, KY 42503
fma46@twc.com
(606)451-9155   MICU#3314

Adams, Jamie (M1)
403 W Washington
Union City, TN 38261
adamsjamie@charter.net
(731)796-1814   GRWT#9408

Aden, Marty (M1)
202 Bennington Place
Wilmington, NC 28412
maadretny@gmail.com
(910)274-8465   MSRR#8400

Agudelo, Gildardo (M1)
Cra 73C # 1A-54
Cali, COLOMBIA, SA
( )   MSCA#8223

Aguiar, Neil (M1)
2005 8th Street SW
Decatur, AL 35601
nlajap@yahoo.com
(256)616-1318   SEGR#0214

Ahn, Da-Wit (David) (M1)
1304 Kakyeng-Dong
Sangdang-Gu Cheongju-City
Choongbook, KOREA
(043)235-0219   SEET#2200

Akai, Anum (M1)
458 Dean Taylor Court
Simpsonville, KY 40067
aakai@uwalumni.com
(502)405-3120   MICU#3100

Akin, Hershel W (M1)
388 Mysen Drive
Cordova, TN 38018
(901)744-8980   GRWT#9100

Alas, William (M1)
105 Waterford Drive Cove
Calera, AL 35040
alas3542085@yahoo.es
(205)966-9411   SEGR#0115

Albarracin, Ruben D (M1)
7411 Magnolia Shadows Lane
Houston, TX 77095
confiaendios@hotmail.com
(281)797-9797   MSTR#8612

Alexander, Merlyn A (M1)
80 N Hampton Lane
Jackson, TN 38305
m_j_alexander@eplus.net
(731)668-8185   GRWT#9100

Allen, Gail (M1)
488 County Road 1650 N
Bethany, IL 61914
kallen1_61914@yahoo.com
(217)665-3387   MINC#5200

Alverson, Elmer L (M1)
354 Roy Davis Road
New Market, AL 35761
1941buddy@att.net
(256)828-4503   SERD#0800

Anderson, Angela (M3)
128 Horse Pin Place
Harvest, AL 35749
divineanderson75@yahoo.com
( )   SERD#0800

Anderson, Barry L (M1)
1790 Faxon Avenue
Memphis, TN 38112
wa4mff@aol.com
(901)458-8232   GRWT#9100

Anderson, Christopher (M1)
117 Big Pine Road
Batesville, AR 72501
csanderson@memphisseminary.edu
(870)805-0886   GRAR#1517

Anderson, Lisa (M1)
1790 Faxon Avenue
Memphis, TN 38112
anderli60@gmail.com
(901)246-8052   GRWT#9305

Ang, John (M1)
5843 S Farm Road 157
Springfield, MO 65810
pastorcares@yahoo.com
(417)886-3487   GRMI#4100

Angulo, Henry (M3)
Verde Limones
(311)734-2253   MSCA#8200

Appling, John (M1)
1722 S Fairway Avenue
Springfield, MO 65804
pegblessings@sbcglobal.net
(417)877-4643   GRMI#4100

Appling, Peggy (M1)
1722 S Fairway Avenue
Springfield, MO 65804
pegblessings@sbcglobal.net
(417)877-4643   GRMI#4100

Arase, Makihiko (M1)
1-350-13 Ogawamachi
Kodaira-shi, Tokyo
187-0032 JAPAN
viator@cb3.so-net.ne.jp
(080)6636-1960   MSJA#8300

Arias, John Jairo (M1)
Calle 144 Sur #496-08 / Apto 202
Caldas, Antioquia
COLOMBIA, SA
(57)317-693-1162   MSAN#8900

Ariza, Fabiola (M1)
COLOMBIA, SA
fatvioleta@hotmail.com
(316)419-8414   MSCA#8200

Arnold, Dwight (M3)
2925 Ragsdale Road
Santa Fe, Tennessee
(931)682-3237   TNCO#7100

Arnold, Will (M1)
6095 Ellington Cove
Milan, TN 38358
willarnold3187@gmail.com
(731)335-3187   GRWT#9121

Aros, Jeremias (M1)
5649 W Roscoe Street
Chicago, IL 60634
jcrcmiasaros@sbcglobal.nct
(773)685-4395   MINC#5200

Arteaga, Gilberto (M3)
Aereo 794
Buenaventura, COLOMBIA, SA
pastorgilbertoa@hotmail.com
( )256-4261   MSCA#8210

Asayama, Masaharu (M1)
6-3-2-308 Toyogaoka
Tama-shi, Tokyo
206-0031, JAPAN
asa@ipcc-21.com
(042)373-2710   MSJA#8300

Ashley, Jack (Nick) (M1)
12278 Herndon Oak Grove Road
Herndon, KY 42236
edencateringusa@aol.com
(812)204-1422   MICO#3606

MINISTERS CONTINUED

Ashton, Christie (M5)
10001 Bailey Cove Road SE
Huntsville, AL 35803
pastor@hopehuntsville.orgt
(256)881-4673 SERD#0800

Attema, Lee (M1)
PO Box 138
San Ignacio Town, Cayo District
BELIZE
lattema@icloud.com
(281)728-6263 MSTR#8100

Attena, Leslie (M1)
PO Box 138
San Ignacio Town, Cayo District
BELIZE
leslieattema@icloud.com
(281)728-6263 MSTR#8100

Atwell, Keith G (M1)
20 Dishman Cemetery Road
Canmer, KY 42722
oldpeacemaker38@live.com
(279)528-2521 MICU#3102

Axton, Durant (M1)
2441 SE Browning Road
Evansville, IN 47725
revpeck@me.com
(812)459-0089 MINC#5124

--=<< B >>==--

Babcock, Edward S, Jr (M1)
200 River Vista Drive Unit 306
Sandy Springs, GA 30339
ejsb1@aol.com
(256)882-9339 SERD#0800

Baltimore, Claud G (M1)
PO Box 1358
1430 Lakehurst Drive
Ada, OK 74821
baltimorejb@earthlink.net
(580)332-2679 MSRR#8400

Bane, Ted (M1)
123 Melanie Drive
Hendersonville, TN 37075
tedjan95@aol.com
(615)975-9343 TNNA#7300

Barkley, Daniel (M1)
2732 Rexford Street
Hokes Bluff, AL 35903
daniel@gadsdencp.com
(256)478-0397 SEGR#0402

Barkley, Kevin (M3)
588 Contest Road
Paducah, KY 42001
kevbark5@yahoo.com
(270)556-3924 MICO#3400

Barna, Clifton (M1)
1012 Adam Court
Cottontown, tn 37066
cliff.barna@gmail.com
(352)598-3246 TNNA#7333

Barnes Nathan (M3)
1139 Kimberly Drive
Goodlettsville, TN 37072
nathanwbarnes@gmail.com
(615)429-0887 TNNA#7319

Barnhouse, Donald Grey, Jr (M1)
51 Harristown Road
Paradise, PA 17562
donaldbarnhouse@gmail.com
(610)337-4015 MICU#3100

Barricklow, Gary (M2)
3012 Winston Meadows
Rio Rancho, NM 87144
garysr@barricklow.com
(505)417-0331 MSDC#8700

Barrios, Janina (M1)
7766 Greenwich Court E
Jacksonville, FL 32227
janina83@hotmail.com
(786)757-0366 SEGR#0100

Barron, Mark (M1)
836 McArthur Street
Manchester, TN 37355
mbarron@cafes.net
(931)728-2975 TNMU#7224

Barry, James (M1)
2912 Roy Road
Tyler, TX 75707
james_barry@bellsouth.net
(903)315-7998 SETG#2100

Barton, Cindy (M1)
600 Green Lane
Tyler, TX 75701
cbarton53@hotmail.com
(442)235-1393 MSTR#8113

Barton, Robert (M1)
22460 Klines Resort Road Lot #290
Three Rivers, MI 49093
csm2ndinfbde2002@yahoo.com
(859)613-2686 MICU#3100

Baugh, Roosevelt (M1)
4101 Hademan Street
Fort Worth, TX 76119
gmf1220@charter.net
(817)536-1315 MSRR#8408

Bautista, Juan (M1)
Tranv 30 No 17F-122
Cali
Colombia, South America
( )442-4562 MSCA#8217

Belizaire, Gama (M3)
26 West Street
Stoughton, MA 02072
gamab2000@gmail.com
(857)349-5588 SEET#2200

Bell, Marc (M1)
3467 State Route 175 N
Bremen, KY 42325
marc.bell1@att.net
(270)846-4203 MICU#3503

Belt, Bernice (M1)
PO Box 8372
Paducah, KY 42002
haroldbelt@comcast.net
(270)217-4623 MICO#5125

Benadom, Dennis (M1)
13314 Sage Street
Trona, CA 93562
galerose91@msn.com
(760)372-4536 MSDC#8503

Bertsch, Michael (M1)
204 Buckleigh Point
Gallatin, TN 37066
mikebertsch14@gmail.com
(423)763-8314 TNNA#7327

Betancur, Sergio (M1)
Iglesia El Rebano
Calle 128 sur #48-13
Caldas, Antioquia, COLOMBIA, SA
sergiobetancurposada@hotmail.com
(574)278-0787 MSCA#8208

Biggs, Jeff (M1)
1504 Cumberland Drive
Fairfield, IL 62837
jeffbiggsonline@gmail.com
(618)842-2219 MINC#5108

Bishop, Brenson (M1)
12000 Hudson View Court
Louisville, KY 40299
pappyvet@gmail.com
(502)641-5925 MICU#3100

Black, Gary G (M1)
11376 AL Highway 21 N
Piedmont, AL 36272
(205)452-2038 SEGR#0400

Blackwelder, Andrew (M1)
43 E Ridgefield Court
Greeneville, TN 37745
ablackwelder@gcpchurch.org
(423)525-3818 SEET#2200

Blair, Fonda (M1)
PO Box 11093
Murfreesboro, TN 37129
fblair4334@gmail.com
(615)605-9755 TNCO#7100

Blair, John (M1)
108 Cliff Drive
Lawrenceburg, TN 38464
jnbblair@charter.net
(931)766-2480 TNCO#7111

Blakeburn, Larry A (M1)
790 Emory Valley Road Apt 714
Oak Ridge, TN 37830
larry@1stcpc.org
(731)676-2978 SEET#2313

Blandon, Juan Esteban (M1)
Calle 51 #15-32
barrio Los Naranjos
Dosquebradas, Risaralda
COLOMBIA, SA
juanestebanblandon@yahoo.com
57(314)680-2246 MSAN#8907

Blanton, D B (M1)
ADDRESS UNKNOWN
( ) GRAR#1100

Blaum, Steve R (M1)
184 900 Street
Middletown, IL 62666
cumberland@frontier.com
(217)871-3339 MINC#5405

Blevins, Ralph (M1)
1623 County Road 2375 E
Geff, IL 62842
pastorreblevins@gmail.com
(618)854-2494 MINC#5107

Blevins, Tom (M1)
50 Blevins Road
Center, KY 42214
(270)565-1792 MICU#3100

Boggs, Barry (M1)
1039 Johnnie Bud Lane
Cookeville, TN 38501
boggsone@hotmail.com
(931)979-1701 TNMU#7274

MINISTERS CONTINUED

Boggs, Robert (M1)
89 Maple Leaf Lane
Leitchfield, KY 42754
(270)259-5546 MICU#3100
Bohon, Chris Michael (M2)
505 Edgehill Road
Joshua, TX 76058
cbohon@pathway.church
(817)228-9494 MSRR#8418
Bond, Bill (M1)
205 Windmere Drive
Chattanooga, TN 37411
bill@wcbj.net
(423)316-0867 SETG#2102
Bond, Richard (M1)
136 N 2nd Avenue
Algood, TN 38506
erbond@frontier.net
(931)319-4399 TNMU#7213
Bondurant, Lee (M1)
10160 Sumatra Street
El Paso, TX 79925
64lee.bondurant@gmail.com
(915)309-7269 MSDC#8700
Bone, W Harold (M1)
28103 Cooperleaf Drive
Bourne, TX 78015
ruaha1@sbcglobal.net
(210)859-5560 MSTR#8100
Borchert, Karen (M1)
PO Box 116
Talbott, TN 37877
mborchert@cn.edu
(865)696-8225 SEET#2218
Borchert, Mark (M1)
PO Box 116
Talbott, TN 37877
mborchert@cn.edu
(865)696-0489 SEET#2218
Boulton, Mitch (M1)
80 Topsy Lane
Savannah, TN 38372
steelermitch@gmail.com
(731)487-2317 GRWT#9220
Bourque, Leo (M1)
1620 Sarahs Cove
Hermitage, TN 37076
bourque120@gmail.com
(615)767-2428 TNNA#7300
Bowen, Greg (M2)
3241 South Fork Road
Glasgow, KY 42141
gbowen@commonwealthbroadcasting.com
(270)576-8011 MICU#3217
Bower, Clay (M1)
1514 Donette Place NE
Albuquerque, NM 87112
cbrev.9497@gmail.com
(704)575-9497 MSDC#8700
Bowers, Sharon G (M1)
1011 Wonder World Drive Apt 1911
San Marcos, TX 78666
sharon.bowers@gmail.com
(512)361-8471 MSTR#8100
Bowling, Andrew (M1)
20945 Highway 16 E
Siloam Springs, AR 72761
(479)524-6576 GRAR#1100
Bowman, Greg (M3)
3241 South Fork Road
Glasgow, KY 42141
( ) MICU#3217

Bozeman, Robert (M1)
582 Bozeman Loop
Belmont, LA 71406
bo@bozemanengineering.com
(318)256-5781 MSTR#8100
Bradberry, Jim (M3)
120 Hummingbird Lane
Searcy, AR 72143
(501)278-9750 GRAR#1205
Bradshaw, James (Jim) (M1)
415 S Red Street
Sheridan, AR 72150
(870)942-2525 GRAR#1100
Brantley, Kevin T (M1)
9801 State Route 81 South
Island, KY 42350
ktbrantley1971@gmail.com
(270)405-2222 MICU#3512
Brasher, Karen (M1)
2931 Barker Cypress Road Apt 415
Houston, TX 77084
ekb077@gmail.com
(205)777-2420 SEGR#0100
Braswell, Jimmy (M1)
1514 E 10th
Odessa, TX 79761
jjcgbraz@cableone.net
(432)967-3765 MSDC#8700
Brewer, Barbara Jean (M1)
500 N Persimmon Circle Apt 501
Rogers, AR 72756
(870)325-6449 GRAR#1100
Brindley, Toy (M1)
149 Joplin Street
Gurley, AL 35748
gurleycpc@gmail.com
(256)776-2331 SERD#0804
Brister, Glenn (M1)
3004 Deleware Avenue
Mcomb, MS 39648
bearmountainpenworks@gmail.com
(706)934-8629 SETG#2100
Brock, Dudley (M1)
490 County Road 1184
Cullman, AL 35057
preacherbrock@att.net
(256)734-0893 SEHO#0213
Brooks, Marcy (M3)
220 W Sevier Heights
Greeneville, TN 37745
marcybrooks52@hotmail.com
(423)747-4500 SEET#2200
Brown, Amy (M1)
679 Freeze Bend Road
Newport, AR 72112
( ) GRAR#1100
Brown, Charles R (M1)
2277 Union Avenue Unit 407
Memphis, TN 38104
(901)246-5837 MSRR#8400
Brown, Dale M (M1)
714 Leyda Street
West Plains, MO 65775
pastorbrown44@yahoo.com
(417)257-0983 GRMI#4100
Brown, Elinor (M1)
350 N Perkins
Memphis, TN 38117
esb@cumberland.org
(901)274-1474 GRWT#9100

Brown, Houston (M3)
866 N McLean
Memphis, TN 38107
hpbrown95@gmail.com
(817)915-9090 MSRR#8400
Brown, Mark (M1)
752 Hawthorne Street
Memphis, TN 38107
dmbrown@utmem.edu
(901)274-1474 GRWT#9100
Brown, Philip (M1)
540 Mt Pisgah Road
Dongola, IL 62926
brownlp75@yahoo.com
(618)827-3516 MICO#5115
Brown, Stephanie S (M1)
475 N Highland Street 6B
Memphis, TN 38122
scrudderbrown7@gmail.com
(817)915-1317 MSRR#8400
Broyles, Byrd (M1)
1856 Culleoka Highway
Culleoka, TN 38451
b3broyles@outlook.com
(931)224-5193 TNCO#7136
Bryan, Hannah (M1)
3601 Dana Drive
Durant, OK 74701
hbryan@choctawnation.com
(580)775-4955 MSCH#6105
Buchanan, Larry (M1)
466 N County Line Road
Calvert City, KY 42029
lbuchanan.tse@gmail.com
(270)519-9292 MICO#3610
Buck, Clinton (M1)
4912 Essexshire Avenue
Memphis, TN 38117
clintobuck@aol.com
(901)409-7432 GRWT#9100
Bulgarelli, Kevin (M3)
208 Silver Rose Boulevard
Burleson, TX 76028
kevinbulgarelli@mac.com
(410)262-4140 MSRR#8400
Bunnell, Robert (Bob) (M1)
329 Lexington Drive
Glasgow, KY 42141
bob_bunnell@yahoo.com
(270)629-6209 MICU#3100
Bunting, Geoff (M1)
9229 Hedgewood Court
Evansville, IN 47725
geoff.bunting@yahoo.com
(812)925-6630 MINC#5200
Burdick, Cynthia Maddux (M1)
16501 SE 113th Street
Newalla, OK 74857
cynthiaburdick02@gmail.com
(823)343-8867 MSRR#8400
Burgess, Ronald D (M1)
116 Harris Ridge Road
Dover, TN 37058
revron4@bellsouth.net
(931)232-5151 TNNA#7322
Burns, Garrett (M1)
387 Forrest Avenue
McKenzie, TN 38201
burnsg@bethelu.edu
(731)535-3126 GRWT#9100

urrows, Arthur L, Jr (M1)
PO Box 511
Hopkinsville, KY 42241
(270)886-1301 MICU#3505

Butcher, Kenny (M1)
403 Kalye Court
Mt Juliet, TN 37122
butcherkenny@yahoo.com
(615)719-1887 TNNA#7208

Butler, Alan (M2)
510 City House Court Apt 406
Memphis, TN 38103
abutler@cumberland.org
(817)937-8488 MSRR#8400

Butler, Jim (M1)
507 W Chestnut Street
Leitchfield, KY 42754
jbutler3026@att.net
(502)635-8587 MICU#3211

Butler, John (M1)
501 Cherokee Drive
Campbellsville, KY 42718
rev.butlerj8134@gmail.com
(270)403-7602 MICU#3104

Butler, Joseph H, Jr (M1)
56 Cline Ridge Road
Winchester, TN 37398
jhbu737@live.com
(931)224-8423 TNMU#7205

Buttram, Jim (M1)
5385 Bungalow Circle
Hixson, TN 37343
littlejimb@gmail.com
(865)938-7418 TNGA#2100

Byford, Ken (M1)
23716 AL Highway 9 N
Piedmont, AL 36272
kenabyford@gmail.com
(205)965-7111 SEGR#0406

Byrd, James F (M1)
1732 Cornishville Road
Harrodsburg, KY 40330
jfbyrd@bluezoomwifi.com
(859)734-0534 MICU#3100

Byrd, Jimmy (M1)
3810 Lake Road
Woodlawn, TN 37191
revjimmybyrd@gmail.com
(615)289-3347 SETG#7304

--=<< C >>==--

Cadenbach, Mark (M1)
91 Elzadah Lane
Salem, AR 72576
cadenbm@nctc.net
(890)955-9250 GRAR#1100

Cajcedo, Efrain (M3)
Aereo 6365
Cali, COLOMBIA, SA
( ) MSCA#8224

Caicedo, Jose Urier (M3)
Cra 4 sur 9C-15
Jamundi, Colombia, South America
joseurier@hotmail.com
(317)675-2580 MSCA#8200

Caldwell, Chris (M1)
829 Chateaugay Road
Knoxville, TN 37923
luke64345@gmail.com
(865)599-1044 SEET#2315

Calero, Aldrin (M1)
Cattara 13 3-81
Guacari, COLOMBIA, SA
( )253-0453 MSCA#8212

Camp, Annetta (M1)
2303 Mill Creek Road
Halls, TN 38040
annetta@cumberlandchurch.com
(731)285-5703 GRWT#9410

Campbell, Thomas D (M1)
7437 Old Clinton Pike
Powell, TN 37849
tdcampbellar@gmail.com
(870)297-2319 SEET#2200

Campos, Eva (M3)
PO Box 451405
Miami, FL 33245
(786)426-5997 SEGR#0100

Cantey, James M (M1)
3505 Elmira Drive
Longview, TX 75605
(903)452-6049 MSTR#8111

Cardona, Nancy (M1)
Calle 51 #15-32
Dosquebradas, Risaralda
COLOMBIA, SA
nancycardona10@yahoo.com
(576)322-2938 MSAN#8900

Carlock, Jon T (M1)
248 Cherry Avenue
McKenzie, TN 38201
carlockj@bethel-college.edu
(731)352-0800 GRWT#9133

Carlton, Gary (M1)
108 Greenbrier Street
Dickson, TN 37055
gwcarlton@yahoo.com
(270)965-4358 TNNA#7300

Carpenter, David (M1)
909 W Elm Street
Olney, TX 76374
olneycpc@brazosnet.com
(940)564-2339 MSRR#8416

Carr, Jill (M1)
1601 Arbour Drive
Lebanon, MO 65536
dig.micah.6.8@gmail.com
(417)532-6760 GRMI#4315

Carter, Billy Ray (M1)
33 Mockingbird Drive
Leitchfield, KY 42754
cartercbc@windstream.net
(270)259-3897 MICU#3221

Carter, Gary (M1)
8311 County Road 1082
Vinemont, AL 35179
garycarter51@gmail.com
(256)443-8389 SEHO#0202

Carter, James L (M1)
6155 Hummingbird Lane
Whitesburg, TN 37891
jandjmt@comcast.net
(423)587-8423 SEET#2200

Carter, Patricia (M1)
2509 Decatur Stratton Road
Decatur, MS 39327
revtree@yahoo.com
(601)604-3813 SEGR#0100

Carver, Gary (M1)
2810 Cabin Road
Chattanooga, TN 37411
sandgatthecabin@epbfi.com
(423)698-2556 SETG#2100

Carwheel, Greg (M2)
12908 Smokey Ranch Drive
Haslet, TX 76052
gcarwheel@gmail.com
(682)215-4516 MSRR#8400

Cassell, C J (M1)
825 Aimes Court
Nashville, TN 37221
n4cjc@comcast.net
(615)594-2693 TNNA#7334

Castaneda, Ricardo (M1)
Calle 65 #98-45 (Interior 174)
Altos de la Macarena-Robledo La
Campina
Medellin, Antioquia, COLOMBIA, SA
rijcah@gmail.com
(574)577-0717 MSAN#8915

Castano, Juan Alexander (M1)
Calle 127 sur #42-38 Apto 301
Caldas, Antioquia, COLOMBIA, SA
juanalexandercastano@hotmail.com
(574)306-4435 MSAN#8906

Castellanos, Sandra (M2)
488 SW 126th Terrace
Davie, FL 33325
sandramcastellanosg@gmail.com
(754)442-4820 SEGR#0100

Chall-Hutchinson, Deborah (M1)
190 Ussery Road
Clarksville, TN 37043
challhut@gmail.com
(931)905-1671 TNNA#7300

Chambers, Jason (M1)
555 Blue Hole Road
Beebe, AR 72012
jmchambers@memphisseminary.edu
(870)807-1930 GRAR#1100

Chambers, Nicholas (M1)
362 Ouachita 54
Camden, AR 71701
nachambrs@hotmail.com
(870)807-0279 GRAR#1303

Chancellor, Hilton (M1)
11905 Preserve Vista
Austin, TX 78738
hiltontex@aol.com
(512)382-1972 MSTR#8100

Chang, Leo (M1)
819 W Division SE
Springfield, MO 65803
(901)287-9901 GRAR#1100

Chapman, Harry W (M1)
4908 El Picador Court
Rio Rancho, NM 87124
wrightrev@gmail.com
(505)620-2427 MSDC#8709

Chen, Steven (M1)
865 Jackson Street
San Francisco, CA 94133
steven@cumberlandsf.org
(415)421-1624 MSDC#8501

Cheung, Luke (M1)
A-D Flat 3/F 338-340 Castle Peak Road
Cheung Sha Wan
Kowloon HONG KONG
luke.cheung@cgst.edu
(852)2794-6781 MSHK#8800

MINISTERS CONTINUED

Chen, Steven (M1)
865 Jackson Street
San Francisco, CA 94133
steven@cumberlandsf.org
(415)421-1624 MSDC#8501

Cheung, Luke (M1)
A-D Flat 3/F 338-340 Castle Peak Road
Cheung Sha Wan
Kowloon HONG KONG
luke.cheung@cgst.edu
(852)2794-6781 MSHK#8800

Christoff, Whitney Brown (M1)
28 S Merton Street
Memphis, TN 38112
(865)387-0002 GRWT#9100

Chin, Kwang Sik (M2)
1168 Palisade Avenue
Fort Lee, NJ 07024
(201)220-3390 SECE#2400

Cho, Kun Ho (M1)
8362 Walker Street Apt 18
Buena Park, CA 90623
pkhch3@gmail.com
(949)241-6167 MSDC#8700

Cho, Sangsook (M1)
7 Falmouth Court
Middletown, CT
(860)830-6808 SECE#2143

Cho, Sung Wan (M1)
304 Cape Liberty Drive
Suwanee, GA 30024
swcho100491@gmail.com
(501)247-5953 GRAR#2135

Choe, Byung-Jae (M1)
876-15 Dokok-1dong
Kangnam-Gu, Seoul, KOREA
(023)463-3939 SEET#2222

Choi, Ezra (M1)
605 Arbor Hollow Circle #2103
Cordova, TN 38018
(901)236-8235 SEET#2200

Choi, Hyoung S (M1)
32132 Huntly Circle
Salisbury, MD 21804
pastor0101@naver.com
(443)880-6776 SETG#2138

Choi, Sean (M1)
1284 New Liberty Way
Braselton, GA 30517
esloveh2@hotmail.com
(901)826-2993 SEKP#2000

Cinco, Carlos (M1)
611 Cheron Road
Madison, TN 37115
pastorcinco2020@gmail.com
(615)586-1269 TNNA#7314

Cintron, Eddie (M3)
5695 S Franklin
Springfield, MO 65810
eddiecintron7@hotmail.com
(417)894-1480 GRMI#4314

Clark, Amber LaCroix (M1)
2353 Blue Springs Road
Decherd, TN 37324
amber.clark@winchestercp.org
(931)967-2121 TNMU#7249

Clark, J Don (M1)
400 University Park Drive Apt 111
Homewood, AL 35209
jdsjcl@charter.net
(205)902-5161 SEGR#0100

Clark, Jeff (M1)
327 Haynes Haven Lane
Murfreesboro, TN 37129
jclark7733@aol.com
(615)896-7733 TNMU#7200

Clark, Michael (M1)
2353 Blue Springs Road
Decherd, TN 37324
mclark37398@gmail.com
(931)967-2121 TNMU#7249

Clark, Tom (M1)
2089 Sumach Church Road
Chatsworth, GA 30705
tom402135@hotmail.com
(270)469-5468 TNGA#2124

Clark, Tommy (M1)
924 Bresslyn Road
Nashville, TN 37205
tommy@wncp.org
(931)703-7542 TNNA#7334

Coffey, Andy (M3)
PO Box 88
Bremen, AL 35033
andycoffey3@gmail.com
(259)590-4995 SEHO#0500

Coker, Robert N (M1)
112 Olympia Drive
Alcoa, TN 37701
nickcoker@bellsouth.net
(865)458-8791 SEET#2302

Cole, Dwayne (M1)
6460 Village Parkway
Anchorage, AK 99504
tadpolejr@aol.com
(907)854-5793 TNCO#7100

Coleman, Bobby D (M1)
107 E Henson
Springdale, AR
bobby.coleman@gmail.com
(870)213-5410 GRAR#1514

Collins, Paul (M1)
915 Warm Sands Drive SE
Albuquerque, NM 87123
preachtheword44@gmail.com
(505)294-3842 MSDC#8700

Colvard, Kevin (M1)
806 23rd Street NW
Cleveland, TN 37311
rev_kev@satx.rr.com
(205)267-9372 MSTR#8100

Condon, Thomas W, Jr (M1)
6508 Victoria Avenue
N Richland Hills, TX 76180
(817)656-9334 MSRR#8400

Condron, Dudley (M1)
1360 Harbert Avenue
Memphis, TN 38104
dudleywcondron@aol.com
(901)726-1488 GRWT#9100

Contini, John (M1)
4344 Poor Ridge Pike
Lancaster, KY 40444
john@hillsideheritagefarm.com
(859)339-0747 MICU#3103

Cook, Douglas (M3)
822 County Road 365 E
Norris City, IL 62869
dcookster2@gmail.com
(618)380-6112 MICO#3400

Cook, Lisa (M1)
4101 Dalemere Court
Nashville, TN 37207
sacredsparksministry@gmail.com
(615)868-4118 TNNA#7300

Corbin, William (M1)
7300 N Lamar Road
Mount Juliet, TN 37122
raven.rest@comcast.net
(615)459-8998 TNNA#7300

Correa, Juan David (M1)
Calle 2 Norte #16-39
Armenia, Quindio, COLOMBIA, SA
jjcedp07@hotmail.com
(318)285-1209 MSEM#8600

Cottingim, Tom (M1)
353 Atwood Drive
Lexington, KY 40515
t.cottingim@insightbb.com
(859)273-3800 MICU#3100

Cowgill, Jana (M3)
1037 Chriswood Drive
Clarkridge, AR 72623
jana.cowgill@gmail.com
(870)421-2106 GRAR#1100

Cox, Jimmy R (M1)
2250 County Road 156
Anderson, AL 35610
dcox01@msn.com
(256)710-1702 SEHO#0508

Craddock, Barry (M1)
147 Moss Way
Glasgow, KY 42141
craddock.barry53@gmail.com
(270)678-7615 MICU#3105

Craig, Aaron (M1)
325 Cherry Avenue
McKenzie, TN 38201
(731)352-6718 MICU#3131

Craig, Peggy Jean (M1)
113 Harbor Town Square #304
Memphis, TN 38013
peggy.jean.craig@cpcg.org
(256)277-1147 GRWT#9310

Craven, Mark (M1)
21 Kingston Stret'
Chattanooga, TN 37414
craven.ma@gmail.com
(423)618-0169 SETG#2113

Crawshaw, Randy (M1)
136 NE 1271 Road
Knob Noster, MO 65336
randy_crawshaw@yahoo.com
(660)563-5149 GRMI#4100

Creamer, Jennifer (M1)
310 5th Street
Pacific Grove, CA 93950
jencreamer@gmail.com
(831)809-9890 SEET#2200

Crisp, Gregory W (M1)
635 Eden Brook Lane
Cordova, TN 38018
(901)266-0406 GRWT#9100

Criss, Paul T (M1)
6831 Salem Road
Lakeland, TN 38002
ptcriss@hotmail.com
(901)626-8462 GRWT#9316

MINISTERS CONTINUED

Criswell, Bradley (M3)
2088 Baird Street
Milan, TN 38358
criswellbj@gmail.com
(731)487-6564 GRWT#9100

Croslin, Dennis (M1
165 Maple Street
Gordonsville, TN .38563
(615)934-2383 TNMU#7246

Cuartas, Joel (M0)
Calle 34 #24A-36
Cali, COLOMBIA, SA
(000)438-2512 MSCA#8211

Cummings, Corey (M1)
399 Lanview Concord Road
Trenton, TN 38382
cummings.corey@gmail.com
(731)845-3173 GRWT#9108

Cunningham, Matthew Dean (M1)
1646 Brighton-Clopton Road
Brighton, TN 38011
mcunningham0528@comcast.net
(901)475-4252 GRWT#9318

--==<< D >>==--

Dalwig, Roger (M1)
1661 Hickory Lane
Corydon, IN 47112
rcd129@hotmail.com
(812)705-5071 MINC#5200

Daniel, Elizabeth (M1)
1818 Memorial Drive
Clarksville, TN 37043
lizzy37@juno.com
(931)645-6956 TNNA#7305

Daniels, Doy L, Jr (M1)
1095 Crestview Drive
Milan, TN 38358
revdrdoy@gmail.com
(731)686-1851 GRWT#9121

Darland, Chris (M1)
1111 Louisville Road
Harrodsburg, KY 40330
revchrisd@yahoo.com
(859)734-2254 MICU#3111

Davenport, Donna (M1)
PO Box 234
Wingo, KY 42088
chamberdonna@yahoo.com
(270)376-5488 MICO#5118

Davenport, Mark A (M1)
1804 Stacie Street
Mt Pleasant, TX 75455
hoginbama@yahoo.com
(205)427-4941 MSTR#8100

Davenport, Vondal (M1)
97 Main Street
Ratcliff, AR 72951
(479)965-2036 GRAR#1100

Davis, C Timothy (M1)
8880 Childress Road
West Paducah, KY 42086
charles0828@earthlink.net
(850)995-8383 SEGR#0100

Davis, Cheyanne (M3)
812 Valley Ridge Road
Burleson, TX 76028
cheyanne@pathway.church
(817)781-5155 MSRR#8400

Davis, Jerry (M2)
604 Nesbitt Hollow Road
McEwen, TN 37101
drjisin@yahoo.com TNNA#7339

Davis, Robert (Toby) (M1)
PO Box 21
Archer City, TX 76351
pastortobydavis@gmail.com
(901)826-5755 GRAR#1100

Davison, Travis (M2)
5940 Highway 412 N
Friendship, TN 38034
travis.edgar.davison@gmail.com
(731)499-3698 GRWT#9100

Daza, Edilberto (M1)
Cra 12 #8-47
Cartago, Valle
Colombia, South America
presbicartago@gmail.com
57(314)794-1905 MSEM#8905

Daza, Johan (M1)
8148 Yellow Stone Drive
Cordova, TN 38016
jdaza@cumberland.org
(281)793-3869 MSAN#8900

De Jimenez, Luciria Aguirre (M1)
AA6365
COLOMBIA, SA
pastorluciana50@yahoo.com.co
(300)686-9161 MSCA#8200

De Vries, Raymond (M1)
2080 Stanford Village Drive
Antioch, TN 37013
raydevries3216@att.net
(615)332-3587 TNNA#7300

De Wees, Jeff (M1)
116 Lancaster Court
Gallatin, TN 37066
pastorjeff@beechcp.com
(931)209-3331 TNNA#7301

Deaton, John (M1)
277 School Lanet
Springfield, PA 19064
deatonjr11@gmail.com
(215)906-7067 SEHO#0500

DeBerry, Martha Jacqueline (M1)
2681 Roosevelt Boulevard Apt 3209
Clearwater, FL 33760
1spiritualdirector@earthlink.net
(931)304-8832 TNMU#7200

Deere, Thomas (Tom) (M1)
460 Yukon Drive
Russellville, AR 72802
tdeere@suddenlinkmail.com
(479)498-0318 GRAR#1100

Delashmit, Steve (M1)
2705 Garrett Drive
Bowling Green, KY 42104
(270)796-8822 MICU#3304

Diamond, Cardelia Howell (M1)
1580 Jeff Road
Huntsville, AL 35806
cpclergymama@gmail.com
(256)837-6014 SERD#0814

Diaz, Esperanza (M1)
Calle 2 Norte #16-19
Armenia, Quindio, COLOMBIA, SA
jjcedp07@hotmail.com
(576)745-0496 MSAN#8903

Diaz, Freddy (M1)
2425 Holly Hall Apt B42
Houston, TX 77054
fredglobeus@yahoo.com
(832)305-2379 MSTR#8606

Diaz, Gloria Villa (M1)
2425 Holly Hall Apt B42
Houston, TX 77054
gloria@newdayinchrist.org
(832)758-5871 MSTR#8100

Diaz, William (M1)
Calle 5 Con Cra 89
Cali, COLOMBIA, SA
nuevaesperanza1983@hotmail.com
( )332-5849 MSCA#8221

Diego, Aida Melendez (M1)
412 SW 87 Place
Miami, FL 33174
revaidamd@yahoo.com
(305)815-1197 SEGR#0100

Dixon, Wendall Logan (M3)
201 Pine Hill Road
Dover, AR 72837
( ) GRAR#1100

Dougherty, Duane A, Jr (M1)
4713 Lake Havasu
Fort Worth, TX 76103
revdad.duane@gmail.com
(903)842-474 MSRR#8415

Douglas, Dwight (M2)
3152 Dothan Street
Memphis, TN 38118
dddouglas@memphisseminary.edu
(901)826-7080 GRWT#9100

Driskell, James P (M1)
154 Mountain Way
Anderson, AL 35610
patprespax@yahoo.com
(256)648-6758 SEHO#0517

Duke, Michael E (M1)
106 Friar Tuck Drive
Dickson, TN 37055
(615)446-6515 TNNA#7300

Dukes, Britta (M1)
5226 W William Cannon Drive
Austin, TX 78749
britta@shpc.org
(512)892-3580 MSTR#8604

Dumas, Byron (M1)
1775 Theresa Drive
Clarksville, TN 37043
bdumas7346@aol.com
(931)552-8772 TNNA#7300

Duncan, Ronnie (M1)
146 Deseree Broyles Road
Chuckey, TN 37641
ronkduncan@icloud.com
(423)552-0321 SEET#2204

Dussan, Hedemarrie (M2)
6248 SW 14th Street
West Miami, FL 33144
hedemarrie@gmail.com
(305)812-0613 SEGR#0100

Dyer, Stuart (M1)
3574 Foxfield Trail
Bartlett, TN 38135
(901)388-0612 GRWT#9100

MINISTERS CONTINUED

--==<< E >>==--

Earheart-Brown, Daniel J (Jay)   (M1)
475 N Highland Street Apt 9L
Memphis, TN 38122
jearheartbrown@gmail.com
(901)463-0007   GRWT#9308

Earheart-Brown, Paul   (M1)
510 City House Court Apt 406
Memphis, TN 38103
paul.earheartbrown@gmail.com
(901)483-0018   GRWT#9100

Eddleman, Keith   (M1)
2787 Stage Park Drive
Memphis, TN 38134
(901)388-9885   GRWT#9100

Edmonds, Wayne   (M1)
112 Dogwood Trail
Eclectic, AL 36024
sweetpea@comlinkinc.net
(334)857-2202   SEGR#0100

Edwards, James Scott   (M3)
226 Jasmine Drive
Alabaster, AL 35007
jedwards53163@bellsouth.net
(205)529-4507   SEGR#0101

Edwards, Jimmie   (M3)
3527 Hinton Road
Clarksville, TN 37043
jimmieedwards@me.com
(931)980-2802   TNNA#7300

Edwards, Joey   (M1)
5526 Highbury
Arlington, TN 38002
edwardsjoey@bellsouth.net
(901)573-7579   GRWT#9100

Edwards, Scott   (M3)
226 Jasmine Drive
Alabaster, AL 35007
jedwards5316@bellsouth.net
(205)358-7456   SEGR#0100

Ensminger, Mike   (M2)
180 Breland Street
Wilsonville, AL 35186
me0573@att.com
(205)529-7878   SEGR#0108

Eppard, Andrew   (M1)
6 Sanford Circle
Greeneville, TN 37743
reformedminister@yahoo.com
(417)770-1153   SEET#2202

Espinoza, Virginia   (M1)
PO Box 132
Boswell, OK 74727
vespinoza@choctawnation.com
(580)434-7971   MSCH#6109

Estep, William   (M1)
239 Skyline Drive
Harriman, TN 37748
(865)882-5114   TNMU#7200

Estes, George R   (M1)
7910 Cloverbrook Lane
Germantown, TN 38138
geoestes@gmail.com
(901)275-4812   MSDC#8700

Evans, Daniel   (M3)
126 Chesapeake Harbor
Hendersonville, TN 37075
gcpcdaniel@comcast.net
(731)613-1806   TNNA#7300

Everett, William   (M1)
1906 Ogburn Chapel Road
Clarksville, TN 37042
weverett62@hotmail.com
(931)220-3854   TNNA#7300

Exley, Cliff   (M3)
PSC 333 Box 985
FPO, AP 96251-00
gtmodawg@gmail.com
(901)430-5095   GRWT#9100

--==<< F >>==--

Fackler, David   (M1)
3409 Benton Road
Paducah, KY 42003
woodlawnpastor@live.com
(270)442-7713   MICO#3400

Fahl, D Frederick (Fred)   (M1)
500 3rd Street
Fulton, KY 42041
dffahl@gmail.com
(270)472-1476   MICO#3419

Fancher, Michael E   (M3)
356 Breeding Road
Edmonton, KY 42129
princo1975@live.com
(270)432-3138   MICU#3101

Fell, Ron   (M1)
PO Box 285
Fairfield, IL 62837
r.fell80@gmail.com
(618)638-3744   MINC#8200

Ferguson, E Blant   (M1)
80 Smoky Mountain Lane Unit 305
Clayton, GA 30525
blantferg@yahoo.com
(706)896-9296   TNNA#7300

Ferrell, Timothy W   (M1)
1850 Dunbar Road
Woodlawn, TN 37191
ferrelltw@aol.com
(931)920-2662   TNNA#7316

Ferrol, Ruben   (M1)
13018 E 28th Street
Tulsa, OK 74134
rubeferrol@msn.com
(610)966-7289   MSRR#8400

Ferry, Aaron   (M1)
3137 Glenbrook Drive
Twinsburg, OH 44087
amferry815@gmail.com
(615)946-3078   TNMU#7200

Fife, Patric   (M1)
73 Jordan Road
Lawrenceburg, TN 38464
pnlfifernak@gmail.com
(931)629-8146   TNCO#7100

Fike, Charles   (M1)
2070 N 1st Street
Milan, TN 38358
(731)686-0224   GRWT#9418

Fisk, James R   (M1)
9 Mills Drive
Bella Vista, AR 72714
jimfisk95@yahoo.com
(479)886-1216   GRAR#1216

Fleming, Christopher   (M1)
3745 Ramona Drive
Paducah, KY 42001
holyday@vci.net
(615)424-8561   MICO#3415

Flores, Fabian   (M3)
Aereo 6365, Cali Valle
COLOMBIA, SA
( )   MSCA#8222

Fly, William   (M1)
2820 Old Sam's Creek Road
Pegram, TN 37143
billyfly3@gmail.com
(865)938-6273   SEET#2200

Fong, Cindi   (M1)
1835 Alemany Boulevard
San Francisco, CA 94112
cfong@redeemersf.org
(415)335-8067   MSDC#8512

Fong, Danny   (M1)
1224 Fairfax Avenue
San Francisco, CA 94124
dfong@redeemersf.org
(415)671-2194   MSDC#8512

Fonseca, Roberto   (M1)
Cll 46 A No 4N 25
Colombia, South America
( )446-3311   MSCA#8218

Ford, John   (M3)
202 Greenfield Drive
Greenwood, MS 38930
trueshepherdjohn@gmail.com
(601)512-5003   GRWT#9100

Foreman, Samuel L   (M1)
22 Weston Lane
Hattiesburg, MS 39402
samfcpc@gmail.com
(601)562-1415   SEGR#0100

Forester, Byron   (M1)
2376 Eastwood Place
Memphis, TN 38112
bforester@bellsouth.net
(901)324-1707   GRWT#9419

Fortner, Terry   (M1)
118 W 5th Avenue
Central City, KY 42330
terryfortner@utlook.com
(270)821-6541   MICU#3100

Fortney, Josh   (M1)
1614 Woodoak Drive
Richardson, TX 75082
jfortney@pathway.church
(214)794-9912   MSRR#8400

Fossey, Donald, II   (M3)
328 Waterloo Road
Cookeville, TN 38506
dfossey@twlakes.net
(931)498-2149   TNMU#7223

Fowler, Scott   (M1)
1900 Alex Mill Road
Montevallo, AL 35115
springcreekchurch@aol.com
(205)901-8478   SEGR#0113

Franco, Ricardo   (M1)
35 Bayrd Terrace Apt 2
Malden, MA 02148
fsfamily64@gmail.com
(781)605-5900   SEET#2200

Franklin, Chris   (M1)
310 Yellow Springs Road
Midway, TN 37809
chrisfranklin104@comcast.net
(423)972-3609   SEET#2208

MINISTERS CONTINUED

Franklin, Curtis   (M1)
3394 Old Mayfield Road
Paducah, KY 42003
brocurtis@fredonia.biz
(270)545-3481   MICO#3410

Freeman, A Daniel   (M1)
210 Dogwood Drive
Greeneville, TN 37743
(423)638-5925   SEET#2200

Freeman, Jesse L, Jr   (M1)
270 Eastside Road
Burns, TN 37029
mptc@bellsouth.net
(615)202-4594   TNNA#7307

Freund, Henry O   (M1)
913 Sam Houston Drive
Dyersburg, TN 38024
freundly@att.net
(731)285-1744   MSDC#8700

Frost, Sherrlyn   (M1)
5557 Surrey Lane
Birmingham, AL 35242
sherrlyn@newhopecpc.org
(205)408-0729   SEGR#0104

Fulton, James   (M1)
1520 Oak Grove Road
Benton, KY 42025
(270)437-4320   MICO#3400

Fung, David   (M1)
19928 Bothell Everett Highway Apt 513
bothell, WA 98012
(403)513-5657   MSDC#8700

Fung, Lawrence   (M1)
367 El Dorado Drive
Daly City, CA 94015
revfung@yahoo.com
(415)535-8754   MSDC#8700

Furr, Wayne   (M1)
706 E 6th Street
Coal Valley, IL 61240
prespreacher@gmail.com
(309)756-9476   MINC#5200

Furuhata, Kazuhiko   (M1)
9-41-15-310 Kamitsuruma-honcho
Minamiku Sagamihara-shi
Kanagawa-ken
cpc.furuhata@gmail.com
252-0318, JAPAN
(501)430-8885   MSJA#8310

--==<< G >>==--

Gaither, Randy   (M1)
No 3 Pacific Street
Belmopan City
BELIZE, CENTRAL AMERICA
rgaither@valuelinx.net
( )   SEGR#0100

Gam, John   (M1)
123 Riviera Road
Birmingham, AL 35209
( )   GRWT#9100

Garcia, Jesus Maria   (M3)
Mazma 38 Casa 34 Barrio Bosques de
Maracibo
jesus.garciagil@hotmail.com
(318)463-7302   MSCA#8200

Garcia, Lucas   (M1)
875 Scenic Highway
Lawrenceville, GA 30045
lucasgarcia924@gmail.com
(678)698-7971   SETG#2149

Garcia, Maria (Mabe)   (M1)
875 Scenic Highway
Lawrenceville, GA 30045
pastoramabegarcia@gmail.com
(678)698-7971   SETG#2149

Garcia, Luz Stella   (M3)
Cll 33 No 34A-22
Cali, Colombia, South America
( )232-5868   MSCA#8200

Gardner, Charles   (M1)
PO Box 1035
Elephant Butte, NM 87935
(719)784-7744   MSRR#8400

Gaskill, Todd   (M1)
47 Brown Teal Road
Fayetteville, TN 37334
revtgaskill@gmail.com
(931)580-2708   TNCO#7121

Gaskin, Tony   (M1)
18 Teal Hollow Road
Kelso, TN 37348
tgaskin46@yahoo.com
(256)338-7893   TNCO#7122

Gates, J B   (M1)
PO Box 289
Enfield, IL 62835
rjjbgate@hamiltoncom.net
(618)963-2306   MINC#5104

Gaviria, Mario   (M1)
Cra 27 #7-48
Cali, COLOMBIA, SA
pastormariogaviria@hotmail.com
(314)773-2601   MSCA#8201

Gehle, Jeffrey A   (M1)
4510 Holly Grove Road
Brighton, TN 38011
jeff@pathway.church
(817)295-5832   MSRR#8418

Gentry, Michele   (M1)
Urb San Jorge casa 28
Km 8 via a La Tebaida
Armenia, Quindio, COLOMBIA, SA
gentry.andes@yahoo.com
(318)285-1161   MSAN#8900

George, Thomas   (M2)
908 N Brown Avenue
Casa Grande, AZ 85222
tgeorge@aerogram.net
(640)447-2676   MSDC#8700

Gerard, Eugene S   (M1)
615 N 42nd Street
Paducah, KY 42001
(270)443-2889   MICO#3400

Gibson, Brian   (M2)
10002 Woodland Ash Drive
Lakeland, TN 38002
briangibson64@gmail.com
(901)674-2162   GRWT#9100

Gillis, Aubrey Thomas   (M1)
110 Blue Sky Lane
Alabaster, AL 35007
tomgillis63@hotmail.com
(251)947-1638   SERD#0800

Gillock, Ed   (M1)
810 Russell Road
Bolivar, TN 38008
(731)609-6744   GRWT#9100

Giraldo, Andres   (M2)
Calle 76 #87-14 Apto 202
Medellin, Antioquia, COLOMBIA, SA
andresgiraldo@une.net.co
(574)422-6669   MSAN#8911

Giraldo, Marcela   (M3)
Calle 68 D #40-15
Manizales, Caldas, COLOMBIA, SA
(576)878-5412   MSAN#8900

Giraldo, William   (M1)
CLL 62 No 18 11
Cali, COLOMBIA, SA
( )439-5436   MSCA#8200

Glenn, Linda H   (M1)
49 Mason Road
Threeway, TN 38343
lindahglenn@click1.net
(731)618-0192   GRWT#9119

Gnewuch-Schmidt, Karen   (M2)
9555 Yukon Street
Westminster, CO 80021
chartreusemonk12@gmail.com
(303)403-4538   MSDC#8700

Goehring, Marty   (M1)
8600 Academy NE
Albuquerque, NM 87111
mmgoehring@heightscpc.org
(505)821-3628   MSDC#8701

Gonzalez, Carlos Humberto   (M3)
Cra 7 E 2-15
Cali, Colombia, South America
carloshg@hotmail.com
(312)889-7919   MSCA#8200

Gonzales, Homer   (M1)
8924 Armistice NE
Albuquerque, NM 87109
hgabq1985@gmail.com
(505)235-0215   MSDC#8700

Gonzales, Miguel   (M1)
200 Bethel Drive
Lenoir City, TN 37772
(865)988-4238   SEET#2320

Gonzalez, Nora   (M1)
2515 Blueberry Lane
Pasadena, TX 77052
(832)202-5572   MSTR#8100

Goodloe, Melissa Reid   (M1)
3741 Highway 59W
Covington, TN 38019
rev.mgoodloe73@gmail.com
(731)412-9657   GRWT#9301

Goodman, Robert   (M1)
756 Kingston Road
Water Valley, KY 42085
rgoodman4gvn@hotmail.com
(580)756-4726   MICO#3401

Goodwill, James L   (M1)
9232 Duckhorn Drive
Charlotte, NC 28277
jim@jimgoodwill.com
(704)526-8729   TNNA#7300

Goodwin, Earl   (M1)
1255 Stevens Road
Bessemer, AL 35022
earlgoodwin@yahoo.com
(205)222-1741   SERD#0800

Gough, Ernest E   (M1)
8366 Highway 70
Nashville, TN 37221
eegough@bellsouth.net
(615)646-4372   TNNA#7300

Graham, Steve   (M1)
804 Sky Blue Drive
Knoxville, TN 37923
eve1ts@hotmail.com
(865)206-0012   SEET#2200

MINISTERS CONTINUED

Gray, Drew (M1)
12304 Wickliffe Road
Kevil, KY 42053
drewgray01@gmail.com
(615)332-8360   MICO#3404

Gray, Isaac (M1)
512 Ed Taft Road
Smithville, TN 37166
revgray08@gmail.com
(870)373-4731   TNMU#7243

Gray, Randall (M1)
1230 New Liberty Big Meadow Road
Knob Lick, KY 42154
(270)432-5322   MICU#3128

Green, Harry N (M1)
45 Wood Way
McMinnville, TN 37110
(931)815-9190   TNMU#7200

Green, Larry (M1)
525 Dearman Street
Smithville, TN 37166
larrylgreen24@aol.com
(615)406-5547   TNMU#7222

Green, Paul (M1)
5228 Anchorage Avenue
El Paso, TX 79924
(915)751-7960   MSDC#8700

Green, Troy (M1)
105 Cobb Hollow Lane
Petersburg, TN 37144
thegreens101@att.net
(931)659-6627   TNCO#7135

Greene, Tammy L (M1)
109 Armitage Drive
Greeneville, TN 37745
tg6386@aol.com
(423)972-5525   SEET#2217

Greenwell, James C (M1)
7165 Wind Whisper Boulevard
Knoxville, TN 37924
greenwelljc@comcast.net
(865)742-1653   SEET#2200

Griffin, Justin (M1)
2625 Beech Bluff Road
Beech Bluff, TN 38313
jjjjgriff@gmail.com
(615)969-2426   GRWT#9210

Grimsley, Roger (M1)
215 N Oak Street
Springfield, TN 37172
( )   GRWT#9100

Guarneros, Stephen H (M1)
141 Angela Trail
Nicholasville, KY 40356
pastorsteve88@yahoo.com
(270)869-7544   MICU#3100

Guasaquillo, Samuel (M3)
Calle 8 No 3-10 Bugalagrande
COLOMBIA, SA
reysoberano777@gmail.com
(311)619-9012   MSCA#8200

Guerrero, Cruzana (M1)
Calle 83 #74-179
Medellin, Antioguia, COLOMBIA, SA
(574)257-0613   MSAN#8919

Guerrero, Josue (M1)
Calle 76 #88-65
Medellin, Antioguia, COLOMBIA, SA
josueggutierrez@yahoo.es
(574)412-3504   MSAN#8919

Guerrero, Luz Dary (M1)
Cra 26D #385-15 Apt 101
Ed Itaparica
Envigado-Antioquia
Colombia, South America
guerrerol500@yahoo.com
(315)412-1100   MSAN#8900

Guin, Larry (M1)
125 Glider Loop
Eagleville, TN 37060
lguin43@hotmail.com
(615)668-5236   TNCO#7123

Guthrie, William (M1)
3217 Miracle Heights Cove
Sherwood, AR 72120
billybarloe@yahoo.com
(501)584-0019   GRAR#1220

Guye, Dean (M1)
2759 Highway 70 E
Dickson, TN 37055
deanjoy@att.net
(615)446-7687   TNNA#7300

--==<< H >>==--

Ha, Ting Bong (M1)
3/F 338-340 Castle Peak Road
Kowloon, HONG KONG
tingbongha@yahoo.com.hk
(852)2386-6563   MSHK#8803

Hackman-Truhan, Deborah (M1)
7314 N Miramar Drive
Peoria, IL 61614
cprevdeb@hotmail.com
(931)537-9040   TNMU#7200

Hagelin, Gerald (M1)
10851 E Old Spanish Trail
Tucson, AZ 85712
azcef@cs.com
(520)275-8110   MSDC#8705

Halford, Angela (M1)
1818 N Taylor Street B-168
Little Rock, AR 72207
angelahalford2000@gmail.com
(769)274-0224   SEGR#0100

Hall, Brad (M1)
1602 Toll Gate Road SE
Huntsville, AL 35801
(256)533-4845   SERD#0800

Hall, Roy W (M1)
1713 Lookout Mountain Drive
Scottsboro, AL 35769
royhall@scottsboro.org
(256)259-9340   SERD#0800

Hamazaki, Takashi (M1)
1551-1-202 Inokuchi Nakai-cho
Ashigarakami-gun
Kanagawa-ken
259-0151, JAPAN
gen22-14@qf7.so-net.ne.jp
(046)543-8550   MSJA#8300

Hamblin, James R (M1)
60 Rolling Meadow Drive
Drummonds, TN 38023
brojim391@gmail.com
(901)840-4747   GRWT#9321

Hamelink, Ronald L (M1)
5045 Starlite Court
Las Cruces, NM 88012
hamronelink@yahoo.com
(575)640-4341   GRAR#1100

Hames, Anne (M1)
118 Paris Street
McKenzie, TN 38201
hamesa@bethelu.edu
(731)352-4066   GRWT#9122

Hamilton, Bruce (M1)
203 W Fifth Street
Mountain View, MO 65548
(352)408-0873   GRAR#1106

Han, Seung Chon (M0)
3075 Landington Way
Duluth, GA 30096
kpc0191@yahoo.com
(678)469-5015   SEKP#2126

Hancock, Paul (M1)
106 Mallard Point
Lebanon, TN 37087
pah4331@gmail.com
(615)4269-4331   TNMU#7233

Hannah, Hugh (M1)
217 Mitchell Road SE
Cleveland, TN 37323
pjhannah23@hotmail.com
(423)473-7852   MSTR#8100

Hansen, Terry (M1)
319 Forest Drive
Humboldt, TN 38343
(417)533-8106   GRMI#4100

Harbour, Ethan (M2)
77 Burton Road
Booneville, AR 72927
ethanharbour@gmail.com
(479)849-6329   GRAR#1100

Hardin, Kenny (M1)
606 Lexington Drive
Glasgow, KY 42141
( )   MICU#3108

Hardisty, Randy (M1)
4908 Redondo Street
Fort Worth, TX 76180
rhardisty@sbcglobal.net
(817)428-3513   MSRR#8409

Harper, Carlton (M1)
255 Glenview Cove
Lenoir City, TN 37771
carltonharperone@gmail.com
(865)317-1296   SEET#2313

Harper, Josh (M1)
227 LaCroix Drive #1
Collierville, TN 38017
jdharperministry@hotmail.com
(615)934-7940   GRWT#9100

Harris, Edward (M1)
10000 Wornall Road Apt 2315
Kansas City, MO 64114
ed121@kcrr.com
(816)214-8977   GRMI#4100

Harris, Robert J (M1)
3441 Clinton Street
Humboldt, TN 38343
pastor@humboldtcpc.org
(731)420-6067   GRWT#9116

Harris, Rodney E (M1)
7420 Conjar Court
Louisville, KY 40214
rodneypat@insightbb.com
(502)368-5501   MICU#3212

Harris, Wendell (M1)
329 N Louis Tittle Avenue
Mangum, OK 73554
wendellharris@itlnet.net
(580)782-2142   MSRR#8400

MINISTERS CONTINUED

Harrison, Richard (M3)
158 Enlow Road
Hodgenville, KY 42748
sundaydrummer75@yahoo.com
(270)505-2102 MICU#3214

Hartman, Gary (M1)
3001 Hines Valley Road
Lenoir City, TN 37771
g37771@att.net
(865)986-4949 SEET#2200

Hartung, J Thomas (M1)
2291 Americus Boulevard W Apt 1
Clearwater, FL 33763
revtom6@aol.com
(727)797-2882 SEGR#0100

Harwell, Keith (M1)
11387 Highway 88
Halls, TN 38040
(731)613-3780 GRWT#9100

Harwell, Sam (M1)
350 Freemont Street
Dyer, TN 38330
sambharl@yahoo.com
(731)414-2153 GRWT#9127

Hassell, Samantha (M1)
510 N Main Street
Sturgis, KY 42459
hassell_samantha@hotmail.com
(270)333-9170 MICO#3625

Hassell, Victor (M1)
510 N Main Street
Sturgis, KY 42459
hassellvictor@hotmail.com
(270)333-9170 MICO#3625

Hawley, David R (M1)
235 Florida Avenue N
Parsons, TN 38363
haw177@aol.com
(731)427-7284 GRWT#9204

Hayes, Brian (M1)
69 Cactus Drive
Benton, KY 42025
cprevbhayes@gmail.com
(270)210-8165 MICO#3422

Hayes, Drew (M1)
6322 Labor Lane
Louisville, KY 40291
dhayes72@gmail.com
(731)796-7076 MICU#3222

Hayes, Jennifer (M1)
7005 Woodmoor Road
Fort Worth, TX 76133
hayesj712@gmail.com
(205)533-1018 TNMU#7200

Hayes, Marcus (M1)
7005 Woodmoor Road
Fort Worth, TX 76133
marcus.hayes@att.net
(270)841-7576 TNMU#7200

Hayes, Sherrad (M1)
1405 N 7th Avenue
Lanett, AL 36863
sherrad.hayes@gmail.com
(706)773-5201 SEGR#0100

Headley, Daniel (M1)
9526 Academy Hills Drive NE
Albuquerque, NM 87111
danieliheadleyp@gmail.com
(720)724-0961 MSDC#8700

Headrick, Anthony (M1)
625 Bakers Bridge Avenue
Suite 105 PMB 197
Franklin, TN 37067
anthony.headrick@va.gov
(208)972-7602 SEGR#0100

Headrick, Christopher (M1)
635 Kensington Manor Drive
Calera, AL 35040
bravespop@gmail.com
(205)240-0979 SEGR#0100

Headrick, Jerry (M1)
7642 Zeigler Boulevard Apt 106
Mobile, AL 36608
willjheadrick@gmail.com
(251)295-0041 SEGR#0100

Heflin, Donna S (M1)
4144 Meadow Court Drive
Bartlett, TN 38135
rdheflin@bellsouth.net
(901)382-8198 GRWT#9100

Heflin, Robert (M1)
4144 Meadow Court Drive
Bartlett, TN 38135
rheflin@cumberland.org
(901)382-8198 TNCO#7100

Heidel, Jason (M1)
218 Morningside Drive
Hopkinsville, KY 42240
heidelj@hotmail.com
(270)498-7380 MICO#3400

Heilbron, Luz Maria (M1)
Cra 12 bis #11-51
Pereira, Risaralda, COLOMBIA, SA
pastorapresbi@hotmail.com
(576)333-9295 MSAN#8916

Henson, Kevin R (M1)
8461 McDaniel Road
Fort Worth, TX 76126
kevin.r.henson@gmail.com
(817)354-1182 MSRR#8400

Heo, Mu Sak (M1)
170 Applewood Drive #210
Lawrenceville, GA 30046
drhou@hanmail.net
(404)644-6514 SETG#2100

Hernandez, Jhonathan (M3)
401 Monument Road Apt 74
Jacksonville, FL 32225
jhoto41@gmail.com
(786)508-8578 SEGR#0100

Herring, C E (Ed), Jr (M1)
969 Campground Circle
Scottsboro, AL 35769
edherring@scottsboro.org
(256)259-2721 SERD#0800

Herston, Terry (M1)
390 County Road 95
Rogersville, AL 35652
tpaw51@gmail.com
(256)247-3004 SEHO#0513

Hess, Jean (M1)
2200 E Dartmouth Circle
Englewood, CO 80113
jeanhess@316denver.com
(303)504-0275 MSDC#8710

Hess, Rick (M1)
2200 E Dartmouth Circle
Englewood, CO 80113
rick@densem.edu
(303)504-0275 MSDC#8710

Hester, Mark S (M1)
724 Brixworth Boulevard
Knoxville, TN 37934
markstephenhester@gmail.com
(865)924-2732 SEET#2307

Ho, Carmen (M2)
Tin Yuet Estate
Tin Shui Wai NT, HONG KONG
ho_carcar@yahoo.com.hk
(852)2617-7872 MSHK#8801

Ho, Jesse (M3)
2/F Welland Plaza
188 Nam Cheong Street
Sam Shui Po
Kowloon, HONG KONG
jessie@taohsien.org.hk
(852)2981-4933 MSHK#8800

Ho, Kelvin (M2)
11 On Wing Centre, 2/F
Pak She Back Street
Cheung Chau, HONG KONG
kelvinskho@gmail.com
(852)2981-4933 MSHK#8801

Hoke, Walter (M1)
215 Navajo Trail
Georgetown, TX 78633
(512)869-1948 MSTR#8100

Holley, Ann (M1)
PO Box 345
Lockesburg, AR 71846
ladyrev1115@yahoo.com
(870)289-3421 GRAR#1100

Hollingshed, Lee (M1)
3612 Harmony Church Grove Road
Dallas, GA 30132
leearmstrong@bellsouth.net
(770)548-0152 SETG#2100

Holmes, Aaron G (M1)
7240 Ellington Cove
Milan, TN 38358
agholmes@charter.net
(731)662-7595 GRWT#9100

Holt, Billy Jack (M1)
5039 Highway 37 N
Clarksville, TX 75426
jackdora@windstream.net
(903)428-9909 MSTR#8125

Hom, Patti (M3)
811 Faxon Avenue
San Francisco, CA 94112
phom@gfccsf.org
(415)486-5998 MSDC#8700

Hong, Soon Gab (M1)
13600 Doty Avenue Apt 4
Hawthorne, CA 90250
lemuelhong@hotmail.com
(972)446-0350 MSRR#8400

Hood, Charles (M1)
6535 Bailey Road
Anderson, AL 35610
hooddad11@gmail.com
(256)229-6251 SEHO#0516

Hood, Larry (M2)
2825 E 17th Street
Odessa, TX 79761
l3lhood@yahoo.com
(432)770-8307 MSDC#8703

Hopkins, Daniel (M1)
1608 Oak Park Boulevard
Calvert City, KY 42029
danielhopkins2469@yahoo.com
(270)205-1847 MICO#5110

MINISTERS CONTINUED

Hopkins, Wayne (M1)
1413 E Unity Church Road
Hardin, KY 42048
(270)437-4481 MICO#3614

Howe, Francis (M1)
129 Manley Street
McKenzie, TN 38201
(731)352-5551 GRWT#9100

Howell, Linda (M1)
PO Box 80050
Keller, TX 76244
sunnylindatrue@gmail.com
(817)564-2236 MSRR#8400

Howell-Diamond, Steven (M1)
106 Ultimate Court
Madison, AL 35757
smdiam@hotmail.com
(931)636-7336 SERD#0800

Howton, Orvie Ray (M1)
4928 Montauk Trail SE
Owens Cross Road, AL 35763
orphowton@yahoo.com
(256)533-9224 SERD#0800

Hoyos, Javier (M3)
Calle 34 24A-36
Cali, COLOMBIA, SA
danlauyanjav@hotmail.com
(316)740-4168 MSCA#8200

Hubbard, Donald (M1)
2128 N Campbell Station Road
Knoxville, TN 37932
djhubbard@mindspring.com
(865)693-0264 SEET#2200

Hubbard, Pratt (M1)
1565 Eli Brown Road
McKenzie, TN 38201
(731)352-9178 GRWT#9100

Hudson, Barney (M1)
10541 Fossil Hill Drive
Fort Worth, TX 76131
barneyrev@gmail.com
(817)851-2960 MSRR#8425

Hudson, Ellen (M3)
301 N Royal Oaks Blvd Apt 2614
Franklin, TN 37067
ellen.hudson17@icloud.com
(731)780-1004 TNCO#7100

Hudson, George Cliff (M1)
4782 Waverly Court
Ooltewah, TN 37363
gchudson3@gmail.com
(423)645-7563 SETG#2106

Hudson, Jennifer (M3)
716 Apache Drive
Marshall, MO 65340
(660)631-3893 GRMI#4100

Huey, Sharon (M1)
3265 16th Street
San Francisco, CA 94103
sharon_huey@yahoo.com
(415)568-7835 MSDC#8700

Hughes, Charles (M1)
114 Gaul Street
Estill Springs, TN 37330
cphugs@cafes.net
(931)649-5189 SERD#0800

Hughes, Douglas (M1)
5545 Hocker Road
Paducah, KY 42001
milburnchapel@gmail.com
(270)488-2588 MICO#3414

Hughes, Richard W (M1)
2954 Bob Wade Lane
Harvest, AL 35749
hughesrichard23@gmail.com
(256)859-3178 SERD#0806

Hullander, Jerry (Butch) (M1)
767 Rifle Range Road
Greeneville, TN 37743
jerryihs@catt.com
(423)802-6156 SETG#2107

Hung, Ella Siu Kei (M1)
2/F Welland Plaza
188 Nam Cheong Street
Sham Shui Po, Kowloon, HONG KONG
ellahung@yahoo.com
(852)2794-2382 MSHK#8809

Hunley, Jearl (M1)
2618 Canterbury Road
Columbus, MS 39705
jdhunley@cableone.net
(662)329-1516 SEGR#0100

Hunley, Terry M (M1)
48 Charleston Square
Jackson, TN 38305
thunley1@charter.net
(731)660-5685 GRWT#9208

Hurley, E C (M1)
#2 Killard Road, Killard
Doonbeg, County Clare, IRELAND
hurleyec@gmail.com
(931)551-6173 TNNA#7300

Hyden, John (M1)
6525 Peytonsville Arno Road
College Grove, TN 37046
john.hyden@wcs.edu
(615)975-9584 TNCO#7100

--==<< I >>==--

Ikushima, Michinobu (M1)
2074 Nakashinden
Ebina-Shi Kanagawa-Ken
243-0422 JAPAN
m.ikushima@tbz.t-com.ne.jp
(046)232-9888 MSJA#8300

Impastato, Paulino (M3)
1547 Mt Zion Church Road
Marion, KY 42064
(270)965-9528 MICO#3400

Ingram, Matthew (M1)
333 Union Station Circle
Calera, AL 35040
matthew.ingram@fpcalabaster.org
(205)663-3123 SERD#0107

Inou, Yuki (M3)
Tokyo Christian University
3-301-5 Uchino Inzai-shi, Chiba
270-1347 JAPAN
yuki_inoh0615@yahoo.co.jp
(047)646-1141 MSJA#8300

Ishitsuka, Keishi (M1)
Nishi Oizumi 6-13-31
Nerima-ku, Tokyo
178-0065 JAPAN
keishi@gmail.com
(080)5896-1139 MSJA#8313

--==<< J >>==--

Jacks, Mathew Derek (M1)
341 Shadeswood Drive
Hoover, AL 35226
pastorderek77@gmail.com
(205)903-8469 SEGR#0111

Jackson, Lamar (M1)
280 Deer Ridge Drive Apt D
Dayton, TN 37321
hljaxn@charter.net
(423)570-9348 SETG#2100

Jackson, Terry (M1)
1461 Mount Pleasant Road
Hernando, MS 38632
(662)429-9741 GRWT#9100

James, William F (M1)
4090 Meadow Field Lane
Bartlett, TN 38135
sparkbill54@gmail.com
(615)653-1396 GRWT#9100

Jang, Won Jeon (M1)
Lot2-C Teresa Subdivision
Tabucan Mandurriao
Iloilo City 5000, Phillippine
( ) SEET#2200

Jarnagin, Mary L (M1)
1026 Clayton Lane Apt 6202
Austin, TX 78723
marjar27@yahoo.com
(512)367-9922 MSTR#8100

Jeffrey, Peter (M1)
4510 Holly Grove Road
Brighton, TN 38011
jeffreyp@hollygrovechurch.com
(615)417-0131 GRWT#9304

Jeffrey, Sarah Ann (M1)
5271 Highway 202 E
Yellville, AR 72687
(870)453-7076 GRAR#1100

Jenkins, Henry (M1)
PO Box 148
Magazine, AR 72943
henryj@magtel.com
(479)969-8352 GRAR#1401

Jenkins, Kevin (M1)
411 E Main Street
Casey, IL 62420
newhoperevkev@gmail.com
(217)609-1120 MINC#5208

Jenkins, William E (M1)
10309 Tammaron Trail
Fort Worth, TX 76140
webkjl@verison.net
(813)579-8994 MSRR#0412

Jett-Rand, Dana (M2)
78 Lester Lane
Martin, TN 38237
msdanajett@yahoo.com
(731)587-0805 GRWT#9100

Jimenez, Jorge Enrique (M2)
Urb Manantiales MzC Casa 6
Armenia, Quindio, COLOMBIA, SA
joenjimu@yahoo.es
(576)749-1166 MSAN#8900

Jobe, J Tommy (M1)
807 Rockwood Drive
Nolensville, TN 37135
cppreacher@united.net
(615)776-7755 TNMU#7240

Johnson, Ken (M1)
122 Ridge Lane
Clinton, TN 37716
kenjoxav122@bellsouth.net
(865)463-7090 SEET#2314

MINISTERS CONTINUED

Johnson, Kris (M3)
130 Essex Street Box 192B
South Hamilton, MA 01982
kris.johnson2198@gmail.com
(808)741-3370 SEET#2200

Johnson, Lanny (M1)
74 Flagstone Drive
Rossville, GA 30741
ljohnson37357@gmail.com
(931)212-1658 TNMU#7200

Johnson, Leslie A (M1)
11716 Price Drive
Oklahoma City, OK 73170
pastorlesliej@gmail.com
(405)248-4232 MSRR#6205

Johnson, Roberta Smith (M1)
397 Ouachita 54
Camden, AR 71701
(870)231-5827 GRAR#1100

Johnson, Rocky L (M1)
1208 Redwood Drive
Clarksville, TN 37042
jjjjgriff@gmail.com
(423)620-7753 TNNA#9300

Johnson, Wesley H (M1)
6222 Crestmoor Lane
Sachse, TX 75048
wes3131@icloud.com
(972)467-3571 MSRR#8400

Jones, Gregory (M1)
4728 Reischa Drive
Nashville, TN 37211
greg1013@aol.com
(931)249-9512 TNNA#7340

Jones, Harold (M1)
650 College Drive
Dalton, GA 30720
harold@personalcharacter.com
(478)320-4222 SETG#2100

Jones, Michael (M1)
120 Jennifer Lane
Branson, MO 65616
(417)334-2058 GRAR#1100

Jones, Steve (M1)
PO Box 368
Burns, TN 37029
stevenejones@bellsouth.net
(615)441-6159 TNNA#7303

Jones, Victor (M1)
7017 Highway 177 S
Jordan, AR 72519
mommom@centurytel.net
(870)499-5882 GRAR#1100

Jones, C William, Jr (M1)
109 Lakewood Drive
Lexington, TN 38351
patfreelandjones@yahoo.com
(731)967-7618 GRWT#9209

Jordan, Matthew (M3)
735 Painter Bottom Road
Pikeville, TN 37367
matthew.jordan3009@hotmail.com
( ) SETG#2100

Jung, Jinook (M1)
1603 Coolhurst Avenue
Sherwood, AR 72120
swch100491@gmail.com
(501)247-5953 GRAR#2135

Justice, Michael (M1)
250 W 5th Street #B
Russellville, KY 42276
(270)726-6673 MICU#3310

--==<< K >>==--

Kang, Eun Hee (M3)
147-15 46th Avenue
Flushing, NY 11355
(718)762-0778 SECE#2400

Kang, Jin Koo (M1)
2310 Hisway
Lawrenceville, GA 30044
agatopia@hanmail.net
(678)462-7526 SEKP#2127

Kang, Myung (M2)
5041 Alabama Street Apt 147
El Paso, TX 79930
dsc3000@hanmail.net
(915)305-9119 MSDC#8700

Karasawa, Kenta (M1)
3-15-10 Higashi
Kunitachi-shi, Tokyo
186-0002 JAPAN
smbno6@gmail.com
(042)575-5549 MSJA#8306

Katsuki, Shigeru (M1)
2-14-16 Higashi-cho
Koganei-shi, Tokyo
184-0011 JAPAN
shigeru.katsuki@nifty.com
(042)231-1279 MSJA#8301

Keenan, Joshua (M3)
6095 Highway 226
Savannah, TN 38372
joshua.keenan16@gmail.com
(731)393-3125 GRWT#9100

Keller, Abby Cole (M1)
162 Owen Lane
Greeneville, TN 37745
abbycolekeller@gmail.com
(423)863-6565 SEET#2206

Kelly, Patrick L (M1)
1449 Rainbow Road
Limestone, TN 37681
(423)727-4067 SEET#2200

Kennedy, Jim (M2)
613 English Ivy Way
Aberdeen, MD 21001
jpkak@comcast.net
( ) SETG#2100

Kennemer, Darren (M1)
8828 Highway 119
Alabaster, AL 35007
dlkennemer@gmail.com
(205)663-3152 SERD#0800

Kerner, Leanne (M1)
9236 Church Road Apt 2041
Dallas, TX 75231
cooldoll@bellsouth.net
(270)851-9709 TNMU#7200

Kessie, John Paul (M1)
138 Pony Grass Lane
Bastrop, TX 78628
jplmkessie@verizon.com
(512)585-1617 MSTR#8100

Keung Yung, Amos Chung (M3)
28 Hong Yip Street
Yuen Long, NT, HONG KONG
amos@xilincpc.org.hk
(522)639-9176 MSHK#8800

Kibler, Taylor (M3)
1070 W Main Street Apt 1720
Hendersonville, TN 37075
taylorkibler@gmail.com
(615)509-7114 MICO#3400

Killeen, Michael (M1)
5211 McCarty Lane
Austin, TX 78749
mike@shpc.org
(512)892-3580 MSTR#8100

Kim, Byong Sam (M1)
2815 Le Bourget Lane
Lincoln, CA 95648
(530)877-4651 MSDC#8700

Kim, Kio Seob (M1)
27-27 Baysied Lane
Flushing, NY 11358
(718)539-3476 SECE#2400

Kim, Paul (M1)
939 Light House Way
Lawrenceville, GA 30043
(678)822-1508 SEKP#2000

Kim, Yoong S (M1)
2770 Farmstead Way
Suwanee, GA 30024
yoongkim1934@yahoo.com
(901)490-8973 SEKP#2000

Kim, Young Ho (Steve) (M1)
B02 Hyundai I-Space 1608-2
Burim Dong, Dong An Gu
AnYang City, Kyunggi Do, S KOREA
paidion4377@naver.com
(231)348-8033 SEET#2200

King, Keith (M2)
3341 S 137th E Avenue
Tulsa, OK 74134
(918)437-5464 MSRR#8400

King, Mark (M1)
713 Baptist Branch Road
Hampshire, TN 38461
pastorking1963@gmail.com
(931)379-7614 TNCO#7129

Kinnaman, Richard T (M1)
2018 Spring Meadow Circle
Spring Hill, TN 37174
kinnaman91@att.net
(615)302-3321 TNCO#7146

Kirkpatrick, Mary Kathryn (M1)
502 S Alley Street
Jefferson, TX 75657
mkkirkpatrick@gmail.com
(903)930-6236 MSTR#8109

Kleinjan, Lori (M1)
6631 Millgrove Park Drive
Bartlett, TN 38135
lkleinj@prodigy.net
(901)372-8413 GRWT#9100

Knight, J Geoffrey (M1)
2119 Avalon Place
Houston, TX 77019
geoff@cphouston.org
(713)522-7821 MSTR#8606

Knight, Melissa (M1)
3514 Westbrook Drive SE
Smyrna, GA 30082
revlissa@gmail.com
(530)632-6472 MSDC#8700

Ko, John Jae (M1)
185 Old Ferris Farm Road
Grand Gorge, NY 12434
spcko@hanmail.net
(718)762-4348 SECE#2141

Koopman, David L (M1)
5606 Brandon Park Drive
Maryville, TN 37804
racewthrev@aol.com
(865)660-2440 SEET#2200

MINISTERS CONTINUED

Krueger, Courtney (M1)
1505 N Moore Road
Chattanooga, TN 37411
ck@firstcumberland.com
(864)933-4912 SETG#2104

Kurtz, David (M1)
244 County Road 4705
Troup, TX 75789
davidk36@yahoo.com
(817)683-4783 MSTR#8104

--==<< L >>==--

Labrada, Hector (M1)
74 Cumberland Drive
McMinnville, TN 37110
( ) TNMU#7200

Ladd, Sherry (M1)
4521 Turkey Creek Road
Williamsport, TN 38487
revsherryladd@gmail.com
(931)682-2263 TNCO#7138

Lain, Judy (M1)
1928 Pine Ridge Drive
Bedford, TX 76021
judylaine5@gmail.com
(817)909-6702 MSRR#8400

Lam, Chris (M3)
2/F Welland Plaza
188 Nam Cheong Street
Shamshuipo, Kowloon, HONG KONG
chrislam@taohsien.org.hk
(852)2981-4933 MSHK#8800

Lam, Dicky (M3)
Flat D 2/F
338-340 Castle Peak Road
Kowloon, HONG KONG
lamdicky912@gmail.com
(852)2386-6563 MSHK#8800

Lam, Janice (M2)
G/F & 1/F 251 Tin Sum Village
Tai Wai, Shatin NT, HONG KONG
janiceyeung929@gmail.com
(852)2693-3444 MSHK#8800

Lancaster, David (M1)
426 Fugua Road
Martin, TN 38237
lancasterd@bethelu.edu
(731)588-5895 GRWT#9130

Lash, Colten (M3)
511 W North Water Street
Bethany, IL 61914
coltenlash@gmail.com
(217)620-1976 MINC#5200

Lathem, W Ray (M1)
452 County Road 1462
Cullman, AL 35055
lathemray@bellsouth.net
(256)734-7146 SEGR#0100

Latimer, James M (M1)
3381 Moss Rose Drive
Memphis, TN 38115
sumnerbacon@me.com
(901)359-9201 GRWT#9100

Lau, Walter (M1)
865 Jackson Street
San Francisco, CA 94133
walter@cumberlandsf.org
(650)583-7878 MSDC#8501

Laurence, Brenda (M1)
2823 Nine Mile Road
Enville, TN 38332
southernmoma@hotmail.com
(731)687-2022 GRWT#9100

Lavender, Michael T (M1)
308 Main Street
Martin, TN 38237
mike_lavender@yahoo.com
(731)253-7308 GRWT#9117

Lawson, James (M1)
1003 W 3rd Street
Fulton, KY 42041
(270)472-5272 MICO#3400

Lawson, Jerry L (M1)
9187 MS Highway 12
Ackerman, MS 39735
lawson@dtcweb.net
(662)285-8295 SEGR#0707

Lawson, John C (M1)
PO Box 645
Daingerfield, TX 75638
sharjohn@windstream.net
(903)645-2183 MSTR#8106

Lawson, Luke (M1)
270 N Ridgeland Circle
Columbus, MS 39705
luke_lawson03@hotmail.com
(662)295-9322 SEGR#0706

Layne, Phillip (M1)
10699 Griffith Highway
Whitwell, TN 37397
44philliplayne@gmail.com
(423)658-6421 SETG#2110

LeNeave, David (M1)
1403 Mt Zion Church Road
Marion, KY 42064
mscpchurch_bd@yahoo.com
(731)414-8232 MICO#5117

Lee, David (M1)
( ) SETG#2100

Lee, Douglas (M1)
70 Sanchez Street
San Francisco, CA 94114
dougblee643@gmail.com
(415)252-9698 MSDC#8510

Lee, George (M1)
314 Kingston Drive
Florence, AL 35633
butchleeautos@yahoo.com
(256)740-0809 SEHO#0501

Lee, Ho-Jin (M1)
7565 Macon Road
Cordova, TN 38018
hojin.lee70@gmail.com
(901)754-7070 GRWT#9322

Lee, Mei Wah (M3)
2/F Welland Plaza, 188 Nam Cheong St
Sham Shui Po Kowloon HONG KONG
vivianyuen@taohsien.org.hk
(852)2783-8923 MSHK#8800

Lee, Sang-Do (M1)
1342 Seocho-2dong, Seocho-Gu
Seoul, KOREA
(023)474-8405 SEET#2200

Lee, Sarah (M1)
( ) SETG#2100

Lee, Siu Yee (M3)
258 Carlos D'Assumpcao Ed Kin Heng
Log 4 A MACAU
leisioi@yahoo.com.hk
(852)2892-1702 MSHK#8800

Lee, Ted Shu Tak (M1)
2/F Welland Plaza
188 Nam Cheong Street
Sham Shui Po, Kowloon, HONG KONG
tedlee@taohsien.org.hk
(852)2783-8923 MSHK#8800

Lee, Timothy Daniel (M1)
186 Blasingame Drive
Columbus, MS 39702
pastor@beershebachurch.com
(601)433-3714 SEGR#0702

Lefavor, David (M1)
414 S Monroe Siding Road
Xenia, OH 45395
david.lefavor@va.gov
(937)262-3394 SEGR#0100

Lerma, Andres Felipe (M3)
Calle 2 Sur Cra 74 17
Cali, Colombia, South America
andestey@hotmail.com
(316)563-8825 MSCA#8200

Lewis, Emily Fowler (M1)
5225 Maple Avenue Apt 5309
Dallas, TX 75235
emilykaye.fowler@gmail.com
(817)983-3559 MSRR#8400

Li, Chun Wai (M1)
1/F Block B
14 Tsat Tsz Mui Road
North Point, Hong Kong
cwli2000hk@gmail.com
(852)2562-2148 MSHK#8805

Li, Siu Fun (M3)
Tin Yuet Estate
Tin Shui Wai NT, HONG KONG
cpyaodao@yahoo.com
(852)2617-7872 MSHK#8800

Liles, Dwight (M1)
8467 Joy Road
Mount Pleasant, TN 38474
dwightliles@att.net
(931)379-0326 TNCO#7100

Lim, Keum-Taek (M1)
1342 Seocho-2dong, Seocho-Gu
Seoul, KOREA
limkt114@hanmail.net
(023)474-8405 SEET#2200

Lim, Seok Heon (M1)
3398 Lake Drive
Lawrenceville, GA 30044
slim3398@gmail.com
(404)667-1800 SEKP#2000

Lindsay, John V (M1)
401 Greenwood Avenue
Marshall, TX 75670
(940)391-1213 MSTR#8113

Lindsey, Tyler (M2)
108 Patterson Street
Paris, TN 38242
alindsey87@bethelu.edu
(270)777-5760 MICU#3100

Linski, David (M2)
1060 Alpine Way
Indian Springs, AL 35124
pastor@greenschapelcpc.org
(205)240-0943 SEGR#0208

Little, Claire (M3)
1736 N Reid Hooker Road
Eads, TN 38028
j.claire.little@gmail.com
(901)734-8569 GRWT#9100

MINISTERS CONTINUED

Little, Russell   (M1)
29 Cotton Row
Medina, TN 38355
russelllittle@bellsouth.net
(731)783-3565   GRWT#9109

Liu, Lai Yuet   (M2)
2/F Fu Tung Shopping Center
Tung Chung
Lantau Island, HONG KONG
(852)2109-1738   MSHK#8800

Lively, James W   (M1)
906 Lyle Circle
Greeneville, TN 37745
jlively@gcpchurch.org
(423)798-1959   SEET#2206

Livingston, Ronald L   (M1)
11314 Maplecrest Drive
Huntsville, AL 35803
hairy404@outlook.com
( )   SERD#0800

Lockhart, Thomas Richie   (M1)
700 County Road 343
Falkner, MS 38629
nmsdiamonddawgs@yahoo.com
(662)837-7281   GRWT#9214

Lockmiller, Lem Jr   (M1)
PO Box 348
Leesburg, AL 35983
(256)490-3021   SEGR#0100

Lofton, Kathy   (M2)
10636 County Road 1500
Ada, OK 74820
kdnlofton@gmail.com
(580)332-0898   MSRR#8400

Logan, Jason   (M1)
709 Cavalier Drive
Clarksville, TN 37040
jason.b.logan.mil@mail.mil
(609)556-3128   TNMU#7200

Lollar, Jeff   (M3)
154 Pathfinder Way
Dalton, GA 30721
jrlollar1873@gmail.com
(705)218-3379   SETG#2100

Lomax, David   (M2)
1501 Robert Cartwright Drive
Goodlettsville, TN 37072
lomaxdavid53@yahoo.com
(615)753-2493   TNNA#7300

Longmire, Ronald L   (M1)
2041 Eckles Drive
Maryville, TN 37804
ronaldlongmire@charter.net
(865)984-1647   SEET#2309

Lopez, Wilson   (M3)
Diag 26M #73A-69
Cali, COLOMBIA, SA
( )422-3940   MSCA#8225

Lorick, Keith   (M1)
127 Chesapeake Boulevard
Madison, AL 35757
keithlorick@knology.net
(256)325-3865   SERD#0808

Louder, Paula   (M1)
98 Gallant Court
Clarksville, TN 37043
plouder223@gmail.com
(615)804-4809   TNNA#7300

Louder, Stephen L   (M1)
98 Gallant Court
Clarksville, TN 37043
slouder81@gmail.com
(931)217-0369   TNNA#7332

Lounsbury, Kristi   (M1 DE)
902 Clearview
Krum, TX 76249
klounsbury@cumberland.org
(940)435-5077   MSRR#8400

Love, James R   (M1)
14382 Sonora Hardin Springs Road
Eastview, KY 42732
(502)862-4119   MICU#3100

Lowe, Randy   (M1)
222 McDougal Drive
Murray, KY 42071
loweshodle@aol.com
(270)753-8255   MICO#3412

Lowrance, John   (M1)
PO Box 871
Dyersburg, TN 38025
jclowrance1@gmail.com
(731)676-4360   GRWT#9422

Lubo, Jaime   (M3)
AA 6365
Montebello, COLOMBIA, SA
( )   MSCA#8223

Lui, Stephen   (M1)
512 16th Avenue
San Francisco, CA 94118
(415)386-2302   MSDC#8700

Luo, Tian-en   (M1)
87 Berta Circle
Daly City, CA 94015
tianenyang555@gmail.com
(650)754-9885   MSDC#8700

Luthy, Dusty   (M1)
2900 Foxcroft Circle
Denton, TX 76209
dustyluthy@gmail.com
(270)933-2722   MICO#3410

Luttrell, Ben   (M1)
608 County Road 992
Iuka, MS 38852
luttrellben993@gmail.com
(931)332-1012   TNMU#7200

--==<< M >>==--

Ma, Choil   (M1)
300 Ringgold Road Apt 503
Clarksville, TN 37042
choilma@yahoo.com
(931)824-2443   SEKP#2000

Macy, William M   (M1)
1358 Ephesus Church Road
Harned, KY 40144
(270)756-2775   MICU#3218

Madden, Judith Ellen   (M1)
100 SW Brushy Mound
Burleson, TX 76028
jmadden@pathway.church
(817)295-5832   MSRR#8418

Madrid, Jorge Alexis   (M3)
Cra 9 #6 N 87 Bello Horizonte
Cali, Colombia South America
sacrydea@hotmail.com
(310)436-0141   MSCA#8200

Magliolo, Sam   (M2)
1113 Hampstead Drive
Madison, MS 39110
smagliolo@comcast.net
(901)486-3527   GRWT#9100

Magrill, J Richard, Jr   (M1)
500 Miller Drive
Marshall, TX 75672
richardmagrill@att.net
(901)685-9454   MSTR#8100

Malinoski, Melissa   (M1)
9087 Fenmore Cove
Cordova, TN 38016
melissalmalinoski@gmail.com
(420)620-0089   GRWT#9100

Malinoski, T J   (M1)
9087 Fenmore Cove
Cordova, TN 38016
tmalinoski@cumberland.org
(901)276-4572   SEET#2200

Malone, John W   (M1)
3693 Highway 67 South
Sommerville, AL 35670
(256)778-8237   SEHO#0500

Marcott, Skyla   (M3)
1980 Mark Avenue
Clarksville, TN 37043
skylamarcott@yahoo.com
(513)907-6055   MICO#3400

Marquez, Alfonso   (M1)
389 Bethel Drive
Lenoir City, TN 37772
amarquez61@bellsouth.net
(865)660-7579   SEET#2320

Marquez, Jose Ignacio   (M3)
8976 W Flagler Street
Miami, FL 33174
jimarquez.aviation@gmail.com
( )   SEGR#0100

Marquez, Martha   (M1)
389 Bethel Drive
Lenoir City, TN 37772
amarquez61@bellsouth.net
(865)660-7579   SEET#2320

Mars, Stan   (M1)
PO Box 274
Mt Pleasant, AR 72561
smars2@liberty.edu
(217)254-5120   GRAR#1100

Marshall, Debbie   (M1)
1494 Bucksnort Road
Covington, TN 38019
dsmarshall05@att.net
(901)494-1251   GRWT#9304

Martin, Theresa   (M1)
116 Crisman Street
Chattanooga, TN 37415
choochootm@usa.net
(423)903-7260   SETG#2100

Martin, Tom   (M1)
116 Crisman Street
Chattanooga, TN 37415
choochootm@usa.net
(423)903-7260 (cell)   SETG#2100

Martin, William E, Jr   (M1)
741 Chapel Hill Road
Marion, KY 42064
juniormartin@yahoo.com
(870)270-3344   MICO#3620

MINISTERS CONTINUED

Martinez, Dagoberto (M1)
Cra 62D #71-113
Bello, Antioquia
COLOMBIA, SA
(574)452-3466 MSAN#8900

Martinez, Soledad (M1)
2801 Biway Street
Ft Worth, TX 76114
shirleymartinez1252@gmail.com
(817)812-8247 MSRR#8400

Masuda, Yasuo (M1)
1-11-20 Kokubu
Ichikawa-shi, Chiba-ken
272-0834 JAPAN
fwgc6854@mb.infoweb.ne.jp
(047)369-7540 MSJA#8314

Mata, Elizabeth (M1)
PO Box 1040
San Elizario, TX 79849
hectoryliz@att.net
(915)704-9930 MSDC#8706

Mata, Hector (M1)
PO Box 1040
San Elizario, TX 79849
hectoryliz@att.net
(915)704-9930 MSDC#8706

Mata, Isaac (M1)
PO Box 1040
San Elizario, TX 79849
isaacmata96@yahoo.com
(915)920-0897 MSDC#8706

Mathews, Nathaniel (M1)
14314 Avenue U
Lubbock, TX 79423
pastor@cpclubbock.com
(931)209-6645 MSDC#8702

Matlock, Robert (M1)
156 Dovenshire Drive
Fairfield Glade, TN 38558
revbobm@msn.com
(931)210-0614 TNMU#7200

Matsumoto, Masahiro (M1)
2-14-1 Minami Rinkan
Yamato-shi, Kanagawa-ken
242-0006 JAPAN
matsumoto@koza-church.jp
(046)275-2767 MSJA#8313

Matsuya, Ryuzo (M1)
72-2 Naka Kibogaoka Asahi-ku
Yokohama, Kanagawa-ken
241-0825 JAPAN
matuyar@yahoo.co.jp
(045)364-8297 MSJA#8302

Matthews, James N (M1)
241 Morning Star Drive
Huntsville, AL 35811
brojim10@att.net
(256)337-2765 SERD#0800

Mayfield, Randall (M1)
12470 Daisywood Drive
Knoxville, TN 37932
mayfield07@comcast.net
(865)769-4756 SEET#2308

Maynard, Geoffery (M1)
1356 Marcia Road
Memphis, TN 38117
(901)409-5269 GRWT#9100

Mays, Ronald B (M1)
124 Summers Lane
Kevil, KY 42053
rbmays@wk.net
(270)247-0070 MICO#3400

McBeth, David (M1)
109 Gloria Place
Jacksonville, NC 28540
dsj3mcbeth@gmail.com
(910)238-4279 SEET#2200

McCallum, Frank (M1)
1500 Coach Estates Road Lot E 16
Murray, KY 42071
mccallum@bbtel.com
(270)580-4796 MICU#3100

McCarty, John (M1)
305 W Martindale Drive
Marshall, TX 75672
mtsjohn@gmail.com
(423)650-8788 MSTR#8100

McCaskey, Charles (M1)
679 Canter Lane
Cookeville, TN 38501
charles@cookevillecpchurch.org
(931)526-4885 TNMU#7200

McCaskey, Mary (M1)
218 Downton Avenue
Cookeville, TN 38501
marykat_61@hotmail.com
(931)260-1422 TNMU#7200

McClanahan, Jo Ann (M1)
215 White Bros Road
Humboldt, TN 38343
joannmcclanahan@hughes.net
(731)784-1176 GRWT#9100

McClung, Andy (M1)
919 Dickinson Street
Memphis, TN 38107
scubarev@att.net
(901)606-6615 GRWT#9314

McClung, Tiffany (M1)
919 Dickinson Street
Memphis, TN 38107
thmcclung@att.net
(901)606-6615 GRWT#9302

McConnell, Donald R (M1)
147 Confederacy Circle
Knoxville, TN 37934
donjoyce515@hotmail.com
(865)288-0230 SEET#2200

McCurley, Don (M1)
4036 McAllister Street
Milan, TN 38358
dcmccurley@hotmail.com
(731)723-3623 GRWT#9100

McDuff, Dwayne (M1)
9770 County Road 5
Florence, AL 35633
fcpdmcduff@comcast.net
(256)764-6354 SEHO#0506

McDuffie, J C (M1)
1985 County Road 1070 N
Fairfield, IL 62837
mactrapper4@frontier.com
(618)842-5624 MINC#5113

McGee, Charles Randall (M1)
9037 Groveland Drive
Dallas, TX 75218
randallmcgee@sbcglobal.net
(214)328-2488 MSRR#8400

McGill, James A (M1)
433 S Walnut Avenue
Cookeville, TN 38501
jam7235@frontiernet.net
(931)526-6936 TNMU#7200

McGowan, Kriss (M1)
885 Mount Calvary Road
Whitwell, TN 37397
krissmcg658@gmail.com
(423)463-8609 SETG#2119

McGowan, Rhonda (M1)
885 Mount Calvary Road
Whitwell, TN 37379
rhondam658@gmail.com
(423)619-5679 SETG#2153

McGuire, James D (M1)
220 Southwind Circle #2
Greenville, TN 37745
jmcguire915@comcast.net
(423)638-6380 SEET#2200

McGuire, Timothy (M1)
PO Box 42
Mt Sherman, KY 42764
brotim.cpc@gmail.com
(270)766-9027 MICU#3509

McInnis, Rodney (M1)
6589 Harbor Place
Gadsden, AL 35907
mcinnisrodneyand@bellsouth.net
(256)454-2399 SEGR#0607

McMichael, Jeff (M1)
224 John Drane Lane
Harned, KY 40144
revmcmichael@outlook.com
(270)617-4016 MICU#3207

McMillan, L Ronald (M1)
675 Kimberly Drive
Atoka, TN 38004
mcmillanron675@yahoo.com
(901)837-1101 GRWT#9100

McNair, Mark (M1)
13 Cedar Lane
Columbia, MS 39429
fryerbuck1385@gmail.com
(901)605-5559 SEGR#0100

McNeese, Mark (M1)
3306 Greenlawn Parkway
Austin, TX 78757
2mam53@gmail.com
(512)517-1042 MSTR#8100

McNeese, Michael C (M1)
16410 Wesley Evans Road
Prairieville, LA 70769
mcneesemc@cox.net
(520)722-1350 MSDC#8700

Mearns, Duawn (M1)
311 Chickasaw Drive
Ada, OK 74820
duawn@covenantcpc.org
(580)332-0799 MSRR#6304

Medlin, Kevin (M1)
316 Dandelion Drive
Lebanon, TN 37087
FAX: (615)444-6671
kmedlin12@hotmail.com
(615)444-7453 TNMU#7220

Meeks, Brittany (M1)
710 N Avalon Street
Memphis, TN 38107
brittany.meeks@garrett.edu
(901)319-3474 GRWT#9100

Meinzer, Alan (M1)
780 Barren Fork Road
Mt. Pleasant, AR 72561
brotheralan@centurylink.net
(870)612-3936 GRAR#1515

MINISTERS CONTINUED

Merritt, Joyce (M1)
3929 Snail Shell Cave Road
Rockvale, TN 37153
(615)574-3047   TNMU#7200

Messer, James (M1)
3653 Old Madisonville Road
Henderson, KY 42420
jcmess@hotmail.com
(270)827-0711   MINC#5304

Micolta, Ruby Mabely (M3)
Anticua 4 Casa 25
Popayan, Colombia, South America
rumami@gmail.com
(318)286-7264   MSCA#8200

Mikel, Jason (M1)
410 Ramblewood Lane
Nolensville, TN 37135
jenkinspastor@gmail.com
(615)243-8938   TNCO#7144

Milby, Elizabeth L (M1)
207 Summersville Road
Greensburg, KY 42743
(270)932-5659   MICU#3100

Miller, Carol (M1)
101 Park Avenue
Dickson, TN 37055
lcarolmiller@comcast.net
(615)411-6656   TNNA#7300

Min, Kim (M1)
55 Magnolia Avenue
Tenafly, NJ 07670
( )   SECE#2444

Mink, R Allan (M1)
1113 Hidden Glen Court
Burleson, TX 76028
alan.mink@pathway.church
(817)295-5832   MSRR#8418

Minor, Mitzi (M1)
875 S Cox
Memphis, TN 38104
(901)278-6115   GRWT#9100

Minton, Grant (M1)
PO Box 270
Auburn, KY 42206
gminton@logantele.com
(270)542-7991   MICU#3301

Mitchell, Cherry (M3)
PO Box 64
Nebo, KY
mitchell9602@bellsouth.net
(270)836-6229   MICO#3400

Miyai, Takehiko (M1)
4-13-24 Higashihara Zama-shi
Kanagawa-ken
228-0004 JAPAN
tacke.m@gmail.com
(046)207-6558   MSJA#8304

Miyajima, Atsushi (M2)
Rua Araja
58 Paraiso Sao Joa
48280-000, Bahia, BRAZIL
ariel.atsushi@gmail.com
(5571)3664-1037   MSJA#8313

Montano, Jhony (M1)
Cra 9 No 6 6N 87 Bello Horizonte
Popayan
Colombia, South America
(092)823-8988   MSCA#8227

Montoya, David (M3)
20900 FM 1093 Apt 11208
Richmond, TX 77407
davinay@hotmail.com
(823)366-6897   MSTR#8100

Montoya, Eduardo (M1)
2436 Anna Way
Elgin, IL 60124
edmontoya@hotmail.com
(630)980-1577   MINC#5203

Moore, Kimberly (M1)
1025 Three Island Ford Road
Charlotte, TN 37036
reverend.kim.moore@gmail.com
(615)545-1595   TNNA#7300

Mora, Wilfredo (M2)
17512 SW 153rd Court
Miami, FL 33187
moraw68@gmail.com
(786)554-1478   SEGR#0100

Morgan, Kenneth P (M1)
5400 Highway 101
Rogersville, AL 35652
kennymorgan330@hotmail.com
(256)247-3890   SEHO#0515

Morgan, Leigh Ann (M3)
PO Box 881
Winchester, TN 37398
( )   TNMU#7200

Morgan, Richard (M1)
1468 Williams Cove Road
Winchester, TN 37398
icthuse3@gmail.com
(931)349-4474   TNMU#7214

Morrow, Charles (M1)
5032 Pine Grove Road
Union, MS 39365
morrowp7@yahoo.com
(601)479-0288   SEGR#0100

Mosley, Steve (M1)
320 N Sherman Circle
Russellville, AR 72802
stevemosley@hotmail.com
(479)880-9498   GRAR#1221

Mosquera, Luis Alfonso (M3)
Calle 3 #36-29, B Juan 23
Cali, Colombia, South America
creer7@hotmail.com
(321)662-7191   MSCA#8200

Mullenix, Robert (M1)
122 Sunnyside Lane
Columbia, TN 38401
glonix@live.comt
(931)379-3617   TNCO#7100

Munoz, Mardoqueo (M1)
816 NW 87th Avenue #101
Miami, FL 33172
tonymardo@comcast.net
(305)801-6424   SEGR#0100

Muraya, Jennifer (M1)
1261 Peabody Avenue Apt 10
Memphis, TN 38104
jmmuraya@memphisseminaary.edu
(469)230-5064   GRWT#9436

Murphree, Hughlen (M1)
4298 County Road 1719
Holly Pond, AL 35083
hmurph@hiwaay.net
(256)796-5352   SERD#0800

Murray, Joshua (M1)
3875 Avalon Boulevard Apt 7
Milton, FL 32583
jdm4428@yahoo.com
(870)723-3286   SEGR#0100

--==<< N >>==--

Nave, Steve (M1)
5172 Fall River Road
Leoma, TN 38468
stevemnave19@gmail.com
(931)424-0020   TNCO#7131

Navrkal, Amy (M3)
302 W 3rd Street
Brookport, IL 62910
brinkleydanne2@gmail.com
(618)638-4218   MICO#3400

Ndoro, Wonder (M1)
111 Roberta Avenue
Memphis, TN 38112
gusungo@yahoo.com
(901)334-5861   GRWT#9100

Neal, Elise Renee (M1)
6800 Tezel Road
San Antonio, TX 78250
pastor@npcsatx.org
(210)680-4825   MSRR#8610

Neese, Dale (M1)
415 59th Street
Clinton, OK 73601
(580)323-7557   MSRR#8400

Nelson, Charles E (M1)
209 Classic Court
Springtown, TX 76082
dundeal10@aol.com
(903)641-5466   MSRR#8410

Newcomb, Troy (M2)
PO Box 858
Salem, KY 42078
newcomb.troy@yahoo.com
(270)210-4902   MICO#3610

Newell, Jennifer (M1)
2322 Maraco Circle
Chattanooga, TN 37421
newelljennifer3@gmail.com
(423)892-5834   SETG#2108

Nichols, Oscar Lee (M1)
1035 N County Road 650E
Trilla, IL 62469
(217)234-6551   MINC#5200

Nichols, Patrick (M3)
508 Brook Highland Lane
Birmingham, AL 35242
patrick.nichols@dcial.com
(205)445-9238   SEGR#0100

Nicholson, Casey (M1)
1020 Tusculum Boulevard
Greeneville, TN 37745
caseynicholson@mac.com
(423)638-4504   SEET#2200

Nickles, Philip (M1)
5821 County Road 1114
Vinemont, AL 35179
phillipnickles996@yahoo.com
(256)734-9847   SEHO#0206

Niswonger, Richard (M1)
20941 Highway 16 E
Siloam Springs, AR 72761
rniswonger@cox.net
(479)524-4081   GRAR#1100

MINISTERS CONTINUED

Niwa, Yoshimasa (M1)
15-402 Narakita Danchi
2913 Naramachi Aoba-ku
Yokohama, Kanagawa-ken
227-0036 JAPAN
rsb09335@nifty.com
(045)961-1540　MSJA#8310

Norris, Caleb (M2)
565 E 10th Street
Cookeville, TN 38501
caleb@cookevillecpchurch.org
(　)　TNMU#7200

Norris, Dakota (M3)
4456 Clarence Murphy Road
Springfield, TN 37172
volsfan2011@gmail.com
(615)681-6346　TNNA#7300

Norris, Freddie (M1)
330 Lexington Drive
Glasgow, KY 42141
(270)651-7932　MICU#3100

Norton, Kitty (M1)
251 Westchase Drive
Nashville, TN 37205
kitty.a.norton@vanderbilt.edu
(615)584-1464　TNNA#7300

Norton, Thomas H (M1)
1049 Lakemont Circle
Winter Park, FL 32792
tomnorton33@gmail.com
(270)505-5218　GRWT#9100

Notley, Sharon (M1)
16500 S Grey Wolf Apt 5
Odessa, TX 79766
sharon_standrewcp@outlook.comt
(432)210-9059　MSDC#8703

Nye, John (M1)
210 Crestview Drive
Mount Juliet, TN 37122
(　)　TNMU#7200

--==<< O >>==--

O'Neal Danhof, Claire (M1)
301 Whispering Hills Street
Hot Springs, AR 71901
acglenn@aol.com
(　)　GRAR#1100

Ocoro, Richard (M3)
Guapi
Cali, Colombia, South America
vpoera@hotmail.com
(315)200-4727　MSCA#8200

Oh, Taeho (M1)
4085 W 7th Street Apt 1
Los Angeles, CA 90005
(213)334-1506　MSDC#8700

Ohi, Keitaro (M1)
1-8-50 Magarimatsu
Hadano-shi Kanagawa-ken
259-1321 JAPAN
keitaro_o@hotmail.com
(046)387-1203　MSJA#8303

Oliveira, Jose (M1)
7310 Jasmine Drive
Hanover Park, IL 60133
valdirsoares@yahoo.com
(630)855-0870　MSDC#8700

Oliver, Lisa (M1)
110 Allen Drive
Hendersonville, TN 37075
lisa.oliver316@gmail.com
(615)474-3954　TNNA#7230

O'Mara, Shelia (M1)
PO Box 170
Gadsden, TN 38337
chaplainshelia@aol.com
(443)699-2321　MSDC#8700

Ordonez, Jeason (M3)
Diag 26 O 96 31
Cali, Colombia, South America
jeamauri@hotmail.com
(312)898-9304　MSCA#8200

Ordway, Wendell (M1)
4775 Calvert City Road
Calvert City, KY 42029
(270)395-7318　MICO#3423

Orozco, Joaquin (M1)
Cra 3 #7-14
Aguadas, Caldas, COLOMBIA, SA
jeob40@hotmail.com
(576)851-4773　MSAN#8900

Orozeo Ariza, Juan Carlos (M2)
Aereo 6365
Cali Vale, COLOMBIA, SA
(　)　MSCA#8200

Orr, Melvin (M1)
806 Washington Street
Newbern, TN 38059
2Orrs.mn@charter.net
(731)627-2445　GRWT#9100

Ortega, Juan (M3)
COLOMBIA, SA
jortegaus@yahoo.com
(574)323-9305　MSAN#8900

Ortiz, Milton (M1)
1257 Magilbra Street
Cordova, TN 38016
mortiz@cumberland.org
(901)486-6679　SEET#2200

Osorio, Fernando (M3)
Aereo 329
Palmira, COLOMBIA, SA
(　)272-7584　MSCA#8215

Ostrander, Shirley (M1)
24069 New Willow Drive #5
Lebanon, TN 65536
(901)827-4830　GRMI#4100

Overton, Janice M (M1)
3320 Pipeline Road
Birmingham, AL 35243
jan@crestlinechurch.org
(205)281-6819　SEGR#0102

Owen, Rick (M1)
3305 Wild Oaks Court
Burleson, TX 76028
rowen@pathway.church
(817)295-5832　MSRR#8418

--==<< P >>==--

Page, Rickey (M1)
1369 Black River Drive
Mt Pleasant, SC 29466
rickey.page59@gmail.com
(615)353-7850　TNNA#7300

Paredes, Fabio (M3)
Carerra 7 # 1-76
La Cruztala, Ipiales, COLOMBIA, SA
(092)773-1036　MSCA#8200

Park, Bo-Seong (M1)
304-28 Sinlim-Dong, Kwanak-Gu
Seoul, KOREA
(002)884-3474　SEET#2200

Park, Jin Soo (M1)
21155 45th Drive
Bayside, NY 11361
jpkorea@daum.net
(516)558-7298　SECE#2137

Park, Sang Hoon (M1)
2980 W Melbourne Street
Springfield, MO 65810
hesed-park@hanmail.net
(417)888-0442　GRMI#4100

Park, Si Hoon (M1)
511 4th Street #B
Palisades Park, NJ 07650
(201)944-7913　SECE#2137

Park, Sung In (M1)
12320 Alameda Trace Circle #1309
Austin, TX 78727
(　)　MSTR#8100

Park, Yang Rae (M1)
4175 Buford Highway
Duluth, GA 30096
barkmoksa@hanmail.net
(770)912-7710　SEKP#2130

Park, Young Jin (M3)
3340 Bentbill Crossing
Cummings, GA 30041
084657@gmail.com
(731)845-3173　SEKP#2000

Park, Young Kwang (M3)
3340 Bentbill Crossing
Cummings, GA 30041
barkmogun@gmail.com
(770)912-8477　SEKP#2000

Parker, Susan (M1)
655 York Drive
Rogersville, AL 35652
park9301@bellsouth.net
(256)247-3877　SEHO#0500

Parks, Sam (M1)
10 Lila Way
Cartersville, GA 60120
wsamparks@aol.com
(615)529-2465　TNMU#7200

Parman, David (M1)
5034 S Monroe School Road
Monroe City, IN 47557
(812)743-2646　MINC#5307

Parrish, Steven (M1)
4610 Dunn Avenue
Memphis, TN 38117
sparrish@memphisseminary.edu
(901)743-9545　TNNA#7300

Patterson, James H (M1)
6705 Ballard Drive #211
Chattanooga, TN 37421
(423)267-8568　SETG#2100

Patton, Malcolm (M1)
921 Harris Drive
Gallatin, TN 37066
bpatton11@comcast.net
(615)452-5557　TNNA#7300

Payne, Robert (Bob) (M1)
PO Box 11
Lauderdale, MS 39335
payne.bob.emmet@gmail.com
(205)856-2427　SEGR#0100

Peach, John (M1)
221 Geronimo Road
Knoxville, TN 37934
peachroot@aol.com
(865)675-5956　SEET#2200

MINISTERS CONTINUED

Pedigo, Russell (M1)
209 Cemetary Street
Morgantown, KY 42261
russell_pedigo@hotmail.com
(870)862-4689 GRAR#1100

Peery, Terry (M1)
1431 Spainwood Street
Columbia, TN 38401
coppreacher@gmail.com
(931)381-6871 TNCO#7143

Pejendino, Socorro (M1)
24 Avenida 0-97 Zona
7 Ciudad de GUATEMALA
(317)654-5750 MSCA#8200

Perez, Jose (M1)
3512 Chesnut Ridge Lane
Birmingham, AL 35216
(205)663-3110 TNMU#7200

Perez, Milagro (M3)
923 SWth 8th Court
Miami, FL 33130
( ) SEGR#0100

Perkins, Ed (M1)
721 E Paris Avenue
McKenzie, TN 38201
(731)352-2754 GRWT#9100

Peters, David J (M1)
4010 Sam Bass Road
Round Rock, TX 78681
(512)244-2152 MSTR#8100

Peterson, Lisa (M1)
7778 Cedar Creek Road
Townsend, TN 37882
petersonli@aol.com
(901)604-0737 SEET#2200

Petty, Linda Lee (M3)
8601 S Mingo Road Apt 3115
Tulsa, OK 74133
linda.petty47@yahoo.com
(918)252-4741 MSRR#8400

Peyton, James L (M1)
1455 County Road 643
Cullman, AL 35055
jakjpeyton@att.net
(256)734-6001 SEHO#0212

Phelps, John (M1)
361 Chaco Road
Yona, GUAM 96915
jbphelps75@yahoo.com
(671)689-6764 MICU#3100

Phillips, Hone (M2)
301 S Walnut Street
Hohenwald, TN 38462
kaitiaki39@gmail.com
(931)306-8000 TNCO#7100

Phillips, Kenneth P (M1)
6419 Town Creek Road East
Lenoir City, TN 37772
(865)986-7344 SEET#2306

Phillips-Burk, Pam (M1)
3325 Bailey Creek Cove N
Collierville, TN 38017
pam@cumberland.org
(256)684-5247 SERD#0800

Piamba, Juan Carlos (M3)
Cra 7 #21N-35
Popayan, COLOMBIA, SA
(092)838-5761 MSCA#8200

Pickard, Ronald (M1)
6292 Golden Drive
Morristown, TN 37814
(423)587-9735 SEET#2200

Pickett, Darrell (M1)
113 Woods Drive
Glasgow, KY 42141
dpickett@glasgow-ky.com
(270)834-6102 MICU#3107

Pickett, Patricia (M1)
1460 Cheatham Dam Road
Ashland City, TN 37015
tovahtoo@aol.com
(615)792-4973 TNNA#7300

Pinion, Phillip (M1)
PO Box 87
Union City, TN 38281
ppinion.tn@gmail.com
(731)885-9175 GRWT#9432

Pittenger, Ronnie M (M1)
207 Cowan Street W
Cowan, TN 37318
cspronnie@gmail.com
(615)832-8832 TNMU#7211

Plachte, Richard (M1)
615 Grover Street
Warrensburg, MO 64093
rap@aerobiz.org
(660)441-4427 GRMI#4100

Polacek, Fred E (M1)
907 Graham Drive
Old Hickory, TN 37138
revfredp@gmail.com
(615)754-5328 TNNA#7300

Ponce, Jesus Adriam (M3)
Carrera 38 #3-31 14 De Julio
Cali, Colombia, South America
dapcristo@hotmail.com
(318)526-6265 MSCA#8200

Porras, Rene Wilgen (M3)
Cra 4 bis #10-51
La Virginia, Risaralda
COLOMBIA, SA
renewilgen@hotmail.com
(576)367-9529 MSAN#8900

Potter, Bruce (M1)
1712 Marion Avenue
South Pittsburg, TN 37380
brucepotter@charter.net
(423)228-4485 SETG#2118

Potts, Danny (M1)
585 State Route 1125 S
Fulton , KY 42041
(270)355-2264 MICO#3400

Pounds, James D (M1)
40 Nellie Lane
Savannah, TN 38372
olivetcp@bellsouth.net
(205)253-3910 SEGR#0105

Powell, Jeff (M1)
694 White Avenue
Henderson, TN 38340
jfpowell2003@yahoo.com
(731)608-2040 GRWT#9215

Prenshaw, Rebecca (M1)
1100 Albermarie Lane
Knoxville, TN 37923
bprenshaw@yahoo.com
(865)531-1954 SEET#2200

Preston, Dennis (M1)
7447 Knottsville Mount Zion Road
Philpot, KY 42366
dpreston@roadrunner.com
(270)925-8144 MICU#3507

Prevost, Abigail (M1)
9111 County Road 747
Cullman, AL 35055
abbyprevost@gmail.com
(270)889-1985 SEHO#0212

Price, Billy (M1)
12510 Buttermilk Road
Knoxville, TN 37932
beavercreekyouth@gmail.com
(901)494-4851 GRWT#2301

Pritchett, Huiling (M2)
5562 S Yank Court
Littleton, CO 80127
whuiling88@yahoo.com
(303)330-3929 MSDC#8700

Prosser, Forest (M1)
1157 Mountain Creek Road
Chattanooga, TN 37405
forestprosser@comcast.net
(423)877-4114 SETG#2100

Prosser, Robert (M1)
1021 Old State Route 76
Henry, TN 38231
(731)243-4467 GRWT#9100

Puckett, Rian (M3)
55 Ham Street
Batesville, AR 72501
bro.rianpuckett@gmail.com
(731)288-7742 GRAR#1510

Puluc, Paul (M3)
1421 Greentree Valley Court
Memphis, TN 38119
paul-tuba@hotmail.com
(830)872-6090 GRWT#9100

Purcell, Rick (M3)
895 Branch Road
Clarksville, TN 37043
rickpurcell@sbcglobal.net
(269)277-7277 TNNA#7338

--==<< Q >>==--

Qualls, Michael (M1)
5355 June Cove
Horn Lake, MS 38637
mqualls1@yahoo.com
(901)377-0526 GRWT#9100

Quevedo, Mariano (M3)
289 Golf Club Lane
McMinnville, TN 37110
( ) TNMU#7200

Quinonez, Wilfrido (M1)
Cra 3 No 36-29, Juan XXIII
BuenaventurValle, COLOMBIA, SA
ipc.divinoredentor@gmail.com
(310)412-1711 MSCA#8206

Quintero, Alexander (M3)
Carrera 13 #3-81
Guacari, COLOMBIA, SA
( ) MSCA#8212

Quinton, Noah (M1)
1617 Faxon Avenue
Memphis, TN 38112
noah.quinton@gmail.com
(270)952-3875 GRWT#9100

--==<< R >>==--

Racines, Jairo (M1)
CLL 39 No 13-40
Cali, COLOMBIA, SA
(311)385-6546 MSCA#8200

MINISTERS CONTINUED

Rackley, Mark (M1)
3060 Highway 140 NE
Rydal, GA 30171
pastormarkbcpcga@gmail.com
(770)382-3790 SETG#2101

Ragsdale, Donnie (M1)
915 S Olive Street
Union City, TN 38261
(731)885-0014 GRWT#9424

Ramiriz, Araceli (M2)
235 Vinewood Road Apt DG
McMinnville, TN 37090
( ) TNMU#7200

Raney, Frankie (M3)
259 Ditto Lane
Rogersville, AL 35652
franey@heavymachinesinc.com
(256)284-8965 SEHO#0500

Ratliff, James L (M1)
13 Hernando Drive
Cherokee Village, AR 72529
kudzu8161@yahoo.com
(901)758-0125 GRWT#9100

Reece, Lyle (M1)
8600 Academy NE
Albuquerque, NM 87111
lreece@heightscpc.org
(505)884-2952 MSDC#8701

Reed, Charles (M1)
36839 Indian Lake Cemetary Road
Dade City, FL 33523
instchuck12@embarqmail.com
(352)567-7427 SEGR#0100

Reed, Laura (M3)
3017 Banyan Hill Lane
Land O'Lakes, FL 34639
lola04@reagan.com
(813)401-2332 SEGR#0100

Reed, Richard (M2)
236 Madison Street
Dyer, TN 38330
richardcplist@hotmail.com
(731)692-3604 GRWT#9101

Reese, Michael (M1)
1114 Palmer Road
Lebanon, TN 37090
michaelhreese@bellsouth.net
(615)443-0457 TNMU#7208

Reeves, Donald (M1)
PO Box 528
Rainsville, AL 35986
reevesd@nacc.edu
(256)228-4057 SERD#0800

Reid, Roger (M1)
637 Colburn Drive
Lewisburg, TN 37091
drrtr@yahoo.com
(931)637-4467 TNCO#7125

Renner, Wallace (M1)
1648 Griffith Avenue
Owensboro, KY 42303
pwrenner@adelphia.net
(270)685-4359 MICU#3501

Reno, Michael (M1)
52 Rolla Gardens
Rolla, MO 65401
rollarenomike@gmail.com
(573)578-5321 GRMI#4309

Restrepo, Johanna (M3)
Ave 4 A Oeste 20-11
Cali, Colombia, South America
rojo_nana@hotmail.es
(318)655-9955 MSCA#8200

Rice, Keith (M1)
PO Box 582
Itasca, TX 76055
rsvkeith@yahoo.com
(254)087-2418 MSRR#8400

Rice, Perryn (M4)
2122 Auburn Drive
Richardson, TX 75081
perryn@lhpres.org
(931)526-6585 MSRR#8411

Richards, Carroll R (M1)
210 Allison Drive
Lincoln, IL 62656
dr_cr@comcast.net
(217)732-7894 MINC#5200

Richter, Justin (M1)
8600 Academy Road NE
Albuquerque, NM 87111
jrichter@heightscpc.org
(505)363-8738 MSDC#8701

Ricketts, Roger (M1)
205 Contantz Drive
Canton, MO 63435
( ) MICU#3100

Ridgely, Michael (M1)
5195 Broad Street S
Trezevant, TN 38258
mdr26347@outlook.com
(731)418-9294 GRWT#9100

Rincon, Alfredo (M1)
12008 Fred Carter
El Paso, TX 79936
yaanaivitaly@yahoo.com
(915)857-1343 MSDC#8704

Rincon, Lyvia (M1)
12008 Fred Carter
El Paso, TX 79936
yaanaivitaly@yahoo.com
(915)857-1343 MSDC#8700

Rippy, James G (M1)
442 Trina Street
Gallatin, TN 37066
lgrippy@live.com
(615)681-7086 TNNA#7300

Rivera, Carlos A (M1)
Calle Dr Jose Maria Vertiz 1410
Departmento 202B, Colonia Portales
Delegacion Benito
Juarez, C.P. 03300 MEXICO
caralrifra@une.net.co
(52)1-55-31058377 MSAN#8900

Rivera, Zenobia (M1)
Cra 12 #8-47
Cartago, Valle, COLOMBIA, SA
zenobiadedaza@yahoo.com.mx
(572)214-5060 MSEM#8905

Rizo, Yency (M3)
Diag 26 H 2 83-35 Marroquin
Cali, Colombia, South America
( )403-7709 MSCA#8200

Rochelle, Jimmy (M1)
609 Woods Drive
Columbia, TN 38401
tnpappy53@yahoo.com
(931)698-6829 TNCO#7133

Rodden, Linda (M1)
PO Box 582
Phillipsburg, MO 65722
lindaleerodden@centurylink.net
(417)588-2207 GRMI#4100

Roddy, Lowell G (M1)
628 Mannington Place
Lexington,, KY 40503
lgroddy@yahoo.com
(931)249-1047 TNNA#7300

Rodgers, Howard (M1)
336 County Road 1216
Vinemont, AL 35179
djbr421@yahoo.com
(256)739-6296 SEHO#0500

Rodriguez, Jairo Hernan (M1)
Cll 42 No 80B 64
Barrio Versalles
Cali-Valle, COLOMBIA, SA
jairo.hrodriguez@hotmail.com
(572)377-8741 MSCA#8200

Rodriguez, Sofonias Velasco (M3)
Brazo Seco Guapi-Cauca
(317)885-9033 MSCA#8200

Roedder, Unhui Grace (M1)
419 S Jonathan Avenue
Springfield, MO 65802
kimroedder@hotmail.com
(417)494-6491 GRMI#4100

Rogers, Andrew (M3)
541 Talpha Drive
Doweltown, TN 37059
awrogers21@gmail.com
(615)597-7963 TNMU#7225

Rogers, John A (M1)
2349 Lynnwood Drive
Paducah, KY 42001
jrogers308@comcast.net
(270)534-1195 MICO#3400

Rogers, Steve (M3)
101 Gillespie Drive Apt 13302
Franklin, TN 37067
(731)882-2229 TNCO#7100

Rojas, Antonio Mena (M1)
1421 1st Street NW
Cullman, AL 35055
antonio.mena.7@facebook.com
(256)531-8193 SEGR#0116

Rolman, William L, Jr (M1)
602 Canyon Drive
Columbia, TN 38401
wlrolman@charter.net
(931)388-2611 TNCO#7130

Romines, Sam (M1)
299 Misty Lane
Bowling Green, KY 42101
sam60romines@hotmail.com
(270)221-5856 MICU#3100

Ros, Ramiro (M1)
107 Bracken Lane
Brandon, FL 33511
bethel@gte.net
(813)633-1548 SEGR#0100

Rosero, Oscar (M3)
Sapuyes Marino Los Monos
(318)415-7077 MSCA#8200

Rowlett, Ron (M1)
336 Alfred Ladd Road E
Franklin, TN 37064
(912)351-0736 SEGR#0100

MINISTERS CONTINUED

Rudolph, Allie D (M1)
855 Old Rosebower Church Road
Paducah, KY 42003
rallie307@aol.com
(270)898-4903 MICO#3400

Ruggia, Mario (Bud) (M1)
603 Rumsey Street
Kiowa, KS 67070
ruggia@aol.com
(620)825-4076 MSRR#8400

Ruiz, Daveiva (M3)
Diagonal 26 F 77-80
Cali, Colombia, South America
daveiva61@gmail.com
(314)668-2610 MSCA#8200

Rush, Kip John (M1)
513 Meadowlark Lane
Brentwood, TN 37027
pastor@brenthaven.org
(615)714-6365 TNNA#7331

Rush, Robert D (M1)
12935 Quail Park Drive
Cypress, TX 77429
robertrush832@gmail.com
(832)843-6124 MSTR#8100

Russell, Albert (M1)
104 Weston Street
Prattville, AL 36066
chemistry.russell@gmail.com
(334)455-3690 SEGR#0407

Russell, Olen (Bud) (M1)
9595 Wickliffe Road
Wickliffe, KY 42087
olen552@aol.com
(270)562-1096 MICO#3414

Rustenhaven, William, III (M1)
PO Box 1303
Marshall, TX 75671
rusty@cumberlandofmarshall.org
(903)935-6609 MSTR#8100

Ryoo, Hwa Chang (M1)
450 Island Road Unit 146
Ramsey, NJ 07446 SECE#2400

--=<< S >>=--

Saldana, Manuel (Alex) (M1)
536 Telop
El Paso, TX 79927
campe13@yahoo.com
(915)317-9349 MSDC#8706

Salisbury, Rebecca (M1)
1033 Twin Oaks Drive
Murfreesboro, TN 37130
(615)410-7801 TNMU#7200

Salyer, Stewart (M1)
2211 Foxfire Road
Clarksville, TN 37040
stewart.salyer@gmail.com
(931)980-2829 TNNA#7302

Sanchez, Josefina (M1)
2625 Benson Gardens Boulevard
Omaha, NE 68134
fsfamily64@gmail.com
(479)970-8654 SEET#2220

Sanchez, Sol Maria (M1)
Av Americas 19 N - 18
Cali Valle
Colombia, South America
solmarias@starmedia.com
( ) MSCA#8200

Sanders, Thomas R (M1)
8480 N 69th East Avenue
Owasso, OK 74055
trsncf@msn.com
(918)269-0043 MSRR#8400

Sandiford, Holton (M2)
4227 E 300th Road
Casey, IL 62420
(217)259-3773 MINC#5200

Sansom, Vernon (M1)
7425 Northampton Boulevard
Knoxville, TN 37931
vernon@sansom.us
(865)556-4107 MSRR#8421

Santillano, Ray Paul (M1)
1270 Polo Road
Columbia, SC 29223
ramon.santillano@us.army.mil
(915)500-4928 MSTR#8100

Sarmiento Paez, Liliana (M1)
Calle 51 #15-32
Los Naranjos Dosquebradas
Colombia, South America
lilianasarmi23@gmail.com
(321)622-2797 MSAN#8900

Satoh, Iwao (M1)
8710 Hickory Falls Lane
Pewee Valley, KY 40056
iwaosatoh@gmail.com
(502)657-9643 MICU3223

Schmoyer, Donna Marie (M1)
613 Mound Street
Monongahela, PA 15063
schmoyerdm@yahoo.com
(817)266-6572 MSRR#8400

Schultz, Don (M1)
708 Gateway Lane
Tampa, FL 33613
(813)960-1473 SEGR#0100

Schwitz, Gary (M1)
PO Box 92
Longview, TX 75606
revschwitz@gmail.com
(903)359-5983 MSTR#8112

Scott, Adrian (M1)
7204 Johnstone Lane
Fort Worth, TX 76133
scott.adrian@zoho.com
(817)205-7760 MSRR#8413

Scott, Jerry (M1)
1580 Dover Road
Morristown, TN 37813
dmjlscott@yahoo.com
(865)809-2621 SEET#2203

Scott, Lisa (M1)
(On File in General Assembly Office)
lascott1979@att.net
(816)332-0604 GRMI#4100

Scott, Nathan (M1)
9696 S Katy Road
Atoka, OK 74525
(580)364-6155 MSCH#6111

Scrivener, Carol (M1)
746 Willowsprings Boulevard
Franklin, TN 37064
csscriv@juno.com
(731)660-6469 GRWT#9100

Scrudder, Norlan (M1)
1514 Irene Lane
Fort Gibson, OK 74434
ndscrudder@gmail.com
(918)949-1326 MSRR#8400

Searcy, James M (M1)
1307 Lucy Way
Knoxville, TN 37912
gsearcy@earthlink.net
(817)293-6132 GRWT#9100

Seki, Nobuko (M1)
2-14-16 Higashi-cho Koganei-Shi
Toyko
184-0011 JAPAN
nobukoseki866@gmail.com
(042)231-1279 MSJA#8300

Seva, Judith (M3)
7685 Tara Circle Apt 204
Naples, FL 34104
jclthgirl12@gmail.com
(239)269-3917 SEGR#0100

Shannon, Randy (M1)
30282 Highway H
Marshall, MO 65340
pastor_randy_shannon@yahoo.com
(660)886-9545 GRMI#4210

Sharpe, Michael G (M1)
3423 Summerdale Drive
Bartlett, TN 38133
(901)276-4572 MSRR#8400

Shatley, Melissa (M3)
339 Ouachita 54
Camden, AR 71701
( ) GRAR#1100

Shauf, Steve (M1)
4630 Mt Sharon Road
Greenbrier, TN 37073
theshaufs@hotmail.com
(270)331-5247 MICO#3400

Shauf, Teresa (M1)
4630 Mt Sharon Road
Greenbrier, TN 37073
theshaufs@hotmail.com
(270)331-5217 MICO#3400

Shelton, Duncan (M3)
533 Carrington Boulevard
Lenoir City, TN 37771
duncanshelton@charter.net
865-635-1338 SEET#2200

Shelton, Steven (M1)
7886 Farmhill Cove
Bartlett, TN 38135
sshelton@cumberland.org
(901)377-0526 GRWT#9100

Shepard, Denny C (M1)
8514 Newsom Station Road
Nashville, TN 37221
(615)662-1114 TNMU#7209

Shepherd, Sandra (M1)
1432 Wexford Downs Lane
Nashville, TN 37211
woolywagon@gmail.com
(615)772-5358 TNNA#7331

Shipley, Howard E (M1)
3800 Dan Drive
Morristown, TN 37814
hshipley@charter.net
(423)581-1092 SEET#2207

Shirley, Betty L (M1)
811 Rotherham Drive
Ballwin, MO 63011
therevbls@prodigy.net
(636)386-3174 MINC#5200

MINISTERS CONTINUED

Shropshire, Patricia (M2)
PO Box 330404
Nashville, TN 37203
patricia.a.shropshire@vumc.org
(517)256-7454 TNNA#7320

Sides, Judy Taylor (M1)
534 Bethany Circle
Murfreesboro, TN 37128
(615)895-1627 TNMU#7231

Simmons, Dyllan (M3)
203 Cambridge Drive
dyllansimmons121999@yahoo.com
(270)534-1770 MICO#3400

Sims, Edward G (M1)
1176 Warfield Boulevard #410
Clarksville, TN 37043
simseg@bellsouth.net
(931)206-5759 TNNA#7300

Sisco, Terra (M1)
811 W Cheyenne Street
Marlow, OK 73055
terrasisco@gmail.com
(618)384-6126 MSRR#6305

Siu, Jonathan Chor K (M1)
251 Tin Sam Estate
Shatin, HONG KONG
cpccksiu@yahoo.com.hk
(852)2693-3444 MSHK#8807

Skidmore, Garland (M1)
2083 US Highway 278 E
Hampton, AR 71744
(870)798-4634 GRAR#1101

Skipper, Steve (M3)
312 E Market Street
Jeffersonville, IN 47130
samuel.skipper@jeffersonkyschools.us
(502)424-0022 MICU#3100

Sledge, Jeff (M1)
241 Long Bow Road
Knoxville, TN 37934
jeffsledge@charter.net
(865)318-5565 SEET#2200

Slickmeyer, Kim (M3)
431 Riley Avenue
Smithville, TN 37166
krslickmeyer@gmail.com
(931)650-1330 TNMU#7200

Small, Kevin (M1)
6492 E 400th Road
Martinsville, IL 62442
revkev61@gmail.com
(618)562-1463 MINC#5211

Smith, Christian (M1)
1094 Tanglewood Drive
Cookeville, TN 38501
csmith2490@gmail.com
(931)265-8896 TNMU#7210

Smith, David R (M1)
PO Box 892
Rosepine, LA 70659
ogreyfox@att.net
(903)297-6074 MSTR#8100

Smith, Griffen (M3)
1801 Westchester Drive
Knoxville, TN 37918
gryffinder2644@gmail.com
(865)804-1571 SEET#2200

Smith, James A (M1)
8301 Poplar Pike
Germantown, TN 38138
james1493@att.net
(901)309-1992 TNNA#7300

Smith, James (M3)
222 Southcrest Drive SW
Huntsville, AL 35802
dr.james.smith@netzero.com
(256)655-6541 SERD#0800

Smith, Jerald D (M1)
502 Blackpatch Drive Apt A102
Springfield, TN 37172
jergensmith@aol.com
(731)427-9316 GRWT#9100

Smith, Kirk (M1)
813 1st Avenue
Fayetteville, TN 37334
kirks37334@att.net
(931)438-8649 TNCO#7108

Smith, Robert A (M1)
PO Box 501
Newbern, TN 38059
ras1957@bellsouth.net
(731)627-3332 GRWT#9409

Smith, Robert H (M1)
5055 S 76th East Avenue Apt D
Tulsa, OK 74145
rhsmith@sstelco.com
(918)671-5520 MSRR#8400

Smith, Steven (M3)
100 Valleyview Drive
Leitchfield, KY 42754
( ) MICU#3100

Smith, Timothy (M1)
214 Jeffrey Drive
Fayetteville, TN 37334
tims38@hotmail.com
(931)438-2820 TNCO#7112

Smyrl, Jerry (M1)
10617 Hagen NE
Albuquerque, NM 87111
gpasmyrl@gmail.com
(505)999-8852 MSDC#8701

Snelling, Linda (M1)
240 Dakota Drive
Waxahachie, TX 75167
lsnelling50@gmail.com
(469)550-9074 MSRR#8400

Snyder, Joel (M1)
224 Lord Lane
Mountain View, AR 72560
snyder.joel@ymail.com
(870)269-9743 GRAR#1504

So, Lai Yuet (M3)
2/F Fu Tung Shopping Centre
Tung Chung
Lantau Island NT, HONG KONG
laiyuet0914@gmail.com
(852)2109-1738 MSHK#8800

So, Patrick (M1)
2/F Fu Tung Shopping Center
Tung Chung
Lantau Island, HONG KONG
cpctwso@uahoo.com.hk
(852)2109-1738 MSHK#8810

Solis, Arcadio (M1)
Crr 42 D1 No 55-69
Guapi, COLOMBIA, SA
( )328-5486 MSCA#8200

Solito, Carlos (M1)
3151 Pleasant Hill Road
Nesbit, MS 38651
fcg9700@gmail.com
(205)329-8514 GRWT#9196

Sontowski, Marian (M1)
17101 N Western Avenue
Edmond, OK 73012
stonegatecpc@gmail.com
(405)340-7281 MSRR#6307

Sosa, Alexandri (M1)
2828 W Kirby Street
Tampa, FL 33614
sosapcus@gmail.com
(813)960-1473 SEGR#0307

Spence, Thomas R (M1)
PO Box 809
Burns Flat, OK 73624
tomspence0302@gmail.com
(580)562-4531 MSRR#6301

Sprenkle, David (M1)
5733 Stone Street
Olive Branch, MS 38654
dsprenkle@memphisseminary.edu
(901)604-8707 GRWT#9213

Spurling, Robert T, Jr (M1)
305 Wayne Drive
Hopkinsville, KY 42240
(865)803-8582 MICO#3611

Steeley, Tim (M1)
PO Box 281
Mt Vernon, MO 65712
timsteeley99@gmail.com
(417)466-4345 GRMI#4102

Stefan, Gregory (M1)
1917 Birchwood Street
East Pearl, PA 17519
pastorstefan@att.net
(931)296-5291 MICU#3100

Stephens, Blake (M1)
2559 Holders Cove Road
Winchester, TN 37398
blsteph@edge.net
(931)308-7335 TNMU#7235

Stephens, Evan (M3)
559 Holders Cove Road
Winchester, TN 37398
( ) TNMU#7200

Stephenson, Joseph (M2)
326 S State Street
Chandler, IN 47610
cpchurchjoe@gmail.com
(812)746-3123 MINC#5200

Stough, Karen (M2)
120 Hunters Hills Drive
Chelsea, AL 35043
raneyday54@aol.com
(205)218-9781 SEGR#0100

Stovall, Jeff (M1)
2829 Trelawny Drive
Clarksville, TN 37043
jeffstovall@juno.com
(931)993-6104 TNNA#7334

Straube, Edgar (M3)
170 Stirrup Lane
Boone, NC 28607
edgarstraube@aol.com
(828)719-8170 SEGR#0100

Straube, Iris (M3)
170 Stirrup Lane
Boone, NC 28607
irisathala@yahoo.com
(828)719-8170 SEGR#0100

MINISTERS CONTINUED

Stutler, Ken   (M3)
1044 Mansker Farms Boulevard
Hendersonville, TN 37075
cpkenstutler@gmail.com
(270)576-8367   TNNA#7300
Stutler, Tim   (M1)
1044 Mansker Farm Boulevard
Hendersonville, TN 37075
tim@goodlettsvillechurch.com
(615)859-5888   TNNA#7328
Sumerlin, Larkin   (M1)
920 Dogwood Circle
Birmingham, AL 35244
larkin.sumerlin@gmail.com
(334)357-0007   SEGR#0100
Sumrall, Phil   (M1)
107 Barnhardt Circle
Fort Oglethorpe, GA 30742
phil.sumrall@gmail.com
(423)903-1938   SETG#2100
Sung, John   (M2)
26 Old Orchard Road
Cherry Hill, NJ 08003
(856)751-0227   SETG#2100
Suttle, Michael   (M1)
507 Ouachita 18
Camden, AR 71701
m_s_suttle@msn.com
(870)836-0008   GRAR#1100
Suzuki, Atsushi   (M1)
53-17 Higashi Kibogaoka
Asahi-ku Yokohama Kanagawa-ken
241-0826 JAPAN
asyuwa98@m10.alpha-net.ne.jp
(045)362-2603   MSJA#8315
Suzuki, Temote   (M2)
9-14-15-310 Honcho Kamitsuruma
Sagamihara-shi, Kanagawa-ken
228-0818 JAPAN
temo_suzuki@hotmail.com
( )   MSJA#8300
Sweet Brockman, Anna   (M1)
635 Country Estates Drive
Winchester, TN 37398
amsweet@memphisseminary.edu
(865)803-8582   TNMU#7249
Sweet, Thomas   (M1)
2711 Windemere Lane
Powell, TN 37849
tsweet1@comcast.net
(865)938-0508   SEET#2301
Sweigart, John M   (M1)
PO Box 876
Dover, AL 72837
(479)229-4041   GRAR#1100
Sze, Joseph   (M1)
Rau Sao Joaquim, 382
Liberdale, Sao Paulo, SP
CEP 015068-000, BRAZIL
WeChat971507345761
pastorsze@yahoo.com
( )   MSDC#8700
Sze, Yat Sung   (M3)
Tin Yuet Estate
Tin Shui Wai NT, HONG KONG
yatsungs@yahoo.com.hk
(852)2617-7872   MSHK#8800

--==<< T >>==--

Tabor, Don M   (M1)
9611 Mitchell Place
Brentwood, TN 37027
dontabor@comcast.net
(615)776-7292   TNNA#7300
Taira, Masanori   (M2)
6-14-3 Minamirinkan Yamato-shi
Kanagawa-ken, JAPAN 242-0006
non.slope@gmail.com
(045)289-1915   MSJA#8305
Talley, Edward   (M1)
404 Serenity Circle
Walland, TN 37886
dptalley@hotmail.com
(205)854-1886   SEGR#0100
Tam, Wai Sun   (M3)
Wing B & C
G/F Ming Wik House
Kin Ming Es
Tseung Kwan O, HONG KONG
tsw428@gmail.com
(852)2706-0111   MSHK#8800
Tamai, Yukio   (M1)
3-17-35-4 Nakashinden
Ebina-shi Kanagawa-ken
243-0422 JAPAN
yukiotamai@icloud.com
(046)234-3426   MSJA#8311
Tan, Pek Hua   (M1)
7 Belhaven Avenue
Daly City, CA 94015
ptan27@yahoo.com
(415)515-0076   MSDC#8700
Tanck, Brian   (M1)
3218 Scenic Drive
Scottsboro, AL 35769
brian.tanck@gmail.com
(630)730-1577   SERD#0800
Tanck, Micaiah Thomas   (M1)
3218 Scenic Drive
Scottsboro, AL 35769
micaiah.thomas@gmail.com
(205)478-5985   SERD#0809
Tang, Po Kau   (M2)
G/1F, 251 Tin Sam Village
Shatin, NT, HONG KONG
cpc_pokau@yahoo.com.hk
(852)2981-4933   MSHK#8800
Taylor, Thomas (Ean)   (M3)
437 Peach Creek Crescent
Nashville, TN 37214
tetaylor91@gmail.com
(615)585-4158   TNNA#7300
Tejada, Jose   (M1)
488 SW 126th Terrace
Davie, FL 33325
jtejadapastor@hotmail.com
(786)817-0972   SEGR#0100
Terpstra, Tami   (M1)
10 Rainbow Crest Drive
Evergreen, CO 80127
tami.terpstra@yahoo.com
(303)350-3604   MSDC#8700
Terrell, Elizabeth   (M1)
2073 Vinton Avenue
Memphis, TN 38104
(901)647-2788   GRAR#1100

Thomas, Don F   (M1)
743 Rain Dance Way
Cordova, TN 38018
thomas63981@comcast.net
(901)412-3695   GRWT#0501
Thomas, Don H   (M1)
4829 Caldwell Mill Lane
Birmingham, AL 35242
dhtatn4ybc@cs.com
(205)747-0785   SEGR#0100
Thomas, Dwight   (M3)
1010 Gill Hodges Road
Portland, TN 37148
dwiight21@gmail.com
(615)906-2224   TNNA#7300
Thomas, Lynn   (M1)
4833 Caldwell Mill Lane
Birmingham, AL 35242
lynndont@gmail.com
(205)601-5770   SEGR#0100
Thomason, Mickey   (M3)
50 Thomason Road
Odenville, AL 35120
mickeythomason@yahoo.com
(205)283-2225   SEGR#0106
Thompson, Dee Ann   (M1)
1299 Mt Sterling Road
Brookport, IL 62910
deethomp5@hotmail.com
(618)445-0310   MICO#3207
Thompson, D J   (M3)
808 Gentry Avenue
Smithville, TN 37166
djthompson272@gmail.com
(615)318-7243   TNMU#7200
Thompson, Eugene   (M1)
1244 S 4th Street Apt 522
Louisville, KY 40203
( )   MICU#3100
Thompson, Tommy   (M1)
9160 Tchulahoma Road
Southaven, MS 38671
(662)393-2552   GRWT#9100
Thompson, W Fay   (M1)
210 Macbeth Lane
Glasgow, KY 42141
(270)646-2218   MICU#3100
Thornton, Jesse   (M1)
2518 IL Highway 15 E
Fairfield, IL 62837
jesstedalehornton@gmail.com
(618)200-0884   MINC#5100
Thornton, Matt   (M3)
773 Cahaba Manor Trail
Pelham, AL 35124
mjamest47@gmail.com
(205)807-6795   SEGR#0100
Tiangping, John   (M3)
331 Plus Park Boulevard #307
Nashville, TN 37217
(615)243-7101   TNNA#7300
Tobler, Garth   (M1)
1641 Pocota Drive Apt 205
Oneonta, AL 35121
gatobler@gmail.com
(205)683-0298   SEGR#0100
Todd, Christopher   (M1)
3303 Decker Street
Bartlett, TN 38134
catodd1964@gmail.com
(901)848-9913   GRWT#9100

MINISTERS CONTINUED

Todd, Laura (M1)
3303 Decker Street
Bartlett, TN 38134
littlelaurarose@yahoo.com
(901)496-1443 GRWT#9217

Tolley, Robert (Butch) (M1)
975 6th Street
Cleveland, TN 37311
butchtolley@hotmail.com
(423)837-6488 SETG#2100

Tompkins, Wayne (M1)
548 E Columbia Road 23
Emerson, AR 71740
wtministries1947@gmail.com
(870)807-2874 GRAR#1100

Topar, Shirley (M1)
1414 Shiloh Road #1012
Plano, TX 75074
s_j_topar@yahoo.com
(616)245-0625 MSRR#8400

Torres, Rodrigo (M3)
Aereo 6365
Cali, COLOMBIA, SA
(011)882-8372 MSCA#8205

Townsend, Mary Anna (M1)
1123 Tyler
Warrensburg, MO 64093
wrenhse1123@gmail.com
(660)909-5966 GRMI#4111

Travieso, Julio (M1)
15913 Countrybrook Street
Tampa, FL 33624
jutra98@aol.com
(813)963-3727 SEGR#0100

Travis, Kermit (M1)
3220 Sharon Highway 89
Dresden, TN 38225
(731)364-2315 GRWT#9124

Treadaway, Kenneth A (M1)
172 Miller County 494
Texarkana, AR 71854
treadaways@ark.net
(870)574-1609 GRAR#1100

Trotter, Wendell (M1)
1516 Fell Avenue NE
Huntsville, AL 35811
wendelltrotter@knology.net
(256)519-6571 TNCO#7100

Troyano, Sergio (M3)
923 SW 8th Court
Miami, FL 33130
( ) SEGR#0100

Truax, Robert Lee, Jr (M1)
2989 Champions Drive Apt 204
Lakeland, TN 38002
(901)266-5927 GRWT#9100

Truitt, Robert D (M1)
1238 Old East Side Road
Burns, TN 37029
rdtjct@aol.com
(615)740-9180 TNNA#7308

Tsui, Jackson (M1)
258 Carlos D'Assumpcao
Ed Kin Heng Long 4 Andar LMN
MACAU
tsuih@yahoo.com
(853)2892-1702 MSHK#8804

Tsui, Sukie (M3)
Wing B & C
G/F Ming Wik House
Kin Ming Es
sukiecpc@yahoo.com.hk
(852)2706-0111 MSHK#8800

Tsujimoto, Mark (M1)
88 S Broadway Unit 3210
Millbrae, CA 94030
mltsuijimoto@gmail.com
(650)697-6901 MSDC#8700

Tubb, Gary Robert (M1)
103 Forest Drive
Mountain Home, AR 72653
grtubb@yahoo.com
(870)424-0603 GRAR#1505

Tucker, Dave (M2)
3901 South Drive
Burleson, TX 76028
kc5cp@gmail.com
(817)506-9197 MSRR#8400

Tucker, Greg (M1)
170 Whitney Drive
Lenoir City, TN 37772
greg.tucker311@outlook.comt
(865)242-4086 SEET#2319

Tucker, James D (M1)
PO Box 34
Mc Daniels, KY 40152
(270)257-8971 MICU#3100

Tucker, Paul (M1)
3801 Brush Hill Pike
Nashville, TN 37216
paultucker@gmail.com
(615)430-9158 TNNA#7325

Turner, Glyn (M1)
601 Wynfal Drive
Holly Ridge, NC 28455
glynturner@hotmail.com
(585)307-7715 SETG#2100

Turner, O Gene (M1)
5160 McSpadden Road
Rives, TN 38253
(731)536-0189 GRWT#9100

Turner, Leonard E, Jr (M1)
12651 Wagon Wheel Circle
Knoxville, TN 37934
pastor@unioncpchurch.com
(865)966-8262 SEET#2315

Twilla, Kevin (M1)
731 Taylorsville Road
Lebanon, TN 37087
( ) TNMU#7220

Tyus, Dwayne (M1)
901 W Old Hickory Boulevard
Madison, TN 37115
dwayne.tyus@gmail.com
(615)720-2564 TNNA#7300

--==<< U >>==--

Underwood, Jerrell M (M1)
1157 E Highway 86
Irvington, KY 40146
(270)536-3706 MICU#3100

Ushioda, Kenji (M1)
2-47-3 Akuwa-higashi Seya-ku
Yokohama, Kanagawa-ken
246-0023 JAPAN
ushioda@jc.ejnet.ne.jp
(046)361-4351 MSJA#8312

--==<< V >>==--

Vacca, Gary (M1)
2203 Creekwood Drive
Murray, KY 42071
(270)978-0818 MICO#3406

Valdez, Diana (M1)
Cra 50 D#62-69
Medellin, Antioquia, COLOMBIA, SA
dianamariavaldezduque@gmail.com
(574)263-2154 MSAN#8915

Valencia, Ana Dolly (M3)
Cll 18 50 C-17
Cali, Colombia, South America
anadollycuartas@hotmail.com
( )513-7754 MSCA#8200

Valencia, Jorge (M1)
Aereo 4290
Cali, COLOMBIA, SA
( )332-5840 MSCA#8200

Valencia, Nulbel (M1)
Diag 11D Casa 11 urbGemelas
Dosquebradas
Risaralda, COLOMBIA, SA
(576)330-7704 MSAN#8900

Van Meter, Bill (M1)
10626 Highway 41
Charleston, AR 72933
revbill46@gmail.com
(479)965-2998 GRAR#1402

Vance, Dennis (M1)
22 Burnette Chapel Road
Sedalia, KY 42079
rvdvance@hotmail.com
(731)420-4261 GRWT#9100

Vance, Joe (M1)
1740 N Friendship Road
Paducah, KY 42001
( ) MICO#3400

Vanderlaan, D Kevin (M1)
17246 Highway K
Aurora, MO 65605
pastorkevin2@gmail.com
(217)620-2723 GRMI#5401

Vargas, Guido (M3)
Calle 73N 7B-08
Popayan, Colombia, South America
g_var9@yahoo.com
(315)326-0308 MSCA#8200

Varilla, Lida Patricia Vargas (M1)
Calle 44 94-68 Barrio La America
Medellin, COLOMBIA, SA
lidapavargas@hotmail.com
(301)657-4906 MSEM#8600

Varilla, Adan Manuel (M1)
Calle 48 D E #96A-30
Medellin, COLOMBIA, SA
adanvarilla@hotmail.com
(300)241-1896 MSEM#8600

Varner Villa, Susan (M1)
11299 Herschel Loop
Daphne, AL 36526
smvarner76@yahoo.com
(804)304-4642 GRAR#1100

Vasquez, Alejandro (M1)
Cra 58 #32A-41 Apt 420
Bello, Antioquia, COLOMBIA, SA
almaesda@une.net.co
(574)451-4816 MSAN#8918

MINISTERS CONTINUED

Vaughan, Jimmy (M2)
1607 E 3rd Street
Fordyce, AR 71742
jvaughan103@hotmail.com
(870)818-1512 GRAR#1309

Velez, Gabriel (M1)
CL 8A #16A-26
Dosquebradas
Risaralda, COLOMBIA, SA
(576)330-1168 MSAN#8900

Velez, Gloria Patricia (M1)
Cra 4 bis #10-51
LaVirginia, Risaralda
COLOMBIA, SA
renewilgen@hotmail.com
(576)385-4517 MSAN#8900

Ventura, Juan (M3)
El Carmelo
i.p.c.divinoredentor@hotmail.es
(321)623-7234 MSCA#8200

Vertrees, Matthew (M3)
442 Herbert Carman Lane
Vine Grove, KY 40175
familylegacy2003@yahoo.com
(270)734-2378 MICU#3100

Viafara, Jesus David (M3)
Cra 26 J 98 13
Cali, Colombia, South America
viafarajdv@gmail.com
(312)203-9074 MSCA#8200

Vick, Joe (M1)
6064 Old Hickory Boulevard
Whites Creek, TN 37189
joervick@gmail.com
(615)519-5249 TNNA#7300

Vickers, Fran (M1)
7225 Old Clinton Pike
Knoxville, TN 37921
franv3@comcast.net
(865)859-0805 SEET#2301

Vowell, Boman (M3)
773 Heather Terrace
Yukon, OK 73099
bowman.s.vowell@gmail.com
(580)309-1563 MSRR#6302

--==<< W >>==--

Wada, Ichiro (M3)
Tokyo Christian University
3-301-5 Uchino Inzai-shi, Chiba
270-1347 JAPAN
ichirowada@gmail.com
(047)646-1141 MSJA#8300

Wagner, Hugh (M1)
12556 Timberline Drive
Garfield, AR 72732
hughawagner@gmail.com
(479)359-0021 MSRR#8400

Walker, Hobert (M1)
PO Box 66
Rutherford, TN 38369
rutherfordcpchurch@gmail.com
(731)665-7236 GRWT#9429

Walker, Michael C (M1)
177 Washington Avenue
Camden, TN 38320
mworator@gmail.com
(423)438-5650 GRWT#9100

Walsh, Devin (M3)
801 East "M" Street
Russellville, AR 72801
(479)890-6716 GRAR#1100

Wan, Sonny (M1)
13 Wexford Place
Aladema, CA 94502
sonny.wan@gmail.com
(510)847-2069 MSDC#8700

Ward, Andrew (M1)
407 Rose Hill Court
Goodlettsville, TN 37072
andrewbward@aol.com
(615)456-9136 TNNA#7300

Ward, Frank (M1)
46 Henderson Cove
Atoka, TN 38004
fdward68@gmail.com
(901)268-6067 GRWT#9100

Warren, Christopher (M1)
906 Prince Lane
Murfreesboro, TN 37129
chris@murfreesborocpc.org
(615)828-8719 TNMU#7232

Warren, Elizabeth (M3)
811 W Wall Street
Morrilton, AR 72110
(501)354-4139 GRAR#1100

Warren, Gordon (M1)
811 Wall Street
Morrilton, AR 72110
jogordonwarren@suddenlink.net
(501)208-1120 GRAR#1219

Warren, Jo (M1)
811 Wall Street
Morrilton, AR 72110
pastorjo47@ymail.com
(501)354-4139 GRAR#1211

Warren, Joy (M1)
906 Prince Lane
Murfreesboro, TN 37129
revjoywarren@gmail.com
(615)828-0407 TNMU#7232

Warren, William (M1)
7139 Toro Cove
Germantown, TN 38138
cpcgww@aol.com
(901)755-8058 GRWT#9100

Washburn, Gloria (M1)
PO Box 1000
Mountain Home, AR 72654
grwashburn07@gmail.com
(870)321-3539 GRAR#1100

Watkins, Robert B (M1)
5405 Kacena Avenue
Marion, IA 52302
watkr@mac.com
(319)431-0990 MINC#5200

Watson, April (M1)
529 W Bellville
Marion, KY 42064
aprilwatson@hotmail.com
(270)965-2850 MICO#3411

Watson, Dale (M1)
1705 Lawnville Road
Kingston, TN 37763
revdwatson@comcast.net
(865)376-2192 SEET#2317

Watson, Johnny E (M1)
7 Hickory Lane
Metropolis, IL 62960
jewatson01@gmail.com
(731)414-3065 GRWT#9100

Watson, Jonathan (M1)
4017 Claude Drive
Smyrna, TN 37167
watsonjonathan@bellsouth.net
(615)630-9153 TNMU#7239

Watson, Micah (M1)
2529 Middle Tennessee Boulevard
Murfreesboro, TN 37130
mwatson4289@gmail.com
(615)692-2742 TNMU#7200

Watt, Eva (M3)
258 Carlos D'Assumpcao
Ed Kin Heng Long 4 Andar LMN
MACAU
eva6e@hotmail.com
(853)2892-1702 MSHK#8804

Watts, Glenn David (M2)
629 High Street
Union City, TN 38261
hongkongbrother@hotmail.com
(502)797-5685 MICU#3100

Wayman, Sam (M1)
707 High Hill Creek Road
LaGrange, TX 78945
samndonnawayman@gmail.com
(979)968-3734 MSTR#8100

Weaver, Dennis (M1)
2589 Magness Road
Benton, KY 42025
dsweaver@memphisseminary.edu
(731)592-9054 MICO#3400

Webb, Lonnie, Sr (M1)
618 N E Street
Duncan, OK 73601
lgwebb.sr@gmail.com
(580)786-8840 MSRR#8400

Webb, William G (M1)
7926 S 78th E Avenue
Tulsa, OK 74133
(918)294-9117 MSRR#8400

Welch, Johnie (M1)
PO Box 1506
Dyersburg, TN 38025
johnniewelch@msn.com
(731)287-9008 GRWT#9100

Weldon, Mark (M1)
2606 Acton Road
Birmingham, AL 35243
weldonm5@gmail.com
(205)913-3033 SEGR#0100

West, David (M1)
2027 Lucille Street
Lebanon, TN 37087
drdavidlwest@aol.com
(615)427-8371 TNNA#7319

West, Earl (M1)
246 Maple Avenue
Greensburg, KY 42743
west5010@windstream.net
(207)932-5010 MICU#3116

West, Fred E, Jr (M1)
510 Cedaredge Drive
New Smyrna, FL 32168
jwest616@earthlink.net
(206)409-8321 SEET#2200

MINISTERS CONTINUED

Westbrook, James   (M1)
1717 Wedgewood Drive
Union City, TN 38261
westbrook731@bellsouth.net
(731)884-0918   GRWT#9100

Westfall, Justin   (M2)
1605 Wickham Drive
Burleson, TX 76028
westfall0@gmail.com
(832)628-7094   MSRR#8400

Weston, Robert E   (M1)
9526 Antoine Forest Drive
San Antonio, TX 78254
rjaweston@gmail.com
(210)347-0232   MSTR#8100

Whaley, Greg   (M2)
4970 Comstock Road
Chapel Hill, TN 37034
grewha@mail.com
(931)364-7637   TNMU#7202

Wheeler, Nathan   (M1)
2084 Linden Avenue
Memphis, TN 38104
nwheeler@cumberland.org
(901)606-9535   GRWT#9100

Whitaker, Perry Eugene   (M1)
1133 Forest Plaza Circle
Hixson, TN 37343
brotherperry@msn.com
(615)691-2933   TNGA#2111

White, Diann   (M1)
9394 Alex Dickson Cove
Bartlett, TN 38133
diannwhite12@yahoo.com
(901)377-7776   GRWT#9110

White, Mack   (M2)
408 W Main Street
Smithville, TN 37166
gnax408@yahoo.com
(615)318-9863   TNMU#7200

Whitworth, Gary W   (M1)
1706 Old Hickory Boulevard
Brentwood, TN 37027
(615)915-4180   TNNA#7300

Whray, Richard "Rocky"   (M1)
201 8th Avenue SE
Winchester, TN 37398
rocklex1017@att.net
(931)636-4844   TNMU#7228

Wieland, Jack G Jr   (M1)
104 N Orchid
Skidmore, MO 64487
jgwieland@hotmail.com
(217)823-4331   MICO#3400

Wiggins, Joe   (M1)
2734 US Highway 41A S
Eagleville, TN 37060
jwigginz@aol.com
(615)274-2011   TNCO#7109

Wilkerson, Patrick   (M1)
903 Park Crest Court
Mount Juliet, TN 37122
patrickwilkerson3@gmail.com
(865)236-7737   SEET#2301

Wilkinson, Michael   (M1)
1174 Tanglewood Street
Memphis, TN 38114
pastormike@kfcpc.comcastbiz.net
(205)533-2001   SEET#2305

Wilkinson, Neal   (M1)
296 Sunset Drive
Lebanon, MO 65536
nwilkinson@whiteoakpond.org
(615)934-7382   GRMI#4315

Williams, Cory   (M1)
585 Tater Hill Road
Newbern, TN 38059
coromis@hotmail.com
(901)486-5981   GRWT#9410

Williams, Dale   (M1)
3156 State Route 2837
Clay, KY 42404
dalewilliams@roadrunner.com
(270)664-2044   MICO#3618

Williams, David J   (M1)
20 Acorn Drive
Harrisburg, IL 629463790
(618)252-1851   MICO#3400

Williamson, Dave   (M1)
PO Box 67
Dolph, AR 72528
(870)499-7448   GRAR#1513

Willis, Danny   (M3)
3328 E 6th Street
Owensboro, KY 42303
dwillis.cpc@gmail.com
(270)993-0882   MICU#3100

Wills, Brent   (M1)
4607 E Richmond Shop Road
Lebanon, TN 37090
bwills9185@yahoo.com
(615)449-3258   TNMU#7218

Wills, Robin   (M3)
4607 E Richmond Shop Road
Lebanon, TN 37090
robinrush24@aol.com
(615-870-4773)   TNMU#7200

Wilson, Brenda   (M1)
35 Collins Drive
Elizabethtown, KY 42701
susieq2007@windstream.net
(270)249-3835   MICU#3100

Wilson, Craig   (M1)
777 Stateline Road East
Southaven, MS 38671
craigwilson2300@yahoo.com
(901)277-4066   GRWT#9306

Wilson, Don   (M1)
7300 Calle Montana NE
Albuquerque, NM 87113
don-wilson07@comcast.net
(505)823-2594   MSDC#8700

Wilson, Kevin   (M1)
2225 North East Road SE
Cleveland, TN 37311
revkev1000@hotmail.com
(423)284-6397   SETG#2112

Wilson, Thomas   (M1)
4543 Lake Vista
Memphis, TN 38128
tomjw217@gmail.com
(901)382-6190   GRWT#9100

Wing So, Patrick Tat   (M1)
2/F Fu Tung Shopping Centre
Tung Chung
Lantau Island, HONG KONG
cpctwso@yahoo.com.hk
(522)109-1738   MSHK#8810

Winn, Don   (M1)
375 Cumberland Mountain Circle
Sunbright, TN 37872
dwinn_ky@yahoo.com
(615)478-9910   SEET#2304

Womack, Carey   (M1)
114 Doris Street
Camden, TN 38320
camdencppastor@bellsouth.net
(731)220-3900   GRWT#9105

Wong, Bruce   (M1)
716 Duncanville Court
Campbell, CA 95008
revbwong@gmail.com
(408)628-1723   MSDC#8700

Wong, Samson   (M2)
CPC Yao Dao Primary School
Tin Yuet Estate
Tin Shui Wai, NT, HONG KONG
wongchishui@yahoo.com.hk
(852)2617-7872   MSHK#8811

Wong, So Li   (M1)
2/F Fu Tung Shopping Centre
Tung Chung, Lantau Island
HONG KONG
soliwong@gmail.com
(852)2109-1738   MSHK#8800

Wood, Gina   (M3)
10919 Gillian Lane
Farragut, TN 37934
ginawood02@gmail.com
(865)679-4332   SEET#2200

Wood, Kevin L   (M1)
339 David Street
McKenzie, TN 38201
revkevbuford1972@gmail.com
(865)228-0710   GRWT#9100

Wood, Wayne   (M1)
HC 61 Box 600
Calico Rock, AR 72519
bexarwood@centurytel.net
(870)297-2205   GRAR#1100

Wright, B J   (M1)
301 25th Street
Phenix City, AL 36867
bojobo3@yahoo.com
(334)298-2896

--==<< X >>==--

--==<< Y >>==--

Yang, Buhwan   (M1)
33 Rockingham Way
Manchester, NJ 08759
yangmoksa@gmail.com
(732)456-2203   SECE#2131

Yano, Fumitsuta   (M1)
424-4 Kamide, Fjinomiya-shi
Shuizuika-ken   JAPAN
(054)454-0313   MSJA#8300

Yarce, Omar   (M1)
3015 N Ocean Blvd Apt 6K
Fort Lauderdale, FL 33308
yarces@yahoo.com
(305)798-0849   SEGR#0100

Yarce, Virginia   (M2)
3015 N Ocean Blvd Apt 6K
Fort Lauderdale, FL 33308
ginnyyarce@gmail.com
(954)213-9064   SEGR#0100

MINISTERS CONTINUED

Yates, Scott (M1)
1632 Lindsey Drive
Columbia, TN 38401
revscottdyates@outlook.com
(615)274-3000 TNCO#7141

Yeung, William Kin Keung (M1)
28 Hong Yip Street
Yuen Long, HONG KONG
william@yuonlongchurch.org
(852)2639-9176 MSHK#8809

Yohena, Takeshi (M3)
7-7-44 Ryokuen Izumi-ku
Yokohama-shi
245-0002 JAPAN
tyohena@uc.catv-yokohama.ne.jp
(045)814-4537 MSJA#8300

York, Danny (M1)
5420 State Route 902
Fredonia, KY 42411
nonnieyork@yahoo.com
(270)350-7262 MICO#3413

Youn, Daniel (M1)
6524 Summer Avenue
Memphis, TN 38134
usyoun61@hotmail.com
(901)381-4790 GRWT#9436

Young, Emily Trapp (M1)
1925 Allsboro Road
Cherokee, AL 35616
ectrapp44@gmail.com
(901)674-2342 GRWT#9305

Young, Lacey Grace (M3)
1211 Michael Drive
Alabaster, AL 35007
laceygrace1918@gmail.com
( ) SERD#0800

Young, Ryan (M2)
1925 Allsboro Road
Cherokee, AL 35616
dennis.ryan.ytoung@gmail.com
( ) TNMU#7200

Young, Taylor (M1)
903 W Old Hickory Boulevard
Madison, TN 37115
taylor@clarksvillecpc.com
(615)30-3344 TNNA#7304

Young, Timothy (M1)
8064 Hummingbird Lane
San Diego, CA 92123
tdy223@gmail.com
(415)350-8201 MSDC#8700

Youngman, Betty (M1)
1471 Creekview Court
Fort Worth, TX 76112
bettyy@swbell.net
(817)492-4100 MSRR#8400

Yu, Alexis (M1)
1761 Willow Way
San Bruno, CA 94066
alexis.yu.k@gmail.com
(415)421-1624 MSDC#8501

Yu, Carver Tat Sum (M1)
2/F Welland Plaza
188 Nam Cheong Street
Sham Shui Po, Kowloon, HONG KONG
ydgrowth@gmail.com
(852)2794-2382 MSHK#8800

Yu, Enoch Jaehyung (M1)
2012 Shenley Park Lane
Duluth, GA 30097
jaeyu117@yahoo.com
(678)600-2787 MSKP#2125

Yu, Grace Siu Tim (M1)
2/F Welland Plaza
188 Nam Cheong Street
Sham Shui Po, Kowloon, HONG KONG
yuleungsiutim@netvigator.com
(852)2783-8923 MSHK#8800

Yu, Pyong San (Sonny) (M1)
139 Silverado Drive
Santa Teresa, NM 88008
pyongsanyu@hotmail.com
(915)329-3451 MSDC#8700

Yu, Wn-yong (M1)
325-1 DongHyen-Dong
Jecheon-city, Choongbuk, KOREA
lifeyu@hanmail.net
(043)652-0540 MMT

Yuen, Amos Pui Chung (M1)
2/F Welland Plaza
188 Nam Cheong Street
Sham Shui Po, Kowloon, HONG KONG
revyuen@taohsien.org.hk
(852)2783-8923 MSHK#8806

Yuen, Susanna (M2)
28 Hong Yip Street
28 Hong Yip Street
Yuen Long, NT, HONG KONG
susanna@yuenlongcpc.org
(522)639-9176 MSHK#8800

Yung, Karen (M2)
Flat D, 2/F
338-340 Castle Peak Road
Kowloon, HONG KONG
(852)2386-6563 MSHK#8800

--==<< Z >>==--

Zahrte, Rebecca (M1)
1550 Anton Road
Madisonnville, TN 42431
rebecca.zahrte@gmail.com
(270)978-3328 MICO#3400

Zumbrunnen, Craig (M1)
1970 W Old Magee Trail Apt 14105
Tucson, AZ 85704
craigzum1@yahoo.com
(580)471-0308 MSRR#8400

ALPHABETICAL INDEX OF CHURCHES

The four letter abbreviation indicates the synod and presbytery of which the congregation
is a member. The four digit number indicates the church number.
(See pages 10-12 for abbreviations of presbyteries.)

316 Fellowship
   CO Englewood.................MSDC#8710

--==<<A>>==--

ACTS Korean
   TN Memphis ....GRWT#9436
Alabaster
   AL Alabaster .... SERD#0107
Algood
   TN Algood........................TNMU#7201
Allsboro
   AL Cherokee ....SEHO#0501
Antioch
   AL Reform ....SEGR#0701
   KY Knob Lick...................MICU#3101
   LA Quitman ....MSTR#8101
Antioch Union
   TN Union City ....GRWT#9401
Appleton
   AR Atkins.......................GRAR#1202
Arkansas Loving
   AR Little Rock ....GRAR#2135
Arlington
   TN Erin ....TNNA#7311
Armenia
   CO Quindio......................MSAN#8903
Asahi Mission
   JA 241-0021 ....MSJA#8315
Ash Hill
   TN Spring Hill ....TNCO#7101
Atwood
   TN Atwood......................GRWT#9101
Auburn
   KY Auburn ....MICU#3301

--==<<B>>==--

Bald Knob
   KY Russellville ....MICU#3302
Baldwin Chapel
   AL Cullman......................SEHO#0202
Banks
   TN Smithville...................TNMU#7202
Barren Fork
   AR Mount Pleasant .... GRAR#1501
Bartow
   GA Rydal...........................SETG#2101
Bates Hill
   TN McMinnville ....TNMU#7203
Bayou de Chien
   KY Water Valley .... MICO#3401
Beaver Creek
   TN Knoxville ....SEET#2301
Beech
   TN Hendersonville........... TNNA#7301
   TN Union City ....GRWT#9402
Beech Grove
   TN Beechgrove ....TNMU#7204
Beersheba
   MS Columbus .... SEGR#0702
Belleview
   TN Franklin......................TNCO#7104
Bells Chapel
   TN Dyer ....GRWT#9403

Belvidere
   TN Belvidere....................TNMU#7205
Ben Lomond
   AR Ben Lomond .... GRAR#1301
Benton
   KY Benton ....MICO#3403
Bertram
   TX Bertram ....MSTR#8605
Betania Mission
   CO Cali ....MSCA#8204
Bethany
   IL Bethany.......................MINC#5401
Bethel
   CO Cali ....MSCA#8205
   KY Center ....MICU#3102
   KY Kevil ....MICO#3404
   MO Wentworth ....GRMI#4102
   TN Atoka.........................GRWT#9301
   TN Clarksville.................. TNNA#7302
Bethel #1
   KY Harrodsburg.................MICU#3103
Bethesda
   AR Camden ....GRAR#1302
   TN Fall Branch...................SEET#2201
   TN Friendship ....GRWT#9404
Beulah
   KY Hartford ....MICU#3501
Big Cove
   AL Brownsboro................. SERD#0801
Blues Hill
   TN McMinnville ....TNMU#7207
Boiling Springs
   TN Portland......................MICU#3303
Bolivar
   TN Bolivar ....GRWT#9202
Booneville
   AR Booneville.................. GRAR#1401
Boonshill
   TN Boonshill....................TNCO#7106
Bowling Green
   KY Bowling Green ....MICU#3304
Bradford
   TN Bradford....................GRWT#9104
Branchville
   AL Odenville.................... SEGR#0106
Brenthaven
   TN Brentwood.................. TNNA#7331
Bridgeport 1st
   PA Bridgeport...................MICU#3131
Brier Creek
   KY Bremen ....MICU#3503
Brunswick
   TN Brunswick ....GRWT#9302
Brush Hill
   TN Nashville..................... TNNA#7325
Burns Flat
   OK Burns Flat..................MSRR#6301
Burnt Prairie
   IL Burnt Prairie ....MINC#5102
Byron
   AR Calico Rock ....GRAR#1508

--==<<C>>==--

Cairo
   MS Cedarbluff................... SEGR#0704
Caleb Mission
   CO Montebello.................MSCA#8223
Calico Rock
   AR Calico Rock ....GRAR#1503
Calvary
   KY Mayfield ....MICO#3405
Camden
   AR Camden......................GRAR#1303
   TN Camden ....GRWT#9105
Camp Ground
   AR Hampton ....GRAR#1101
   IL Anna ....MICO#5103
   TN Decaturville.................GRWT#9204
   TN Erin ....TNNA#7312
Campbellsville
   KY Campbellsville.............MICU#3104
Campground
   IL Greenville ....MINC#5402
Cane Ridge
   TN Cane Ridge .... TNNA#7326
Caneyville
   KY Caneyville...................MICU#3201
Cartago
   CO Valle...........................MSAN#8906
Casa De Fe
   MA Malden ....SEET#2220
Casey
   IL Casey ....MINC#5201
Casey's Fork
   KY Marrowbone ....MICU#3105
Caulksville
   AR Ratcliff .... GRAR#1402
Cedar Flat
   KY Edmonton ....MICU#3106
Cedar Hill
   TN Greeneville..................SEET#2202
Cedar Springs
   TN Whitwell ....SETG#2119
Central
   CO Cali .... MSCA#8208
Champ
   TN Mulberry ....TNCO#7108
Chandler
   IN Chandler......................MICO#5302
Chapel Hill
   TN Chapel Hill..................TNCO#7109
Charleston
   TN Cleveland ....SETG#2102
Charlotte
   TN Charlotte .... TNNA#7303
Chattanooga 1st
   TN Chattanooga ....SETG#2104
Cheung Chau
   HO Cheung Chau.............MSHK#8801
Chinese
   CA San Francisco.............MSDC#8501
Christ
   FL Lutz.............................SEGR#0303
Christ Church
   AL Huntsville....................SERD#0814

ALPHABETICAL INDEX OF CHURCHES CONTINUED

Clark's Grove
  TN Maryville.....................SEET#2302
Clarksville
  TN Clarksville................... TNNA#7304
Claybrook
  TN Jackson.......................GRWT#9205
Clear Point
  KY Horse Cave .... MICU#3107
Cleveland
  TN Cleveland....................SETG#2108
Clifton Mills
  KY Irvington .... MICU#3202
Clinton
  OK Clinton....................... MSRR#6302
Cloyd's
  TN Mt Juliet....................TNMU#7208
Coal Creek
  OK Coalgate..................... MSCH#6102
Coker
  AL Coker........................... SEGR#0705
Colonial
  TN Memphis ....GRWT#9305
Columbia 1st
  TN Columbia....................TNCO#7110
Columbus
  MS Columbus .... SEGR#0706
Comeback
  NJ Wallington ....SECE#2446
Commerce
  TN Watertown..................TNMU#7209
Concord
  AL New Market .... SERD#0802
  TN Trenton........................GRWT#9106
  TN Waverly .... TNNA#7306
  TX Troup...........................MSTR#8104
Cookeville 1st
  TN Cookeville..................TNMU#7210
Cool Springs CC
  TN Lavinia.......................GRWT#9107
Cool Springs GC
  TN Trimble.......................GRWT#9408
Cornerstone Community
  TN Chattanooga ....SETG#2107
Corntassel
  TN Madisonville ....SEET#2304
Covenant
  OK Ada .... MSRR#6304
Cowan
  TN Cowan ....TNMU#7211
Coyle
  KY Hudson .... MICU#3203
Crestline
  AL Birmingham .... SEGR#0102
Cristo Salva
  TN Memphis ....GRWT#9196
Cristo Vive
  TN Madison .... TNNA#7314
Crossroads
  AR Little Rock ....GRAR#1102
Cumberland Chapel
  IL Fairfield ....MINC#5104
Cumberland Valley
  TN McEwen...................... TNNA#7307

--==<<D>>==--

Daingerfield
  TX Daingerfield ....MSTR#8106
Davidson Chapel
  TN Trenton........................GRWT#9108
Den-en Mission
  JA 228-0818 .... MSJA#8310

Denton
  TX Denton......................... MSRR#8404
Desert Gardens
  AZ Tucson......................... MSDC#8705
Dibrell
  TN McMinnville ....TNMU#7212
Dickson
  TN Dickson .... TNNA#7308
Dilworth
  AR Horatio .... GRAR#1304
Divino Redentor
  CO Buenaventura.............. MSCA#8206
Donelson
  TN Nashville .... TNNA#7327
Dosquebradas
  CO Risaralda.....................MSAN#8907
Double Springs
  TN Humboldt ....GRWT#9109
Dover
  AR Dover .... GRAR#1203
  TN Morristown ....SEET#2203
Dresden
  TN Dresden ....GRWT#9110
Dry Fork
  TN Bethpage .... TNNA#7309
Dry Valley
  TN Cookeville..................TNMU#7213
Dukes
  KY Hawesville................... MICU#3204
Dyer
  TN Dyer ....GRWT#9409
Dyersburg 1st
  TN Dyersburg ....GRWT#9410

--==<<E>>==--

E T Allen
  AR Ashdown .... GRAR#1307
East Point
  AL Cullman....................... SERD#0206
Eastlake
  OK Oklahoma City .... MSRR#6205
Ebenezer
  IL Chicago...........................MINC#5203
  IL Thompsonville...............MICO#5105
  TN Mason ....GRWT#9303
  TN Mercer.........................GRWT#9206
  TN Whitwell ....SETG#2110
Ebenezer Hall
  IL Buncombe......................MICO#5106
Ebina Shion No Oka
  JA 243-0422 .... MSJA#8311
Edgefield
  AL Stevenson .... SERD#0813
El Camino
  FL Miami .... SEGR#0310
El Rebano
  CO Antioquia ....MSEM#8905
El Redil
  GA Lawrenceville ....SETG#2149
Elk Creek
  MO West Plains .... GRMI#4304
Elm River
  IL Cisne.............................MINC#5107
Elmira Chapel
  TX Longview ....MSTR#8111
Elora
  TN Elora...........................TNCO#7111
Emaus
  CO Buenaventura.............. MSCA#8219
Enon
  MS Ackerman .... SEGR#0707

Ephesus
  KY Harned .... MICU#3205
Erin
  MS Union........................... SEGR#0601

--==<<F>>==--

Fairfield
  IL Fairfield ....MINC#5108
Fairview
  KY Bremen .... MICU#3504
  TN Afton ....SEET#2204
Faith
  AL Cullman....................... SEHO#0213
  MI St Clair Shores ....MINC#5501
  OK Tulsa .... MSRR#6201
  TN Bartlett ....GRWT#9308
Faith Fellowship
  TN Columbia.....................TNCO#7146
  TN Lenoir City....................SEET#2319
Faith-Hopewell
  AR Batesville .... GRAR#1502
Falling Water
  TN Hixson.........................SETG#2111
Falls Chapel
  AR Lockesburg .... GRAR#1308
Fayetteville
  TN Fayetteville ....TNCO#7112
Fellowship
  AR Camden....................... GRAR#1309
  AR Mountain Home.......... GRAR#1505
Fiducia
  TN Prospect.......................TNCO#7113
Filipos
  CO Cali .... MSCA#8211
First Hispanic
  FL Tampa .... SEGR#0307
Flat Lick
  KY Herndon .... MICO#3606
Flint Springs
  TN Cleveland....................SETG#2112
Flintville
  TN Flintville......................TNCO#7115
Florence 1st
  AL Florence....................... SEHO#0506
Fomby
  AR Ashdown .... GRAR#1310
Fort Smith
  AR Fort Smith .... GRAR#1406
Franklin
  TN Franklin.......................TNCO#7116
Fredonia
  KY Fredonia...................... MICO#3608
Freeport
  TX Freeport.......................MSTR#8103
Freedom
  KY Harned .... MICU#3207
Fullerton
  IL Farmer City ....MINC#5404
Fulton
  TN South Fulton...............GRWT#9412

--==<<G>>==--

Gadsden
  AL Gadsden....................... SEGR#0402
Garfield
  KY Garfield....................... MICU#3208
Gasper River
  KY Auburn........................ MICU#3306
Georgetown
  IL Georgetown ....MINC#5204

ALPHABETICAL INDEX OF CHURCHES CONTINUED

ALPHABETICAL INDEX OF CHURCHES CONTINUED

Liberty
  KY Campbellsville............. MICU#3116
  KY Murray .... MICO#3406
  TN Clarksville................... TNNA#7315
  TN McMinnville .... TNMU#7222
Lick Branch
  KY Glasgow...................... MICU#3117
Lincoln 1st
  IL Lincoln .... MINC#5405
Lisman
  KY Clay .... MICO#3613
Little Muddy
  KY Morgantown .... MICU#3310
Livingston 1st
  TN Livingston .... TNMU#7223
Lockesburg
  AR Lockesburg .... GRAR#1311
Lone Star
  OK Coalgate..................... MSCH#6105
Longview 1st
  TX Longview .... MSTR#8112
Loudon
  TN Loudon......................... SEET#2307
Louisville 1st
  KY Louisville.................... MICU#3212
Louisville Japanese
  KY Pewee Valley .... MICU#3223
Lubbock
  TX Lubbock .... MSDC#8702
LuzD.L.Naciones
  TN McMinnville .... TNMU#7252

--==<<M>>==--

Macau
  MA Andar LMN................ MSHK#8804
Macedonia
  KY Dalton .... MICO#3614
Madison 1st
  TN Madison .... TNNA#7329
Madisonville
  KY Madisonville............... MICO#3615
Magnolia
  KY Magnolia...................... MICU#3214
Manchester
  TN Manchester.................. TNMU#7224
Manizales
  CO Caldas .... MSAN#8914
Mansfield
  MO Mansfield .... GRMI#4308
Maple Springs
  TN Beech Bluff .... GRWT#9210
Maranatha
  CO Guapi .... MSCA#8220
  TX San Elizario................. MSDC#8706
Mariah
  TN Waverly....................... TNNA#7317
Marietta
  AR Charleston................... GRAR#1408
  TN Knoxville .... SEET#2308
Marion 1st
  KY Marion .... MICO#3616
Marlow
  OK Marlow .... MSRR#6305
Mars Hill
  AR Pottsville .... GRAR#1211
Marshall
  MO Marshall..................... GRMI#4210
  TX Marshall .... MSTR#8115
Martin
  TN Martin .... GRWT#9117

Maryville 1st
  TN Maryville...................... SEET#2309
Mason Hall
  TN Kenton......................... GRWT#9415
Mata de Sao Joao
  BR Bahia........................... MSJA#8313
Maud
  AL Cherokee .... SEHO#0509
McAdoo
  TN Clarksville................... TNNA#7318
McCains
  TN Columbia...................... TNCO#7126
McGee Chapel
  OK Broken Bow .... MSCH#6106
McKenzie
  TN McKenzie..................... GRWT#9118
McLeod Chapel
  MS Macon.......................... SEGR#0708
McMinnville
  TN McMinnville .... TNMU#7225
Medina
  TN Medina .... GRWT#9119
Megumi
  JA 207-0023 .... MSJA#8309
Mercy
  TN Lenoir City.................. SEET#2320
Meridian
  TN Greenfield .... GRWT#9120
Meridianville
  AL Meridianville............... SERD#0808
Mesquite
  TX Mesquite .... MSRR#8412
Milan
  TN Milan........................... GRWT#9121
Milburn Chapel
  KY West Paducah............... MICO#3416
Mill Creek
  TN Puryear........................ GRWT#9122
Mohawk
  TN Mohawk........................ SEET#2208
Monroe Chapel
  KY Hardyville.................... MICU#3119
Monroe City
  IN Monroe City................. MINC#5307
Monteagle
  TN Monteagle .... TNMU#7227
Morella
  TN Kenton......................... GRWT#9416
Morgantown
  KY Morgantown .... MICU#3311
Morning Sun
  TN Cordova....................... GRWT#9314
Morningside
  IN Evansville .... MINC#5304
Mt Ararat
  TN Union City .... GRWT#9417
Mt Carmel
  AR London......................... GRAR#1212
  KY White Plains .... MICO#3617
  TN Franklin....................... TNCO#7127
  TN Huntland .... TNMU#7228
  TN Oliver Springs............. SEET#2310
  TN Somerville................... GRWT#9315
Mt Denson
  TN Springfield.................... TNNA#7319
Mt Gilead
  IL Greenville .... MINC#5406
Mt Hester
  AL Cherokee .... SEHO#0510
Mt Hope
  TX Joinerville .... MSTR#8117

Mt Joy
  TN Mount Pleasant .... TNCO#7129
Mt Lebanon
  TN Spring Hill .... TNCO#7130
Mt Liberty
  TN Charlotte .... TNNA#7320
Mt Moriah
  KY Summer Shade............. MICU#3120
  TN Pulaski......................... TNCO#7131
Mt Nebo
  TN Iron City...................... TNCO#7132
Mt Olive
  AR Melbourne................... GRAR#1517
  KY Big Clifty.................... MICU#3216
  TN Dyer............................ GRWT#9418
Mt Olivet
  IN Washington .... MINC#5308
  KY Bowling Green .... MICU#3312
Mt Pleasant
  AL Muscle Shoals .... SEHO#0511
  KY Caneyville................... MICU#3217
  KY Sullivan...................... MICO#3618
  TN Afton .... SEET#2209
  TN Mount Pleasant .... TNCO#7133
Mt Sharon
  TN Greenbrier................... TNNA#7321
Mt Sinai
  TN Nashville .... TNNA#7330
Mt Sterling
  IL Brookport .... MICO#5117
Mt Tabor
  TN Murfreesboro .... TNMU#7230
Mt Vernon
  KY Leitchfield.................. MICU#3218
  TN Ramer.......................... GRWT#9213
  TN Rockvale..................... TNMU#7231
Mt View
  TN Dover .... TNNA#7322
Mt Zion
  IL Dongola .... MICO#5118
  MS Columbus .... SEGR#0709
  MS Falkner........................ GRWT#9214
  TX Greenville .... MSRR#8414
Mu Min
  HO Landau Island............. MSHK#8810
Murfreesboro
  TN Murfreesboro .... TNMU#7232

--==<<N>>==--

Naruse
  JA 194-0041 .... MSJA#8305
Neal's Chapel
  KY Glasgow...................... MICU#3122
Nebo
  AL Lexington .... SEHO#0512
Needham
  KY Eastview .... MICU#3219
New Beginning
  TN Memphis .... GRWT#9306
New Bethel
  TN Columbia...................... TNCO#7134
  TN Greeneville.................. SEET#2210
  TN Selmer......................... GRWT#9215
New Bethlehem
  TN Newbern...................... GRWT#9420
New Ebenezer
  TN Troy............................ GRWT#9422
New Hope
  AL Birmingham .... SEGR#0104
  AR Batesville .... GRAR#1510
  IL Yale............................. MINC#5208

ALPHABETICAL INDEX OF CHURCHES CONTINUED

ALPHABETICAL INDEX OF CHURCHES CONTINUED

Russellville
  AR Russellville .... GRAR#1216
Ruth Chapel
  TN Livingston .... TNMU#7241
Rutherford
  TN Rutherford .... GRWT#9429

--==<<S>>==--

Sacramento
  KY Sacramento .... MICU#3512
Sagamino
  JA 228-0004 .... MSJA#8304
Salem
  AR Salem .... GRAR#1514
  KY Greensburg .... MICU#3127
  MS Walnut Grove .... SEGR#0607
  MO Warrensburg .... GRMI#4216
  TN Gadsden .... GRWT#9430
  TN Greeneville .... SEET#2216
Samaria
  CO Cali .... MSCA#8217
San Lucas
  CO Palmira .... MSCA#8215
San Marcos
  CO Cali .... MSCA#8218
San Pablo
  CO Guacari .... MSCA#8212
Sandy Springs
  TX Whitesboro .... MSRR#8420
Santa Fe
  TN Santa Fe .... TNCO#7138
Savannah 1st
  TN Savannah .... GRWT#9224
Scottsboro
  AL Scottsboro .... SERD#0809
Searcy
  AR Searcy .... GRAR#1218
Selmer Court Avenue
  TN Selmer .... GRWT#9225
Senda de Libertad
  CO South America .... MSAN#8919
Seven Springs
  KY Center .... MICU#3128
Sewanee
  TN Sewanee .... TNMU#7242
Seymour
  MO Seymour .... GRMI#4313
Sharing
  NY College Point .... SECE#2141
Sharon
  TN Sharon .... GRWT#9130
Shatin
  HO Shatin NT .... MSHK#8807
Shaver
  AR Paris .... GRAR#1413
Shawnee Mound
  MO Chilhowee .... GRMI#4111
Shell Chapel
  AR Pine Bluff .... GRAR#1108
Shepherd/Hills
  TX Austin .... MSTR#8604
Sherwood
  AR Sherwood .... GRAR#1220
Shibusawa
  JA 259-1321 .... MSJA#8307
Shiloh
  IL Virginia .... MINC#5409
  KY Campbellsville .... MICU#3129
  MS Corinth .... GRWT#9226
  TN Greeneville .... SEET#2217

TN McKenzie .... GRWT#9131
TN Palmyra .... TNNA#7338
TX Clarksville .... MSTR#8125
TX Midlothian .... MSRR#8421
Shinar
  IA New London .... MINC#5410
Short Creek
  KY Falls of Rough .... MICU#3221
Sidney
  AR Batesville .... GRAR#1515
Silverdale
  TN Chattanooga .... SETG#2106
Smithville
  TN Smithville .... TNMU#7243
South Pittsburg
  TN South Pittsburg .... SETG#2123
Spring Creek
  AL Montevallo .... SEGR#0113
  MO Dunnegan .... GRMI#4113
Spring Hill
  IL Beecher City .... MINC#5411
Springfield
  AL Rogersville .... SEHO#0515
Springfield 1st
  MO Springfield .... GRMI#4314
St Andrew
  TX Odessa .... MSDC#8703
St John
  TX Arlington .... MSRR#8413
St Luke
  TN Madison .... TNNA#7332
  TX Fort Worth .... MSRR#8407
St Mark
  TX Fort Worth .... MSRR#8408
St Timothy
  TX Bedford .... MSRR#8419
Steam Mill
  MS Union .... SEGR#0608
Stevenson
  AL Stevenson .... SERD#0810
Stonegate
  OK Edmond .... MSRR#6307
Stone Oak
  TX San Antonio .... MSTR#8608
Sturgis
  KY Sturgis .... MICO#3625
Sudanese
  TN Gallatin .... TNNA#7341
Sugar Grove
  KY Marion .... MICO#3626
Suggs Creek
  TN Mount Juliet .... TNMU#7244
Sulphur Springs
  AR Louann .... GRAR#1315
Sumach
  GA Chatsworth .... SETG#2124
Sumkim Presby
  KO Seoul .... SEET#2222A
Swan
  TN Centerville .... TNCO#7140

--==<<T>>==--

Talbott
  TN Talbott .... SEET#2218
Tao Hsien
  HO Kowloon .... MSHK#8806
Trezevant
  TN Trezevant .... GRWT#9132
Trimble Camp Ground
  AR Dolph .... GRAR#1504

Trinity
  AR Morrilton .... GRAR#1219
  TX Fort Worth .... MSRR#8409
Trona
  CA Trona .... MSDC#8503
Troy
  TN Troy .... GRWT#9432
Tulua Mission
  CO Tulua .... MSCA#8226
Tusculum
  TN Nashville .... TNNA#7333

--==<<U>>==--

Union
  AL Vance .... SEGR#0114
  TN Knoxville .... SEET#2315
Union Chapel
  IL Galatia .... MICO#5123
Union City
  TN Union City .... GRWT#9433
Union Grove
  TN Columbia .... TNCO#7141
Union Hill
  AL Anderson .... SEHO#0516
  TN Brush Creek .... TNMU#7246
Union North
  IL Fairfield .... MINC#5124
United
  IL Norris City .... MINC#5119
Unity
  KY Hardin .... MICO#3422

--==<<V>>==--

Vaughn's Chapel
  KY Calvert City .... MICO#3423
Village
  IL Norris City .... MICO#5125
Virtue
  TN Knoxville .... SEET#2316

--==<<W>>==--

Walkertown
  TN Afton .... SEET#2222
Walkerville
  AR Magnolia .... GRAR#1317

Walnut Grove
  AL New Hope .... SERD#0811
  AR Magazine .... GRAR#1414
Warrensburg
  MO Warrensburg .... GRMI#4115
Watertown
  TN Watertown .... TNMU#7247
Waverly
  TN Waverly .... TNNA#7339
Waynesboro
  TN Waynesboro .... TNCO#7142
Welti
  AL Cullman .... SEHO#0212
West Nashville
  TN Nashville .... TNNA#7334

West Point
  TN Columbia .... TNCO#7143
West Union
  TN Millington .... GRWT#9321
Westside
  NM Rio Rancho .... MSDC#8709

ALPHABETICAL INDEX OF CHURCHES CONTINUED

Wheatcroft
    KY Wheatcroft .... MICO#3627
White Oak Pond
    MO Lebanon .... GRMI#4315
Whitwell
    TN Whitwell .... SETG#2122
Willoughby
    TN Bulls Gap .... SEET#2219
Willow Creek
    IL Martinsville .... MINC#5211
Winchester 1st
    TN Winchester .... TNMU#7249
Wisdom
    KY Knob Lick .... MICU#3130
Woodlawn
    KY Paducah .... MICO#3417
Woodward's Chapel
    TN Obion .... GRWT#9434

--==<<X>>==--

Xi Lin
    HO Yuen Long .... MSHK#8809

--==<<Y>>==--

Yao Dao
    HO NT .... MSHK#8811
Yorkville
    TN Yorkville .... GRWT#9435
Young's Chapel
    TN Kingston .... SEET#2317

--==<<Z>>==--

Zamora
    CO Antioquia .... MSAN#8918
Zion
    TN McKenzie .... GRWT#9133
Zion Valley
    TX Chico .... MSRR#8425

LOCATION INDEX OF CHURCHES

The four letter abbreviation indicates the synod and presbytery of which the congregation
is a member. The four digit number indicates the church number.
(See pages 10-13 for abbreviations of presbyteries.)

ALABAMA

AL Alabaster
  Alabaster .... SERD#0107
AL Anderson
  Union Hill .... SEHO#0516
AL Bessemer
  Hopewell .... SEGR#0101
  Pleasant Hill .... SEGR#0710
AL Birmingham
  Crestline .... SEGR#0102
  New Hope .... SEGR#0104
  Roca De Salvacion .... SEGR#0115
  Rocky Ridge................... SEGR#0105
AL Brownsboro
  Big Cove .... SERD#0801
AL Cherokee
  Allsboro.......................... SEHO#0501
  Maud .... SEHO#0509
  Mt. Hester .... SEHO#0510
AL Cleveland
  Greens Chapel............... SEGR#0208
AL Coker
  Coker.............................. SEGR#0705
AL Cullman
  Baldwin Chapel.............. SEHO#0202
  East Point .... SERD#0206
  Faith .... SEHO#0213
  House Prayer Cullman .. SEGR#0116
  Welti............................... SEHO#0212
AL Decatur
  House of Prayer.............. SEGR#0214
AL Florence
  Florence 1st................... SEHO#0506
AL Gadsden
  Gadsden.......................... SEGR#0402
AL Glencoe
  Glencoe .... SEGR#0404
AL Gurley
  Gurley .... SERD#0804
AL Helena
  Helena .... SEGR#0108
AL Homewood
  Homewood......................SEGR#0111
AL Huntsville
  Christ Church .... SERD#0814
  Hope................................ SERD#0812
  Huntsville 1st .... SERD#0806
AL Lexington
  Nebo................................ SEHO#0512
AL Meridianville
  Meridianville.................. SERD#0808
AL Millbrook
  Grace Community.......... SEGR#0407
AL Montevallo
  Spring Creek .... SEGR#0113
AL Moulton
  Hickory Grove .... SEHO#0507
AL Muscle Shoals
  Mt. Pleasant................... SEHO#0511
AL New Hope
  Walnut Grove .... SERD#0811
AL New Market
  Concord.......................... SERD#0802
AL Odenville
  Branchville..................... SEGR#0106
AL Piedmont
  Piedmont .... SEGR#0406

AL Reform
  Antioch........................... SEGR#0701
AL Rogersville
  Hurricane........................ SEHO#0508
  Old Mt Bethel .... SEHO#0513
  Rogersville 1st .... SEHO#0517
  Springfield...................... SEHO#0515
AL Scottsboro
  Goosepond .... SERD#0803
  Scottsboro .... SERD#0809
AL Sheffield
  Park Terrace .... SEHO#0514
AL Stevenson
  Edgefield .... SERD#0813
  Stevenson .... SERD#0810
AL Vance
  Union............................... SEGR#0114

ARIZONA

AZ Tucson
  Desert Gardens............... MIDC#8705

ARKANSAS

AR Ashdown
  E T Allen .... GRAR#1307
  Fomby .... GRAR#1310
AR Atkins
  Appleton......................... GRAR#1202
AR Batesville
  Faith-Hopewell .... GRAR#1502
  New Hope .... GRAR#1510
  Sidney .... GRAR#1515
AR Ben Lomond
  Ben Lomond................... GRAR#1301
AR Booneville
  Booneville .... GRAR#1401
AR Calico Rock
  Byron.............................. GRAR#1508
  Calico Rock.................... GRAR#1503
AR Camden
  Bethesda......................... GRAR#1302
  Camden .... GRAR#1303
  Fellowship...................... GRAR#1309
AR Charleston
  Marietta.......................... GRAR#1408
AR Dolph
  Trimble Camp Ground .. GRAR#1504
AR Dover
  Dover.............................. GRAR#1203
AR Fayetteville
  Grace .... GRAR#1405
AR Fort Smith
  Fort Smith .... GRAR#1406
AR Grapevine
  Pine Ridge......................GRAR#1105
AR Hampton
  Camp Ground.................GRAR#1101
AR Hector
  Hector............................. GRAR#1207
AR Horatio
  Dilworth .... GRAR#1304
AR Hot Springs
  Lake Hamilton .... GRAR#1221
AR Jordan
  Rodney........................... GRAR#1513

AR Little Rock
  Arkansas Loving .... GRAR#2135
  Crossroads......................GRAR#1102
AR Lockesburg
  Falls Chapel .... GRAR#1308
  Lockesburg.....................GRAR#1311
AR London
  Mt Carmel .... GRAR#1212
AR Louann
  Sulphur Springs............. GRAR#1315
AR Magazine
  Old Union....................... GRAR#1409
  Walnut Grove .... GRAR#1414
AR Magnolia
  Walkerville .... GRAR#1317
AR Melbourne
  Mt Olive .... GRAR#1517
AR Monticello
  Rose Hill ....GRAR#1106
AR Morrilton
  Trinity............................ GRAR#1219
AR Mount Pleasant
  Barren Fork .... GRAR#1501
AR Mountain Home
  Fellowship...................... GRAR#1505
AR Oxford
  Oxford............................GRAR#1511
AR Palestine
  Palestine ....GRAR#1103
AR Paris
  Shaver .... GRAR#1413
AR Pine Bluff
  Pine Bluff 1st.................GRAR#1104
  Shell Chapel ....GRAR#1108
AR Pineville
  Pineville .... GRAR#1512
AR Pottsville
  Mars Hill ....GRAR#1211
AR Ratcliff
  Caulksville .... GRAR#1402
AR Russellville
  Russellville.................... GRAR#1216
AR Salem
  Salem.............................. GRAR#1514
AR Searcy
  Gum Springs .... GRAR#1205
  Pleasant Grove .... GRAR#1214
  Searcy............................. GRAR#1218
AR Sherwood
  Sherwood .... GRAR#1220

BRAZIL

BR Bahia
  Mata de Sao Joao .... GRAR#8313

CALIFORNIA

CA San Francisco
  Chinese.......................... MSDC#8501
  Grace.............................. MSDC#8510
  Redeemer .... MSDC#8512
CA Trona
  Trona .... MSDC#8503

LOCATION INDEX OF CHURCHES CONTINUED

COLOMBIA

CO Antioquia
    Horeb-Central .... MSAN#8915
    El Rebano .... MSEM#8905
    La Rosa De Saron .... MSAN#8911
    Senta de Libertad .... MSAN#8919
    Zamora .... MSAN#8918
CO Buenaventura
    Divino Redentor .... MSAN#8206
    Emaus .... MSCA#8219
CO Caldas
    Manizales .... MSAN#8914
CO Cali
    Betania Mission .... MSAN#8204
    Bethel .... MSCA#8205
    Central .... MSCA#8208
    Filipos .... MSCA#8211
    Nueva Esperanza .... MSCA#8221
    Nueva Jerusalen .... MSCA#8222
    Principe De Paz .... MSCA#8201
    Renacer .... MSCA#8225
    Rey de Reyes .... MSCA#8228
    Samaria .... MSCA#8217
    San Marcos .... MSCA#8218
CO El Cerrito
    Getsemani .... MSCA#8210
CO Guacari
    San Pablo .... MSCA#8212
CO Guapi
    Maranatha .... MSCA#8220
CO Montebello
    Caleb Mission .... MSCA#8223
CO Palmira
    San Lucas .... MSCA#8215
CO Popayan
    Popayan .... MSCA#8227
CO Quindio
    Armenia .... MSAN#8903
CO Risaralda
    Dosquebradas .... MSAN#8907
    La Virginia .... MSCA#8913
    Pereira .... MSAN#8916
CO Tulua
    Tulua Mission .... MSCA#8226
CO Valle
    Cartago .... MSAN#8906

COLORADO

CO Englewood
    316 Fellowship .... MSDC#8710

FLORIDA

FL Lutz
    Christ .... SEGR#0303
FL Miami
    El Camino .... SEGR#0310
FL Tampa
    First Hispanic .... SEGR#0307
FL Wimauma

GEORGIA

GA Chatsworth
    Sumach .... SETG#2124
GA Cumming
    Korean Livingstone .... SETG#2130
GA Lawrenceville
    El Redil .... SETG#2149

GA Rydal
    Bartow .... SETG#2101

HONG KONG

HO Cheung Chau
    Cheung Chau .... MSHK#8801
HO Kowloon
    Kowloon .... MSHK#8803
    Tao Hsien .... MSHK#8806
HO Landau Island
    Mu Min .... MSHK#8810
HO NT
    Yao Dao .... MSHK#8811
HO North Point
    North Point .... MSHK#8805
HO Shatin NT
    Shatin .... MSHK#8807
HO Tseung Kwan O NT
    Po Lam .... MSHK#8808
HO Yuen Long
    Xi Lin .... MSHK#8809

ILLINOIS

IL Anna
    Camp Ground .... MICO#5103
IL Annapolis
    Pleasant Grove .... MICO#5210
IL Beecher City
    Spring Hill .... MINC#5411
IL Bethany
    Bethany .... MINC#5401
IL Brookport
    Mt. Sterling .... MICO#5117
IL Buncombe
    Ebenezer Hall .... MICO#5106
IL Burnt Prairie
    Burnt Prairie .... MINC#5102
IL Casey
    Casey .... MINC#5201
IL Chicago
    Ebenezer .... MINC#5203
IL Cisne
    Elm River .... MINC#5107
IL Dongola
    Mt Zion .... MICO#5118
IL Fairfield
    Cumberland Chapel .... MINC#5104
    Fairfield .... MINC#5108
    Lebanon North .... MINC#5113
    Union North .... MINC#5124
IL Farmer City
    Fullerton .... MINC#5404
IL Galatia
    Lebanon South .... MINC#5114
    Union Chapel .... MICO#5123
IL Georgetown
    Georgetown .... MINC#5204
IL Greenville
    Campground .... MINC#5402
    Mt. Gilead .... MINC#5406
IL Lincoln
    Lincoln 1st .... MINC#5405
IL Martinsville
    Willow Creek .... MINC#5211
IL Norris City
    United .... MINC#5119
    Village .... MICO#5125
IL Petersburg
    Petersburg .... MINC#5408

IL Simpson
    Gilead .... MICO#5110
IL Thompsonville
    Ebenezer .... MICO#5105
IL Trilla
    Good Prospect .... MINC#5205
IL Virginia
    Shiloh .... MINC#5409
IL Yale
    New Hope .... MINC#5208

INDIANA

IN Chandler
    Chandler .... MICO#5302
IN Evansville
    Morningside .... MINC#5304
IN Monroe City
    Monroe City .... MINC#5307
IN Petersburg
    Knights Chapel .... MINC#5306
IN Washington
    Mt Olivet .... MINC#5308

IOWA

IA New London
    Shinar .... MINC#5410

JAPAN

JA 184-0011
    Higashi Koganei .... MSJA#8301
JA 186-0002
    Kunitachi Nozomi .... MSJA#8306
JA 194-0041
    Naruse .... MSJA#8305
JA 207-0023
    Megumi .... MSJA#8309
JA 228-0004
    Sagamino .... MSJA#8304
JA 228-0818
    Den-en Mission .... MSJA#8310
JA 241-0021
    Asahi Mission .... MSJA#8315
JA 241-0825
    Kibougaoka .... MSJA#8302
JA 242-0006
    Koza .... MSJA#8303
JA 243-0422
    Ebina Shion No .... MSJA#8311
JA 245-0016
    Izumi Mission .... MSJA#8312
JA 259-1321
    Sibusawa .... MSJA#8307
JA 272-0834
    Ichikawa Grace Mission . MSJA#8314

KENTUCKY

KY Auburn
    Auburn .... MICU#3301
    Gasper River .... MICU#3306
KY Beaver Dam
    Point Pleasant .... MICU#3313
KY Benton
    Benton .... MICO#3403
    Oak Grove .... MICO#3412
KY Big Clifty
    Mt Olive .... MICU#3216

KY Bowling Green
  Bowling Green .... MICU#3304
  Mt Olivet .... MICU#3312
KY Bremen
  Brier Creek .... MICU#3503
  Fairview .... MICU#3504
KY Calvert City
  Oakland .... MICO#3413
  Vaughn's Chapel .... MICO#3423
KY Campbellsville
  Campbellsville .... MICO#3104
  Good Hope .... MICU#3109
  Liberty .... MICU#3116
  Shiloh .... MICU#3129
KY Caneyville
  Caneyville .... MICU#3201
  Mt Pleasant .... MICU#3217
KY Center
  Bethel .... MICU#3102
  Seven Springs .... MICU#3128
KY Clay
  Lisman .... MICO#3613
  Oak Grove Union .... MICO#3619
KY Dalton
  Macedonia .... MICO#3614
KY Eastview
  Needham .... MICU#3219
KY Edmonton
  Cedar Flat .... MICU#3106
KY Falls of Rough
  Short Creek .... MICU#3221
KY Fredonia
  Fredonia .... MICO#3608
  Good Spring .... MICO#3609
KY Garfield
  Garfield .... MICU#3208
KY Glasgow
  Glasgow .... MICU#3108
  Lick Branch .... MICU#3117
  Neal's Chapel .... MICU#3122
KY Greensburg
  Greensburg .... MICU#3110
  Salem .... MICU#3127
KY Greenville
  Greenville .... MICU#3505
KY Guthrie
  Gill's Chapel .... MICU#3307
KY Hardin
  Unity .... MICO#3422
KY Hardyville
  Monroe Chapel .... MICU#3119
KY Harned
  Ephesus .... MICU#3205
  Freedom .... MICU#3207
KY Harrodsburg
  Bethel #1 .... MICU#3103
  Harrodsburg .... MICU#3111
KY Hartford
  Beulah .... MICU#3501
KY Hawesville
  Dukes .... MICU#3204
KY Herndon
  Flat Lick .... MICO#3606
KY Hopkinsville
  Hopkinsville .... MICO#3611
KY Horse Cave
  Clear Point .... MICU#3107
KY Hudson
  Coyle .... MICU#3203
KY Irvington
  Clifton Mills .... MICU#3202
  Irvington .... MICU#3210

KY Kevil
  Bethel .... MICO#3404
  Pleasant Valley .... MICU#3418
KY Knob Lick
  Antioch .... MICU#3101
  Wisdom .... MICU#3130
KY Leitchfield
  Leitchfield .... MICU#3211
  Mt Vernon .... MICU#3218
KY Lewisburg
  Green Ridge .... MICU#3308
  Lewisburg .... MICU#3309
KY Louisville
  Heartsong .... MICU#3222
  Louisville 1st .... MICU#3212
KY Madisonville
  Madisonville .... MICO#3615
KY Magnolia
  Magnolia .... MICU#3214
KY Marion
  Marion First .... MICO#3616
  Piney Fork .... MICO#3620
  Sugar Grove .... MICO#3626
KY Marrowbone
  Casey's Fork .... MICU#3105
KY Mayfield
  Calvary .... MICO#3405
  Rozzell Chapel .... MICO#3419
KY Morgantown
  Little Muddy .... MICU#3310
  Morgantown .... MICU#3311
KY Murray
  Liberty .... MICO#3406
  North Pleasant Grove ..... MICO#3411
KY Nebo
  Rose Creek .... MICO#3622
KY Owensboro
  Owensboro .... MICU#3509
KY Paducah
  Grace Covenant .... MICO#3415
  Highland .... MICO#3414
  New Hope .... MICO#3410
  Woodlawn .... MICO#3417
KY Pewee Valley
  Louisville Japanese .... MICU#3223
KY Providence
  Providence 1st .... MICU#3621
KY Radcliff
  Radcliff .... MICU#3220
KY Russellville
  Bald Knob .... MICU#3302
KY Sacramento
  Poplar Grove .... MICU#3511
  Sacramento .... MICU#3512
KY Salem
  Hopewell .... MICO#3610
KY Sturgis
  Sturgis .... MICO#3625
KY Sullivan
  Mt. Pleasant .... MICO#3618
KY Summer Shade
  Mt Moriah .... MICU#3120
KY Summersville
  Oak Forest .... MICU#3123
KY Water Valley
  Bayou de Chien .... MICO#3401
KY West Paducah
  Milburn Chapel .... MICU#3416
KY West Somerset
  High Point .... MICU#3314
KY Wheatcroft
  Wheatcroft .... MICO#3627

KY White Plains
  Mt Carmel .... MICO#3617

KOREA

KO Seoul
  Korea 1st .... SEET#2221
  Sumkim Presby .... SEET#2222A

LOUISANA

LA Pleasant Hill
  Progress .... MSTR#8123
LA Quitman
  Antioch .... MSTR#8101

MACAU, PORTUGUESE PROVINCE

MA Andar LMN
  Macau .... MSHK#8804

MASSACHUSETTS

MA Malden
  Casa De Fe .... SEET#2220

MARYLAND

MD Beverly
  Pilgrim .... SEET#2332
MD Salisbury
  Our Good .... SETG#2138

MICHIGAN

MI Lincoln Park
  Grace .... MINC#5502
MI St Clair Shores
  Faith .... MINC#5501

MISSISSIPPI

MS Ackerman
  Enon .... SEGR#0707
MS Cedarbluff
  Cairo .... SEGR#0704
MS Columbus
  Beersheba .... SEGR#0702
  Columbus .... SEGR#0706
  Mt Zion .... SEGR#0709
MS Corinth
  Shiloh .... GRWT#9226
MS Falkner
  Mt Zion .... GRWT#9214
MS Macon
  McLeod Chapel .... SEGR#0708
MS Morton
  Groverton .... SEGR#0602
MS Olive Branch
  Olive Branch .... GRWT#9312
MS Union
  Erin .... SEGR#0601
  Steam Mill .... SEGR#0608
MS Walnut
  Hopewell .... GRWT#9207
MS Walnut Grove
  Salem .... SEGR#0607

MISSOURI

MO Aurora
  Orange .... GRMI#4108

LOCATION INDEX OF CHURCHES CONTINUED

MO Chilhowee
Shawnee Mound............. GRMI#4111
MO Conway
Happy Home .... GRMI#4306
MO Dunnegan
Spring Creek .... GRMI#4113
MO Greenfield
God's Grace .... GRMI#4104
MO Knob Noster
Pleasant Grove .... GRMI#4109
MO Lamar
Hopewell .... GRMI#4105
MO Lebanon
White Oak Pond............. GRMI#4315
MO Mansfield
Mansfield....................... GRMI#4308
MO Marshall
Marshall .... GRMI#4210
MO Martinville
Pierson........................... GRMI#4312
MO Phillipsburg
Phillipsburg................... GRMI#4311
MO Salem
New Hope .... GRMI#4309
MO San Antonio
Harmony .... GRMI#4203
MO Seymour
Seymour .... GRMI#4313
MO Springfield
Korean............................ GRMI#4316
Oak Grove...................... GRMI#4310
Springfield 1st .... GRMI#4314
MO Warrensburg
Salem.............................. GRMI#4216
Warrensburg .... GRMI#4115
MO Wentworth
Bethel .... GRMI#4102
MO West Plains
Elk Creek .... GRMI#4304

NEW JERSEY

NJ Tinton Falls
Hope Korean .... SECE#2131
NJ Wallington
Comeback .... SECE#2446

NEW MEXICO

NM Albuquerque
Heights .... MSDC#8701
NM Rio Rancho
Westside .... MSDC#8709

NEW YORK

NY College Point
Sharing .... SECE#2141
NY Flushing
One Way........................... SECE#2137

OKLAHOMA

OK Ada
Covenant .... MSRR#6304
OK Atoka
Pigeon Roost................. MSCH#6109
OK Broken Bow
McGee Chapel .... MSCH#6106
OK Burns Flat
Burns Flat...................... MSRR#6301
OK Clinton
Clinton........................... MSRR#6302

OK Coalgate
Coal Creek .... MSCH#6102
Lone Star....................... MSCH#6105
OK Eagletown
Panki Bok...................... MSCH#6108
OK Edmond
Stone Gate .... MSRR#6307
OK Honobia
Rock Creek.................... MSCH#6111
OK Marlow
Marlow .... MSRR#6305
OK Oklahoma City
Eastlake .... MSRR#6205
OK Tulsa
Faith .... MSRR#6201
OK Tupelo
Round Lake .... MSCH#6112

PENNSYLVANIA

PA Bridgeport
Bridgeport .... MICU#3131

TENNESSEE

TN Afton
Fairview .... SEET#2204
Mt Pleasant.................... SEET#2209
Walkertown .... SEET#2222
TN Algood
Algood............................TNMU#7201
TN Atoka
Bethel .... GRWT#9301
TN Atwood
Atwood............................ GRWT#9101
Pleasant Green .... GRWT#9129
TN Bartlett
Faith .... GRWT#9308
TN Beech Bluff
Maple Springs .... GRWT#9210
TN Beechgrove
Beech Grove.................. TNMU#7204
TN Bell Buckle
Green Hill....................... TNCO#7118
TN Belvidere
Belvidere....................... TNMU#7205
TN Bethel Springs
New Salem .... GRWT#9216
TN Bethpage
Dry Fork .... TNNA#7309
TN Bolivar
Bolivar............................ GRWT#9202
TN Boonshill
Boonshill........................ TNCO#7106
TN Bradford
Bradford .... GRWT#9104
Oliver's Chapel.............. GRWT#9127
TN Brentwood
Brenthaven .... TNNA#7331
TN Brighton
Holly Grove .... GRWT#9304
TN Brunswick
Brunswick .... GRWT#9302
TN Brush Creek
Union Hill .... TNMU#7246
TN Bulls Gap
Pilot Knob .... SEET#2213
Willoughby.................... SEET#2219
TN Camden
Camden .... GRWT#9105
TN Cane Ridge
Cane Ridge..................... TNNA#7326

TN Centerville
Swan................................TNCO#7140
TN Chapel Hill
Chapel Hill.....................TNCO#7109
TN Charlotte
Charlotte........................ TNNA#7303
Mt Liberty .... TNNA#7320
TN Chattanooga
Chattanooga 1st..............SETG#2104
Cornerstone Community TNNA#2107
Red Bank........................SETG#2105
Silverdale.......................SETG#2106
TN Chuckey
Pleasant Hill .... SEET#2214
Pleasant Vale .... SEET#2215
TN Clarksville
Bethel .... TNNA#7302
Clarksville .... TNNA#7304
Liberty............................ TNNA#7315
McAdoo .... TNNA#7318
New Providence .... TNNA#7305
TN Cleveland
Charleston ....SETG#2102
Cleveland ....SETG#2108
Flint Springs...................SETG#2112
Prospect United..............SETG#2116
TN College Grove
Harpeth Lick ....TNCO#7119
TN Columbia
Columbia 1st ....TNCO#7110
Faith Fellowship.............TNCO#7146
McCains ....TNCO#7126
New Bethel.....................TNCO#7134
Pleasant Mount..............TNCO#7136
Union Grove...................TNCO#7141
West Point ....TNCO#7143
TN Cookeville
Cookeville 1st ....TNMU#7210
Dry Valley ....TNMU#7213
TN Cordova
Korean............................ GRWT#9322
Morning Sun .... GRWT#9314
TN Cowan
Cowan ....TNMU#7211
TN Cunningham
Locust Grove................. TNNA#7316
TN Decaturville
Camp Ground................ GRWT#9204
TN Dickson
Dickson .... TNNA#7308
TN Dover
Mt View......................... TNNA#7322
TN Dresden
Dresden .... GRWT#9110
TN Dukedom
Good Springs .... GRWT#9112
TN Dunlap
Pikeville ....SETG#2153
TN Dyer
Bells Chapel.................. GRWT#9403
Dyer................................ GRWT#9409
Mt Olive .... GRWT#9418
TN Dyersburg
Dyersburg 1st .... GRWT#9410
Roellen .... GRWT#9428
TN Eagleville
Rocky Glade..................TNMU#7240
TN Elora
Elora...............................TNCO#7111
TN Erin
Arlington .... TNNA#7311
Camp Ground............... TNNA#7312

LOCATION INDEX OF CHURCHES CONTINUED

LOCATION INDEX OF CHURCHES CONTINUED

TN Rutherford
Rutherford.....................GRWT#9429
TN Santa Fe
Santa Fe.........................TNCO#7138
TN Savannah
Olivet.............................GRWT#9220
Savannah 1st ....GRWT#9224
TN Selmer
New Bethel....................GRWT#9215
Selmer Court Avenue ....GRWT#9225
TN Sewanee
Sewanee ....TNMU#7242
TN Sharon
Hopewell.......................GRWT#9115
New Salem ....GRWT#9124
Sharon ....GRWT#9130
TN Smithville
Banks.............................TNMU#7202
Smithville......................TNMU#7243
TN Somerville
Mt Carmel ....GRWT#9315
TN South Fulton
Fulton ....GRWT#9412
TN South Pittsburg
Richard City...................SETG#2118
South Pittsburg..............SETG#2123
TN Sparta
Hickory Valley ....SETG#7251
Old Zion........................TNMU#7234
TN Spring Hill
Ash Hill.........................TNCO#7101
Mt Lebanon....................TNCO#7130
TN Springfield
Mt Denson..................... TNNA#7319
TN Stewart
New Hope .... TNNA#7337
TN Talbott
Talbott ....SEET#2218
TN Telford
Oakland ....SEET#2211
TN Trenton
Concord..........................GRWT#9106
Davidson Chapel...........GRWT#9108
TN Trezevant
Trezevant.......................GRWT#9132
TN Trimble
Cool Springs............ GCGRWT#9408
Trimble..........................GRWT#9431
TN Troy
New Ebenezer ....GRWT#9422
Protemus ....GRWT#9426
Troy...............................GRWT#9432
TN Union City
Antioch Union...............GRWT#9401
Beech.............................GRWT#9402
Mt Ararat.......................GRWT#9417
Union City.....................GRWT#9433
TN Unionville
Kingdom ....TNCO#7123
TN Watertown
Commerce.....................TNMU#7209
Watertown ....TNMU#7247
TN Waverly
Concord.......................... TNNA#7306
Halls Creek.................... TNNA#7313
Mariah .... TNNA#7317
Waverly .... TNNA#7339
TN Waynesboro
Waynesboro...................TNCO#7142

TN Whitwell
Cedar Springs..................SETG#2119
Ebenezer.........................SETG#2110
Kelly's Chapel ....SETG#2120
New Hope ....SETG#2115
Oak Grove.......................SETG#2121
Whitwell..........................SETG#2122
TN Winchester
Goshen ....TNMU#7214
Gum Creek ....TNMU#7215
Harmony ....TNMU#7216
Owens Chapel ....TNMU#7235
Winchester 1st..............TNMU#7249
TN Yorkville
Yorkville........................GRWT#9435

TEXAS

TX Arlington
St John..........................MSRR#8413
TX Austin
Shepherd/Hills................MSTR#8604
TX Bedford
St Timothy.....................MSRR#8419
TX Bertram
Bertram ....MSTR#8605
TX Burleson
Pathway.........................MSRR#8418
TX Chico
Zion Valley....................MSRR#8425
TX Clarksville
Shiloh............................MSTR#8125
TX Daingerfield
Daingerfield....................MSTR#8106
TX Dallas
Lake Higlands ....MSRR#8411
TX Denton
Denton...........................MSRR#8404
TX Fort Worth
St Luke..........................MSRR#8407
St Mark..........................MSRR#8408
Trinity............................MSRR#8409
TX Freeport
Freeport.........................MSTR#8103
TX Georgetown
Oak Grove......................MSTR#8607
TX Greenville
Mt Zion ....MSRR#8414
TX Houston
Houston 1st ....MSTR#8606
Nueva Vida....................MSTR#8612
TX Jefferson
Jefferson ....MSTR#8109
TX Joinerville
Mt Hope ....MSTR#8117
TX Longview
Elmira Chapel ....MSTR#8111
Longview 1st..................MSTR#8112
Pine Tree ....MSTR#8113
TX Lubbock
Lubbock ....MSDC#8702
TX Marshall
Marshall ....MSTR#8115
TX Mesquite
Mesquite........................MSRR#8412
TX Midlothian
Shiloh ....MSRR#8421
TX Millsap
Newberry.......................MSRR#8415
TX Odessa
St Andrew......................MSDC#8703

TX Olney
Olney.............................MSRR#8416
TX Round Rock
Round Rock ....MSTR#8611
TX San Antonio
Northminster ....MSTR#8610
Stone Oak.......................MSTR#8608
TX San Elizario
Maranatha ....MSDC#8706
TX Troup
Concord..........................MSTR#8104
TX Whitesboro
Sandy Springs ....MSRR#8420
TX Winnsboro
Pine Hill ....MSTR#8122

CUMBERLAND PRESBYTERIAN CHURCH IN AMERICA
Denominational Center
www.cpcoga.org
226 Church Street, NW, Huntsville, AL 35801
Denomination Mailing Address: PO Box 18009, Huntsville, AL 35804
(256)536-7481 OR (256)682-3405
midgettvanessapca@gmail.com

Moderator of the General Assembly:
Reverend Dr. Theodis Acklin, 3315 Mastin Lake Road, Huntsville, AL 3581
(256)468-9585   tedacklin@att.net

Vice-Moderator of the General Assembly:
Reverend Michael Jones, 205 Burwell Road, Harvest, AL 35749
(256)852-8075   mljones3028@gmail.com

Administrative Director of the Cumberland Presbyterian Church in America:
Elder Vanessa K. Midgett, 118 Thunderbird Drive, Harvest, AL 35749
(256)682-3405   vkm118@aol.com

Stated Clerk of the General Assembly:
Elder Vanessa K. Midgett, 118 Thunderbird Drive, Harvest, AL 35749
(256)682-3405   vkm118@aol.comt

Engrossing Clerk of the General Assembly:
Reverend Lela Fencher, 620 Live Oak Circle, Fairfield, AL 35064
(205)706-8633   fencherl@bellsouth.net

Church Paper: *THE CUMBERLAND FLAG*
Edi: Elder Brenda Sutherlin, PO Box 456, Trinity, AL 35673
(256)227-1408   kerry sutherlin@bellsouth.net

SYNODS - PRESBYTERIES - STATED CLERKS

Alabama Synod - Elder Debra Smith, 102 Stornaway Court, Madison, AL 35758
(256)542-8162   djsmith878@yahoo.com
1. Birmingham Presbytery - Rev. Annett Pullom, 1313 Thirty-Fifth Street West, Birmingham, AL 35218
(205)781-6020   pastoralpullom@gmail.com
2. Florence Presbytery - Rev. Dr. Nancy Fuqua, 1963 County Road 406, Town Creek, AL 35672
(256)566-1226   fuq23@bellsouth.net
3. Huntsville Presbytery - Rev. Dr. Theodis Acklin, 3315 Mastin Lake Road, Huntsville, AL 35810
(256)468-9585   tedacklin@att.net
4. South Alabama Presbytery - Elder Minnie McMillan, 54 Riverview Avenue, Selma, AL 36701
(334)875-9617   mmcmillan54@hotmail.com
5. Tennessee Valley Presbytery - Rev. Critis Fletcher, 68 Mattie Street, Russellville, AL 35654
(256)412-2640   gepolar@bellsouth.net
6. Tuscaloosa Presbytery - Rev. Jacqueline Lang, 250 New Cumberland Road, Carrollton, AL 35447
(205)292-1048   jackielang53@gmail.com

Kentucky Synod - Elder Leon Cole, Jr., PO Box 335, Warren, MI 48090
(248)770-1540   llcole1951@yahoo.com
1. Cleveland, Ohio Presbytery - Elder Greg Scruggs, 3274 Milikin Court, Cleveland Heights, OH 44118
(216)645-9584   gsagi57@yahoo.com
2. Ohio Valley Presbytery - Elder Mary Henton, 8816 W Manslick Road, Louisville, KY 40272
(502)396-6119   henton819@gmail.com
3. Purchase Presbytery - Elder Sherell Sparks, 79 Paradise Lane, Metropolis, IL 62960
(618)203-2799   relld2000@yahoo.com

Tennessee Synod - Rev. Christopher Martin, 205 North Point Road, Sweetwater, TN 37874
(423)371-9986   cj85martin@gmail.com
1. Elk River Presbytery - Elder Jacquelyn Cooper, 4705 Indian Summer Drive, Nashville, TN 37207
(615)440-3010   jmcooper12@comcast.net
2. Hiwassee Presbytery - Rev. Stephanie Martin, 205 North Point Road, Sweetwater, TN 37874
(423)489-7633   stephanie.nicole@yahoo.com
3. New Hopewell Presbytery - Rev. Deborah Montague, 417 Archwood Street, North Jackson, TN 38305
(731)935-7213   montague1@gmail.com

Texas Synod - Elder Gladys Brandon, 719 Olive Street, Waco, TX 76704
(254)498-6905   gladysbrandon@sbcglobal.net
1. Angelina Presbytery - Elder Tom Jones, 739 County Road 4720, Troup, TX 75789
(972)415-3200   tomjones91154@yahoo.com
2. Brazos River Presbytery - Rev. Joan Jefferson, 2710 Jeffries #110, Dallas, TX 75215
(254)855-7308   fieldsjrosyjoan@aol.com
3. East Texas Presbytery - Rev. Kay Ward Creed, PO Box 1316, Henderson, TX 75653
(903)657-7169   kcrn760@suddenlink.net

CUMBERLAND PRESBYTERIAN CENTER OFFICES
8207 TRADITIONAL PLACE
CORDOVA, TENNESSEE 38016
www.cumberland.org

Central Telephone for Center Offices: (901)276-4572, Historical Foundation Telephone: (901)276-8602

BOARD OF STEWARDSHIP, FOUNDATION AND BENEFITS
www.cumberland.org/bos

Phone (901)276-4572	FAX (901)272-3913
Robert Heflin, Executive Secretary	
rah@cumberland.org	Ext-207
Alan Butler, Coordinator of Benefits	
rmd@cumberland.org	Ext-204
Kathryn Gilbert Craig, Administrative Assistant	
kgc@cumberland.org	Ext-206

CENTRAL ACCOUNTING

Phone (901)276-4572	FAX (901)272-3913
Dan Scherf, Accounting Supervisor	
dscherf@cumberland.org	Ext-233

CP RESOURCES

resources@cumberland.org	(901)276-4581

GENERAL ASSEMBLY OFFICE
www.cumberland.org/gao

Phone (901)276-4572	FAX (901)272-3913
Michael Sharpe, Stated Clerk	
msharpe@cumberland.org	Ext-225
Elizabeth Vaughn, Assistant to the Stated Clerk	
eav@cumberland.org	Ext-226

HISTORICAL FOUNDATION OF THE CPC & CPCA
www.cumberland.org/hfcpc

Phone (901)276-8602	FAX (901)272-3913
Susan Knight Gore, Archivist	skg@cumberland.org
Missy Rose, Archival Assistant	jmr@cumberland.org

OUR UNITED OUTREACH
www.cumberland.org/ouo

Cliff Hudson, Development Director	
gchudson3@gmail.com	Ext-210

REGIONAL DIRECTORS

Calotta Edsell	cedsell@hotmail.com
Arkansas & West Tennessee Presbyteries	(864)915-6105
Carolyn Harmon	richardharmon09@comcast.net
Presbytery of East Tennessee	(423)639-3037
Jeff McMichael	revmcmichael@outlook.com
Covenant, Cumberland & North Central Presbyteries	(270)617-4016

MINISTRY COUNCIL
www.cpcmc.org

Phone (901)276-4572	FAX (901)276-4578
Edith Old, Director of Ministries	
eold@cumberland.org	Ext-228
Executive Assistant to the Director of Ministries	

PASTORAL DEVELOPMENT MINISTRY TEAM

Phone (901)276-4572	FAX (901)276-4578
Pam Phillips-Burk, Team Leader	
pam@cumberland.org	Ext-203

COMMUNICATIONS MINISTRY TEAM

Phone (901)276-4572	FAX (901)276-4578
Matthew Gore, Publications Manager/Editor	
mhg@cumberland.org	Ext-221
Sowgand Sheikholeslami, Senior Art Director	
sowgand@cumberland.org	Ext-211

DISCIPLESHIP MINISTRY TEAM

Phone (901)276-4572	FAX (901)276-4578
Elinor Brown, Team Leader	
esb@cumberland.org	Ext-205
Cindy Martin, CP Resources Distribution Manager	
chm@cumberland.org	Ext-252
Jodi Rush, Children & Family Ministry	
jhr@cumberland.org	Ext-223
Nathan Wheeler, Youth & Young Adult Ministry	
nwheeler@cumberland.org	Ext-218
Chris Fleming, Adult Ministry	
cfleming@cumberland.org	Ext-219

MISSIONS MINISTRY TEAM

Phone (901)276-4572	FAX (901)276-4578
Milton Ortiz, Team Leader	
mortiz@cumberland.org	Ext-234
Jinger Ellis, Manager, Finance and Administration	
jellis@cumberland.org	Ext-230
Kristi Lounsbury, Congregational Ministries	
klounsbury@cumberland.org	Ext-203
Howell-Diamond, Cardelia, Women's Ministry	
chd@cumberland.org	Ext-264
Johan Daza, Cross-Culture Immigrant Ministries USA	
jdaza@cumberland.org	Ext-202
T.J. Malinoski, Evangelism & New Church Development	
tmalinoski@cumberland.org	Ext-232
Lynn Thomas, Global Cross-Culture Missions	
lynndont@gmail.com	Ext-261

OTHER CHURCH OFFICES

BETHEL UNIVERSITY
www.bethelu.edu

325 Cherry Avenue, McKenzie, TN 38201

Phone (731)352-4000	FAX (731)352-6387

Walter Butler, President
David Huss, Vice President for Finance
Dale Henry, Vice President for Development
Cindy Mallard, Vice President for College of Arts & Sciences
Joe Hames, Vice President of Health Sciences
Kimberly Martin, Vice President of Professional Studies
Phyllis Campbell, Chief Academic Officer
Michelle Mitchell, Special Assistant to the President for Strategic Initiatives

CHILDREN'S HOME
cpch@cpch.org   www.cpch.org

909 Greenlee Street, Denton, TX 76201
Mail Address: Drawer G, Denton, TX 76202

Phone (940)382-5112	FAX (940)387-0821
	(940)595-0564
Courtney Banatoski, President/CEO	
cbanatoski@cpch.org	
Mary Dickerman, Director of Development	(972)765-1180
mdickerman@cpch.org	

MEMPHIS THEOLOGICAL SEMINARY
www.MemphisSeminary.edu

168 East Parkway South, Memphis, TN 38104-4395

Phone (901)458-8232	FAX (901)452-4051

Jody Hill, President
Cassandra Price-Perry, Vice-President of Operations/CFO
Peter Gathje, Vice-President of Academic Affairs/Dean
Barry Anderson, Executive Director of Student Services

PROGRAM OF ALTERNATE STUDIES
www.MemphisSeminary.edu/program-of-alternate-studies

168 East Parkway South, Memphis, TN 38104-4395

Phone (901)334-5853	FAX (901)452-4051

Michael Qualls, Director
mqualls@MemphisSeminary.edu
Karen Patten, Administrative Assistant
kpatten@MemphisSeminary.edu

CUMBERLAND PRESBYTERIAN CENTER
E-MAIL ADDRESSES & TELEPHONE EXTENSION LIST
(901) 276-4572
Hours: Monday-Thursday 8:00am-5:00pm (CDT), Friday 8:00am-12:00 pm (CDT)

Staff	Email	Ext
Alan Butler	abutler@cumberland.org	204
Andy McClung	amcclung@cumberland.org	256
Cardelia Howell-Diamond	chd@cumberland.org	(ext. rings Cardelia's cell) 264
Chris Fleming	cfleming@cumberland.org	(ext. rings Chris' cell) 219
Cindy Martin	cmartin@cumberland.org	252
Dan Scherf	dscherf@cumberland.org	233
Edith Busbee Old	eold@cumberland.org	228
Elinor Brown	ebrown@cumberland.org	205
Elizabeth Vaughn	evaughn@cumberland.org	226
Jinger Ellis	jellis@cumberland.org	230
Jodi Rush	jrush@cumberland.org	(ext. rings Jodi's cell) 223
Johan Daza	jdaza@cumberland.org	202
Kathryn Gilbert Craig	kcraig@cumberland.org	206
Kristi Lounsbury	klounsbury@cumberland.org	(ext. rings Kristi's cell) 263
Lynn Thomas	lynndont@gmail.com	(ext. rings Lynn's cell) 261
Matthew Gore	mhg@cumberland.org	221
Mike Sharpe	msharpe@cumberland.org	225
Milton Ortiz	mortiz@cumberland.org	234
Missy Rose	mrose@cumberland.org	215
Nathan Wheeler	nwheeler@cumberland.org	218
Pam Phillips-Burk	pam@cumberland.org	203
Robert Heflin	rheflin@cumberland.org	207
Shipping		256
Sowgand Sheikholeslami	sowgand@cumberland.org	211
Susan Gore	sgore@cumberland.org	214
T.J. Malinoski	tmalinoski@cumberland.org	232

Our United Outreach

Cliff Hudson　　　**gchudson3@gmail.com**　　　**(ext. rings Cliff's cell) 210**

Building Lobby:	
8175 Building	227
8207 Building	231
Fax Numbers:	
8175 Building	901-272-3913
8207 Building	901-276-4578

Conference Rooms:	
8175 Building	220
8207 Building	208
Other Offices:	
MTS	901-458-8232
Bethel University	731-352-4000
Children's Home	940-382-5112
Historical Foundation	901-276-8602

www.ingramcontent.com/pod-product-compliance
Lightning Source LLC
Chambersburg PA
CBHW051345290326
41933CB00042B/3176